TIMELINES OF AFRICAN-AMERICAN HISTORY

TIMELINES OF AFRICAN- AMERICAN HISTORY

500 YEARS OF BLACK ACHIEVEMENT

Tom Cowan, Ph.D., and Jack Maguire

Senior Consultant: Richard Newman, W.E.B. Du Bois Institute at Harvard University

Editorial Consultant: Emory J. Tolbert, Howard University

A ROUNDTABLE PRESS/PERIGEE BOOK

Perigee Books
are published by
The Berkley Publishing Group
200 Madison Avenue
New York, NY 10016

A Roundtable Press Book
Directors: Susan E. Meyer, Marsha Melnick
Executive Editor: Amy T. Jonak
Art Direction: Martin Lubin
Editorial Assistant: Megan Keiler

First edition: September, 1994

Published simultaneously in Canada.

Library of Congress Cataloging-in-Publication Data

Cowan, Thomas Dale.
　　Timelines of African-American history :five hundred years of
Black achievement / Tom Cowan and Jack Maguire ; introduction by
Richard Newman. —1st ed.
　　　p.　cm.
　　"A Roundtable Press/Perigee book."
　　Includes index.
　　ISBN 0-399-52127-5
　　1. Afro-Americans—History—Chronology　I. Maguire, Jack, 1945–.
　　II. Title.
E185.C86　1994　　　　　　　　　　　　　　　　　94-12771
973'.049673—dc20　　　　　　　　　　　　　　　　CIP

Printed in the United States of America

1 2 3 4 5 6 7 8 9 10

CONTENTS

ACKNOWLEDGMENTS

Our ambitious task was made possible by referring to the seminal research on African-American history performed by groundbreaking scholars before us. We are particularly indebted to Peter M. Bergman and HarperCollins for giving us permission to draw from the comprehensive volume *The Chronological History of the Negro in America* (Harper & Row, 1969).

Among the other sources of factual information we referred to are: *Before Freedom Came: African-American Life in the Antebellum South,* edited by Edward D. C. Campbell, Jr., with Kym S. Rice (Museum of the Confederacy and University Press of Virginia, 1991); *Before the Mayflower: A History of Black America,* by Lerone Bennett, Jr. (Penguin Books, 6th revised edition, 1993); *The Blacks in America: 1492–1976,* edited by Irving J. Sloan (Oceana Publications, 1977); *A Documentary History of the Negro People in the United States,* volumes 1–4, edited by Herbert Aptheker (Citadel Press/Carol Publishing Group, 1990–92); *Historical and Cultural Atlas of African Americans,* by Molefi K. Asante and Mark T. Mattson (Macmillan, 1992); *I, Too, Sing America,* by Paula L. Woods and Felix H. Liddell (Workman Publishing, 1992); *Milestones in 20th-Century African-American History,* by Alton Hornsby, Jr. (Visible Ink Press, 1993); *The Negro Almanac: A Reference Work on the African American,* edited by Harry A. Ploski and James Williams (John Wiley & Sons, 4th edition, 1983); and *A Pictorial History of Blackamericans,* by Langston Hughes, Milton Meltzer, and C. Eric Lincoln (Crown Publishers, 5th revised edition, 1983).

Finally we are grateful to Richard Newman for reviewing our manuscript and correcting errors and inaccuracies. Even with the most careful readings, of course, some errors may slip through, for which we take full responsibility.

INTRODUCTION

It has not yet been given a name, but we are currently in the midst of an African-American Renaissance, a rebirth considerably more far-reaching than the familiar Harlem Renaissance or New Negro movement of the 1920s.

What are some of the contemporary signs and evidences? Books by black writers are on the best-seller lists and working their way into the literary canons. Black music has become American music and is fast becoming the music of the world. Black style, dress, and speech more and more define international popular culture. The black heritage, with its African roots, is a badge of pride and an incentive to action. The "lost, strayed, or stolen" history of people of color in this country is becoming part of the school curriculum at all levels. Scholars are realizing that the American past cannot be understood apart from its black components and are working to fill in the gaps in our knowledge of the African-American past.

This book is an aspect of this new Renaissance. It is a response to the widespread and growing interest and enthusiasm on the part of black and white people alike for the history and culture of African Americans. It is a celebration of the long struggle of black people for freedom in this country, a struggle with many triumphs, but one which is not yet over. It is a guide to the central facts and key information necessary for an understanding of the black experience itself as well as of its true place as an integral part of the American experience.

What this book does is make available in chronological sequence the dates of major events in African-American history from the 15th century to the present day. It is not only a survey over time, however. The events of each year are divided into subject categories like politics and civil rights, sports, literature and journalism, the military, and visual arts. This means it is possible to trace any of these themes across the years as well as within each year.

Another feature is that this book lists not only the significant dates of black history and politics, but it recognizes the vital importance of African-American culture as well. Areas like music, art, and film, which are not always included in standard histories, are deliberately incorporated here. This inclusion not only provides a breadth of view, it reveals something of the scope of the black influence on American life.

Of course, the authors had to be selective, and so not everything is here. Of course, there are errors despite careful checking, sometimes because basic research to determine accurate dates and information remains to be done. Frederick Douglass said he never met a slave who knew the date of his own birth; sometimes information is simply unknown. Many of the crucial documents of African-American history—newspapers, for example—were never saved, because no one thought them important, and their information is lost.

Despite these limitations, the authors have brought together a treasury of information. Because of the chronological arrangement, it will be possible to see connections that were simply not evident before. Think of this book as an introduction: behind and beyond every fact listed here is a story: of a useful life, of a creative act, of a blow for freedom, of an event that made a difference. Let the simple fact recorded here spark your interest to discover more. You will not be disappointed. The full stories behind these facts are still little known, but they are the stuff of drama as well as of history.

RICHARD NEWMAN

1492

EXPLORATION

Pedro Alonzo Niño, a black man, serves on Christopher Columbus's ship on the first Spanish voyage to the New World. Sailors of African ancestry are members of all the major Spanish expeditions to the Americas, including those of Balboa, Ponce de León, Cortés, Pizarro, and Menéndez.

1513

EXPLORATION

Thirty black men in Balboa's expedition help construct the first road across the Isthmus of Panama.

1526

POLITICS AND CIVIL RIGHTS

Spanish explorers bring the first Africans into what is now the United States. Imported into the Carolinas as slaves to build a Spanish fortress, the blacks escape to Native American communities farther inland. This is the first recorded slave revolt in North America.

Contemporary Events, 1502 ■ The first African slaves are brought to Latin America.

EXPLORATION

Cabeza de Vaca and his black companion, Esteban, the only survivors of the Spanish Narváez expedition to Florida, explore the southeastern region of North America for six and a half years.

EXPLORATION

The black explorer Esteban helps search for the Seven Cities of Cibola. He travels in territory that is now Arizona and New Mexico.

EXPLORATION

African craftspeople and farmers are among the Spanish settlers who establish the city of St. Augustine, Florida.

Contemporary Events, 1538 ■ Gerardus Mercator employs the word "America" for the first time. **1585** ■ The English found a settlement on Roanoke Island off the coast of North Carolina.

POLITICS AND CIVIL RIGHTS

The British government sanctions the slave trade by granting monopolies to English trading companies.

POLITICS AND CIVIL RIGHTS

Twenty black indentured servants arrive in Jamestown, Virginia, on board a Dutch ship. They are probably the first African Americans in the North American English colonies.

POLITICS AND CIVIL RIGHTS

In Jamestown, Virginia, John Phillip, a black man, testifies in court against a white man.

In New York's Hudson River Valley, Africans are imported as slaves to work on the farms of Dutch settlers.

ADDITIONAL EVENTS

In Virginia, William Tucker is perhaps the first African American born in the English colonies.

POLITICS AND CIVIL RIGHTS

Slaves are introduced into the colony of Connecticut.

POLITICS AND CIVIL RIGHTS

The colony of Massachusetts enacts a law that protects slaves who run away from their owners because of abusive treatment.

The First Black Virginians

The first Africans arrived in Virginia in 1619 on board a Dutch vessel. They were indentured servants, bound to service for a period of years, after which they would legally become free. White immigrants arrived in the colonies under the same conditions. In the early years there was no implication of racial inferiority for blacks bound to servitude. During the first 40 or 50 years, the black Virginians eventually realized their freedom, bought land, engaged in commerce, and enjoyed political rights. Some even owned other indentured servants of African ancestry.

Contemporary Events, 1607 ■ The English colony of Jamestown is founded in Virginia.
1620 ■ The **Mayflower** arrives on Cape Cod, and the English Pilgrims found the Plymouth Colony.
1630 ■ The town of Boston is settled by John Winthrop and other English Puritans.

The Africans and the Dutch

In New Amsterdam, the Dutch colony located on the present site of Manhattan, at least some Africans and Dutch settlers were on equitable social terms. The Dutch-governed Bouweire Chapel had 40 black members in 1641, the year that records indicate two African Americans, Antony van Angola and Lucie d'Angola, were married there.

POLITICS AND CIVIL RIGHTS

The colony of Maryland imports black slaves.

RELIGION AND EDUCATION

In Louisiana, French Catholics advocate educational opportunities for people of color, including slaves.

POLITICS AND CIVIL RIGHTS

The New England slave trade begins when a ship from Salem, Massachusetts, sails to the West Indies with a cargo of Native American slaves, who are exchanged for Africans and goods.

POLITICS AND CIVIL RIGHTS

The English colonies begin to enact punitive laws to discourage slaves and indentured servants from running away and sympathetic people from sheltering them.

POLITICS AND CIVIL RIGHTS

In legalizing the slavery of "lawful" captives, Massachusetts sets a precedent later followed by all the New England colonies.

POLITICS AND CIVIL RIGHTS

In Virginia a person can be fined 20 pounds of tobacco for each night that he or she hides or gives refuge to a runaway slave.

Contemporary Events, 1636 ■ Harvard College is founded in Massachusetts. **1642** ■ Compulsory education is introduced in Massachusetts.

1643

POLITICS AND CIVIL RIGHTS

The New England Confederation sponsors an intercolonial agreement that a suspected runaway slave can be convicted simply by a statement of certification from a government magistrate.

1644

BUSINESS AND EMPLOYMENT

The Dutch grant land to the first 11 African Americans brought to their colony at New Netherland. The land given the black settlers includes property that today lies in Brooklyn and Greenwich Village.

1645

POLITICS AND CIVIL RIGHTS

Ships sailing out of Boston bring slaves from Africa to the West Indies, where they are exchanged for sugar, tobacco, and wine, which in turn are sold for manufactured goods on return to Massachusetts. This lucrative venture establishes what will become New England's triangular trade route.

1649

STATISTICS

The colony of Virginia has over 300 African slaves.

1651

POLITICS AND CIVIL RIGHTS

In Northampton County, Virginia, Anthony Johnson founds a community of African Americans, which consists of a dozen homesteaders, each of whom receives a land grant for imported servants.

The Johnson Estate

Evidence that some members of the first generation of blacks in Virginia lived and worked on approximately the same terms as whites of the same class is seen in the rise of the Anthony Johnson family. Johnson came to Virginia from England about 1621 as an indentured servant. After working off his years of servitude, he earned money, bought land, and began to bring in other indentured servants, both black and white. Under the headright system, anyone who brought new workers into the colony was given 50 acres of land for each person. Johnson received 250 acres in Northampton County in 1651. Over the next few years, Johnson's sons added another 650 acres for bringing in 13 servants. In time the Johnson settlement on the Pungoteague River was one of the wealthiest African-American communities in the area.

Contemporary Events, 1643 ■ John Winthrop brings the first telescope to America.
1649 ■ An act providing for religious tolerance is passed in Maryland.

Lost Firsts

How many "firsts" in American history were due to African-American ingenuity and inventiveness will never be known. Much has been lost in history, and in many cases, whites took credit for insights they received from their slaves or servants. One example that has survived is the 1648 decision by the governor of the Virginia colony to begin the production of rice. On the advice of "our Negroes," he wrote, rice was planted because the land and climate seemed comparable to that "in their Country."

POLITICS AND CIVIL RIGHTS

Rhode Island legislators pass the first colonial law limiting servitude. Applying to both blacks and whites, the statute limits bondage to no more than 10 years.

THE MILITARY

In Massachusetts, African Americans, Indians, and Scots are required to train for the colonial militia.

POLITICS AND CIVIL RIGHTS

In some parts of Virginia black and white homesteaders live in integrated settlements. Some African Americans, such as Benjamin Doyle, own land totaling several hundred acres.

THE MILITARY

Connecticut forbids African Americans serving in the military.

POLITICS AND CIVIL RIGHTS

A fugitive slave law in Virginia gives legal recognition to slavery.

POLITICS AND CIVIL RIGHTS

Virginia declares that a mother's status determines whether a child is born free or into slavery.

Contemporary Events, 1660 ■ The British parliament initiates a series of Navigation Acts to regulate commerce with the colonies.

1663

POLITICS AND CIVIL RIGHTS

In Gloucester County, Virginia, a major slave revolt by both black slaves and white indentured servants is foiled when a servant exposes the conspiracy.

In Maryland a law is passed that all blacks brought into the colony are automatically slaves.

Also in Maryland, a free white woman who marries a black is considered a slave as long as her husband is alive.

1664

POLITICS AND CIVIL RIGHTS

Maryland forbids marriage between black men and white women.

RELIGION AND EDUCATION

Maryland no longer grants freedom to slaves who become Christians. A new law states that baptism does not change the status of a slave.

1667

POLITICS AND CIVIL RIGHTS

The British "Act to Regulate the Negroes on the British Plantations" places severe restrictions on African Americans. Slaves cannot leave a plantation without a pass and can never leave on Sunday; they cannot carry weapons or possess horns or other signaling devices. Whipping is the punishment for striking a Christian the first time, branding on the face for a second offense.

1670

POLITICS AND CIVIL RIGHTS

Virginia repeals a law that allows freed slaves and indentured servants to vote.

Contemporary Events, 1664 ■ The Dutch surrender the settlement of New Netherland to the Duke of York, thus creating the English colony of New York.

Virginia also passes a law declaring that anyone arriving by sea who is not a Christian can be held a slave for life—a statute applied primarily to recently arrived Africans.

STATISTICS

The governor of Virginia estimates that the colony now has over 2,000 slaves.

BUSINESS AND EMPLOYMENT

England charters the Royal African Company to compete with the French and Dutch in the slave trade.

POLITICS AND CIVIL RIGHTS

In Maryland a law declares that children born to white mothers and black fathers are to be free, as are the children born to free African-American women.

POLITICS AND CIVIL RIGHTS

This is the last year that indigenous people from non-Christian nations may enter the colony of Virginia as free men and women. Later, they are considered slaves.

RELIGION AND EDUCATION

In Virginia a law makes it illegal for slaves to attend Quaker meetings held for educational purposes.

Contemporary Events, 1675–76 ■ King Philip's War (named after a Native American leader) causes massive destruction and loss of life for New England settlers and native peoples. **1681** ■ William Penn is granted the territory of Pennsylvania. **1682** ■ Quakers begin extensive settlement of Pennsylvania.

1686

BUSINESS AND EMPLOYMENT

In the Carolinas a law prohibits African Americans from engaging in any trade or business.

1688

POLITICS AND CIVIL RIGHTS

The first recorded protest against slavery by a white group in the English colonies occurs at a monthly meeting of Quakers in Germantown, Pennsylvania, but is shelved by the yearly meeting.

1689

THE MILITARY

King William's War begins, and one of the first casualties in Massachusetts is an African American killed at Falmouth.

1691

POLITICS AND CIVIL RIGHTS

The existence of free African Americans in Virginia is seen as a threat by white colonists, who pass a strict law to restrict manumissions.

1692

POLITICS AND CIVIL RIGHTS

Maryland passes a law that white men who marry or have children by black women must spend seven years in servitude. There are also penalties for black men, free or slave, who have sexual relations with white women.

Tituba, a slave from Barbados, is one of the first three accused of witchcraft in the hysteria in Salem, Massachusetts.

Slave Codes

Frontier conditions required the keeping of firearms for hunting and protection, but whites believed guns would encourage slave revolts. As early as 1636 Virginia stipulated the militia should be all-white. Blacks were forbidden to have or bear arms. In time the prohibition against firearms, intended to prevent slave uprisings, evolved into extensive slave codes to control every aspect of slave life. Slaves could not own property, assemble when or where they wished, or leave the plantation without written permission from their owners. Crimes committed by blacks generally received more severe punishments than similar crimes committed by whites. Murder, rape, and arson (seen as attacks against white society) were punishable by death. Lesser offenses received the brutal punishments of maiming, whipping, and branding. Many places in the North enacted equally severe codes against African Americans. However, in time of war, when settlements needed as many armed troops as possible for defense, slave codes were relaxed, and blacks were enlisted with whites.

Contemporary Events, 1689 ■ Massachusetts colonists rebel against the high-handed rule of Governor Edmund Andros, seizing him and sending him to England as a prisoner.

The African Homelands

Where did the men and women sold into slavery in the colonial period come from? Where did their parents and grandparents call home? Most left West Africa along a 3,000-mile coastline, after being caught in the interior local wars, kidnapped by African slave traders, or sold into slavery for violating tribal laws. Their people were Mandingos, Binis, Sengalese, Hausas, Yorubas, Ibos, Efiks, Krus, Fantins, Ashantis, and Dahomeans. They were people of many different cultures, religions, languages, traditions, and racial stocks.

POLITICS AND CIVIL RIGHTS

George Keith, a dissident Quaker, publishes "An Exhortation," the first printed protest against slavery in British North America.

RELIGION AND EDUCATION

A Quaker importing slaves into Pennsylvania can be expelled from the Society of Friends.

Contemporary Events, 1693 ■ The College of William and Mary is founded in Virginia.

1700

POLITICS AND CIVIL RIGHTS

The slave trade operates out of Boston and supplies Africans to Virginia and the New England colonies.

In his pamphlet *The Selling of Joseph,* judge Samuel Sewall of Massachusetts argues against slavery and advocates emancipation and education of African-American slaves.

RELIGION AND EDUCATION

Quaker leader George Fox urges slave owners to provide religious instruction for their slaves. William Penn, the Quaker governor of Pennsylvania, establishes a monthly meeting for African Americans.

STATISTICS

In British North America there are 27,817 slaves, about 22,600 in the South.

1701

RELIGION AND EDUCATION

The Society for the Propagation of the Gospel in Foreign Parts is organized by the Church of England to instruct African Americans in Christianity.

1704

BUSINESS AND EMPLOYMENT

Advertisements for slaves occupy a major place in the first newspaper printed in the colonies, the *Boston Newsletter.*

RELIGION AND EDUCATION

A French immigrant, Elias Neau, opens the Catechism School for African Americans at New York's Trinity Church.

Contemporary Events, 1701 ■ Yale University is founded in Connecticut. **1704** ■ In Deerfield, Massachusetts, Native Americans kill about 50 people and capture many others, taking them to Canada.

Legal Recognition of Slavery in the Colonies

Each of the 13 original colonies over time legally recognized slavery. The following list shows those dates:

Massachusetts	1641
Connecticut	1650
Virginia	1661
Maryland	1663–64
New York	1665
South Carolina	1682
Pennsylvania	1700
New Jersey	1702
Rhode Island	1703
New Hampshire	1714
North Carolina	1715
Delaware	1721
Georgia	1755

POLITICS AND CIVIL RIGHTS

In Virginia, African Americans are slaves for life unless they were Christians in their native lands or were free in a Christian country.

Massachusetts declares intermarriage between blacks and whites to be illegal and institutes fines for ministers who perform them. This law will not be repealed until 1843.

POLITICS AND CIVIL RIGHTS

New York and Virginia pass laws stating that slaves cannot become free by Christian baptism.

THE MILITARY

Free blacks serve in the Massachusetts militia.

STATISTICS

Virginia has 12,000 African Americans.

POLITICS AND CIVIL RIGHTS

The government of Virginia officially frees a slave named Will for his service in exposing a slave revolt.

STATISTICS

There are 44,866 slaves in the British colonies.

Contemporary Events, 1706 ■ Benjamin Franklin is born in Boston.

1711

POLITICS AND CIVIL RIGHTS

Quaker sentiment persuades the colonial government to outlaw slavery in Pennsylvania, but the law is vetoed by the British government.

LITERATURE AND JOURNALISM

Poet Jupiter Hammon is born October 17 into slavery in Long Island.

1712

POLITICS AND CIVIL RIGHTS

In New York City a slave revolt leaves 9 whites dead, and some 20 African Americans rebels are either killed or commit suicide.

1715

STATISTICS

The total population for the English colonies in North America stands at 434,600, of whom 58,850 are of African ancestry.

1716

POLITICS AND CIVIL RIGHTS

Slave ships begin delivering black slaves to Louisiana.

BUSINESS AND EMPLOYMENT

A Massachusetts pamphlet declares that slavery discourages new settlements on the frontier by limiting job opportunities for whites.

1717

RELIGION AND EDUCATION

In Massachusetts, the Puritan clergyman Cotton Mather holds evening classes to instruct African Americans and Indians.

Contemporary Events, 1714 ■ Tea is introduced into colonial life. **1718** ■ Virginia's lieutenant governor, Alexander Spotswood, offers rewards for dead or living pirates. The infamous Blackbeard is captured and beheaded.

SCIENCE AND TECHNOLOGY

Onesimus, a slave in the household of Cotton Mather, tells the minister about medical inoculations performed in Africa by tribal healers. Mather informs Dr. Zabdiel Boylston of this practice, and the doctor performs the first smallpox inoculations in North America on his son and two slaves.

POLITICS AND CIVIL RIGHTS

The Pennsylvania Assembly attacks the practice of blacks and whites living together as "wicked and scandalous."

POLITICS AND CIVIL RIGHTS

Free African Americans in Virginia are forbidden by law to carry weapons or to meet or visit slaves.

A group of Philadelphians petitions the colonial government to enact legislation to discourage the intermarriage of blacks and whites.

RELIGION AND EDUCATION

A Virginia religious tract advocates baptism and educational opportunities for African Americans, Native Americans, and people of mixed blood. It also argues that slave owners should be exempt from taxes on baptized slave children under age 18.

RELIGION AND EDUCATION

In Williamsburg, Virginia, a black Baptist church is founded.

Contemporary Events, 1725 ■ William Bradford starts the first New York newspaper, the **New York Gazette.**

STATISTICS

African-American slaves in British North America number approximately 75,000.

RELIGION AND EDUCATION

In New Orleans, Ursuline nuns begin teaching African Americans and Indians.

STATISTICS

In a total population of 654,950, the British colonies contain 91,021 African-American slaves, with 17,323 living in the North and 73,698 in the South.

SCIENCE AND TECHNOLOGY

Astronomer and mathematician Benjamin Banneker is born November 9 in Maryland to free parents.

POLITICS AND CIVIL RIGHTS

Prince Hall, abolitionist leader and the founder of African-American freemasonry, is born.

RELIGION AND EDUCATION

In Bethlehem, Pennsylvania, Moravians organize a mission to minister to African Americans.

Maroons

From the mid-17th to the mid-19th centuries, many runaway slaves established communities in the mountains, swamps, and wilderness areas from South Carolina and Florida to Louisiana and the West Indies. Called Maroons from the Spanish term **cimarrones,** which meant runaways, these escaped slaves lived with the constant risk of being captured and returned to slavery. Maroons lived in largely self-sufficient camps, often with Native Americans, providing their food from the land and forests and supplementing their needs by occasional raids on plantations and towns. In 1672 the colony of Virginia passed a law to encourage the recapturing and killing of Maroons. Other colonies followed. In 1733 South Carolina offered a 20-pound reward to anybody who captured and returned a Maroon. During the second decade of the 19th century Maroons allied themselves with Native Americans to resist the annexation of Florida by the United States. At this time Maroon rebellions in North and South Carolina and in Virginia led to retaliation by armed militia. Some Maroon settlements survived into the Civil War era.

Contemporary Events, 1732 ■ James Oglethorpe is granted a charter for the colony of Georgia. **1734** ■ The Great Awakening, a religious revival, starts in Northampton, Massachusetts. **1735** ■ The trial of John Peter Zenger, a New York newspaper editor, is a landmark case for freedom of the press.

The Middle Passage

Undoubtedly the most brutal link in the journey from Africa to the Western Hemisphere was the infamous Middle Passage: the crossing of the Atlantic. Slaves were branded, chained two by two, and forced into intolerably cramped quarters, often into shelves not more than 18 inches high. They could not move, the air was suffocatingly foul and hot, they endured dysentery and other illnesses with no relief or attempt on the part of the crew to maintain clean quarters. The voyage might last from 6 to 10 weeks. One captain described the conditions: "They had not so much room as a man in his coffin, either in length or breadth." Some slaves killed those near them in order to have more air and room. Others committed suicide. The dead, if found, were thrown overboard. Some were not discovered until they reached port, and a live slave might arrive chained to a dead body. It is estimated that in the 1700s between 50,000 and 100,000 Africans were brought each year.

1739

POLITICS AND CIVIL RIGHTS

Three slave revolts occur in South Carolina in which dozens of blacks and whites are killed. In the Stono Rebellion, led by a slave named Cato, 30 whites are killed.

1740

POLITICS AND CIVIL RIGHTS

A South Carolina law prevents slaves from raising livestock.

SCIENCE AND TECHNOLOGY

The first written account of an African-American dentist practicing in the colonies appears in a Pennsylvania newspaper. The article states that an African American named Simon is able to "bleed and draw teeth."

STATISTICS

There are 150,024 slaves in the colonies, 126,066 in the South and 23,958 in the North.

1741

POLITICS AND CIVIL RIGHTS

In New York City, 11 African Americans are burned at the stake, 18 are hanged, and 70 are sold into slavery in the South in response to a series of arsonist attacks, although there is no evidence that the victims were involved.

1743

RELIGION AND EDUCATION

Mr. Garden's school to educate and train young African Americans opens in Charleston, South Carolina, with support from both black and white citizens of the city.

Contemporary Events, 1741 ■ New York City is the site of the first strike, in which bakers protest the regulation of bread prices.

STATISTICS

Approximately 42,000 African Americans live in the colony of Virginia.

BUSINESS AND EMPLOYMENT

Jean Baptiste Point du Sable, whose trading post evolves into the city of Chicago, is born in Haiti to an African slave woman and a French seaman.

LITERATURE AND JOURNALISM

Poet and storyteller Lucy Terry Prince composes "Bars Fight," a poem about the 1704 Indian attack known as the Deerfield Massacre in Massachusetts.

THE MILITARY

New Jersey raises a troop of 500 free African Americans and Native Americans to fight the French in Canada.

RELIGION AND EDUCATION

The Presbyterian church begins a program of education for African Americans in Virginia.

THE MILITARY

South Carolina allows African Americans to serve in the colonial militias during war, but not to exceed half the male slave population aged 16 to 60, and only in integrated units where they will not be more than one-third of the white soldiers. Freedom is granted to any slave who kills or captures an enemy.

Contemporary Events, 1746 ■ Princeton University is founded in New Jersey.

1750

POLITICS AND CIVIL RIGHTS

In Framingham, Massachusetts, Crispus Attucks escapes from his master. Attucks will be one of the first colonials killed in the Boston Massacre in 1770.

RELIGION AND EDUCATION

Near Newburgh, New York, James Varick, founder and first bishop of the African Methodist Episcopal Zion Church, is born.

STATISTICS

At midcentury the slave population reaches 236,400, which is approximately 20% of the total colonial population. Over 206,000 slaves live in the South.

1752

POLITICS AND CIVIL RIGHTS

Eighteen African-American slaves work at Mount Vernon when George Washington acquires the property. During his ownership of the estate, the number of slaves will increase to 200.

1753

RELIGION AND EDUCATION

Patriot and minister Lemuel Haynes is born July 18 in West Hartford, Connecticut. He will serve in the Revolutionary War and become the first black minister ordained in the Congregational Church.

LITERATURE AND JOURNALISM

Poet Phillis Wheatley is born in Africa. Brought to America as a girl, she will be honored as a poet in both New England and London.

THE MILITARY

Soldier and patriot James Robinson is born. After winning a medal

Contemporary Events, 1752 ■ The first general hospital for the colonies is opened in Philadelphia by Thomas Bond.

for bravery at the Battle of Yorktown and being promised his freedom for fighting for the Americans, Robinson will be sold into slavery after the Revolution.

SCIENCE AND TECHNOLOGY

Benjamin Banneker constructs a clock that strikes the hour, although he has never seen one.

RELIGION AND EDUCATION

Quakers begin to discourage slave owning among their members. Philadelphia Quakers bar any member who deals in the slave market.

POLITICS AND CIVIL RIGHTS

Paul Cuffe, shipowner and advocate of African resettlement, is born in Cuttyhunk, Massachusetts.

RELIGION AND EDUCATION

Among Quakers there is little agreement regarding slavery. Some oppose the institution; others, especially in the South, tolerate slavery and are even engaged in it. New England Quakers make it an offense against the Society of Friends to import slaves.

Richard Allen, the founder and first bishop of the African Methodist Episcopal Church, is born February 14 to slave parents in Philadelphia.

LITERATURE AND JOURNALISM

The poem "An Evening Thought, Salvation by Christ, with Peniten-

Exercise on a Slave Ship

Human beings cannot remain bound up in cramped quarters for great lengths of time without serious circulation and other health problems. A permanently disabled slave would not command a high price. To alleviate the problem, captains required slaves to be brought on deck, where they were forced under the lash to dance for exercise. For many, this was an act of sacrilege and a violation of ancestral traditions, for they came from cultures where dance was a sacred act: to honor the spirits and maintain the customs of one's people.

Contemporary Events, 1754 ■ The French and Indian War, a nine-year struggle between England and France and their Native American allies, begins.

tial Cries," by Jupiter Hammon, is printed as a broadside, one of the first known publications by an African American.

STATISTICS

There are 325,806 slaves in the British colonies in North America. Of that number, 40,033 reside in the North, and 285,773 live in the South.

SCIENCE AND TECHNOLOGY

The first known African-American physician, James Derham, is born into slavery in Philadelphia.

RELIGION AND EDUCATION

John Chavis, the first African American to study at Princeton, is born. He will become a Presbyterian preacher and educator, teaching the sons of prominent white families.

SPORTS

Boxer Bill Richmond is born to free parents on Staten Island, New York. He will become one of the first African-American athletes to fight competitively.

POLITICS AND CIVIL RIGHTS

In his work *The Rights of the British Colonies*, Massachusetts legislator James Otis argues that slaves have a right to be free.

BUSINESS AND EMPLOYMENT

Abijah Prince, a former slave and one of the founders of Sunderland, Vermont, acquires 100 acres in Guilford, Vermont.

1766

POLITICS AND CIVIL RIGHTS

Slaves in Massachusetts begin a court action against their masters, charging them with trespass in an unsuccessful attempt to challenge the legality of slavery.

1767

POLITICS AND CIVIL RIGHTS

Denmark Vesey, leader of an important slave revolt in South Carolina, is born.

1769

POLITICS AND CIVIL RIGHTS

Thomas Jefferson's first legislative proposal as a member of the Virginia House of Burgesses is a bill to provide for the emancipation of slaves. It is rejected.

BUSINESS AND EMPLOYMENT

Emanuel Bernoon, a successful African-American caterer and owner of a Rhode Island oyster house, dies, leaving a house and estate valued at 539 pounds, a large sum of money at the time.

1770

RELIGION AND EDUCATION

A school for African Americans is set up in Philadelphia by Quaker Anthony Benezet.

THE MILITARY

Crispus Attucks is one of three men killed by British soldiers on March 5 in the Boston Massacre, one of the precipitating events of the American Revolution.

Contemporary Events, 1767 ■ The British Parliament passes the Townshend Acts, imposing import duties on many common items, including tea.

STATISTICS

Of the 2,312,000 estimated total population of the 13 British colonies in North America, 462,000 are slaves.

THE MILITARY

Aaron, an African American from Rhode Island, is among the revolutionaries who burn the British revenue ship *Gaspee* at Providence.

POLITICS AND CIVIL RIGHTS

A group of slaves in Massachusetts files a petition asking for the right to earn money to purchase their freedom. In the course of the Revolutionary War, other similar petitions will be filed.

Caesar Hendricks, a slave in Massachusetts, sues his master in court "for detaining him in slavery." Hendricks is freed and awarded damages by an all-white jury.

Sally Hemings, Thomas Jefferson's slave mistress, is born in Virginia.

RELIGION AND EDUCATION

An African-American Baptist church is started in Silver Bluff, South Carolina. Nearby, George Liele begins his preaching career.

LITERATURE AND JOURNALISM

In London Phillis Wheatley of Boston publishes *Poems on Various Subjects, Religious and Moral*, the first book published by an African American and the second by an American woman.

VISUAL ARTS

Scipio Moorhead is honored in a poem written by Phillis Wheatley, entitled "To S.M., a Young African Painter, on Seeing His Works." Moorhead, a Boston slave, reportedly painted Wheatley's portrait, and this rendering was engraved as the frontispiece to her book. The first known advertisement by an African-American portraitist appears in the *Massachusetts Gazette*.

1774

POLITICS AND CIVIL RIGHTS

African Americans file another petition with the Massachusetts General Court asking for freedom as a natural right.

The Continental Congress calls for an end to the slave trade, and Thomas Jefferson argues for the abolition of slavery in "A Summary of the Rights of British America."

RELIGION AND EDUCATION

Benjamin Franklin and other Philadelphians open a school for African Americans to educate slaves for eventual freedom.

THE MILITARY

In Massachusetts the Committees of Safety organize Minutemen companies, which enlist both black and white volunteers.

1775

POLITICS AND CIVIL RIGHTS

The first antislavery society, the Pennsylvania Society for the Abolition of Slavery, is organized in Philadelphia.

THE MILITARY

Among the Minutemen who stand against the British at Concord Bridge on April 19 are Peter Salem, Samuel Craft, Caesar and John Ferrit (father and son), and Pomp Blackman.

At the Battle of Bunker Hill, Peter Salem, a former slave, kills Major Pitcairn, the British commander who gave the order to fire at the Minutemen at Lexington. Fourteen other African Americans fight beside Salem.

Primas Black and Epheram Blackman are among the Green Mountain Boys of Vermont who capture Fort Ticonderoga.

George Washington endorses a recommendation of the Continental Congress to bar African Americans from service in the army. However, the British governor of Virginia offers freedom to any slave who joins the British army.

African-American Soldiers in the Revolutionary War

In spite of various bans on black soldiers in the Revolutionary armies, some 8,000 to 10,000 African Americans served between 1775 and 1783. About 5,000 served as regular soldiers; others as guerrilla fighters, spies, and naval crewmen, including ship pilots. African Americans were both in mixed regiments and in a few all-black regiments. Black soldiers fought at White Plains, Saratoga, Stony Point, Princeton, Rhode Island, Monmouth, Yorktown, and other major battles. South Carolina and Georgia, however, generally opposed the involvement of African-American soldiers. In South Carolina slaves were used as laborers and on general work teams in the militias until the General Assembly prohibited the use of slaves in the war effort in any capacity. Yet when the need for manpower was acute, some slaves were freed in order to fight.

Contemporary Events, 1774 ■ The First Continental Congress meets to protest recent British laws. **1775** ■ The Second Continental Congress convenes. ■ Massachusetts Minutemen fire on British troops along the route from Boston to Lexington and Concord.

The Problem of Manumission

Freeing one's slaves was a legal act, requiring court documentation and bureaucratic red tape. In many states the laws for manumission were rigid and cumbersome, making it extremely difficult to free slaves. The point behind such legislation was to prevent the growth of the free African-American population, which was perceived as threatening by white society, both as competition for jobs and as a source of social unrest. Free blacks, intentionally or by their mere presence, encouraged slaves to rebel, run away, or demand greater freedoms. In 1775 North Carolina passed a law forbidding manumission of slaves, except as a reward for certain services. Later acts supported the intent of this law. Freed slaves were captured and sold back into slavery with 20% of the price going to the informer who had helped in the capture. Former slaves from North Carolina living in Philadelphia petitioned Congress for redress of grievances. The request was debated and rejected by a vote of 50 to 33.

EXPLORATION

A slave guides Daniel Boone's party from Virginia into Kentucky.

STATISTICS

There are over half a million slaves in North America.

POLITICS AND CIVIL RIGHTS

The Continental Congress adopts the draft of the Declaration of Independence that does not include Jefferson's proposed statement on slavery.

THE MILITARY

George Washington reverses his decision of the previous year and allows free African Americans to serve in the Continental Army. Lafayette praises African-American military efforts to protect Washington's retreat onto Long Island.

African-American soldiers Prince Whipple and Oliver Cromwell are members of the troops who cross the Delaware with Washington to attack the British in New Jersey.

Bill Richmond, a young slave, is the hangman at the execution of Nathan Hale, accused by the British of being an American spy. Later, Richmond will become a heavyweight boxer in Europe.

Eight hundred slaves join the British troops on Staten Island in exchange for their freedom.

POLITICS AND CIVIL RIGHTS

By drawing up a state constitution that forbids slavery, Vermont becomes the first state to abolish slavery.

RELIGION AND EDUCATION

New Jersey begins a program for the education of African-American children.

Contemporary Events, 1776 ■ The Declaration of Independence is signed. **1777** ■ The British suffer a major defeat at Saratoga, New York.

THE MILITARY

Pompey Lamb, posing as a vegetable seller, gains access to the British fort at Stony Point, New York. Lamb's spying and his efforts during the battle later assist General Anthony Wayne and the Revolutionary forces in capturing the garrison.

Prince Whipple, an African-American soldier serving in Rhode Island, is among the detachment that captures two British officers who are held as bargaining chips for the release of the American General Lee.

Edward Hector, an African American in the artillery regiment at the Battle of Brandywine, refuses to abandon his ammunition wagon at the order to retreat and heroically collects other abandoned weapons as he brings his wagon, team, and munitions to safety.

During the winter retreat at Valley Forge, Washington's men desert in large numbers, but African Americans do so at a lower rate than white soldiers.

THE MILITARY

An African-American battalion is formed in Rhode Island made up of 300 former slaves. The troops will kill 1,000 Hessians, whom the British use as mercenaries. They are paid comparably with white soldiers, and guaranteed their freedom when the war ends. In the Battle of Rhode Island, 125 black soldiers, over 90 of them ex-slaves, hold off British-Hessian troops for four hours while the American forces successfully retreat.

POLITICS AND CIVIL RIGHTS

African Americans in New Hampshire use Jefferson's arguments in the Declaration of Independence on their own behalf, petitioning the state legislature to grant their freedom because it is "an inherent right of the human species." The 20 African Americans cite "life and freedom" and "perfect equality with other men" as inalienable rights granted by God.

Contemporary Events, 1778 ■ Congress ratifies an alliance with France.

Petitions for Freedom

From the earliest days, African Americans petitioned colonial governments for their freedom. Individuals demanded freedom in their particular cases, and collectively small groups of African Americans, both free and slave, sent petitions to local assemblies, pointing out the evil of slavery and demanding its abolition. Some individual complaints were granted. During the Revolutionary era, black protestors made use of revolutionary propaganda to enhance their cause, pointing out, for example, the incongruity for white Americans to shout "liberty or death," while holding hundreds of thousands of black Americans in bondage.

POLITICS AND CIVIL RIGHTS

Pennsylvania passes a gradual emancipation act.

Paul Cuffe, Adventure Childe, Paul Cuve, Samuel Gray, Pero Howland, Pero Russell, and Pero Coggeshall, all free African Americans living in Dartmouth, Massachusetts, petition the general court to exempt them from taxation because they are denied suffrage and other rights of citizenship. Through these efforts, free African Americans gain the rights and privileges of citizenship in Massachusetts.

RELIGION AND EDUCATION

Lott Cary is born into slavery in Virginia. As a Baptist missionary sponsored by the American Colonization Society, Cary will sail with 28 settlers to found Liberia in the 1820s.

THE MILITARY

As part of their bounty for enlisting in the Revolutionary army, volunteers in South Carolina are promised young and healthy slaves.

THE MILITARY

James Armistead, a Virginia slave, infiltrates General Cornwallis's headquarters as a servant and is hired by the British to spy on the Americans. But Armistead, a double agent, passes key information about the size and movements of British troops to Lafayette, and this information greatly contributes to Cornwallis's defeat.

African-American troops fight in the Battle of Yorktown, Virginia, where General Cornwallis surrenders, ending the Revolutionary War.

THE MILITARY

Disguised as a male soldier named "Robert Shurtliff," Deborah Gannett, an African-American woman, serves for 17 months in the Continental Army.

Contemporary Events, 1780 ■ Benedict Arnold is discovered to be a traitor after he betrays West Point to the British.

34

Quaco Honeyman, a Rhode Island slave, receives his freedom in exchange for espionage services during the Revolutionary War.

About 5,000 slaves escape from America on British ships leaving Savannah.

1783

POLITICS AND CIVIL RIGHTS

Virginia grants freedom to slaves who fought for the patriots in the Revolutionary War.

The Massachusetts Supreme Court declares slavery illegal in the commonwealth.

BUSINESS AND EMPLOYMENT

Samuel "Black Sam" Fraunces, a prosperous tavern owner in New York who supplied American forces with food and money, hosts the occasion for George Washington's farewell address to his troops.

RELIGION AND EDUCATION

In Philadelphia the Quakers vote to admit the first African-American member to the Society of Friends.

THE MILITARY

Oliver Cromwell, an African-American soldier who crossed the Delaware with Washington and fought at the battles of Brandywine, Monmouth, and Yorktown, receives from Washington a "Badge of Merit for six years' faithful service."

About 3,000 slaves escape on British ships from New York harbor, and more than 6,000 flee with the British from Charleston, South Carolina.

1784

POLITICS AND CIVIL RIGHTS

Gradual abolition acts are passed in Rhode Island and Connecticut. In New Jersey all African Americans who served in the Revolutionary War are freed.

Contemporary Events, 1783 ■ The Treaty of Paris officially ends the Revolutionary War.

BUSINESS AND EMPLOYMENT

In Virginia, a protest by unemployed white seamen influences a law limiting the number of slaves who can work on Virginia's ships.

RELIGION AND EDUCATION

The Methodist Church orders its members to free their slaves within one year because slavery is contrary to the will of God. But the order is suspended because of objections from churches in the southern states.

George Liele, an African-American Baptist missionary, leaves for Jamaica.

LITERATURE AND JOURNALISM

Poet Phillis Wheatley dies February 28.

SPORTS

Tom Molineaux, the most honored and successful boxer in the nation's early years, is born into slavery in Washington, D.C.

POLITICS AND CIVIL RIGHTS

The New York Society for Promoting the Manumission of Slaves is established, with John Jay, the future chief justice, as president.

David Walker, militant abolitionist and author of *Walker's Appeal,* is born September 28 of free parents in Wilmington, North Carolina.

POLITICS AND CIVIL RIGHTS

New Jersey passes a law forbidding the importation of slaves.

POLITICS AND CIVIL RIGHTS

The Constitutional Convention agrees to the three-fifths compro-

---

Contemporary Events, 1786 ■ Shays's Rebellion breaks out among farmers and poor settlers in western Massachusetts over unequal representation in state government.

mise—namely, that for taxation and representation purposes five slaves will be counted as the equivalent of three whites.

At the Constitutional Convention a North Carolina delegate proposes the basis for a fugitive slave law, which passes with little debate and becomes part of the Constitution. It is a federal offense to harbor or assist a runaway slave.

The Continental Congress passes the Northwest Ordinance, which forbids slavery in the territory that will become the states of Ohio, Indiana, Illinois, Michigan, and Wisconsin.

In Philadelphia the Free African Society is organized by Absalom Jones and Richard Allen.

African Americans petition the Massachusetts legislature for funds to return to Africa, the first recorded effort for repatriations.

During the debates over the Constitution, James Madison records in his diary, "Where slavery exists, the republican theory [of government] becomes still more fallacious."

BUSINESS AND EMPLOYMENT

Prince Hall, a Revolutionary War veteran, obtains a charter for a black Masonic lodge in Boston.

RELIGION AND EDUCATION

The New York manumission society organizes the African Free School with 40 pupils.

African Americans in Boston, led by Prince Hall, petition the Massachusetts government for equal school facilities for black students.

1788

POLITICS AND CIVIL RIGHTS

The Negro Union in Newport, Rhode Island, calls for free African Americans to emigrate to Africa, a position the Philadelphia Free African Society opposes.

RELIGION AND EDUCATION

Andrew Bryan, a follower of George Liele, establishes a Baptist church in Savannah, Georgia, and becomes its first pastor.

Contemporary Events, 1788 ■ **The Federalist Papers** are published as a collection of essays. ■ Georgia, Connecticut, Massachusetts, Maryland, South Carolina, New Hampshire, Virginia, and New York are admitted to the Union.

The Free African Society

In 1787 Richard Allen and Absalom Jones founded the Free African Society in Philadelphia, a precursor to many later organizations promoting self-reliance, as well as abolitionist societies. Based on religious principles, the organization gained a national reputation for its work and stirred pride among many African Americans throughout the country. The Free African Society advocated and worked for the abolition of slavery and provided medical assistance and other forms of welfare for the poor. Surreptitiously, it served as a communications pipeline for African Americans in the South.

Enslaving Free African Americans

It was a widespread practice in many areas to capture free African Americans and sell them into slavery, whether they were runaways, ex-slaves who had been manumitted, or even people born to free parents. In 1788 a protest lead by Boston black activist Prince Hall requested that the Massachusetts government look into the case of a group of free African Americans who had been captured and sold into slavery in the French colony of Martinique. The Americans refused to work in spite of being beaten and intimidated. Massachusetts Governor John Hancock joined the cause, and the Americans were returned. Boston rejoiced and passed a law against the slave trade.

A New Jersey law makes it mandatory for slave owners to teach their slaves to read. The fine for not doing so is five pounds.

SCIENCE AND TECHNOLOGY

James Derham, an ex-slave, is a prominent New Orleans doctor.

LITERATURE AND JOURNALISM

Josiah Henson is born into slavery in Charles County, Maryland. He will later escape and become an inspiration for "Uncle Tom" in Harriet Beecher Stowe's novel *Uncle Tom's Cabin.*

BUSINESS AND EMPLOYMENT

Jean Baptiste Point du Sable, a frontier entrepreneur of African ancestry from Haiti, establishes a trading post at "Eschikagou" on the southern shore of Lake Michigan. Du Sable's permanent settlement will grow into the city of Chicago.

RELIGION AND EDUCATION

Henry Evans, an African American, organizes a white Methodist church in Fayetteville, North Carolina.

A special committee is appointed by the Pennsylvania Abolition Society to assure the education of free African Americans.

The Brown Fellowship Society of Charleston, South Carolina, is organized by free people of mixed blood. With a membership fee of $50, the organization maintains a clubhouse and cemetery, sponsors educational opportunities for free African Americans, and provides assistance to widows and orphans.

STATISTICS

The first census taken in the new nation shows that African Americans make up 19.3% of the population; 59,466 are free and 697,897 are slaves.

Contemporary Events, 1789 ■ George Washington becomes the nation's first president on April 30 in New York City. ■ North Carolina is admitted to the Union. **1790** ■ Rhode Island becomes a state.

1791

POLITICS AND CIVIL RIGHTS

An African-American revolt in Louisiana results in the execution of 23 slaves and the exile of 3 white sympathizers.

About a dozen abolition societies are active from Massachusetts to Virginia.

SCIENCE AND TECHNOLOGY

Benjamin Banneker, African-American mathematician and astronomer, works on the survey to create the District of Columbia.

1792

SCIENCE AND TECHNOLOGY

Benjamin Banneker begins publication of his yearly almanac.

THE MILITARY

Congress passes a law that only white males may enroll in militias during peacetime.

1793

POLITICS AND CIVIL RIGHTS

The nation's first fugitive slave law is passed. It allows a slave owner to pursue runaway slaves into another state, and with court approval, capture them and take them home. The law makes it a federal crime to harbor a runaway slave or prevent an arrest.

A state law in Virginia forbids free African Americans from entering the state.

In Camden, South Carolina, 23 free black men and women, supported by sympathetic whites, sign a petition protesting the state's poll tax.

SCIENCE AND TECHNOLOGY

White inventor Eli Whitney introduces the cotton gin, which will

---

Contemporary Events, 1791 ■ The first 10 amendments, known as the Bill of Rights, are added to the U.S. Constitution. ■ Vermont becomes a state. ■ The Bank of the United States is chartered. **1792** ■ Washington is reelected to a second term as president. ■ Kentucky becomes a state.

St. Thomas Episcopal Church

In 1791 African Americans in Philadelphia, led by Absalom Jones, who had worshipped in the Methodist Church, organized St. Thomas Episcopal Church. Jones, who with Richard Allen founded the Free African Society in 1787, was ordained and became the church's first rector, as well as the first black Episcopal minister in the United States. The church was dedicated in 1794 and became the first African-American Episcopal congregation in the nation. However, the following year the Episcopal Convention voted that the black church could not participate in the annual meeting of the Pennsylvania diocese. The new congregation was forbidden to send either a minister or lay deputies.

make cotton growing profitable in many places throughout the South, thus instilling new life into the slave economy.

POLITICS AND CIVIL RIGHTS

The American Convention of Abolition Societies is formed in Philadelphia by delegates from nine states. It condemns slavery and the slave trade and calls for an end to legal restrictions on free blacks.

RELIGION AND EDUCATION

On July 17 Richard Allen founds the Bethel Church in Philadelphia, the first African Methodist Episcopal church.

Absalom Jones and Richard Allen win praise from the mayor for their medical and nursing work in the white community during the yellow fever epidemic of 1793 in Philadelphia.

RELIGION AND EDUCATION

Amos Fortune, a former slave and a leading businessman in Jaffrey, New Hampshire, founds the Jaffrey Social Library and gives money for a town school.

PERFORMING ARTS

For the first time, an African-American actor plays a role that is not a comic part. In James Murdock's *The Triumph of Love,* a black actor portrays a romantic character.

POLITICS AND CIVIL RIGHTS

The African Society is organized in Boston.

RELIGION AND EDUCATION

The Zion Church, a black Methodist congregation, is organized in New York City by James Varick and others.

Contemporary Events, 1794 ■ The Whiskey Rebellion in western Pennsylvania is crushed by federal troops. ■ Toussaint L'Ouverture joins black forces in Haiti and by 1801 leads them to control of both Haiti and Santo Domingo. **1796** ■ John Adams is elected president. ■ Tennessee becomes a state.

1797

POLITICS AND CIVIL RIGHTS

Four African Americans fleeing reenslavement in North Carolina send the first recorded petition to the United States Congress asking for freedom, not only for themselves but for "our relief as a people."

Sojourner Truth is born Isabella Bomefree in Hurley, New York. She will become one of the leading abolitionists and advocates for women's rights.

George Washington writes in his will that, on the death of his wife, all his slaves are to be freed. This decision by the nation's first president lends moral support to the growing abolitionist movement.

LITERATURE AND JOURNALISM

George Moses Horton, a slave who will become a janitor at the University of North Carolina, is born in Chapel Hill. Later he will make money by writing and selling love poems that white male students send to their girlfriends.

1798

BUSINESS AND EMPLOYMENT

John C. Stanley, who will become one of the wealthiest people in Craven County, North Carolina, is freed. After becoming a barber, Stanley will invest in plantations and use his influence to purchase and free many slaves.

James Forten establishes his sail-making shop in Philadelphia and invents a sail-handling device.

RELIGION AND EDUCATION

In Boston, Primus Hall conducts a school for African American pupils in his home.

VISUAL ARTS

The first advertisement by Joshua Johnston, a portrait artist believed to be of African descent, appears in the December 19 issue of the *Baltimore Intelligencer*.

Contemporary Events, 1798 ■ The Department of the Navy is established. ■ Congress passes the Alien and Sedition Acts, making the naturalization process for citizenship more difficult and allowing for the arrest of writers, editors, and speakers charged with criticizing the government.

THE MILITARY

The United States Navy issues its first restrictions against enlisting African Americans on men-of-war and in the Marine Corps. In spite of the regulations, some blacks manage to enlist, such as George Diggs, who serves as quartermaster on *Experiment,* and William Brown, who becomes a "powder monkey" on the *Constellation.*

EXPLORATION

James P. Beckwourth is born in Virginia to a Revolutionary War veteran and a slave woman. Later he will become a mountain man, explorer, and fur trader.

PERFORMING ARTS

In Boston, Gottlieb Graupner, a German immigrant who will later found the Boston Philharmonic Society, performs one of the early racist minstrel shows, complete with blackface and southern black dialect.

1800

POLITICS AND CIVIL RIGHTS

Gabriel Prosser plans a revolt of about 1,000 slaves in Richmond, Virginia, with the goal of seizing the capital and taking over the state. The effort is thwarted by the militia, and Prosser and his followers are executed.

Free African Americans in Philadelphia formally petition the U.S. Congress to pass new legislation to end slavery, the slave trade, and the fugitive slave law. Congress votes 85 to 1 against the proposal and strongly discourages any such petitions in the future.

Nat Turner is born in Southampton, Virginia. He will become a popular preacher and lead a major slave rebellion in 1831.

STATISTICS

There are 1,002,037 African Americans in the United States according to the U.S. census, making up 18.9% of the total population.

1801

POLITICS AND CIVIL RIGHTS

Playing on the fear of slave revolts in the southern states, the American Convention of Abolition Societies goes on record in favor of a system of gradual emancipation.

RELIGION AND EDUCATION

James Varick and other religious leaders incorporate the Zion Church as the "African Methodist Episcopal Church in New York."

The General Assembly of the Presbyterian Church appoints John Chavis, an African American, as a missionary to slaves.

1802

POLITICS AND CIVIL RIGHTS

Ohioans write a state constitution forbidding slavery and allowing free African Americans to vote.

Contemporary Events, 1800 ■ The federal government moves from Philadelphia to the new capital in Washington, D.C. ■ Thomas Jefferson is elected president. **1801** ■ The Pasha of Tripoli declares war on the United States, and President Jefferson sends warships to the Mediterranean.

Slaves as Skilled Workers

While most African-American slaves were engaged in agricultural work, some plantation and many urban slaves were employed in a variety of skilled and semiskilled tasks. Many black workers were carpenters, masons, bricklayers, and iron workers; others helped construct bridges, streets, canals, railroad lines, public buildings, and private homes. Plantation owners found it economically advantageous to teach some slaves industrial skills so that they could be hired out during off-seasons. In some parts of the South, more slaves were engaged in skilled work than were whites, a condition that caused resentment among working-class whites.

In various counties in Virginia and North Carolina rumors of slave revolts are widespread, leading to the arrest and execution of many African Americans suspected of involvement.

1803

POLITICS AND CIVIL RIGHTS

South Carolina opens slave trade with South America and the West Indies.

In New York City, protesting African Americans burn houses and riot for several days, resulting in arrests and convictions.

PERFORMING ARTS

Newport Gardner's composition "Crooked Shanks" is published.

1804

POLITICS AND CIVIL RIGHTS

By this year all the northern states have passed antislavery laws or measures to allow the gradual emancipation of the current slave population.

Ohio passes the first in a series of "black codes" to restrict the rights and movement of free African Americans. Other northern states will enact similar laws.

1805

POLITICS AND CIVIL RIGHTS

In the case of *Thompson* v. *Wilmot*, the court decides that a slave who was promised freedom after a certain amount of time should be granted freedom and awarded over $600 in damages because his owner refused to uphold the contract.

BUSINESS AND EMPLOYMENT

In Maryland free African Americans are forbidden by law to sell corn, wheat, or tobacco without a special license.

Contemporary Events, 1803 ■ Ohio becomes a state. ■ The Louisiana Territory is purchased from France. **1804** ■ The Lewis and Clark expedition starts out from St. Louis, Missouri. **1805** ■ The Lewis and Clark expedition reaches the Pacific Coast.

RELIGION AND EDUCATION

A Baptist church, with both white and black members, is established in Mississippi by Joseph Willis, a free African American.

SCIENCE AND TECHNOLOGY

Mathematician and inventor Benjamin Banneker dies in Maryland October 9.

Norbert Rillieux, the inventor who will revolutionize the sugar-refining industry, is born March 17 in New Orleans.

POLITICS AND CIVIL RIGHTS

Congress passes a law to abolish the importation of slaves from Africa, but illegal cargoes of slaves continue to arrive up to the time of the Civil War.

Abolitionist and Mason Prince Hall dies in Boston December 4.

RELIGION AND EDUCATION

John Gloucester organizes the First African Presbyterian Church in Philadelphia.

George Bell, Nicholas Franklin, and Moses Liverpool, three African Americans, build the first schoolhouse for black students in the nation's capital.

LITERATURE AND JOURNALISM

Charles Bennett Ray, who will become editor of the *Colored American* in the 1830s, is born December 25 in Falmouth, Massachusetts.

THE MILITARY

A British naval ship stops the United States frigate *Chesapeake* and impresses four men on the grounds that they are fugitive British sailors. One of the four men is David Martin, an African American from Massachusetts.

Contemporary Events, 1807 ■ The United States passes the Embargo Act against England and France.

The Poll Tax

The poll tax was used from colonial times into the mid-20th century to prevent or discourage free African Americans from voting. The first poll tax in South Carolina was levied in 1760 and amended at various times in its details. In 1787, for example, the law applied to men and women, ages 16 to 50. Two years later, it was changed to cover every free black citizen regardless of age or sex, requiring each to pay 25 cents for the next 10 years, in addition to other forms of taxation. For many free African Americans (as well as for many whites) this was a severe economic hardship. Protests from both blacks and whites were sent periodically to the state legislature. In 1809 some relief was granted by a dispensation for people who were unable to earn a living due to physical disabilities.

PERFORMING ARTS

Ira Frederick Aldridge is born July 24 in New York City. He will become an internationally known Shakespearean actor.

POLITICS AND CIVIL RIGHTS

A federal law abolishing the importation of slaves goes into effect January 1.

STATISTICS

The slave population reaches one million.

POLITICS AND CIVIL RIGHTS

Joseph Jenkins Roberts is born to free parents in Petersburg, Virginia. In 1847 he will be instrumental in winning independence for the American colony of Liberia and become its first president.

RELIGION AND EDUCATION

The Abyssinian Baptist Church is founded July 5 in New York.

The First African Baptist Church in Philadelphia is organized. A Baptist church is also established in Boston.

James W. C. Pennington is born into slavery in Maryland. He will become the only black member of the Hartford (Connecticut) Central Association of Congregational Ministers, and in 1843 will represent Connecticut at the World Anti-Slavery Convention in London.

POLITICS AND CIVIL RIGHTS

In its efforts to curtail slavery, New York State passes two laws. One requires slave owners to teach slave children how to read the Bible. The other forbids New Yorkers to import slaves for any purpose.

Charles Lenox Remond is born in Salem, Massachusetts. He will

Contemporary Events, 1808 ■ James Madison is elected president. **1810** ■ More than a million people have settled in the territory between the Appalachian Mountains and the Mississippi River.

46

become a leading antislavery advocate in New England and recruit for the 54th regiment of the Massachusetts volunteer infantry.

BUSINESS AND EMPLOYMENT

A federal law makes it illegal to hire an African American as a United States mail carrier.

An insurance company organized in Philadelphia is the first one known to be managed by African Americans.

STATISTICS

According to the U.S. census, 1,377,808 African Americans live in the United States, making up 19% of the total population. Slaves account for 1,191,362, while only 186,466, or 13.5% of the black population, is free.

1811

POLITICS AND CIVIL RIGHTS

Federal and state troops crush a revolt by several hundred slaves in Louisiana, not far from New Orleans.

In Georgia, slaves can receive a jury trial only for crimes involving capital punishment. Trials for slaves accused of lesser crimes and misdemeanors are held before a justice of the peace.

Any free African American who enters the state of Delaware is given 10 days' notice to leave, after which he or she is fined $10 a week. Any free black citizen of Delaware who leaves the state for six months is no longer considered a resident and cannot return.

RELIGION AND EDUCATION

Daniel Alexander Payne is born to free parents in Charleston, South Carolina. Payne will become a bishop in the African Methodist Episcopal Church and serve as president of Wilberforce University.

1812

POLITICS AND CIVIL RIGHTS

Martin Robinson Delany is born May 6 in Charles Town, Virginia.

Contemporary Events, 1812 ■ Louisiana becomes a state. ■ James Madison is reelected president. ■ The United States declares war on Great Britain.

He will become the first African-American major in the United States Army, a medical doctor, a writer, and a black nationalist, of whom Frederick Douglass will say, "I thank God for making me a man simply; but Delany always thanks Him for making him a black man."

RELIGION AND EDUCATION

The General Conference of the Methodist Church adopts a resolution that any member who owns slaves and lives in a state where manumission of slaves is legal must free his slaves in order to become a minister in the church.

THE MILITARY

African Americans account for one-sixth of the seamen in the navy during the War of 1812.

In Georgia and North Carolina, free African Americans must seek special approval to be allowed to serve in the state militia.

RELIGION AND EDUCATION

In Philadelphia a school building for African Americans, costing over $3,000, is financed by the Pennsylvania Abolition Society.

LITERATURE AND JOURNALISM

James McCune Smith is born in New York City. He will become a medical doctor and prolific writer.

THE MILITARY

In a sea battle off Boston between the American frigate *Chesapeake* and the British *Shannon*, a major proportion of the American seamen are African Americans.

Andrew Jackson awards the title of "major" to a black man named Jeffrey who rallies Americans in a successful stand against the British at the Battle of Fort Boyer in Alabama.

Commander Oliver Hazard Perry defeats the British at the Battle of Lake Erie and praises the 50 African Americans on his ship as "among my best men."

Contemporary Events, 1813 ■ Tecumseh, chief of the Shawnee, is killed by American troops at the Battle of the Thames in Ontario.

1814

THE MILITARY

After the British burn Washington, D.C., over 2,500 African Americans under the leadership of James Forten, Richard Allen, and Absalom Jones are enlisted by the Vigilance Committee of Philadelphia to construct defenses to keep the British from burning the city. Similar plans in Baltimore are carried out by African-American workers, both free and slave, along with whites.

John Day is one of the many African-American gunners at the Battle of Lake Champlain. He continues to serve in the U.S. Navy in the Mediterranean until 1816.

Charles Black, who serves with honors at Lake Champlain, is the third generation in his family to fight America's wars.

1815

POLITICS AND CIVIL RIGHTS

In the Northwest Territory the tolerant attitude of white settlers toward blacks triggers a migration of southern blacks to that region.

Paul Cuffe takes 38 African Americans to Sierra Leone on his ship.

Civil rights preacher and abolitionist Henry Highland Garnet is born into slavery December 23 in Maryland.

BUSINESS AND EMPLOYMENT

In Louisiana free African Americans are allowed to serve in an all-black police corps.

THE MILITARY

African-American officers command approximately 600 black soldiers under Andrew Jackson at the Battle of New Orleans. More than 1,000 soldiers of African descent, some from Santo Domingo, fight against the British at this historic battle.

In Florida 300 fugitive slaves-turned-farmers from Georgia and 30 Creek Indians seize the former British Fort Blount and create an asylum for runaway slaves. In a year U.S. troops will destroy the stronghold, killing about 270 former slaves.

Contemporary Events, 1814 ■ Francis Scott Key writes the lyrics that will become the national anthem, "The Star-Spangled Banner." ■ The Treaty of Ghent ends the War of 1812. Territories that had been seized by the United States or Great Britain during the war are restored to their prewar status.

The American Colonization Society

As a way of eliminating free African Americans, whose very existence was an inspiration to slaves, many white leaders favored colonization in Africa. In 1816 they formed the American Colonization Society to fund and orchestrate the emigration of free African Americans. In 1822 the society established the state of Liberia as a colony for ex-slaves and free blacks.

A few African Americans—including Daniel Coker, AME leader, and John Russwurm, editor of the first black newspaper—advocated emigration as a way of escaping a racist society. Most African Americans, however, viewed colonization in Africa as a betrayal of the desire of most blacks to achieve their place in America. James Forten, in particular, was an outspoken opponent, seeing the plan as an attempt to remove black abolitionists from America, where they were working for emancipation and full civil rights for their people.

1816

POLITICS AND CIVIL RIGHTS

The American Colonization Society is founded in Washington, D.C., with the support of many leading white politicians, who hope it will "solve" the race problem in the United States by promoting the return of free African Americans to Africa.

RELIGION AND EDUCATION

A library and a school taught by an African-American teacher are set up for black students in Wilmington, Delaware.

In Philadelphia, the African Methodist Episcopal (AME) Church is formally organized, and Richard Allen becomes its bishop.

LITERATURE AND JOURNALISM

William Wells Brown is born in Lexington, Kentucky. He will become a popular lecturer in the antislavery communities, a doctor, a historian, and a writer.

William Cooper Nell is born in Boston. In the 1850s Nell, an educator and antislavery advocate, will write about African Americans who served in the Revolutionary War and the War of 1812.

1817

POLITICS AND CIVIL RIGHTS

Along with other African Americans, Richard Allen and James Forten lead a protest in Philadelphia against the attempts of the American Colonization Society to drive black Americans "from the land of our nativity."

Captain Paul Cuffe, Revolutionary era leader and businessman, dies in Westport, Massachusetts, September 9.

Frederick Douglass is born February 14 into slavery in Maryland. He will become the leading black abolitionist, orator, and civil rights advocate of the 19th century.

Author, clergyman, and abolitionist Samuel Ringgold Ward is born in Maryland.

Contemporary Events, 1816 ■ James Monroe is elected president. ■ Indiana becomes a state. **1817** ■ Mississippi becomes a state. ■ Writer and naturalist Henry David Thoreau is born. ■ Construction begins on the Erie Canal between Buffalo and Albany, linking the Great Lakes with the Hudson River.

BUSINESS AND EMPLOYMENT

John Jones is born free in North Carolina. He will become one of America's wealthiest African Americans, a civil rights advocate, and the first black elected Cook County commissioner in Chicago.

RELIGION AND EDUCATION

John Mifflin Brown, writer, educator, and bishop in the AME Church, is born in Delaware.

LITERATURE AND JOURNALISM

Victor Sejour, one of Paris's most successful commercial playwrights, is born in New Orleans. In 1844 his first play, *Diegareas,* will be produced by Le Théâtre-Français.

RELIGION AND EDUCATION

The Pennsylvania Augustine Society, an organization to promote educational opportunities, is founded by free African Americans.

Absalom Jones, religious leader and cofounder of the Free African Society, dies February 13 in Philadelphia.

THE MILITARY

At the Battle of Suwanee an army of black soldiers and Seminole warriors is defeated by Andrew Jackson. The conflict ends the First Seminole War.

POLITICS AND CIVIL RIGHTS

In the Missouri territory, a law forbids the right of assembly to African Americans, whether slave or free. It is also illegal there to teach slaves to read. However, when Missouri becomes a state in 1821, its state constitution will grant slaves court-assigned legal defense, trial by jury, and a uniform punishment code for both free whites and black slaves.

Contemporary Events, 1819 ■ The United States purchases Florida from Spain. ■ Alabama becomes a state. ■ Poet Walt Whitman is born.

1820

POLITICS AND CIVIL RIGHTS

The Missouri Compromise is reached, admitting Missouri into the Union as a slave state (in 1821), but prohibiting slavery in all the Plains states that will be formed north of latitude line 36 degrees, 30 minutes. Theoretically, states formed south of this line could become slave states.

Carrying 86 African Americans, the *Mayflower of Liberia* sets sail from New York on February 6, headed for colonization in Sierra Leone.

1821

POLITICS AND CIVIL RIGHTS

To qualify for voting rights in New York, African Americans must own more property and reside longer in the state than white people.

Harriet Tubman is born into slavery in Maryland. She will become one of the most courageous workers in the Underground Railroad.

RELIGION AND EDUCATION

In New York the African Methodist Episcopal Zion Church is formally founded and holds its first annual conference.

LITERATURE AND JOURNALISM

Benjamin Lundy, a white Quaker, begins publishing *The Genius of Universal Emancipation* in Ohio, an antislavery journal that attracts the services of William Lloyd Garrison. Lundy strongly endorses voluntary emigration for African Americans.

Writer and lifelong civil rights activist William Still is born. He will publish an account of the Underground Railroad.

SCIENCE AND TECHNOLOGY

The earliest known patent given to an African-American inventor is for Thomas L. Jennings's invention to dry-clean clothes.

PERFORMING ARTS

The African Company, the first all-black actors guild, is founded in

Contemporary Events, 1820 ■ James Monroe is reelected president. ■ The U.S. Land Law sets $1.25 as the minimum price for an acre of land.

New York. They perform *Richard III* in the African Grove Theatre in lower Manhattan.

POLITICS AND CIVIL RIGHTS

Denmark Vesey, a former slave in Charleston, South Carolina, plans an insurrection to seize arsenals, guardhouses, and munition supplies; take the city; and kill all whites. His plans run aground when government officials learn of the conspiracy from slave informers. The rebels are arrested, and Vesey and 34 others are executed.

African-American members of the American Colonization Society officially establish the recently purchased colony of Liberia as a haven for ex-slaves and expatriated African Americans.

In Tennessee it becomes illegal for blacks and whites to marry.

Hiram Rhoades Revels is born free in Fayetteville, North Carolina. He will become a U.S. Army chaplain during the Civil War and in 1870 a U.S. senator from Mississippi.

RELIGION AND EDUCATION

James Varick becomes bishop of the African Methodist Episcopal Zion Church in New York on July 30.

The first public school for African Americans in Philadelphia is opened. Originally called the Bird School, it will later be renamed for James Forten, the black entrepreneur and civil rights leader.

LITERATURE AND JOURNALISM

Poet and militant abolitionist James Whitfield is born April 10 in Massachusetts.

POLITICS AND CIVIL RIGHTS

A U.S. circuit court in Washington, D.C., upholds a principle that later will be overturned by the Dred Scott decision—namely, that removal of a slave into a free state, where slavery is not legally protected by the law, bestows freedom on that slave.

Contemporary Events, 1823 ■ The Monroe Doctrine states that the Americas are no longer open to further European colonization.

In Mississippi it is illegal to teach slaves to read or write. The law also forbids meetings of more than five African Americans, free or slave. Punishment for these infractions is up to 39 lashes.

LITERATURE AND JOURNALISM

Abolitionist lecturer and journalist Mary Ann Shadd Cary is born October 9 in Wilmington, Delaware. She will publish and edit the *Provincial Freeman,* a Canadian newspaper.

PERFORMING ARTS

West-Indian-born playwright Henry Brown presents his *Drama of King Shotaway* at the African Grove Theatre in New York.

1824

RELIGION AND EDUCATION

The city government of New York begins financial support of the African Free School, which has 600 pupils.

Dartmouth College administrators are persuaded by a student protest to admit African Americans.

LITERATURE AND JOURNALISM

George B. Vashon, whose romantic narrative poetry will celebrate the Haitian Revolution and its heroes, is born July 24.

1825

POLITICS AND CIVIL RIGHTS

Josiah Henson, the alleged model for Harriet Beecher Stowe's character "Uncle Tom," leads a group of runaway slaves from Maryland to freedom in Kentucky. Henson later flees to Canada, where he founds a settlement of former slaves.

U.S. congressman from Alabama and successful businessman Benjamin S. Turner is born into slavery in North Carolina.

BUSINESS AND EMPLOYMENT

Free African Americans cannot sell tobacco in Maryland without a

---

Contemporary Events, 1824 ■ John Quincy Adams is elected president by the House of Representatives, as none of the four candidates carried a majority in the popular election. ■ The Sunday School Union is formed to promote religious instruction for young children.

certificate from a justice of the peace that has been witnessed by two white citizens.

RELIGION AND EDUCATION

Richard Harvey Cain, AME minister, publisher, and U.S. congressman from South Carolina, is born April 12 in Virginia.

LITERATURE AND JOURNALISM

Poet and novelist Frances Ellen Watkins Harper is born September 24 in Baltimore of free parents.

SCIENCE AND TECHNOLOGY

Alexander Thomas Augusta, the first black surgeon in the U.S. Army, is born March 8 in Norfolk, Virginia.

PERFORMING ARTS

Ira Aldridge begins to appear in major roles on the London stage.

1826

POLITICS AND CIVIL RIGHTS

A mob of whites in Cincinnati attempts unsuccessfully to drive the black population of 690 residents from the city.

Activist Sarah Remond is born June 6 in Salem, Massachusetts.

BUSINESS AND EMPLOYMENT

Restrictions in North Carolina forbid free blacks from selling certain articles and from selling or trading outside the county of their residence without a special license.

RELIGION AND EDUCATION

Two of the first African Americans to graduate from college are Edward A. Jones of Amherst and John Russwurm of Bowdoin.

Peter Williams, Jr., is ordained to the ministry in the Episcopal Church and becomes the rector of St. Phillip's Church in New York City.

LITERATURE AND JOURNALISM

Poet James Madison Bell is born in Ohio. He will help recruit for

African-American Businesses

Even before the Civil War, some African-American businessmen founded companies that became successful and hired both white and black employees. These entrepreneurs, however, always ran the risk of resentment from white businesses and customers. Henry Boyd of Cincinnati is a case in point. When he came to Ohio in 1826, racial prejudice prevented him from finding employment as a cabinetmaker. He went into home construction, eventually partnering with a white man. As he grew more successful, he built a factory to manufacture bed frames and other articles of furniture, his company eventually occupying four buildings and employing 50 workers. A creative businessman and inventor, Boyd devised a machine for making bed rails (although he had to obtain a patent for his invention under the name of a white man). Resentful whites frequently vandalized his buildings, and Boyd went out of business after his plant was destroyed by fire.

Contemporary Events, 1826 ■ Both Thomas Jefferson and John Adams die within hours of each other on July 4, the 50th anniversary of the Declaration of Independence, which they both signed.

the raid on Harpers Ferry, and after the Civil War become active in the Republican Party in Ohio.

PERFORMING ARTS

Ira Aldridge stars as "Othello" in Shakespeare's play in London.

POLITICS AND CIVIL RIGHTS

Ten thousand African Americans are freed in New York when the state abolishes slavery on July 4.

LITERATURE AND JOURNALISM

In New York City on March 16 John Russwurm and Samuel E. Cornish begin publication of *Freedom's Journal*, the first African-American-owned newspaper. Its goal is "to arrest the progress of prejudice, and to shield ourselves against its consequent evils."

POLITICS AND CIVIL RIGHTS

William Lloyd Garrison becomes involved in the antislavery movement and writes an article for the *National Philanthropist*, an antislavery journal published in Boston, in which he attacks slavery and the restrictions against educating slaves, notably in South Carolina.

BUSINESS AND EMPLOYMENT

A new ruling by the U.S. postmaster general provides limited work opportunities for African Americans. Under white supervision, blacks are allowed to carry mail from stagecoaches to post offices. This is a departure from the 1810 prohibition against African Americans working as letter carriers.

RELIGION AND EDUCATION

The Reading Room Society is founded in Philadelphia by businessman William Whipper. Membership fees and monthly dues finance the library, which offers a program for educating blacks and provides a center for antislavery activists.

Contemporary Events, 1828 ■ Andrew Jackson is elected president. ■ Construction begins on the Baltimore and Ohio Railroad. ■ Noah Webster publishes **The American Dictionary of the English Language.**

LITERATURE AND JOURNALISM

Three antislavery publications are founded: the *Free Press* in Bennington, Vermont; the *New England Weekly Review*, and the *Liberalist* in New Orleans.

VISUAL ARTS

Landscape painter Edward M. Bannister is born in New Brunswick, Canada. He will help start the Providence Art Club in Rhode Island.

1829

POLITICS AND CIVIL RIGHTS

Walker's Appeal, written by African-American activist David Walker, is published in Boston. The pamphlet calls upon slaves to rise up against their masters, and its circulation is prohibited in the South.

In Cincinnati an estimated 1,200 African Americans flee to Canada after mobs of whites loot and burn their homes.

Mexico abolishes slavery, but American settlers, most of whom migrated from southern slave states, force the Mexican government to reestablish it in the northern province called Texas.

Attorney John Mercer Langston is born into slavery in Virginia. He will serve as minister resident to Haiti, chargé d'affaires to Santo Domingo, and U.S. representative from Virginia.

BUSINESS AND EMPLOYMENT

Robert Bogle, one of the first African-American professional caterers, is honored in a poem posthumously acknowledging his career in Philadelphia.

RELIGION AND EDUCATION

The state of Ohio returns the school tax levied on the property owned by African Americans, since the law forbids them from attending public schools.

In Charleston, South Carolina, Daniel A. Payne, a free African American, opens a school for black children that will thrive until 1834, when it is closed in the aftermath of a state law prohibiting free blacks from teaching other African Americans, slave or free.

Abolition Societies along the Ohio

By the mid-1820s there were 130 abolition societies in the United States, most of them operating along the Ohio River and in what would become the border states between North and South during the Civil War. There were 106 societies in Kentucky, Tennessee, the western counties of Virginia (which split from the state during the Civil War to become West Virginia), and in the southern sections of Ohio, Indiana, and Illinois (the territories where slavery was forbidden by the Northwest Ordinance in 1787). In the 1820s membership in these 106 abolition societies grew to over 5,000 members, a sizable percentage of the 6,625 members nationwide.

Contemporary Events, 1829 ■ The first American encyclopedia, **The Encyclopaedia Americana,** is published in Philadelphia by Francis Lieber.

James Theodore Holly is born free in Washington, D.C. He will become a bishop in the Episcopal Church, a historian of the black revolution in Haiti, and in 1874 the bishop of Haiti.

POLITICS AND CIVIL RIGHTS

The first National Negro Convention meets in Philadelphia. The organization enlists the support of African-American churches to launch programs to improve the status of blacks in the United States and work against the colonization movement.

BUSINESS AND EMPLOYMENT

The largest livery stable owner in Washington, D.C., is an African American, William Wormley, who invests in the construction of a school building. Wormley's sister and other educators conduct classes there, until the building and Wormley's business are destroyed by riots and fires in 1835.

RELIGION AND EDUCATION

The first African-American Roman Catholic bishop, James Augustine Healy, is born April 6 in Georgia to a slave woman and an Irish planter. He will administer the diocese covering the states of Maine and New Hampshire for 25 years.

PERFORMING ARTS

In Louisville, Kentucky, a white song-and-dance man, Thomas D. "Daddy" Rice, creates a comic character named "Jim Crow." Based on an elderly black stable hand who danced and sang in a "humorous" fashion as he went about his work, the stock character "Jim Crow" will become a standard feature in white minstrel shows in the United States and Europe.

POLITICS AND CIVIL RIGHTS

On January 1 William Lloyd Garrison launches the *Liberator*, which argues that slavery is sinful and calls for immediate emancipation of

Contemporary Events, 1830 ■ Daniel Webster debates Robert Y. Hayne over the issue of states' rights. ■ Poet Emily Dickinson is born.

all slaves without compensation to their owners. This publication signals a change in the antislavery movement, which becomes increasingly belligerent and political.

In Southampton County, Virginia, Nat Turner, a charismatic preacher, leads a bloody slave rebellion, killing approximately 50 whites. Backlash is swift and merciless, involving 3,000 soldiers and militiamen who slaughter blacks indiscriminately. Turner is eventually caught and hanged.

The first Annual Convention of the People of Color in Philadelphia, comprised of delegates from five states, opposes the American Colonization Society's program of emigration to Africa in favor of resettling free blacks in Canada. It also advocates bettering the condition of free African Americans and funding an industrial training college in New Haven, Connecticut.

In Ohio, African Americans are not allowed to serve on juries.

BUSINESS AND EMPLOYMENT

In South Carolina, African Americans are prohibited by law from making or selling liquor.

RELIGION AND EDUCATION

James Walker Hood, who will become bishop of the African Methodist Episcopal Zion Church, is born.

LITERATURE AND JOURNALISM

Free African-American women in Philadelphia organize a club, the Female Literary Society, to promote and critique members' writings.

1832

POLITICS AND CIVIL RIGHTS

The New England Anti-Slavery Society is formed. About one-quarter of the first 72 members are African American.

Joseph H. Rainey, U.S. congressman from South Carolina, is born June 21 in Georgetown, South Carolina.

Emigrationist and scholar Edward Wilmot Blyden is born August 3 in St. Thomas.

Contemporary Events, 1831 ■ U.S. Chief Justice John Marshall, ruling against the longstanding concept that Native Americans constituted "foreign nations," declares that the U.S. government alone holds sovereignty over tribal peoples living in the United States.

African-American Urban Population

In the 1830s the African-American population in several southern cities was larger than the white population. In Charleston, Savannah, New Orleans, and Richmond, African Americans were a majority; and in Mobile and Norfolk they were almost a majority. But white populations grew faster than black populations, and by 1860, no city had a black majority. The shift was due to two major trends. First, white immigration outpaced black immigration, as more whites arrived and fewer African Americans were brought into urban areas. Second, urban whites intentionally sold slaves to rural areas to reduce the urban black population in fear of possible slave revolts.

RELIGION AND EDUCATION

African-American circuit rider William Paul Quinn begins his itinerant missionary work in the Midwest, eventually founding 47 churches in Illinois, Indiana, Ohio, and western Pennsylvania.

In Boston the Afric-American Female Intelligence Society is organized to sponsor cultural and literary events for free black women.

STATISTICS

A healthy male field hand, aged 18 to 25, can be bought for $500.

POLITICS AND CIVIL RIGHTS

The American Anti-Slavery Society is organized in Philadelphia by William Lloyd Garrison, Robert Purvis, George B. Vashon, and other abolitionists. This biracial nationwide organization calls for the immediate and uncompensated emancipation of slaves. By 1840 the society will have 2,000 local chapters, with a membership of over 200,000. Its activities include publication of periodicals, pamphlets, and books and an unrelenting petitioning of Congress.

BUSINESS AND EMPLOYMENT

In Georgia a law forbids employing African Americans in printing offices in any capacity that requires knowledge of reading or writing.

RELIGION AND EDUCATION

Oberlin College is founded in Ohio. From its earliest days the college, a center for clandestine abolitionist activity, welcomes black students on equal terms with whites. By the Civil War, one-third of the student body will be African American. Three black students from Oberlin will join John Brown's raid at Harpers Ferry.

POLITICS AND CIVIL RIGHTS

A white mob attacks the African-American section of Philadelphia, killing a black man and destroying over 30 homes. Riots also occur in

---

Contemporary Events, 1833 ■ The Whig party is formed by political forces opposed to Andrew Jackson. ■ President Jackson removes government funds from the Bank of the United States in order to destroy its political power.

other cities, such as Trenton, New Jersey, and Rochester, New York.

Parliament abolishes slavery within the British Empire, freeing over 700,000 people. This act increases the moral pressure on Americans to abolish slavery.

Alonzo J. Ransier, lieutenant governor of South Carolina and U.S. representative, is born January 3 in Charleston to free parents.

BUSINESS AND EMPLOYMENT

An organization for free African-American mechanics, called "Les Artisans," is founded in New Orleans.

In New York David Ruggles opens the first black-owned bookshop, which will be burned by a white mob in 1835.

RELIGION AND EDUCATION

In the aftermath of slave uprisings led by preachers like Nat Turner, southern slave owners begin to force slaves to attend church services conducted by white ministers. In some places African-American ministers are outlawed, black churches are closed, and slaves are required to attend services in their masters' churches.

Henry McNeal Turner, bishop in the AME Church, emigrationist, and the first black chaplain in the United States Army, is born in South Carolina.

Patrick Francis Healy, the first African American to earn a doctorate, is born February 7 in Georgia. He will become president of Georgetown University.

Rufus L. Perry, Baptist missionary, minister, and noted journalist, is born into slavery in Tennessee.

SCIENCE AND TECHNOLOGY

Henry Blair of Maryland receives a patent for his invention of a corn-planting machine.

1835

POLITICS AND CIVIL RIGHTS

In a message to Congress, President Andrew Jackson, a southerner, calls for restrictions on abolitionist literature sent through the mails.

Contemporary Events, 1834 ■ Abraham Lincoln enters politics in Illinois as an assemblyman in the state legislature. ■ Cyrus Hall McCormick receives a patent for his reaping machine.

Underground Railroad

Crossing the Ohio River or the Chesapeake Bay, tens of thousands of fugitive slaves risked their lives and the lives of their friends and families to reach freedom. No one knows how many people fled during the 30 years before the Civil War. Estimates range from 40,000 to 100,000. In addition to the official Underground Railroad "agents" along the precarious route to freedom, either in the United States or Canada, countless average men and women risked their lives to harbor one or several fleeing slaves for a night before they continued on to the next station. Whigs, Democrats, Quakers, Baptists, people from many walks of life took part—even those who were not fully convinced of the abolitionist position. Frederick Douglass, commenting on the genuine sense of humanity that emerged in many cases, said that people "were better than their theology, and truer to humanity than to their politics."

He notes the "painful excitement produced in the South" by "inflammatory appeals [and] addresses to the passions of the slaves" to work for freedom.

An African-American abolitionist from Ohio, Amos Dresser, is arrested for passing out antislavery literature in Nashville. He is tried, beaten, and driven from the city.

North Carolina becomes the last southern state to deny suffrage to all African Americans, by repealing its 1776 provision that all freemen who meet the property requirement can vote, regardless of color.

Sally Hemings, slave mistress of Thomas Jefferson, dies in Virginia.

BUSINESS AND EMPLOYMENT

In Georgia a law is passed to prohibit African Americans from working in drugstores and pharmacies where they have access to poison and other lethal substances.

THE MILITARY

The Second Seminole War breaks out. By the time it ends in 1843, some 500 fugitive slaves who were living with the Seminoles will be reenslaved.

1836

POLITICS AND CIVIL RIGHTS

Congress passes the infamous "gag rule," which prohibits any antislavery bill or petition from being introduced, read, or discussed. All such petitions are to be tabled, unread. A direct violation of the Constitutional right of petition, the rule will not be repealed until 1845.

Disagreement over whites and blacks mixing in public extends even to antislavery societies. In New York, the Women's Anti-Slavery Society does not admit African Americans as members. A request to have a black minister address the American Anti-Slavery Society is rejected by members on the grounds that it would be a breach of correct social mores. In some places, however, whites and blacks work together publicly for the antislavery cause.

Contemporary Events, 1835 ■ Fighting breaks out in Texas with Americans seizing important Mexican towns, and Texas declares its right to secede from Mexico. ■ Writer Samuel L. Clemens (Mark Twain) is born. ■ Industrialist Andrew Carnegie is born.

RELIGION AND EDUCATION

Under pressure from slave owners, the Methodist Church votes to avoid confrontation over the issue of abolition, stating that civil and political relationships between masters and slaves should not be the concern of religion.

Independent missionary Amanda Berry Smith is born into slavery January 23 in Maryland. The AME church does not ordain women, so Smith will pursue her own preaching career throughout the nation and on three other continents.

SCIENCE AND TECHNOLOGY

Henry Blair receives a second patent for his cotton-planting machine.

1837

POLITICS AND CIVIL RIGHTS

In Alton, Illinois, Elijah Lovejoy is murdered and his printing press destroyed by angry mobs. The editor, who advocated immediate abolition, had endured attacks against his printing office in previous years for championing antislavery positions. Lovejoy's murder will become a *cause célèbre* among journalists and abolitionists, linking the issues of antislavery and free speech.

Canadian blacks gain the right to vote.

Pinckney B. S. Pinchback, lieutenant governor of Louisiana and U.S. senator, is born May 10 in Georgia to a white planter and a slave mother.

BUSINESS AND EMPLOYMENT

U.S. congressman from Alabama and labor leader James T. Rapier is born November 13 in Florence, Alabama. He will be instrumental in setting up Alabama's first African-American labor convention.

RELIGION AND EDUCATION

The first National Negro Catholic Congress takes place in Washington, D.C.

Francis L. Cardozo, educator and minister, is born February 1 in Charleston, South Carolina.

Contemporary Events, 1836 ■ Texas wins independence from Mexico, and General Sam Houston becomes the first president of the Republic of Texas. ■ Arkansas becomes a state. ■ Martin Van Buren is elected president. **1837** ■ Michigan becomes a state. ■ The financial panic of 1837 begins.

Frederick Douglass

The foremost African-American leader in the antislavery movement was Frederick Douglass. Born into slavery in Maryland, Douglass worked as a house servant, where he learned to read and write, and then as field hand, where he experienced the brutality inflicted on rural slaves. He became a preacher in his teens. In 1838 Douglass escaped, disguised as a sailor, and took a train to New York. Within three years he was speaking publicly about the horrors of slavery as no one had ever spoken before. In 1845 he published his autobiography at the risk of being captured and reenslaved as a fugitive. He also founded the **North Star,** an important abolition newspaper. "If there is no struggle, there is no progress," Douglass wrote in 1881. "Those who profess to favor freedom, and yet deprecate agitation, are men who want crops without plowing up the ground."

LITERATURE AND JOURNALISM

Hosea Easton's *A Treatise on the Intellectual Character and Political Condition of the Colored People of the United States* is published in Boston.

Samuel E. Cornish, pastor of the African Presbyterian Church in New York, begins the *Weekly Advocate.* Within a few months, he renames it the *Colored American.*

Slavery in the United States: A Narrative of the Life and Adventures of Charles Ball, a Black Man, is published.

SCIENCE AND TECHNOLOGY

After studying medicine in Scotland, James McCune Smith begins a medical practice in New York. Later he will pioneer methods for calculating mortality rates for insurance companies.

VISUAL ARTS

Quiltmaker Harriet Powers is born October 29 in Georgia.

THE MILITARY

In December John Horse, an African-American commander of the Seminole Indians, helps defeat U.S. troops at the Battle of Okeechobee in Florida.

STATISTICS

The price of a healthy male field slave, 18 to 25 years old, is $1,300.

POLITICS AND CIVIL RIGHTS

Frederick Augustus Washington Bailey escapes from slavery in Maryland, traveling by train to New York disguised as a sailor. He will change his name to Frederick Douglass.

Charles Lenox Remond becomes a professional abolitionist. The first African-American lecturer employed by an antislavery society, Remond begins as a Garrisonian, preaching nonviolence; he later advocates armed slave revolts.

BUSINESS AND EMPLOYMENT

According to the Abolition Society of Philadelphia, only 350 out of

Contemporary Events, 1838 ■ The Cherokees are forcibly removed from their land in Georgia and relocated in what will become Oklahoma.

997 African-Americans with trade credentials in that city actually work at their trades.

In many areas, jobs on wharves and in domestic service formerly filled by African Americans are now going to Irish immigrants.

RELIGION AND EDUCATION

Minister and teacher John Chavis dies June 13.

LITERATURE AND JOURNALISM

William Whipper and other African-American leaders begin publishing the *National Reformer*, a journal of the Moral Reform Society that advocates nonviolent methods for abolishing slavery.

David Ruggles begins a black quarterly magazine, *Mirror of Liberty*, in New York City.

1839

POLITICS AND CIVIL RIGHTS

The Liberty Party is formed by James G. Birney and other abolitionists, notably African-American leaders Samuel Ringgold Ward and Henry Highland Garnet. The new party will run candidates for president in 1840 and 1844.

Samuel Ringgold Ward is hired by the American Anti-Slavery Society. Later he will be forced to flee to Canada and live in exile.

On board the Spanish slave ship *L'Amistad*, 54 African slaves, led by Cinque, seize the ship off the coast of Cuba and sail to Long Island. Defended by John Quincy Adams, they will win their freedom in a celebrated Supreme Court case.

The State Department refuses to give an African American from Philadelphia a passport on the grounds that blacks are not citizens in Pennsylvania because suffrage is limited to whites.

Robert Smalls, state senator and U.S. congressman from South Carolina, is born into slavery in Beaufort, South Carolina.

BUSINESS AND EMPLOYMENT

Wealthy Memphis banker and businessman Robert R. Church, Sr., is born June 18 in Mississippi.

Contemporary Events, 1839 ■ Charles Goodyear discovers how to vulcanize rubber, giving it elasticity and strength. ■ Industrialist John D. Rockefeller is born.

Ship captain Michael Healy is born September 22 in Georgia. His life will be an inspiration for Jack London's *Sea Wolf*.

RELIGION AND EDUCATION

A school for African-American boys is founded that evolves over the years into Cheyney State College in Pennsylvania.

1840

POLITICS AND CIVIL RIGHTS

Charles Lenox Remond, the American delegate to the World's Anti-Slavery Convention in London, refuses to take his seat when women delegates are segregated from the main floor into the gallery.

In Indiana it becomes illegal for whites to marry people with one great-grandparent who was African American. Fines up to $5,000 and prison terms up to 20 years are established for violators, and ministers who perform such marriages can be fined up to $10,000.

James Milton Turner, educator and minister to Liberia, is born May 16 in Missouri. He will win a claim for congressional funds for African-American members of the Cherokee Nation.

RELIGION AND EDUCATION

Bishop John Wesley Gaines is born. He will help establish the African Methodist Episcopal Church in the South and found Morris Brown College in Atlanta.

PERFORMING ARTS

Frank Johnson founds an orchestra in Philadelphia that will eventually tour overseas and perform before Queen Victoria.

STATISTICS

The U.S. census reports that the African-American population is 2,873,648, or 16.1% of the total population.

Of the 2,255 African Americans living in Cincinnati, one-fourth belong to temperance organizations, a number significantly greater than for whites, whose membership is less than one-tenth.

Contemporary Events, 1840 ■ William Henry Harrison is elected president. ■ According to the sixth national census, the population is 17 million.

POLITICS AND CIVIL RIGHTS

Cinque and other African slaves who rebelled aboard the *L'Amistad* are ordered freed by the U.S. Supreme Court.

Slaves transported from Hampton Roads, Virginia, to New Orleans aboard the ship *Creole* revolt, overpower the crew, and sail for the Bahamas, where they are given asylum and freedom by the British.

Black abolitionist Charles Lenox Remond returns from the World Anti-Slavery Convention in Britain with a petition titled "Address from the People of Ireland," with 60,000 signatures. It urges Irish Americans to oppose slavery and all forms of discrimination.

In Boston, African Americans are forced to march at the rear of the funeral procession for President William Henry Harrison.

In South Carolina, African Americans working in cotton mills are not allowed to look out the same windows as whites.

In Atlanta courts, blacks and whites are required to swear on different Bibles.

Blanche K. Bruce, the first African American to serve a full term in the U.S. Senate, is born in Virginia.

LITERATURE AND JOURNALISM

The first book-length study of northern urban African Americans by an African American appears. Although the book is published anonymously, the author of *Sketches of the Higher Classes of Colored Society in Philadelphia* claims to be black.

James W. C. Pennington, an ex-slave, writes *The Origin and History of the Colored People,* a textbook for children.

The pioneer quarterly *African Methodist Episcopal Church Magazine* begins publication in Brooklyn. In 1847 it will be renamed the *Christian Herald,* and in 1852 it will become the *Christian Recorder.*

VISUAL ARTS

Lithographer and painter Grafton Tyler Brown is born in Harrisburg, Pennsylvania.

Antislavery Centers

Certain key areas became centers of abolitonist activity in the 1840s and 1850s. Boston, continuing its Revolutionary War tradition of speaking out against oppression, was home to many abolitionists and sponsored abolitionist programs and speakers. New York saw a large number of escaped slaves arrive in the 1840s. Oberlin, Ohio, the home of Oberlin College, became a seat of abolitionist activity due to the college's liberal and humanitarian policies since its founding in 1833. Rochester, New York, where Frederick Douglass continued his fight against slavery, was also in an area that had a long tradition of radical social thinkers. In Rochester, Douglass published the **North Star,** an important abolitionist newspaper. Like Oberlin, the city was close to the Canadian border, an important consideration for Underground Railroad activities.

Contemporary Events, 1841 ■ President Harrison dies after one month in office and is succeeded by Vice President John Tyler.

1842

POLITICS AND CIVIL RIGHTS

In *Prigg* v. *Pennsylvania*, the U.S. Supreme Court decides that a "personal liberty" law enacted by Pennsylvania is constitutional, and that individual states cannot be made to enforce the Fugitive Slave Law of 1793. The result is that other northern states pass "personal liberty" laws.

The capture of escaped slave George Latimer in Boston is the first of many famous fugitive slave cases. Boston abolitionists purchase Latimer from his owner, and Frederick Douglass appears in print in support of the action.

Rhode Island grants suffrage to African Americans.

The Webster-Ashburton Treaty between the United States and Great Britain states that both nations will station ships off the African coast to thwart the slave trade.

Abolitionist Philadelphia businessman James Forten dies.

Robert B. Elliott, U.S. congressman from South Carolina, is born, probably in England.

Robert C. DeLarge, U.S. congressman from South Carolina, is born in Aiken, South Carolina.

Florida's first African-American congressman, Josiah T. Walls, is born December 30 in Virginia.

BUSINESS AND EMPLOYMENT

Bloodshed erupts between African Americans and Irish Americans working in Pennsylvania mines.

RELIGION AND EDUCATION

Bishop and educator Lucius Henry Hosley is born. He will compile a hymnal for the Colored Methodist Episcopal Church.

VISUAL ARTS

Painter Robert S. Duncanson first exhibits his paintings at the Western Art Union exhibition in Cincinnati.

Contemporary Events, 1842 ■ The Webster-Ashburton Treaty establishes the U.S.-Canadian border at the 49th parallel. ■ Social reformer Dorothea Dix begins a crusade to reform U.S. prisons and asylums.

1843

POLITICS AND CIVIL RIGHTS

The Liberty Party is the first national political party to allow African Americans to participate fully in leadership roles. Blacks serve as delegates, speakers, and officials at the party's national convention.

Isabella Bomefree, an ex-slave, changes her name to Sojourner Truth, symbolizing her religious mission to travel around the country speaking on behalf of abolition and women's rights.

At a convention of African Americans in Buffalo, New York, Henry Highland Garnet calls for a slave revolt and general strike, a position condemned by Frederick Douglass and other abolitionists.

Vermont and Massachusetts pass "personal liberty" laws, making it illegal for state officials to assist federal agents in recapturing fugitive slaves.

The Massachusetts legislature legalizes interracial marriages by repealing a 1786 law.

BUSINESS AND EMPLOYMENT

A Mississippi law allows county police authorities to make exceptions to local laws forbidding free African Americans from living and pursuing a trade in certain areas.

RELIGION AND EDUCATION

Richard Henry Boyd is born into slavery in Mississippi. Later a Baptist minister, Boyd will found the National Baptist Publishing Board.

LITERATURE AND JOURNALISM

In New Orleans, Creole writers start a journal of poems, stories, and articles. Called *L'Album Littéraire, Journal des Jeunes Gens, Amateurs de la Littérature*, the monthly is so successful that it becomes a biweekly.

Martin Robinson Delany starts the newspaper *Mystery* in Pittsburgh.

1844

POLITICS AND CIVIL RIGHTS

Attorney and abolitionist John Henry Smyth is born into slavery in

Sojourner Truth

Sojourner Truth was born Isabella Bomefree in Ulster County, New York, in 1797. She escaped from slavery in 1826. After a religious vision, she decided to become a traveling missionary and changed her name to Sojourner. When she asked God for a second name, she explained, "The Lord gave me Truth because I was to declare the truth to the people." In the 1840s Sojourner Truth became an important abolitionist lecturer, winning audiences with her eloquent opposition to slavery. She also voiced her strong support of women's rights. In 1867 she declared, "There is a great stir about colored men getting their rights, but not a word about colored women; and if colored men get their rights and not colored women theirs, you see the colored men will be masters over the women, and it will be just as bad as it was before."

Contemporary Events, 1843 ■ Congress funds Samuel F. B. Morse's project to build the first telegraph line from Washington to Baltimore. ■ "Oregon Fever" sweeps the country, sending thousands to the Northwest.

Richmond, Virginia. He will serve as minister resident and consul general of Liberia.

James Edward O'Hara, two-term congressman from North Carolina, is born February 26 in New York.

The first African American U.S. congressman from Louisiana, Charles Edmund Nash, is born in Opelousas, Louisiana.

RELIGION AND EDUCATION

In Boston, African Americans begin a series of meetings to fight the segregated school system.

Educator and lawyer Richard T. Greener is born in Philadelphia. He will be the first African American to receive a degree from Harvard.

SCIENCE AND TECHNOLOGY

Inventor Elijah McCoy is born May 2 in Ontario, Canada. He will receive over 70 patents, most involving the lubricating of machinery. His name will become the reference in the popular phrase "the real McCoy."

1845

BUSINESS AND EMPLOYMENT

Macon B. Allen becomes the first licensed African-American attorney by passing the bar exam in Worcester, Massachusetts.

LITERATURE AND JOURNALISM

Creole poet Armand Lanusse inspires 17 black poets in New Orleans to publish an anthology of their works, *Les Cenelles*.

Frederick Douglass publishes the first of his three autobiographies, *Narrative of the Life of Frederick Douglass*, describing his experiences as a slave.

PERFORMING ARTS

African-American dancer William Henry Lane, known as "Juba," receives top billing in a white minstrel company.

VISUAL ARTS

Sculptor Edmonia Lewis is born June 14 in Albany, New York. She

---

Contemporary Events, 1844 ■ The Democratic campaign slogan is "54°40' or Fight," threatening American expansion up to the Russian border in Canada. ■ Democrat James K. Polk is elected president. **1845** ■ Texas and Florida become states. ■ The U.S. Naval Academy opens in Annapolis, Maryland.

will work in the neoclassical style popular in her day and live most of her life in Italy.

1846

POLITICS AND CIVIL RIGHTS

Moses Dickson and 11 other African-American leaders form a secret society in St. Louis called the Knights of Liberty. Dedicated to the abolition of slavery, the order reputedly gains 47,240 members in 10 years, although its activities are unknown, until it reemerges in Independence, Missouri, in 1871, calling itself the Temple and Tabernacle of the Knights and Daughters of Tabor.

The U.S. House of Representatives adopts an amendment to an appropriations bill, called the Wilmot Proviso, barring slavery in any territory captured during the Mexican War. It is not, however, passed by the Senate.

BUSINESS AND EMPLOYMENT

An experiment in independent farming is begun in upstate New York when abolitionist Gerrit Smith grants 3,000 African Americans 40 to 60 acres of land each. In two years only 30 black families succeed, most failing because of poor soil and lack of funds to sustain the enterprise. Land ownership is a requirement for suffrage.

RELIGION AND EDUCATION

Historian John W. Cromwell is born September 5 in Virginia.

SCIENCE AND TECHNOLOGY

Norbert Rillieux, an African-American inventor, receives a patent for an evaporating pan that will revolutionize sugar-refining methods here and in Central America.

1847

POLITICS AND CIVIL RIGHTS

The New England Anti-Slavery Society elects Frederick Douglass as its president.

Contemporary Events, 1846 ■ The United States declares war on Mexico. ■ Iowa becomes a state. **1847** ■ American troops capture Mexico City.

In the circuit court in St. Louis, Dred Scott files a lawsuit to gain his freedom.

In Kentucky a move to replace the 1793 Fugitive Slave Law with more severe legislation begins the process that will result in the stringent Fugitive Slave Law of 1850.

The commonwealth of Liberia declares itself an independent republic, and Virginian Joseph Jenkins Roberts becomes its first president.

John R. Lynch, U.S. congressman from Mississippi, is born September 10 in Louisiana. He will become the first African American to preside over a Republican National Convention.

BUSINESS AND EMPLOYMENT

William Alexander Leidesdorff, of Danish and African parentage and a successful businessman and local politician in California, launches the first steamboat in San Francisco Bay.

Isaiah Thornton Montgomery is born into slavery in Mississippi. He will establish Mount Bayou, Mississippi, a self-sufficient model agricultural community of 3,000 people, and help found the National Negro Business League.

LITERATURE AND JOURNALISM

On December 3, Frederick Douglass and Martin R. Delany begin publishing the *North Star* in Rochester, New York, one of the leading abolitionist newspapers of the era. It will be renamed *Frederick Douglass's Paper* in 1850.

ADDITIONAL EVENTS

Blacks and whites organize the Independent Order of Good Samaritans and Daughters of Samaria to promote temperance. In time African Americans gain more voting privileges, become more numerous, and white members drop out. African Americans gain control and elect a black Grand Sire in 1877.

POLITICS AND CIVIL RIGHTS

Frederick Douglass speaks at the first Women's Rights Convention, held at Seneca Falls, New York.

Contemporary Events, 1848 ■ The Treaty of Guadalupe Hidalgo ends the Mexican War, giving the United States what will become Texas, New Mexico, California, Utah, Nevada, Arizona, and parts of Colorado. ■ Wisconsin becomes a state. ■ Zachary Taylor is elected president.

African-American abolitionists attend the newly formed Free Soil Party's convention in Buffalo, New York.

William and Ellen Craft succeed in a dramatic escape from slavery in Georgia. Ellen, who has light skin, poses as a slaveholder and her husband acts as her slave. They later write a classic narrative, *Running a Thousand Miles for Freedom*.

In Virginia, postmasters must turn over abolitionist literature to the local authorities for burning.

LITERATURE AND JOURNALISM

West Virginia politician, pastor, and newspaperman Christopher Harrison Payne is born in Virginia. He will found the *West Virginia Enterprise*, the *Pioneer*, and the *Mountain Eagle*.

SCIENCE AND TECHNOLOGY

Lewis Temple invents the toggle harpoon for whaling.

Lewis Latimer, inventor of the carbon filiment for electric lights, is born September 4 in Chelsea, Massachusetts.

1849

POLITICS AND CIVIL RIGHTS

A precedent for the "separate but equal" theory of segregation arises in Massachusetts, when the state's Supreme Court decides against Benjamin F. Roberts's claim for damages because the city of Boston refused to admit his daughter Sarah to a white public school.

Harriet Tubman escapes from slavery in Maryland and begins working for the Underground Railroad. She will assist more than 300 slaves in their escape to freedom.

Ohio repeals a law requiring African Americans to post bond before entering the state.

Abolitionist, author, bookseller, and Underground Railroad worker David Ruggles dies in Northampton, Massachusetts, December 26.

BUSINESS AND EMPLOYMENT

Waller Jackson becomes the first known African American to join the Gold Rush in California.

Contemporary Events, 1849 ■ The Minnesota Territory is established.

Harriet Tubman

Harriet Tubman's life in slavery was characterized by punishment, abuse, and harassment. When she escaped from slavery in 1849, she vowed to help others. She made 19 trips into the South to lead some 300 other slaves into the northern states or to Canada. Northern abolitionists sponsored her financially, while southerners placed a $40,000 bounty on her head. She recruited soldiers for John Brown's raid on Harpers Ferry. When the Civil War broke out, Tubman served in the Union army, ostensibly as a nurse, but with her knowledge of people and places in the South, she also engaged in scouting and espionage activities. After the war she concentrated on helping poor children and the elderly. At the 1896 meeting of the National Federation of Afro-American Women, she spoke about the need for homes for the elderly, and she later established a residence for the aged in Auburn, New York.

RELIGION AND EDUCATION

Author and essayist Martin R. Delany is admitted to Harvard Medical School.

Avery College is founded in Allegheny City, Pennsylvania.

James Monroe Gregory, the first graduate of Howard University, is born January 23 in Lexington, Virginia.

LITERATURE AND JOURNALISM

Henry Bibb publishes his slave narrative. In 1851 he will create an organization in Canada to buy land for escaped slaves.

Writer, lawyer, and civil rights leader Archibald H. Grimké is born August 17 in South Carolina.

George Washington Williams, author of *History of the Negro Race in America from 1619 to 1890,* is born October 16 in Pennsylvania.

1850

POLITICS AND CIVIL RIGHTS

The 1850 Compromise ends slave trade in Washington, D.C., but it also provides for a strong federal fugitive slave law.

September James Hamlet, a free African American in New York, is arrested under the new fugitive slave law. Residents raise money, buy his freedom, and prevent him from being sent to the South.

Vermont passes a law requiring state attorneys to defend fugitives.

Harriet Tubman returns for the first time to Baltimore and brings her sister and two children out of slavery.

Residents of Lehigh County, Pennsylvania, demand that all African Americans be expelled from the state.

BUSINESS AND EMPLOYMENT

In New York the American League of Colored Workers is formed with Samuel R. Ward as president. Composed of skilled African-American workers, the union's mission is to train craftspeople and stimulate business opportunities for African Americans.

RELIGION AND EDUCATION

In New York City approximately the same percentage of black and white children regularly attend school.

LITERATURE AND JOURNALISM

Bishop Daniel A. Payne publishes his book *Pleasures and Other Miscellaneous Poems.*

Hallie Quinn Brown, author of a 1926 collection of women's biographical sketches titled *Homespun Heroines,* is born March 10 in Pittsburgh.

SCIENCE AND TECHNOLOGY

In Ohio, David Clay manufactures a plow, custom-made to any size, capable of plowing depths from 8 to 20 inches.

EXPLORATION

Pioneer James Beckwourth discovers a pass through the Sierra Nevada mountains that will be used by settlers migrating to California.

Contemporary Events, 1850 ■ California becomes a state. ■ President Zachary Taylor dies in office, and Vice President Millard Fillmore succeeds him. ■ Nathaniel Hawthorne publishes **The Scarlet Letter.**

ADDITIONAL STATISTICS

According to the U.S. census, the African-American population is 3,638,808 or 15.7% of the total population. Of these, 434,495 African Americans are free.

A prime male field slave can be bought for $1,600.

1851

POLITICS AND CIVIL RIGHTS

Virginians rewrite their constitution so that emancipated slaves automatically return to slave status if they remain in the state for more than 12 months.

The new state of California does not allow African Americans to testify in court against whites.

On October 1 U.S. forces arrest William "Jerry" Henry, a runaway slave who settled in Syracuse, New York, but thousands of citizens raid the sheriff's office and help him escape to Canada.

In Boston, African-American abolitionists storm a courtroom and rescue a fugitive slave.

In Christiana, Pennsylvania, African Americans fight off slave catchers, killing one and wounding another.

LITERATURE AND JOURNALISM

Frederick Douglass publishes *Lectures on American Slavery.*

The Liberty Party's official paper merges with Frederick Douglass's *North Star.*

African-American abolitionist William C. Nell publishes *Services of Colored Americans in the Wars of 1776 and 1812.*

Poet Albery Allson Whitman is born into slavery in Kentucky. His poetry using black dialect is considered the best in that genre prior to the work of Paul Laurence Dunbar.

SCIENCE AND TECHNOLOGY

In Philadelphia, the Colored American Institute for the Promotion of the Mechanic Arts and Sciences exhibits inventions, paintings, and craftwork by African-American artisans.

Contemporary Events, 1851 ■ Herman Melville publishes **Moby Dick.**

PERFORMING ARTS

After singer Elizabeth Taylor Greenfield debuts at the Buffalo Musical Association, she is called the "Black Swan."

VISUAL ARTS

Robert S. Duncanson paints *Blue Hole, Little Miami*, regarded as a classic in the Hudson River school style.

POLITICS AND CIVIL RIGHTS

Physician and writer Martin R. Delany, losing hope in the United States as a congenial home for African Americans, advocates Central or South America as a possible site for an African-American state.

In a speech in Rochester, New York, Frederick Douglass asks what the Fourth of July means to the slave. He points out, "To drag a man in fetters into the grand illuminated temple of liberty, and call upon him to join you in joyous anthems, were inhuman mockery and sacreligious irony." Underlining "this Fourth of July is *yours*, not *mine*," he accuses the national holiday of being a "sham."

A Kentucky law denies free African Americans entry to the state. Violators face imprisonment.

Sojourner Truth reportedly delivers her "Ain't I a Woman?" speech at the Second National Women's Suffrage Convention, held in Akron, Ohio.

Congressman George H. White is born December 18 in North Carolina. He will introduce an antilynching bill in the House.

RELIGION AND EDUCATION

In the Georgia state legislature a bill to allow slaves to receive an education is introduced as a strategy to raise their monetary value.

LITERATURE AND JOURNALISM

Martin R. Delany publishes *The Condition, Elevation, Emigration and Destiny of the Colored People of the U.S., Politically Considered*.

In Cleveland, W. H. H. Day begins editing a new African-American publication, the *Alienated American*.

African Americans in Business

In spite of the severe restriction of "black laws," some African Americans, mostly free, but occasionally slave, managed to pursue successful business ventures. Simon Gray, a slave, captained a lumber company flatboat on the Mississippi River, working, living, and even vacationing with his family as a free person. In Ohio, African-American plasterers Knight and Bell were contracted to plaster public buildings in Hamilton County. Mifflin Gibbs and John Lester jointly owned a successful store in San Francisco. Samuel T. Wilcox's grocery store in Cincinnati did $140,000 worth of yearly business in the decade before the Civil War. In Atlanta, Roderick Badger, a free man, was a dentist.

Contemporary Events, 1852 ■ Harriet Beecher Stowe's **Uncle Tom's Cabin** is published. The most popular novel of the century, it influences northern sentiment against slavery. ■ Franklin Pierce is elected president.

SCIENCE AND TECHNOLOGY

Inventor Jan E. Matzeliger is born in Dutch Guiana. His shoe-lasting machine, eventually purchased by the United Shoe Machinery Company of Boston, will revolutionize the shoe industry.

1853

POLITICS AND CIVIL RIGHTS

Over 780 African Americans migrate to Liberia.

The *New York Herald Tribune* claims African Americans are racially inferior to whites and endorses emigration as a desirable policy.

A national black convention meets in Rochester, New York, and founds the National Council of Colored People. James W. C. Pennington of New York is elected president. With 140 delegates from nine states, it is the most representative of the early African-American conventions.

In Pennsylvania, free African Americans petition the state legislature to provide security for them when they travel through slave states.

Virginia imposes a poll tax on free African-American men and plans to use the revenue to deport African Americans.

Congressman George Washington Murray is born into slavery September 22 in South Carolina.

RELIGION AND EDUCATION

Anthony Bower establishes an African-American branch of the YMCA in Washington, D.C.

When black children are no longer allowed to attend schools near Philadelphia, abolitionist Robert Purvis refuses to pay taxes and decries the "infamously despotic denial" of his and others' rights.

LITERATURE AND JOURNALISM

William Wells Brown publishes *Clotel, or the President's Daughter* in London, an antislavery novel about one of Thomas Jefferson's children by his slave mistress Sally Hemings.

The Narrative of Sojourner Truth is published.

Writer Octavia Victoria Rogers Albert, author of *House of Bondage,* is born December 24 in Oglethorpe, Georgia.

Contemporary Events, 1853 ■ In the Gadsden Purchase the United States acquires what is now southern New Mexico and Arizona from Mexico. ■ New York Central Railroad is formed.

PERFORMING ARTS

African Americans are not allowed to attend concert singer Elizabeth Taylor Greenfield's New York debut at Metropolitan Hall. As a protest, Greenfield sings a separate concert for African Americans at the Broadway Tabernacle.

1854

POLITICS AND CIVIL RIGHTS

In Cleveland, at the National Emigration Convention of the Colored People, representatives from 11 states discuss the benefits of an African-American colony as an alternative to U.S. oppression.

Fugitive Anthony Burns is captured in Boston and sent back to slavery in the South. Abolitionists take up his cause and try unsuccessfully to purchase his freedom.

The New England Emigration Aid Society plans to settle ex-slaves in the Kansas Territory as part of its goal to create a free state.

Abraham Lincoln makes his first public statement about slavery, saying that he is opposed to its extension into the western territories.

RELIGION AND EDUCATION

The first school for African-American children in San Francisco is established by the St. Cyprian AME Church.

Ashmun Institute is founded in Oxford, Pennsylvania. It will later be renamed Lincoln University.

James Augustine Healy, the first African-American Catholic priest in North America, is ordained at Notre Dame Cathedral in Paris.

LITERATURE AND JOURNALISM

Frances Ellen Watkins Harper publishes *Poems on Miscellaneous Subjects.*

SCIENCE AND TECHNOLOGY

Martin R. Delany receives public recognition for his work in Pittsburgh during a serious cholera epidemic.

John V. DeGrasse is the first African American admitted to the Massachusetts Medical Society.

Anthony Burns

The case of Anthony Burns became a **cause célèbre** in the abolition struggle. Burns, an escaped slave, was captured in Boston May 24, 1854. A mass protest of citizens threatened to rescue Burns from federal agents. Eventually over 2,000 U.S. soldiers were called out to escort Burns to a ship in Boston harbor, which returned him to the South on June 3. Boston citizens raised $1,200 to purchase Burns's freedom, but his owner refused to sell him. Eventually Burns was freed, attended college, and served as pastor of Zion Baptist Church in Canada.

Contemporary Events, 1854 ■ Congress passes the Kansas-Nebraska Act. ■ The Republican Party is founded to oppose the opening of the West to slavery.

Marching Bands

The military tradition was always stronger in the South than elsewhere, and European march music was extremely popular at midcentury. By the 1850s all southern cities sponsored military bands, including some composed of African-American musicians, to play at military events and parades. Usually members of the black bands were free African Americans and house slaves who learned the European marches from white bands. After Emancipation, when field hands joined the bands, African rhythms and musical constructions influenced the style of the black marching bands.

PERFORMING ARTS

Songwriter James A. Bland is born October 22 in Flushing, New York. He will write over 600 songs, including "Carry Me Back to Old Virginny," which will become Virginia's state song in 1940.

Violinist and orchestra leader Walter F. Craig is born December 20 in Princeton, New Jersey.

1855

POLITICS AND CIVIL RIGHTS

Because he is black, James W. C. Pennington is forcibly removed from a horsecar in New York City after he refuses to get off. He later sues the company and wins his case.

Frederick Douglass is the first African American nominated for a state office, when the New York Liberty Party designates him for New York secretary of state.

On his election as clerk of Brownhelm Township in Ohio, John Mercer Langston becomes the first known African American to be elected to public office. In 1888 he will be elected to the U.S. Congress from Virginia.

RELIGION AND EDUCATION

Massachusetts abolishes segregated schools, and black and white children begin attending Boston schools together without any racial incidents.

J. W. E. Bowen, Methodist educator, is born December 3 in New Orleans.

LITERATURE AND JOURNALISM

Frederick Douglass publishes his second autobiographical work, *My Bondage and My Freedom.*

In San Francisco the *Mirror of the Times,* an African-American newspaper, begins publication. It is both edited and owned by Mifflin Wistar Gibbs.

William Cooper Nell publishes *The Colored Patriots of the American Revolution,* a revised version of his 1851 publication with an introduction by Harriet Beecher Stowe.

Contemporary Events, 1855 ■ The law stipulates that all children born overseas of U.S. citizens are guaranteed citizenship.

PERFORMING ARTS

Richard Milburn, an African-American barber in Philadelphia, is credited as composer on the sheet music for "Listen to the Mocking Bird."

VISUAL ARTS

In Cincinnati, James Presley Ball, one of the first African-American daguerrotypists, publishes the narration for his popular panorama, which depicts the history of black people in the United States.

1856

POLITICS AND CIVIL RIGHTS

Through the State Convention of Colored Citizens, African Americans in Illinois establish the Negroes of the Repeal Association to work for the elimination of the state's "black laws."

Proslavery settlers attack Lawrence, Kansas, because of its abolitionist sentiments. In revenge white abolitionist John Brown leads a raid on a proslavery settlement at Pottawatomie Creek in Kansas and kills five men.

BUSINESS AND EMPLOYMENT

Biddy Mason is awarded her freedom by a Los Angeles County court after living in California for three years. She will become a philanthropist and a major landowner in Los Angeles.

RELIGION AND EDUCATION

Wilberforce University is established for African Americans in Ohio.

In Kentucky, Berea College is founded. Its policy of integration will survive until 1907, when the U.S. Supreme Court rules that it must follow a state law requiring segregated schools.

Booker T. Washington, founder of Tuskegee Institute, is born April 5 in Hale's Ford, Virginia.

LITERATURE AND JOURNALISM

Editor and writer Timothy Thomas Fortune is born October 3 in Florida. He will work for various newspapers and in 1887 found the Afro-American League.

Contemporary Events, 1856 ■ James Buchanan is elected president.

Journalist John Edward "Bruce Grit" Bruce is born February 22 in Maryland.

SCIENCE AND TECHNOLOGY

Inventor Granville T. Woods is born April 23 in Columbus, Ohio. He will invent steam boilers, automobile air brakes, a telegraph system for moving trains, and other devices, many purchased by the General Electric and Bell Telephone companies.

The first doctor to perform open-heart surgery, Daniel Hale Williams is born January 18 in Pennsylvania. He will help found Provident Hospital in Chicago.

1857

POLITICS AND CIVIL RIGHTS

The Dred Scott case is settled May 5 by the U.S. Supreme Court. The decision declares that African Americans are not citizens, that residence in a free state does not bestow freedom on a slave, and that slavery cannot be excluded from the western territories.

The U.S. Land Office denies African Americans public land grants in the West on the grounds that they are not citizens.

Oregon votes 8 to 1 to include a clause in the state constitution to prevent the further movement of African Americans into the state.

In opposition to the Fugitive Slave Law of 1850, Maine and New Hampshire grant freedom and citizenship to African Americans.

Congressman Henry Plummer Cheatham is born December 27 in North Carolina.

LITERATURE AND JOURNALISM

In London, Frank Webb publishes *The Garies and Their Friends*, a novel about discrimination and the caste system.

1858

POLITICS AND CIVIL RIGHTS

John Brown rescues 11 slaves from Missouri and takes them to Canada, where he holds an antislavery convention.

Contemporary Events, 1858 ■ Minnesota becomes a state.

A Philadelphia streetcar company allows African Americans to ride only on the front platforms of its cars.

Debating Stephen A. Douglas in Illinois, Abraham Lincoln declares his opposition to slavery as an institution, but states that equality between the white and black races is not achievable.

A Maryland law prohibits African Americans, both free and slave, from having or using boats on the Potomac River.

RELIGION AND EDUCATION

Teacher and administrator Anna Julia Cooper is born August 10 in Raleigh, North Carolina. She will be founder and president of Frelinghuysen University, a school for African Americans.

LITERATURE AND JOURNALISM

William Wells Brown publishes *The Escape, or the Leap to Freedom* in Boston, probably the first play by an African American.

Novelist Charles Waddell Chesnutt is born June 20 in Cleveland.

1859

POLITICS AND CIVIL RIGHTS

Hoping to instigate a slave revolt, abolitionist John Brown raids the federal arsenal at Harpers Ferry, Virginia, on October 16 with a band that includes five African Americans. Lewis Leary and Dangerfield Newby are killed. John Copeland and Shields Green are later hanged with Brown. Osborne Anderson survives the attack and writes *A Voice from Harpers Ferry*.

Georgia prohibits slave owners from manumitting slaves through wills or other means after their deaths.

A new law in Louisiana makes it easier to reenslave free blacks.

In Arkansas, a law requires free African Americans to leave the state by the end of the year or to find masters who will "not allow [them] to act as free."

The Southern Commercial Convention, held at Vicksburg, Mississippi, supports the reopening of the African slave trade.

Citizens of North Carolina are forbidden by law to sell alcoholic beverages to free blacks except for medicinal purposes.

Contemporary Events, 1859 ■ Oregon becomes a state.

Slavery in Illinois

The Land of Lincoln illustrates the persistence of slavery in the "free" northern states. In 1814, when Illinois was still a territory where slavery was prohibited since the Northwest Ordinance of 1787, it was legal to hire slaves and bring them into the territory from outside for specific work projects. In 1818, on admission to statehood, Illinois officially forbade slavery in its constitution. However, on the eve of the Civil War, an Illinois law allowed African Americans to be advertised and sold at auction if they failed to produce proof of freedom or post bond guaranteeing good behavior. Another law prohibited free African Americans and mulattoes from entering the state.

The last slave ship before the Civil War, the *Clothilde*, lands a shipment of slaves at Mobile Bay, Alabama.

BUSINESS AND EMPLOYMENT

At a slave owners' convention in Baltimore, businessmen advocate the removal of free African Americans from the state on the grounds that they monopolize certain industries, such as hotel labor, coach services, and transportation. The idea is rejected by a majority, who feel that the state's economy depends on the labor of free blacks.

RELIGION AND EDUCATION

The Ohio Supreme Court rules that children who are three-eighths African American cannot attend schools for whites.

African Methodist Episcopal Zion bishop and editor George Wylie Clinton is born in South Carolina.

LITERATURE AND JOURNALISM

The *Afro-American Magazine*, a literary journal, begins publication.

On September 5, Harriet E. Wilson publishes *Our Nig*, probably the first novel written by an African-American woman.

VISUAL ARTS

Painter Henry Ossawa Tanner, the first African American elected to the National Academy of Design, is born June 21 in Pittsburgh. In his early work he will draw directly on black subject matter; after moving to Paris in the 1890s he will emphasize religious themes.

1860

POLITICS AND CIVIL RIGHTS

All the New England states except Connecticut have granted African Americans equal suffrage rights with whites. Connecticut continues to vote against African-American suffrage as late as 1865.

On the eve of the Civil War, approximately 500 black Canadians have participated in treks to the South to help slaves escape.

In Virginia, a law allows free African Americans to be sold into slavery for committing offenses punishable by imprisonment.

Contemporary Events, 1860 ■ Abraham Lincoln is elected president in November, precipitating rebellion in the southern states. ■ On December 20, South Carolina secedes from the Union, followed by other slave states, which form a separate national government.

Sylvester Gray, a free black settler in Wisconsin since 1856, petitions Congress concerning the revocation of his land claim by the General Land Office. The office argues Gray was not, according to the Dred Scott decision, a citizen and therefore not entitled to government land grants.

President Buchanan advocates a fugitive slave amendment to the Constitution.

BUSINESS AND EMPLOYMENT

Runaway slave Barney Ford arrives in Colorado, where he will build a Denver hotel and become a successful businessman.

ADDITIONAL STATISTICS

The African-American population is 4,441,830 or 14.1% of the whole population. Slaves account for 3,953,760 of this number.

In Virginia, healthy male field slaves are sold for $1,000; in New Orleans, $1,500.

1861

POLITICS AND CIVIL RIGHTS

In his inaugural address as president of the Confederate States of America, Jefferson Davis declares that slavery is "necessary to self-preservation."

William C. Nell, the first African American to hold a civilian job with the federal government, is appointed a post office clerk in Boston.

RELIGION AND EDUCATION

The American Missionary Association receives permission to begin opening schools for freed African Americans in areas under U.S. military occupation in the South.

Mary Peake, an African-American teacher, begins classes at a school for freedmen at Fortress Monroe, Virginia.

LITERATURE AND JOURNALISM

In January Harriet Jacobs publishes *Incidents in the Life of a Slave Girl: Written by Herself.*

Journalist and social worker Victoria Earle Matthews is born May 27

Contemporary Events, 1861 ■ Fort Sumter falls. ■ President Lincoln declares the southern states in rebellion and raises an army.

1860 Population

In 1860 the vast majority of African Americans lived in the South, most as slaves. In northern states, African Americans constituted less than 1% of the population. In Rhode Island, Connecticut, New York, New Jersey, Pennsylvania, Ohio, and California, they were more than 1% but less than 5%. In the border and Confederate states, African Americans counted for as few as 10% in Missouri and as many as 58.6% in South Carolina.

Nonenlisted African Americans

Although African Americans asked to serve in the Union army from the first days of the Civil War, throughout the first year they served the war effort in a nonmilitary capacity, mainly because Lincoln feared that to raise black troops would alienate the border states that had not seceded. African Americans volunteered in great numbers and served in the Union army in many nonmilitary capacities: scouts; pioneers; teamsters; wagoners; blacksmiths; carpenters; masons; construction workers engaged in building fortifications, highways, railroads, and bridges; laundry and hospital attendants; camp attendants, waiters, and cooks; and longshoremen. Some African Americans served military personnel as servants and orderlies until the war ended.

in Fort Valley, Georgia. She will found the White Rose Mission in New York in 1897.

THE MILITARY

Frederick Douglass says both slaves and free African Americans should be called into military service, as a "liberating army, to march into the South and raise the banner of emancipation."

Union Brigadier General Benjamin F. Butler is the first officer to treat runaway slaves as contraband of war and prevent their return to their owners.

General John C. Fremont proclaims that slaves belonging to owners who fight against the Union should be freed. Lincoln overrides Fremont's proclamation.

Hilton Head, an island off the coast of South Carolina, becomes an official center for fugitive slaves, who are enjoined to grow cotton for the federal government.

Nicholas Biddle is the first known African American in uniform to be wounded in the Civil War.

The Confederate government runs into opposition from slave owners when it tries to hire slaves for the war effort. Instead, it resorts to impressment of slaves to work in various capacities related to defense.

On the state level, Confederate governments recruit free African Americans for military service, including women to work in camps and hospitals.

1862

POLITICS AND CIVIL RIGHTS

In April slavery is ended in the District of Columbia.

Lincoln meets with African-American leaders, urging them to advocate colonization of free blacks outside the country. This is the first time a group of African Americans confers with an American president.

In June, Lincoln signs a bill ending slavery in the western territories.

In September, Lincoln announces the Emancipation Proclamation,

Contemporary Events, 1862 ■ Military setbacks for the Confederates occur in the battles of Shiloh and Antietam.

which will abolish slavery as of January 1, 1863, in the seceded states of the Confederacy (where his authority is not recognized).

The National Freedmen's Relief Association is formed in New York to help slaves adjust to freedom. Similar groups are organized in Philadelphia, Cincinnati, and Chicago.

Editor and activist Ida B. Wells Barnett is born into slavery in Holly Springs, Mississippi, July 6. She will become a crucial voice in the antilynching campaign.

BUSINESS AND EMPLOYMENT

African-American workers in the North are seen as strikebreakers by white laborers attempting to unionize, while in the South, severe labor shortages convince most states to impress African Americans into job positions left vacant by whites who joined the military.

RELIGION AND EDUCATION

At Oberlin, Mary Jane Patterson is probably the first African-American woman to graduate from college.

THE MILITARY

Congress authorizes the recruitment of African Americans for military service. Three generals had previously organized African-American regiments without government approval.

The first African-American regiment to be officially mustered into the Union army is the First Louisiana Native Guards, a troop of free men from New Orleans.

The first engagement of African-American troops is at Island Mound, Missouri, where the First Kansas Colored Volunteers drive off a superior force of Confederates.

African-American forces hold off Confederate attacks on contraband camps on St. Simon Island, Georgia, and St. Helena Island, South Carolina.

Robert Smalls daringly sails a Confederate ship, the *Planter*, out of Charleston harbor and delivers it to a Union squadron. He is made a pilot in the navy and later promoted to commander.

1863

POLITICS AND CIVIL RIGHTS

On January 1, the Emancipation Proclamation frees all American slaves, except those living in states and areas of states that are not in rebellion.

Lincoln on Slavery

Although Abraham Lincoln was opposed to slavery, he was not considered an abolitionist. His stance was shaped by practical, economic concerns at well as moral ones. When he emerged in Illinois politics, he argued against the extension of slavery into the western territories because he wanted the West to be a place for free white labor, and he thought slavery would depress wages. Later, in his "House Divided" speech, he argued for the preservation of the Union, saying that the nation could not survive half free and half slave. As president, Lincoln felt he did not have the authority to abolish slavery because it was written into the Constitution. Only an amendment could change the Constitution. Yet, because the Confederate states had withdrawn from the covenant of the U.S. Constitution, he felt he could proclaim emancipation there. With the Emancipation Proclamation, Lincoln put the war effort on the moral ground of working to abolish slavery. But a constitutional amendment was still needed to eradicate the "peculiar institution" from the entire nation.

The New York City draft riots, instigated primarily by Irish workers who cannot afford $300 to hire substitutes for the draft, turn mercilessly on African Americans. White rioters believe they are being asked to fight to free slaves, who will in turn take their jobs.

Civil and women's rights advocate Mary Church Terrell is born September 23 in Memphis.

RELIGION AND EDUCATION

At Wilberforce University Daniel A. Payne becomes the first African-American president of a U.S. college.

Episcopal clergyman George Freeman Bragg is born January 25 in North Carolina.

Minister and YMCA official Jesse Moorland is born September 10 in Coldwater, Ohio. His personal library will form the basis of the Moorland-Spingarn Research Center at Howard University.

Intellectual Kelly Miller is born July 18 in Winnsboro, South Carolina.

THE MILITARY

In the summer 30 African-American regiments are officially accepted by the federal government as part of the Union army.

The Bureau for Colored Troops is established.

Military commanders are forbidden to return runaway slaves.

Frederick Douglass encourages African-American men to volunteer for the U.S. Colored Troops.

Lieutenant Colonel Alexander T. Augusta, the highest ranking black officer, is appointed "surgeon of the U.S. Colored Troops."

Sergeant William H. Carney, of the 54th Massachusetts Colored Infantry, displays outstanding heroism in the Battle of Fort Wagner, South Carolina. Thirty-seven years later he will receive the Congressional Medal of Honor for his bravery.

The 54th Massachusetts Regiment attacks and captures Morris Island, South Carolina, but suffers 42% casualties.

About one-fourth of all African Americans, mostly escaped slaves, sheltered in federal refugee camps will die because of poor sanitary conditions and lack of supplies.

African-American troops and their commanding officers captured

Contemporary Events, 1863 ■ After the western counties separate from Virginia, which had seceded, they are admitted by President Lincoln as the new state of West Virginia.

by Confederate armies are often murdered or subjected to forced labor. President Lincoln retaliates with an "eye for an eye" policy, threatening to execute or condemn to a life of hard labor one Confederate soldier for every African American so treated by the Confederate army.

POLITICS AND CIVIL RIGHTS

Frederick Douglass endorses John C. Fremont for Republican presidential candidate, in protest over Lincoln's conservative and uncertain position on postwar Reconstruction policies.

The Republican National Convention makes abolition of slavery a plank in its platform.

Among the Reconstruction positions of Congress's Wade-Davis Bill is the requirement that the seceded states must abolish slavery in their new constitutions before readmission to the Union.

The National Negro Convention, meeting in Syracuse, New York, calls for black suffrage.

A new state legislature elected in the Louisiana Territory occupied by federal troops votes to abolish slavery but refuses to grant African Americans the right to vote.

BUSINESS AND EMPLOYMENT

Congress passes a bill forbidding discrimination in hiring U.S. mail carriers.

Facing severe labor shortages, the Confederate government attempts to impress 20,000 slaves, but owners refuse to cooperate.

RELIGION AND EDUCATION

In Kansas, Western University is founded by the African Methodist Episcopal Church.

LITERATURE AND JOURNALISM

The *New Orleans Tribune* is founded by Louis C. Roudanez and published in both English and French. It will become the first daily African-American newspaper.

Contemporary Events, 1864 ■ Lincoln is reelected president.

The Fort Pillow Massacre

In many instances, Confederate troops indiscriminately executed African-American troops when they were captured. At Fort Pillow, Tennessee, on April 12, 1864, Confederate General Nathan B. Forrest ordered the killing of 300 black soldiers garrisoned there, along with women and children. The Fort Pillow massacre is considered one of the most despicable atrocities committed during the Civil War.

SCIENCE AND TECHNOLOGY

Rebecca Lee, one of the first African-American female physicians, graduates from New England Female Medical College on March 1.

Agricultural scientist George Washington Carver is born January 10 into slavery in Missouri.

THE MILITARY

Lieutenant Colonel Alexander T. Augusta, an army surgeon with the U.S. Colored Troops, receives $7 a month pay, the same as an enlisted man, until he brings pressure through Senator Henry Wilson and the secretary of war to receive compensation commensurate with his rank.

In June, Congress authorizes equal pay, arms, equipment, and medical services for whites and African Americans.

Fourteen black soldiers and 23 white soldiers will receive Congressional Medals of Honor for fighting at the Battle of Chaffin's Farm near Richmond, Virginia.

Confederate General Nathan Bedford Forrest and his troops massacre approximately 300 African-American military prisoners at Fort Pillow, Tennessee.

African-American troops in the Union army are the first to take control of key points on the James River in Virginia.

1865

POLITICS AND CIVIL RIGHTS

The 13th Amendment, officially abolishing slavery in the United States, is passed by Congress on January 31 and ratified by the end of the year.

Abolitionist Henry Highland Garnet, the first African American to speak in the nation's Capitol, delivers an address in the House of Representatives on the end of slavery.

The new state constitutions in the South, written by all-white legislators, contain "black codes" to regulate and control African Americans, once slavery is abolished. So severely do the codes restrict black freedom that virtual slavery is reestablished in many places.

In Pulaski, Tennessee, the Ku Klux Klan is started to control African

Contemporary Events, 1865 ■ On April 9, Confederate Robert E. Lee surrenders to General Ulysses S. Grant at Appomattox, thus ending the Civil War. ■ President Abraham Lincoln is assassinated, and Vice President Andrew Johnson becomes president.

Americans through terror and intimidation and minimize Union influence in the South.

In South Carolina any white man can arrest an African American he sees committing a misdemeanor.

John Rock becomes the first African-American attorney admitted to practice before the U.S. Supreme Court.

In New York the city council tries to prevent African Americans from marching in Lincoln's funeral procession when Irish immigrants object. The police commissioner, however, assigns police protection so that black marchers can participate safely.

BUSINESS AND EMPLOYMENT

In Baltimore the African-American-owned Chesapeake Marine Railroad and Dry Dock Company is founded. This company will employ over 300 black workers.

Of the estimated 120,000 skilled artisans in the South, 100,000 are African Americans. Over the next 25 years, the black artisan will virtually disappear as white society reserves skilled crafts for whites.

The Freedmen's Savings and Trust is chartered by Congress.

RELIGION AND EDUCATION

Atlanta University is begun by the American Missionary Association.

Adam Clayton Powell, Sr., civil rights activist and pastor of the Abyssinian Baptist Church in New York, is born in Virginia.

LITERATURE AND JOURNALISM

George Moses Horton publishes a volume of poetry, *Naked Genius*.

The only African-American journalist writing for a major daily newspaper, the *Philadelphia Press*, Thomas Morris Chester describes the Union army's triumphant occupation of the Confederate capital at Richmond.

In New Orleans the first convention of black journalists is chaired by P. B. S. Pinchback, who will later found the New Orleans *Louisianian*.

PERFORMING ARTS

African-American singer and entertainer Charles Hicks organizes the Georgia Minstrels, a troupe that will tour Europe as Haverly's European Minstrels.

THE MILITARY

In the closing days of the war, Virginia legislature allows the Confederate army to enlist slaves if compensation is given to owners. Fol-

The Black Codes of Reconstruction

Immediately after Emancipation the southern state legislatures passed harsh laws to control the lives of African Americans. Blacks without work were declared vagrant and indentured to whites. Orphans were indentured to white masters until they reached adulthood. African Americans could not testify in court. Curfews kept blacks off the streets after sundown. Passes were required for travel, and in some states African Americans had to post bonds when they entered the state or be subject to arrest. Freedom of assembly was prohibited. The right to bear arms was forbidden. In some places, African Americans could be hired only as contract laborers, or they were required to have a special license to engage in any work other than farm or domestic service. The result of these laws was virtual reenslavement.

The Freedmen's Bureau

Famine was widespread throughout the South following the Civil War; few crops had been planted during the war. Thousands of people were displaced and without homes or means of livelihood. The U.S. War Department's Bureau of Refugees, Freedmen, and Abandoned Lands, or simply the Freedmen's Bureau, was charged to issue provisions, clothing, and fuel to refugees and freedmen, and to rent abandoned or confiscated lands up to 40 acres to any refugee or freedman. In the first four years after the war, the Freedmen's Bureau issued 15 million rations to African Americans and 6 million to impoverished whites. The bureau also supervised labor contracts, set up schools, provided medical assistance, and established special courts if justice was not being carried out in the regular judicial system. The bureau was allowed to die in 1872 by congressional inaction.

lowing this policy, the Confederate Congress allows the army to enlist slaves, but without altering the master-slave relationship. Slaves receive the same pay and rations as white soldiers.

Over the course of the war, about 10% of the total Union army is composed of African-American troops. Over 186,000 African Americans serve in the Union army, with 38,000 losing their lives. It is estimated that one-fourth of the Union navy is African American.

The Freedmen's Bureau (officially the Bureau of Refugees, Freedmen, and Abandoned Lands) is established within the War Department to provide food, clothing, fuel, medical assistance, and economic help to former slaves, as well as white refugees in the South.

General William T. Sherman's Special Field Order No. 15 assigns areas of land in South Carolina and Florida for exclusive settlement by African Americans. A year later, the land, which was not to exceed 40 acres per family, is given back to its owners when President Andrew Johnson reverses the policy.

Aaron Anderson, while serving aboard the USS *Wyandanch*, fights in the battle of Mattox Creek, for which he receives the Navy Medal of Honor.

1866

POLITICS AND CIVIL RIGHTS

The nation's first Civil Rights Act is passed in Congress over President Andrew Johnson's veto. The law confers citizenship on African Americans and assures all citizens equal rights under the law.

The 14th Amendment, guaranteeing African Americans citizenship and overruling the Dred Scott decision, is passed by Congress. It will be ratified in 1868.

In Massachusetts, Edward G. Walker and Charles L. Mitchell become the first African Americans elected to a northern state legislature.

Riots, instigated by white Democrats, break out in Memphis and New Orleans.

Thaddeus Stevens's proposal to distribute public and confiscated lands in the South to freedmen in 40-acre lots is defeated in the House of Representatives 126 to 37.

Contemporary Events, 1866 ■ In New York City the Metropolitan Museum of Art is established. ■ The American Society for the Prevention of Cruelty to Animals is founded.

Frederick Douglass and other African-American leaders meet with President Johnson to advocate voting rights for former slaves, but Johnson remains opposed.

BUSINESS AND EMPLOYMENT

In Baltimore the National Labor Union advocates the unionization of African-American workers to prevent their use as strikebreakers.

In New Orleans, Louisiana; Norfolk, Virginia; and Beaufort, South Carolina; military banks are created to help African Americans whose deposits are not guaranteed protection by commercial banks.

RELIGION AND EDUCATION

Rust College in Holly Springs, Mississippi, and Morgan State College in Baltimore (originally the Centenary Biblical Institute) are founded by the Methodist Episcopal Church.

Fisk University is founded in Nashville on January 9 by the American Missionary Association.

George Alexander McGuire, first bishop of the African Orthodox Church, is born March 26 in Antigua.

PERFORMING ARTS

Composer and concert baritone Harry Thacker Burleigh is born December 2 in Erie, Pennsylvania. He will introduce the African-American spiritual to the concert stage.

VISUAL ARTS

Robert S. Duncanson is selected by the London *Art Journal* as one of the best contemporary landscape painters.

THE MILITARY

Two African-American calvary units, made up of Civil War veterans, are organized to serve in the West.

EXPLORATION

Explorer and Arctic authority Matthew Alexander Henson is born August 8 in Culver City, Maryland. He will accompany Robert Peary on seven Arctic expeditions.

1867

POLITICS AND CIVIL RIGHTS

Congress passes the first of a series of Reconstruction acts, which place the South under military rule, require new state constitutions, and enfranchise African Americans.

Massachusetts Senator Charles Sumner unsuccessfully introduces legislation giving the Freedmen's Bureau authority to provide homes and schools for African Americans.

Although African Americans are a numerical minority, after voter registration, they constitute a majority of voters in South Carolina, Georgia, Florida, Alabama, Mississippi, and Louisiana.

The new state constitutions, written after the Reconstruction Acts have been passed, guarantee African Americans suffrage, civil rights, public education, and other democratic reforms.

Mississippi's first Republican Convention is held with one-third of its members former slaves.

In April the Ku Klux Klan holds its first national convention in a hotel in Nashville. Its first Grand Wizard is ex-Confederate General Nathan Bedford Forrest.

In Charleston, Richmond, New Orleans, Mobile, and other cities African-American demonstrators stage ride-ins on streetcars.

Monroe Baker becomes mayor of St. Martin, Louisiana. The businessman is probably the first African American to be elected mayor of a town.

BUSINESS AND EMPLOYMENT

Businesswoman and civic leader Maggie Lena Walker is born September 26 in Richmond. She will found the Saint Luke Penny Savings Bank in Virginia.

Madame C. J. Walker is born December 23 in Delta, Louisiana. Her beauty-care products will make her one of the first black woman millionaires.

RELIGION AND EDUCATION

Howard University in Washington, D.C., is chartered by Congress on March 2.

Morehouse College is established in Augusta, Georgia.

In Alabama the American Missionary Association sets up Emerson and Talladega colleges.

Johnson C. Smith College is founded in Charlotte, North Carolina.

Contemporary Events, 1867 ■ Nebraska becomes the 37th state. ■ The United States purchases Alaska from Russia.

The Peabody Fund is created to finance educational endeavors for freed slaves.

PERFORMING ARTS

Actor Ira Aldridge dies August 7 in Poland.

SPORTS

The Excelsiors of Philadelphia beat the Brooklyn Uniques 37 to 24 in a black baseball club championship.

POLITICS AND CIVIL RIGHTS

Congress passes a law over President Andrew Johnson's veto giving African Americans living in the District of Columbia voting rights.

The 14th Amendment, guaranteeing citizenship, is ratified.

The 15th Amendment, guaranteeing that the right to vote shall not be denied because of "race, color, or previous condition of servitude," is passed by Congress. It will be ratified in 1870.

The governor of Florida requests federal troops to counteract Klan violence, but his request is ignored.

White legislators in Georgia evict African-American legislators on the grounds that the right to hold office had not been specifically applied to recently freed slaves.

Oscar J. Dunn becomes lieutenant governor of Louisiana, the highest elective office yet held by an African American.

In St. Landry Parish in Louisiana, the Ku Klux Klan pursues Republicans through the countryside for two days, killing or wounding over 200. Throughout Louisiana, hundreds of African Americans are killed prior to the year's election.

John W. Menard of Louisiana becomes the first African American elected to Congress, but he is denied his seat.

P. B. S. Pinchback and James J. Harris become the first African-American delegates to the Republican National Convention, held in Chicago.

On July 6, the South Carolina General Assembly opens with a majority of African-American legislators: 88 blacks to 67 whites. This is the

Mississippi under Reconstruction

Mississippi was one of the most racially divided states, and one of the most economically devastated by the Civil War. Between 1868 and 1874, African-American and white state legislators began reforming the entire state with remarkable vision and foresight. The new state constitution had provisions against racial discrimination and property qualifications for voting and juries. A biracial educational system was established, with two schools for African Americans and a university for training black professionals. The University of Mississippi was reorganized. Public accommodations were open to both races. Mississippi elected the only two African Americans to serve in the U.S. Senate until the 1960s: Hiram Revels and Blanche K. Bruce.

Contemporary Events, 1868 ■ President Andrew Johnson is impeached. By one vote, the Senate finds him not guilty of the offenses for impeachment. ■ Ulysses S. Grant is elected president. ■ Louisa May Alcott publishes **Little Women.**

only time in American history there is an African-American majority in a state legislature.

Francis L. Cardozo is appointed secretary of state in South Carolina, the first African-American cabinet officer in a state government.

W. E. B. Du Bois, one of the nation's foremost African-American scholars, authors, editors, and civil rights leaders, is born February 23 in Great Barrington, Massachusetts.

RELIGION AND EDUCATION

Hampton Normal and Agricultural Institute is founded in Virginia.

Howard University Medical School opens.

Educator John Hope is born June 2 in Augusta, Georgia. He will become president of Morehouse College and later the Atlanta University system.

LITERATURE AND JOURNALISM

William Wells Brown publishes *The Negro in the American Rebellion.*

PERFORMING ARTS

Opera singer Sissieretta Jones is born in Portsmouth, Virginia. She will found Black Patti's Troubadours and become one of the first African-American singers to perform at the White House, in 1892.

The great ragtime composer and pianist Scott Joplin is born November 12 in Texarkana, Texas.

VISUAL ARTS

Edmonia Lewis completes her sculpture *Forever Free,* celebrating the Emancipation Proclamation.

ADDITIONAL STATISTICS

The Freedmen's Bureau provides 2.5 million rations to refugees and former slaves.

POLITICS AND CIVIL RIGHTS

Ebenezer Don Carlos Bassett becomes U.S. minister to Haiti, probably the first African American to receive a diplomatic appointment.

Contemporary Events, 1869 ■ The National Woman Suffrage Association and the American Woman Association are organized.

BUSINESS AND EMPLOYMENT

Nine of the 142 representatives at the annual National Labor Union conference are African Americans. The conference encourages African Americans to form their own unions and send delegates to the national conferences.

The National Negro Labor Union is organized in Washington, D.C.

RELIGION AND EDUCATION

Tougaloo College is founded in Mississippi.

In New Orleans, Dillard University is chartered.

LITERATURE AND JOURNALISM

Frances Ellen Watkins Harper publishes *Moses: A Story of the Nile.*

PERFORMING ARTS

Composer and conductor Will Marion Cook is born January 27 in Detroit. His operetta *Clorindy; or the Origin of the Cakewalk* will introduce syncopated ragtime to New York audiences in the 1890s.

THE MILITARY

Two African-American infantry regiments are formed, bringing the total number of black soldiers to 12,500.

1870

POLITICS AND CIVIL RIGHTS

The 15th Amendment, guaranteeing the right to vote to all male citizens, is ratified March 30. On April 9, the American Anti-Slavery Society disbands, believing its work is done.

When the Mississippi state legislature convenes, about one-fourth of its members are African Americans.

The Mississippi legislature elects Hiram R. Revels to fill the U.S. Senate seat formerly held by Jefferson Davis. On March 16 Revels makes the first official speech by an African American before the Senate when he argues against Georgia's readmission to the Union without assurances to protect black citizens.

Joseph H. Rainey from South Carolina is seated as the first African-American congressman. Four other African Americans are elected

The Seating of Hiram R. Revels

When Mississippi had two U.S. Senate vacancies in 1870, black legislators in the state government demanded that at least one of the vacancies go to an African American. State senator Hiram Revels was elected and appointed by the military governor of Mississippi. When Revels presented his credentials in Washington, a three-day debate ensued on whether he should be seated. Some senators questioned the right of a military governor to certify elections. Others raised the racial issue of whether Revels had been a citizen long enough to serve in the U.S. Senate. The vote was 48 to 8 in favor of seating Revels. Among his more important votes was a change in the naturalization law striking out the word "white."

Contemporary Events, 1870 ■ John D. Rockefeller founds the Standard Oil Company.

to the 42nd Congress: Robert C. DeLarge and Robert B. Elliott from South Carolina, Benjamin S. Turner from Alabama, and Josiah T. Walls from Florida. Jefferson F. Long from Georgia is elected to fill an unexpired term in the 41st Congress.

Judge Jonathan Jasper Wright becomes the first African American elected to a major judicial position when he is selected for the South Carolina Supreme Court.

Massachusetts Senator Charles Sumner introduces a civil rights bill to guarantee equal rights in public accommodations, such as hotels, theaters, schools, churches, cemeteries, and transportation.

The governor of North Carolina sends the militia into areas where the Ku Klux Klan has killed 13 African Americans. He is later impeached for his action.

RELIGION AND EDUCATION

Literacy among African Americans stands at 18.6%.

Richard T. Greener is the first African American to graduate from Harvard College.

Membership in the black Baptist churches reaches a half million.

The Colored Methodist Episcopal Church is founded by freedmen leaving the predominantly white Methodist Church.

LeMoyne-Owen College is established in Memphis.

LITERATURE AND JOURNALISM

Newspaper publisher Robert Sengstacke Abbott is born in Georgia. He will found the crusading *Chicago Defender* in 1905, the first big-city African-American newspaper.

THE MILITARY

Because of Indian wars in the West, recruitment of African-American soldiers steps up.

ADDITIONAL STATISTICS

The census reports that the 4,880,009 African Americans in the United States comprise 12.7% of the total population.

POLITICS AND CIVIL RIGHTS

The Congressional Investigating Committee reports that in South Carolina the Ku Klux Klan has murdered 35 men; whipped 262 men and women; and destroyed the property of 101 African Americans. Similar atrocities are reported for other states.

The Ku Klux Klan Act is passed, giving federal courts jurisdiction over cases involving terrorism against freedmen and empowering the president to suspend habeas corpus, declare martial law, and send in troops to maintain order.

Representative Jefferson F. Long from Georgia, the second African-American congressman to be seated, is the first to make an official speech in the House.

The first African-American congressman from a northern state (Illinois) and the first following Reconstruction, Oscar DePriest is born March 9 in Alabama.

RELIGION AND EDUCATION

In Independence, Missouri, Moses Dickson founds the International Order of 12 of the Knights and Daughters of Tabor. Claiming some 200,000 members in 1900, the secret organization is dedicated to spreading Christianity, education, temperance, and home ownership.

A law school is established at Howard University.

Alcorn Agricultural and Mechanical College, the first land grant school, begins classes in Lorman, Mississippi.

LITERATURE AND JOURNALISM

Hampton Institute Press is founded.

Albery Allson Whitman is thought to have published his first book, *Essays on the Ten Plagues and Miscellaneous Subjects*. All copies of it will eventually be lost.

James Weldon Johnson, poet, teacher, anthologist, diplomat, and NAACP officer, is born June 17 in Jacksonville, Florida. His poem "Lift Every Voice and Sing" will be set to music and become known as the "Negro national anthem."

SCIENCE AND TECHNOLOGY

Miles Vandahurst Lynk is born June 3 in Texas. He will found the first African-American medical journal, the *Medical and Surgical Observer*, and help organize the National Medical Association.

Contemporary Events, 1871 ■ The Chicago fire occurs. ■ P. T. Barnum opens "The Greatest Show on Earth" in Brooklyn. ■ Grand Central Terminal opens in New York City.

Lynchings

When Reconstruction ended in 1877 and federal troops withdrew from the South, turning state governments over to racist white Democratic majorities, an era of brutal suppression of blacks began in earnest. Lynchings were one of the most widespread forms of lawless intimidation. In 1872, at least 12 African Americans were lynched in the South. Twenty years later, in 1892, there were 255 black victims known to be lynched, and they were often tortured in the process. According to one tally, within a 35-year period, no fewer than 3,200 African-American men and women were lynched, many involving burnings and mutilations.

PERFORMING ARTS

The Fisk Jubilee Singers tour America and Europe to raise money for the college.

Joseph H. Douglass, grandson of Frederick Douglass and renowned violinist, is born July 3 in Washington, D.C.

VISUAL ARTS

Sculptor and ceramicist Isaac Hathaway is born in Kentucky.

POLITICS AND CIVIL RIGHTS

The Freedmen's Bureau, established by Congress to assure African Americans fair treatment after the Civil War, goes out of existence due to Congress's unwillingness to renew its authority.

Congress allows the Ku Klux Klan Act to expire.

Congress passes an Amnesty Act, which allows former Confederate officials to hold office.

On June 5 the Republican National Convention in Philadelphia becomes the setting for major participation by African-American delegates. Robert B. Elliott (who chairs the delegation from South Carolina), Joseph Rainey (also from South Carolina), and John R. Lynch (from Mississippi) speak at the convention.

P. B. S. Pinchback begins his one-month term as the first African-American governor of Louisiana, following the impeachment of Governor Henry Clay Warmoth.

Civil rights activist and editor William Monroe Trotter is born April 7 near Chillicothe, Ohio.

RELIGION AND EDUCATION

At Howard University Charlotte Ray becomes the first African-American woman to graduate from law school.

LITERATURE AND JOURNALISM

Frederick Douglass publishes *U. S. Grant and the Colored People*.

William Still publishes *Underground Railroad*.

Poet Paul Laurence Dunbar is born June 27 in Dayton, Ohio. He

Contemporary Events, 1872 ■ Ulysses S. Grant is reelected president. ■ Congress establishes Yellowstone as the nation's first national park.

will gain attention for his "dialect" poetry, but he will also write serious poems in standard English.

SCIENCE AND TECHNOLOGY

Inventor Elijah McCoy earns a patent for a steam engine lubricator.

Inventor T. J. Byrd receives four patents for improvements or new devices related to coupling horses to carriages.

PERFORMING ARTS

Cleveland Luca, founder of the Luca Family Quartet and composer of the Liberian national anthem, dies in Liberia on March 27.

THE MILITARY

John H. Conyers, Sr., is the first African American to be admitted to the Naval Academy at Annapolis.

SPORTS

African-American baseball player Bud Fowler plays for a Newcastle, Pennsylvania, team.

1873

POLITICS AND CIVIL RIGHTS

The Colfax massacre occurs in Louisiana, triggered by accusations of fraud in the election of 1872. About 100 whites indiscriminately slaughter over 60 African-American members of the Colfax community. Federal troops are sent in but fail to capture any of the white vigilantes.

Puerto Rico abolishes slavery.

PERFORMING ARTS

Composer, songwriter, and bandleader W. C. Handy is born November 16 in Alabama. His popular hits, including "St. Louis Blues" and "Memphis Blues," will establish the genre.

Composer J. Rosamond Johnson, brother of James Weldon Johnson, is born August 11 in Jacksonville, Florida. With Robert Cole, he will produce such popular songs as "Under the Bamboo Tree" and "Nobody's Looking But the Owl and the Moon."

Contemporary Events, 1873 ■ Banks collapse and the financial panic of 1873 begins.

The Freedmen's Savings and Trust Company

In 1865 the federal government founded the Freedmen's Savings and Trust Company, a bank to do business exclusively with African Americans. Headquartered in Washington, D.C., it eventually had approximately 40 branches, with total deposits of almost $3,300,000 from many thousands of African-American patrons. Frederick Douglass described it as "the black man's cow and the white man's milk." In 1874, as part of the nationwide economic depression that began the previous year, the bank failed.

VISUAL ARTS

Landscape painter William A. Harper is born in Canada.

1874

POLITICS AND CIVIL RIGHTS

Blanche K. Bruce from Mississippi is the first African American elected to a full term in the Senate.

BUSINESS AND EMPLOYMENT

Frederick Douglass is elected president of the already-failing Freedmen's Savings and Trust; the bank closes a few months later.

RELIGION AND EDUCATION

African-American Catholic priest Patrick F. Healy, S.J., is inaugurated president of Georgetown University in Washington, D.C.

James Theodore Holly is elected Episcopal bishop of Haiti.

Bibliophile, journalist, and lecturer Arthur A. Schomburg is born January 24 in Puerto Rico.

SCIENCE AND TECHNOLOGY

Inventor Elijah McCoy receives a patent for an ironing table.

PERFORMING ARTS

Guitarist Justin Holland publishes *Comprehensive Method for the Guitar*, a standard instructional guide.

1875

POLITICS AND CIVIL RIGHTS

Charles Sumner's bill introduced in the U.S. Senate in 1870 is enacted as the nation's second Civil Rights Act. It recognizes "the equality of all men before the law" and enacts stiff penalties for denying any citizen "full and equal enjoyment of . . . inns, public conveyances, . . . theaters, and other places of public amusement."

Educator and activist Mary McLeod Bethune is born July 10 in South Carolina. She will establish the National Council of Negro

---

Contemporary Events, 1875 ■ *Alexander Graham Bell invents the telephone.*

Women, serve as an adviser to President Franklin D. Roosevelt, and help run the National Youth Administration.

RELIGION AND EDUCATION

Knoxville College is established in Tennessee by Presbyterians.

The first African-American Roman Catholic bishop, James A. Healy, is consecrated in Portland, Maine.

LITERATURE AND JOURNALISM

The Convention of Colored Newspapermen is held in Cincinnati to help make African-American newspapers self-sustaining.

Historian Carter Godwin Woodson is born December 19 in Virginia. He will found the Association for the Study of Negro Life and History, edit its scholarly *Journal of Negro History*, and establish Negro History Week.

Writer Alice Ruth Moore Dunbar-Nelson is born July 19 in New Orleans.

SCIENCE AND TECHNOLOGY

Inventor A. P. Ashbourne receives a patent for a process for preparing coconut oil for domestic use.

SPORTS

Riding Aristides, jockey Oliver Lewis wins the first Kentucky Derby ever held.

1876

POLITICS AND CIVIL RIGHTS

The Supreme Court decides in *United States* v. *Cruikshank* that the "right of suffrage is not a necessary attribute of national citizenship . . . [and that] the right to vote in the States comes from the States."

In *United States* v. *Reese*, the Supreme Court decides that "the 15th Amendment to the Constitution does not confer the right of suffrage" but only allows the government to provide a punishment for denying the vote to anyone based on "race, color, or previous condition of servitude."

President U. S. Grant sends federal troops to restore order in Ham-

Contemporary Events, 1876 ■ The National Baseball League is founded. ■ Colorado becomes the 38th state.

burg, South Carolina, after a heavily armed white mob kills several African Americans.

When the election of P. B. S. Pinchback to the U.S. Senate from Louisiana is contested, Senator Blanche K. Bruce speaks in his favor, but Pinchback is nevertheless denied a seat.

In Alabama a law prevents white and black prisoners being detained in the same cell.

RELIGION AND EDUCATION

Edward Bouchet receives a doctorate in physics from Yale University, becoming the first African American to receive a Ph.D. from a U.S. school.

Meharry Medical College is founded at Central Tennessee College in Nashville.

SCIENCE AND TECHNOLOGY

D. C. Fisher receives a patent for a furniture caster.

PERFORMING ARTS

Popular vaudeville and musical comedy star Bert Williams is born in the Bahamas. Teamed with George Walker, Williams will entertain audiences, and after Walker's death, he will become the first black member of the Ziegfeld Follies.

VISUAL ARTS

At the Centennial Exposition in Philadelphia, African-American landscape painter Edward M. Bannister and sculptor Edmonia Lewis win critical acclaim for their work. Bannister's painting *Under the Oaks* is awarded the bronze medal.

THE MILITARY

African-American cavalryman and Indian scout Isaiah Dorman warns General George A. Custer about the presence of hostile Sioux near the Little Bighorn River in the Dakotas. His warning, however, is not heeded.

ADDITIONAL EVENTS

In Philadelphia's Fairmont Park, a monument is dedicated to Richard Allen, one of the founders of the Free African Society and the first bishop of the African Methodist Episcopal Church. This is the first known monument erected by African Americans to honor a black leader.

POLITICS AND CIVIL RIGHTS

After the presidential election between Samuel J. Tilden and Rutherford B. Hayes ends in an electoral college dispute, the Democrats trade the presidency for Republican assurance that Democrats will be able to control southern state governments without federal interference. Hayes is chosen as president, but the trade-off effectively brings an end to Reconstruction.

White majorities regain control of state governments in the South and reinstate severe laws regulating African Americans.

BUSINESS AND EMPLOYMENT

Six African-American entrepreneurs in northwestern Kansas found the American Nicodemus Town Company.

LITERATURE AND JOURNALISM

Albery Allson Whitman, a former slave, publishes his long poem *Not a Man and Yet a Man.*

SCIENCE AND TECHNOLOGY

Inventor of the traffic light and gas mask Garrett A. Morgan is born in Kentucky.

PERFORMING ARTS

Cornetist Charles "Buddy" Bolden, thought to lead the first jazz band, is born September 6 in New Orleans.

VISUAL ARTS

Sculptor Meta Vaux Warrick Fuller is born June 9 in Philadelphia.

Sculptor May Howard Jackson is born in Philadelphia.

THE MILITARY

On June 15, after four years of ostracism by whites, Henry O. Flipper becomes the first African American to graduate from West Point.

SPORTS

Jockey Isaac Murphy wins at Churchill Downs.

African Americans in Congress during Reconstruction

From 1869 to 1877, when Reconstruction ended, 14 African Americans served at one time or another in the U.S. House of Representatives. Two, both from Mississippi, served in the U.S. Senate. African-American congressmen made commendable efforts to fight for Reconstruction legislation to ensure black rights in the former Confederate states and legislation to benefit the poor, both black and white, in all parts of the nation. Their progressive voting record, however, produced short-lived legislation in the South. The laws were either rescinded or allowed to expire after federal troops were withdrawn in 1877, when southern planters with northern industrialist support regained power.

Contemporary Events, 1877 ■ The Great Railroad Strike spreads violently across the country.

POLITICS AND CIVIL RIGHTS

A Democrat-controlled Congress weakens the U.S. Army by withholding funds and strips the president of power to send federal troops to oversee fair elections in the South.

According to a report by the U.S. attorney general, elections in several southern states are characterized by ballot stuffing on the part of white Democrats and widespread intimidation to prevent blacks from voting.

In *Hall* v. *DeCuir* the U.S. Supreme Court protects segregation by ruling that states cannot outlaw segregation on streetcars, railroads, and similar forms of public transportation.

LITERATURE AND JOURNALISM

Poet, educator, and lawyer George B. Vashon dies October 5 in Mississippi.

Poet and literary critic William Stanley Braithwaite is born in Boston. He will edit the *Anthology of Magazine Verse* from 1913 to 1929.

SCIENCE AND TECHNOLOGY

African-American inventor J. R. Winters devises a fire escape ladder.

Inventor W. A. Lavalette receives a patent for a variation on the printing press.

PERFORMING ARTS

James Bland publishes his song "Carry Me Back to Old Virginny."

Actor Charles S. Gilpin is born November 19 in Richmond, Virginia. He will star in Eugene O'Neill's *Emperor Jones* at the Provincetown Playhouse in New York in 1920.

Dancer, vaudeville star, and movie actor Bill "Bojangles" Robinson, dubbed the "King of Tap Dancers," is born May 25 in Richmond, Virginia.

SPORTS

Heavyweight boxing champion Jack Johnson is born in Galveston. He will lose only 3 bouts out of 100 fights between 1899 and 1908.

Contemporary Events, 1878 ■ Yellow fever kills approximately 14,000 people in the southern part of the United States.

International cycling star Marshall "Major" Taylor is born November 8 in Indianapolis.

1879

POLITICS AND CIVIL RIGHTS

Spurred on by activists like Henry Adams in Louisiana and Benjamin "Pap" Singleton in Tennessee, thousands of African Americans begin a mass exodus from the rural South, moving to the North and West, especially Kansas.

In opposition to the black migration out of the South, an armed group of southern whites threatens to "close" the Mississippi River by blockading river landings and sinking all boats carrying African Americans. The federal government threatens to intervene, and the shipping companies resume operations.

Civil rights activist and religious leader Nannie Burroughs is born May 2 in Orange, Virginia.

BUSINESS AND EMPLOYMENT

Approximately 1.25 million African Americans will join the newly formed Colored Farmer's Alliance, which along with the all-white Farmer's Alliance is a precursor of the Populist Movement.

PERFORMING ARTS

Pioneer jazz cornetist William "Bunk" Johnson is born December 27 in New Orleans.

SPORTS

Jockey Isaac Murphy enters 75 races and wins 35, including the Travers Stakes at Saratoga.

1880

POLITICS AND CIVIL RIGHTS

In *Strauder* v. *West Virginia*, the U.S. Supreme Court rules that laws preventing African Americans from serving on juries violate the 14th Amendment.

Contemporary Events, 1880 ■ James A. Garfield is elected president. ■ Andrew Carnegie develops the first large steel furnace.

U.S. Senator Blanche K. Bruce of Mississippi receives eight votes for vice president at the Republican National Convention.

In Florida, protests by poor whites are successful in getting officials to ignore the literacy tests for voting written into the 1868 state constitution to prevent African Americans from voting. The tests were slated to go into effect in 1880.

BUSINESS AND EMPLOYMENT

In Virginia's lucrative oyster industry, approximately half the oystermen are African Americans.

RELIGION AND EDUCATION

The National Baptist Convention, the Foreign Mission Baptist Convention of the U.S.A., and the American National Baptist Convention are all founded.

LITERATURE AND JOURNALISM

William Wells Brown publishes *My Southern Home.*

Poet Angelina Weld Grimké is born February 27 in Boston.

PERFORMING ARTS

Cakewalk dancer and ragtime singer Aida Overton Walker is born February 14 in New York.

SPORTS

Jockey Barrett Lewis wins the Kentucky Derby riding Fonso.

1881

POLITICS AND CIVIL RIGHTS

In his first message to Congress, President Chester A. Arthur expresses the opinion that African Americans can be excluded from voting if they are not literate.

Tennessee passes a law requiring railroad companies to provide segregated first-class cars for African Americans, instead of making all black passengers ride second class. Eventually all southern states pass similar "Jim Crow" laws.

Frederick Douglass is named recorder of deeds in Washington, D.C.

Contemporary Events, 1881 ■ President James A. Garfield is assassinated; Vice President Chester A. Arthur takes office.

The only two African Americans elected to Congress are Robert Smalls of South Carolina and John R. Lynch of Mississippi.

RELIGION AND EDUCATION

Tuskegee Institute, offering secondary education and teacher training, opens September 19 with 30 students and one teacher, Booker T. Washington. The school is funded by an appropriation of $2,000 from the Alabama legislature.

Allen University in Columbia, South Carolina, is founded by the African Methodist Episcopal Church.

Spelman College opens in Atlanta.

SCIENCE AND TECHNOLOGY

The first incandescent electric lamp with carbon filament is patented by Lewis Latimer. He will also make drawings for Alexander Graham Bell's telephone and become chief draftsman for General Electric and Westinghouse.

Architect Julian Francis Abele is born in Philadelphia. His designs will contribute to Philadelphia's Museum of Art, the Free Library, and buildings on the campus of Duke University.

PERFORMING ARTS

The Callender Minstrels make their first European tour.

Thirteen bands from African-American fraternal organizations in New Orleans play at the funeral ceremonies for President Garfield.

Bandleader James Reese Europe is born February 22 in Alabama.

1882

POLITICS AND CIVIL RIGHTS

There are 48 recorded lynchings.

The U.S. Supreme Court rules in *Pace* v. *Alabama* that a state law meting out harsher punishments for sexual relations between unmarried people of different races than for the same offenses committed by people of the same race is a violation of the equal protection clause of the 14th Amendment.

The white Populist leader Tom Watson of Georgia is elected to the

Contemporary Events, 1882 ■ The American Baseball Association is founded. ■ The United States bans Chinese immigrants for 10 years.

African-American Inventors

In the 1880s some of the most important inventions that furthered the increased mechanization of industry were developed by African Americans, an irony considering the fact that black workers were largely barred from skilled industrial jobs. In 1883 Jan Matzeliger revolutionized the shoe industry with his lasting machine. The following year John J. Parker invented a screw for tobacco presses and set up his own foundry to manufacture it. In 1884 Granville T. Woods began turning out inventions in electronics, telegraphy, air brake systems, and steam boilers. He sold many of his inventions to the major companies that were changing U.S. industry and the American way of life: American Bell Telephone Company, General Electric Company, and Westinghouse Air Brake Company.

state legislature by African Americans who support his position on providing free education for blacks and bringing an end to the convict lease system.

RELIGION AND EDUCATION

Lane College is founded in Jackson, Tennessee, by the Colored Methodist Episcopal Church.

Religious leader Father Divine is born George Baker in Maryland. The popular preacher will create an interracial movement that provides meals and housing during the Depression.

LITERATURE AND JOURNALISM

George Washington Williams publishes his two-volume *History of the Negro Race in America.*

Poet, biographer, and historian Benjamin Brawley is born in Columbia, South Carolina.

Novelist Jessie Fauset is born April 27 in Camden, New Jersey.

SCIENCE AND TECHNOLOGY

William B. Purvis patents a device for fastening paper bags. He will also receive 10 patents for the manufacturing of paper bags.

THE MILITARY

Thomas Boyne, a U.S. Cavalry sergeant, receives the Congressional Medal of Honor for bravery in the Indian Wars in New Mexico.

SPORTS

Jockey Babe Hurd wins the Kentucky Derby riding the horse Apollo.

1883

POLITICS AND CIVIL RIGHTS

There are 52 recorded lynchings.

The U.S. Supreme Court rules in a series of cases that the Civil Rights Act of 1875 is unconstitutional, going beyond the authority of Congress.

Abolitionist Sojourner Truth dies November 26 in Battle Creek, Michigan.

Contemporary Events, 1883 ■ The first skyscraper, with 10 stories, is built in Chicago. ■ The Brooklyn Bridge opens.

The first African American to serve as a Democrat in Congress, Arthur W. Mitchell is born in Alabama on December 22. He will represent Illinois from 1934 to 1942.

Black militant Hubert Harrison is born April 27 in St. Croix.

LITERATURE AND JOURNALISM

Poet Anne Spencer is born February 6 in Henry County, Virginia.

SCIENCE AND TECHNOLOGY

The shoe industry is revolutionized by a shoe-lasting machine invented by Jan Matzeliger, who receives a patent March 20.

H. H. Reynolds patents an improvement for railroad-car window ventilators.

Scientist and physician William A. Hinton is born in Chicago. A leading authority on venereal diseases, he will develop the Hinton Test and Davies-Hinton Test for detecting syphilis.

Marine biologist Ernest Everett Just is born August 14 in Charleston, South Carolina. He will investigate chromosome makeup in animals and important aspects of cellular theory.

PERFORMING ARTS

Singer Mamie Smith, the first African-American woman to record a blues song, is born May 26 in Cincinnati.

Pianist and composer Eubie Blake is born February 7 in Baltimore.

SPORTS

Coach and athletic entrepreneur Edwin Bancroft Henderson is born in Washington, D.C., November 24. Considered the "Father of Black Sports," he will organize the Negro Athletic Conference, the Interscholastic Athletic Association, and the Colored Inter-Collegiate Athletic Association.

1884

POLITICS AND CIVIL RIGHTS

There are 50 recorded lynchings.

Efforts to disfranchise black voters in the South result in the African-

---

Contemporary Events, 1884 ■ Grover Cleveland is elected president. ■ *The Adventures of Huckleberry Finn* by Mark Twain is published.

American vote dropping by one-third in Louisiana, one-fourth in Mississippi, and one-half in South Carolina.

John R. Lynch is the first African American to preside over the Republican National Convention, where he gives the keynote address.

RELIGION AND EDUCATION

Paine College in Augusta, Georgia, is established.

The African Methodist Episcopal Church *Review* is founded.

LITERATURE AND JOURNALISM

T. Thomas Fortune publishes the first issue of *New York Freeman,* later named *New York Age.*

SCIENCE AND TECHNOLOGY

The first African-American medical society, the Medico-Chirugical Society of Washington, D.C., is founded April 24.

Granville Woods receives his first two patents, for a steam boiler furnace and a telephone transmitter.

PERFORMING ARTS

Actress Rose McClendon is born August 27 in North Carolina.

VISUAL ARTS

Artist William Edouard Scott is born in Indianapolis.

Filmmaker Oscar Micheaux is born January 22 in Illinois.

SPORTS

The horse Buchanan wins at the Kentucky Derby; both trainer, William Bird, and jockey, Isaac Murphy, are African Americans.

Moses Fleetwood Walker, a bare-handed catcher, plays for Toledo in the old major league American Association.

1885

POLITICS AND CIVIL RIGHTS

There are 74 recorded lynchings.

Martin R. Delany, emigrationist and cofounder of the African Civilization Society, dies January 24.

Contemporary Events, 1885 ■ The new immigration from eastern and southern Europe begins. ■ The Washington Monument is dedicated.

RELIGION AND EDUCATION

Morris Brown University is founded in Atlanta by the African Methodist Episcopal Church.

Samuel David Ferguson becomes the first African-American missionary bishop (assigned to Liberia) in the Protestant Episcopal Church.

LITERATURE AND JOURNALISM

The *Philadelphia Tribune* begins publication.

SCIENCE AND TECHNOLOGY

Sarah Goode receives a patent for a folding cabinet bed.

PERFORMING ARTS

Folksinger Huddie "Leadbelly" Ledbetter is born in Louisiana. In the 1930s his concerts stimulate a revival in American folk music.

Ferdinand "Jelly Roll" Morton, the first great jazz composer, is born in Gulfport, Louisiana.

Jazz cornetist Joseph "King" Oliver is born May 11 in Louisiana. In the 1920s his band will make the first series of recordings by an African-American jazz band.

VISUAL ARTS

Photographer James Conway Farley wins an award at the New Orleans World Exposition.

SPORTS

Jockey Erskine Henderson wins the Kentucky Derby riding the horse Joe Cotton.

The Cuban Giants, considered the first black professional baseball team, are formed.

1886

POLITICS AND CIVIL RIGHTS

There are 74 recorded lynchings.

Congressman William L. Dawson is born in Albany, Georgia. He will become the first African American to chair a standing congressional committee after Reconstruction.

Contemporary Events, 1886 ■ The American Federation of Labor is founded with Samuel Gompers as president. ■ The Haymarket Square riot breaks out in Chicago.

BUSINES AND EMPLOYMENT

The National Colored Farmers' Alliance and Cooperative Union is established.

RELIGION AND EDUCATION

Timothy Drew, founder of Moorish Science, precursor of the Nation of Islam, is born January 8 in rural North Carolina.

LITERATURE AND JOURNALISM

Poet Georgia Douglas Johnson is born September 10 in Atlanta.

Scholar and literary critic Alain Leroy Locke is born September 13 in Philadelphia.

PERFORMING ARTS

George W. Chadwick's *Second Symphony* is published, incorporating African-American folk songs into symphonic arrangements.

Singer Gertrude "Ma" Rainey, "Mother of the Blues," is born April 26 in Columbus, Georgia. She will record with Louis Armstrong, Fletcher Henderson, and others.

VISUAL ARTS

Photographer James VanDerZee is born June 29 in Lenox, Massachusetts. He will be known for his images of Harlem.

1887

POLITICS AND CIVIL RIGHTS

There are 70 recorded lynchings.

Black nationalist Marcus M. Garvey is born August 17 in Jamaica. His Universal Negro Improvement Association will find widespread support in the 1920s.

LITERATURE AND JOURNALISM

Charles Chesnutt's "The Goophered Grapevine" is published in the *Atlantic Monthly*.

George Washington Williams's *History of the Negro Troops in the War of Rebellion* is published.

Writer Gussie Davis publishes *The Lighthouse by the Sea*.

Contemporary Events, 1887 ■ Frank J. Sprague develops the first electric street railway and builds a 12-mile trolley line in Richmond, Virginia.

PERFORMING ARTS

Musician Cora "Lovie" Austin is born September 19 in Chattanooga, Tennessee.

Thomas Montgomery Gregory, a founder of the Howard University Players, is born August 31 in Washington, D.C.

VISUAL ARTS

Sculptor Sargent Johnson is born October 7 in Boston.

SPORTS

The Union Giants, a semiprofessional African-American baseball team, are founded in Chicago.

Jockey Isaac Lewis wins the Kentucky Derby, while Isaac Murphy wins four big races, including the St. Louis Derby.

1888

POLITICS AND CIVIL RIGHTS

There are 69 recorded lynchings.

In Mississippi blacks and whites are required to use separate waiting rooms in railroad stations.

BUSINESS AND EMPLOYMENT

The Savings Bank of the Grand Fountain United Order of True Reformers in Richmond, Virginia, and the Capital Savings Bank in Washington, D.C., both African-American banks, are founded.

LITERATURE AND JOURNALISM

The *Freeman* begins publication in Indianapolis.

Poet Fenton Johnson is born May 7 in Chicago.

PERFORMING ARTS

Alcide "Slow Drag" Pavageau, bassist, is born March 7.

VISUAL ARTS

Folk painter Horace Pippin is born February 22 in West Chester, Pennsylvania.

Blacks in Industry

During the 1880s the burgeoning American industry provided jobs for skilled and unskilled laborers and reshaped the face of America. Expansion swept through the railroad, mining, lumber, steel, and construction industries, fueling the rapid growth of cities and the development of the West. But African-American workers were denied most of the skilled jobs, and were hired primarily as unskilled workers or strikebreakers. In contrast to the days before the Civil War, when the majority of the construction workers in the South were black, by 1890 less than one-third of plasterers and less than one-fifth of carpenters were African Americans. The same year found only 8,000 black steelworkers, 800 machinists, and 200 boilermakers. The major unions barred black laborers, and tolerated segregated unions only to protect themselves from strikebreakers.

Contemporary Events, 1888 ■ Benjamin Harrison is elected president.

SPORTS

Jockey Pike Barnes wins the first Futurity race, held at Sheepshead in Brooklyn.

1889

POLITICS AND CIVIL RIGHTS

There are 92 recorded lynchings.

Frederick Douglass is appointed minister to Haiti.

BUSINESS AND EMPLOYMENT

The People's Building and Loan Association in Virginia is created by the Hampton Institute to provide loans to black homeowners.

An African-American bank, the Mutual Trust Company, is founded in Chattanooga, Tennessee.

Union leader and civil rights activist Asa Philip Randolph is born April 15 in Crescent City, Florida. He will found the Brotherhood of Sleeping Car Porters and the Negro American Labor Council.

LITERATURE AND JOURNALISM

Henry O. Flipper publishes *The Colored Cadet at West Point*.

SPORTS

Amherst College in Massachusetts has two African-American varsity football players, William Tecumseh Sherman Jackson and William Henry Lewis.

Jockey Pike Barnes wins the Champagne Stakes.

1890

POLITICS AND CIVIL RIGHTS

There are 85 recorded lynchings.

The U.S. Supreme Court decides in *In re Green* that states have full jurisdiction over the selection of presidential electors, which in effect disfranchises black voters.

The U.S. Supreme Court decides in *Louisville, New Orleans, and Texas Railroad* v. *Mississippi* that states' efforts to segregate railroad cars are

---

Contemporary Events, 1889 ■ North Dakota, South Dakota, Montana, and Washington become states. ■ Oklahoma is opened to settlement by non–Native Americans. **1890** ■ Idaho and Wyoming become states. ■ U.S. troops kill about 200 Native Americans at Wounded Knee in South Dakota.

constitutional.

The Mississippi State Constitutional Convention rewrites its Reconstruction constitution, adding provisions that require a poll tax of $2; bar voters convicted of bribery, burglary, theft, arson, perjury, murder, and bigamy; and bar voters who cannot read, understand, and "interpret" any section of the state constitution. The convention passes the new constitution without submitting it to a popular vote. This "Mississippi Plan" to eliminate black voters is adopted by other southern states.

One of the first modern African-American protest organizations, the National Afro-American League, is organized in Chicago with Joseph C. Price its first president.

BUSINESS AND EMPLOYMENT

African Americans found the Alabama Penny Savings and Loan Company in Birmingham. It will survive the financial depression of 1893, which causes larger banks in Birmingham to fail.

African Americans own 120,738 farms.

RELIGION AND EDUCATION

The U.S. census indicates that 18.7% of African Americans in the South attend school. The literacy rate also rises to 42.9%, compared with 30% in 1880.

Susie Elizabeth Frazier becomes the first black woman teacher in the New York City public school system.

There are 12,159 African-American ministers in the Protestant denominations.

The Morrill Act is amended to provide land-grant funds for African-American education in places with segregated public school systems.

The Blair Bill to reduce illiteracy among southern blacks by providing federal funds for education is defeated in the U.S. Senate by a vote of 37 to 31.

Savannah State College is founded in Georgia.

Mordecai W. Johnson, Howard University's first African-American president, is born January 12 in Paris, Tennessee.

LITERATURE AND JOURNALISM

Octavia Victoria Rogers Albert's *The House of Bondage,* a collection of slave narratives, is published posthumously.

Poet and novelist Claude McKay, a major force in the Harlem Renaissance, is born in Jamaica September 15.

The Lodge Bill

Crucial to safeguarding the rights of African-American voters was the need for federal supervision of national elections. Representative Henry Cabot Lodge of Massachusetts introduced a bill to provide for this in 1890. If passed, federal officials would have had the authority to decide upon the qualifications of voters and place their ballots into ballot boxes over the objections of local officials. The bill passed in the House by 155 to 149 votes. A southern filibuster killed the bill in the Senate. In later sessions of Congress, an alliance between southern Democrats and Silver Republicans prevented Lodge's bill from being considered. By the election of 1892, the Democratic national platform officially denounced the election bill. African Americans in the South continued to suffer discrimination and intimidation at the ballot box until the 1960s.

SCIENCE AND TECHNOLOGY

William B. Purvis is granted a patent for a fountain pen.

PERFORMING ARTS

Banjoist Johnny St. Cyr is born April 17.

VISUAL ARTS

Sculptor Nancy Elizabeth Prophet is born March 19 in Rhode Island.

Painter Palmer C. Hayden is born January 15 in Widewater, Virginia.

SPORTS

George "Little Chocolate" Dixon wins the world bantamweight boxing championship.

Pike Barnes wins the Belmont and Alabama Stakes.

Isaac Murphy wins the Kentucky Derby.

1891

POLITICS AND CIVIL RIGHTS

There are 112 recorded lynchings.

Southern whites try unsuccessfully to segregate delegates from the National Colored Farmers' Alliance at the National Populist Convention in Cincinnati. The alliance has 1,300,000 members.

Railroads are now racially segregated in Alabama. Georgia becomes the first state to segregate streetcars.

After passing in the House, Representative Henry Cabot Lodge's bill calling for federal supervision of elections is killed in the Senate by a southern filibuster.

The first African-American congressman from North Carolina, John Adams Hyman, dies September 14 in Washington, D.C.

Edward R. Dudley, assistant attorney general for New York State, ambassador to Liberia, and state supreme court justice, is born in South Boston, Virginia.

BUSINESS AND EMPLOYMENT

In Texas cotton pickers unionize and strike for higher wages.

Contemporary Events, 1891 ■ Stanford White designs the first Madison Square Garden. ■ The second of two volumes of Emily Dickinson's poems, published posthumously, appears.

RELIGION AND EDUCATION

North Carolina Agricultural and Technical State University is founded in Greensboro.

West Virginia State College is founded in Institute, West Virginia.

LITERATURE AND JOURNALISM

Folklorist, novelist, and short-story writer Zora Neale Hurston is born January 7 in Eatonville, Florida.

Novelist Nella Larsen is born April 13 in Chicago.

SCIENCE AND TECHNOLOGY

On May 4, African-American physician Daniel Hale Williams opens Provident Hospital in Chicago, which includes a school to train black doctors and nurses.

PERFORMING ARTS

The Creole Show, a play by Sam T. Jack, opens in Haverhill, Massachusetts, featuring African-American women for the first time as leading performers in a stage play.

An African-American group from New Orleans, the Onward Brass Band, wins first prize in a New York City music contest.

Lillian Evanti, one of the founders of the National Negro Opera Company, is born August 12 in Washington, D.C.

VISUAL ARTS

Artist Alma W. Thomas is born September 22 in Columbus, Georgia.

Archibald J. Motley, Jr., the first major African-American painter to depict the life of urban blacks, is born October 7 in New Orleans.

THE MILITARY

Charles H. Garvin, the first African-American physician to be commissioned during World War I, is born October 27 in Jacksonville, Florida.

SPORTS

Isaac Murphy is the first jockey to win three Kentucky Derbys.

1892

POLITICS AND CIVIL RIGHTS

There are 160 recorded lynchings.

Racism plays a major role in southern elections. In Georgia, white

Ida B. Wells Barnett

The woman credited with beginning a campaign to stop lynching, Ida B. Wells, was born in Holly Springs, Mississippi. She was educated at Rust College, taught in Memphis, and became editor and part-owner of the **Memphis Free Speech.** During the 1880s she observed the growing trend of lynching. In 1892, because she exposed those behind the lynching of three black Memphis businessmen, angry whites destroyed her offices and drove her out of the city. Wells went to Chicago and married Ferdinand Barnett, founding editor of the **Chicago Conservator.** She chaired the Anti-Lynching Bureau of the National Afro-American Council and proved statistically that the southern white fantasy that black men raped white women was not the cause of lynchings. "Nowhere in the civilized world, save the United States, do men go out in bands, to hunt down, shoot, hang to death a single individual," she pointed out in 1928. One of the founders of the NAACP, Ida B. Wells Barnett died in 1931.

Democrats murder 15 African Americans during the campaign. In Augusta, Georgia, Democrats stuff the ballot boxes, creating a total number of votes twice the number of registered voters.

Congress grants a pension to Harriet Tubman for her work during the Civil War as a scout, nurse, and spy.

BUSINESS AND EMPLOYMENT

In St. Louis African-American longshoremen strike for higher wages.

LITERATURE AND JOURNALISM

A secret society of African Americans, the Virginia Organization of True Reformers, publishes the *Reformer,* a newspaper that will reach a weekly circulation of 8,000 by 1900.

African-American educator Anna Julia Cooper publishes *A Voice from the South.*

Baltimore's *Afro-American* newspaper begins publication.

Frances Ellen Watkins Harper publishes her only novel, *Iola Leroy: Or, Shadows Uplifted.*

SCIENCE AND TECHNOLOGY

Andrew Beard is granted a patent for his rotary engine.

PERFORMING ARTS

The World's Fair Colored Opera Company gives the first performance by African Americans at New York's recently opened Carnegie Hall.

Sissieretta Jones, known as "Black Patti," is invited to sing at the White House.

Jazz clarinetist Johnny Dodds is born April 12.

Jazz trumpeter Mutt Carey is born August 28.

VISUAL ARTS

Sculptor Augusta Savage is born February 29 near Jacksonville, Florida.

Self-taught artist Minnie Evans is born December 12 in rural North Carolina.

Contemporary Events, 1892 ■ Grover Cleveland is elected president.

SPORTS

The Calumet Wheelmen, an African-American athletic club, is organized in New York.

William Henry Lewis, captain of the Amherst football team, is named All-American.

George "Little Chocolate" Dixon wins the world's featherweight boxing championship by defeating Jack Skelly, a white man, in New Orleans. The city's major newspaper criticizes the event for bringing the two fighters together on equal terms.

The first African-American intercollegiate football game is played between Livingstone and Biddle College (now Johnson C. Smith).

POLITICS AND CIVIL RIGHTS

There are 117 recorded lynchings.

BUSINESS AND EMPLOYMENT

E. P. McCabe, an African-American entrepreneur, takes part in the Oklahoma Land Rush. He is the founder of two all-black Oklahoma towns, Liberty and Langston.

RELIGION AND EDUCATION

Sociologist Charles S. Johnson is born July 24 in Bristol, Virginia. He will found the National Urban League's magazine, *Opportunity*, and serves as president of Fisk University.

LITERATURE AND JOURNALISM

Paul Laurence Dunbar's first collection of poetry, *Oak and Ivy*, is published.

SCIENCE AND TECHNOLOGY

At Provident Hospital in Chicago, Daniel Hale Williams sutures the pericardium of a stabbing victim, thus performing the world's first open-heart surgery.

Aviator Bessie Coleman, the first black woman to obtain a pilot's license, is born January 20 in Texas.

Contemporary Events, 1893 ■ There is a major financial panic. ■ The World's Columbian Exposition is held in Chicago.

PERFORMING ARTS

Songwriter Perry Bradford is born February 14.

Country blues singer William "Big Bill" Broonzy is born June 26 in Scott, Mississippi.

Singer "Mississippi" John Hurt is born July 3.

VISUAL ARTS

Henry O. Tanner completes *The Banjo Lesson,* one of his most famous paintings.

SPORTS

Willie Simms wins the Belmont Stakes.

1894

POLITICS AND CIVIL RIGHTS

There are 135 recorded lynchings.

Congress repeals the 1870 Enforcement Act's provision to provide federal marshals and election supervisors to see that election practices in local communities do not violate African Americans' right to vote.

J. Ernest Wilkins, assistant secretary of labor in the Eisenhower administration, is born in Farmington, Missouri.

BUSINESS AND EMPLOYMENT

The major railroad unions, including socialist Eugene V. Debs's American Railway Union, bar African Americans from membership.

RELIGION AND EDUCATION

E. Franklin Frazier, head of the sociology department at Howard University and the first African-American president of the American Sociological Society, is born September 24 in Washington, D.C.

LITERATURE AND JOURNALISM

Walter Stowers and William H. Anderson publish *Appointed,* the first African-American novel to deal with the racism of the Jim Crow era. It details the effects of convict labor, peonage, disfranchisement, segregation, and lynching.

Contemporary Events, 1894 ■ Hawaii becomes a republic.

John Mercer Langston, a former congressman, publishes his autobiography *From the Virginia Plantation to the National Capitol*.

Jean Toomer, author of the experimental novel *Cane*, is born December 26 in Washington, D.C.

PERFORMING ARTS

The greatest of all blues singers, Bessie Smith is born April 15 in Chattanooga, Tennessee.

Comedienne Jackie "Moms" Mabley is born March 19 in Brevard, North Carolina.

Musician Charles "Cow Cow" Davenport is born April 23.

Singer Lucille Hegamin is born November 29.

Jazz pianist James P. Johnson is born February 1 in New Brunswick, New Jersey. His Harlem stride piano technique will influence Fats Waller and Duke Ellington.

Nightclub hostess Ada Bricktop Smith is born August 14 in Alderson, West Virginia.

VISUAL ARTS

Architect Paul Revere Williams is born February 18 in Los Angeles. He will design the Hollywood YMCA and houses for Frank Sinatra, Lon Chaney, and others.

SPORTS

For the second year, Willie Simms wins the Belmont Stakes.

1895

POLITICS AND CIVIL RIGHTS

There are 112 recorded lynchings.

Booker T. Washington gives his "Atlanta Compromise" speech at the Cotton States Exposition in Atlanta. He urges African Americans to put aside the fight for equality and cultivate friendly relations with southern whites, while pursuing a practical education that prepares them for earning a livelihood. Political and social equality, he argues, will follow black self-reliant economic achievement.

South Carolina revises its state constitution to disfranchise African

The Atlanta Compromise

Booker T. Washington, the principal of a small teacher-training school in Tuskegee, Alabama, gained national attention when he made a speech in Atlanta at the Cotton States Exposition on September 18, 1895. Reconstruction had been thwarted by the white South, and African Americans were subject to violence, lynchings, disfranchisement, legalized segregation, and the economic enslavement of sharecropping. Washington's address, in effect, agreed to accept white domination. He urged blacks to surrender the struggle for civil rights, to accommodate themselves to segregation, to take responsibility for their situation and pull themselves up by their own bootstraps. Whites embraced Washington and his philosophy, and he was heralded by the white press as the new spokesperson for American blacks. His supporters claimed Washington was doing the only practical thing that could be done under the circumstances, but his wholesale capitulation led to his famous speech being forever referred to as the "Atlanta Compromise.

Contemporary Events, 1895 ■ American interests in Cuba are threatened as insurrection breaks out against Spanish rule.

Americans by requiring poll taxes, property qualifications, educational tests, and two years' residency.

Frederick Douglass, leading abolitionist and civil rights advocate, dies at age 78 in Washington, D.C., February 20.

Charles Hamilton Houston, civil rights lawyer, is born September 3 in Washington, D.C.

RELIGION AND EDUCATION

The Foreign Mission Baptist Convention of the U.S.A., the American National Baptist Convention, and the American National Educational Baptist Convention consolidate into the National Baptist Convention of the U.S.A.

W. E. B. Du Bois receives a Ph.D. in history from Harvard University.

LITERATURE AND JOURNALISM

Paul Laurence Dunbar's book of poetry *Majors and Minors* receives a favorable review by William Dean Howells in *Harper's Weekly*.

Ida B. Wells Barnett publishes the first statistics on lynching in her pamphlet "The Red Record."

SCIENCE AND TECHNOLOGY

The Frederick Douglass Memorial Hospital and Training School for Nurses is founded in Philadelphia.

The black National Medical Association is founded in Atlanta, since African Americans are barred from established medical groups.

PERFORMING ARTS

John W. Ishaw produces the all-black musical *The Octoroon.*

Composer William Grant Still, the first African American to conduct a major symphony orchestra, is born May 11 in Woodville, Mississippi.

Singer Alberta Hunter is born April 1 in Memphis.

Choral director Eva Jessye is born January 20 in Coffeyville, Kansas.

Singer Lizzie Miles is born March 31.

Vaudevillian Jodie Edwards, known as "Butterbeans," is born July 19.

Actor Rex Ingram is born October 20 near Cairo, Illinois. He will play "De Lawd" in the film version of *The Green Pastures* in 1936.

Songwriter Andy Razaf (originally Razafkeriefo) is born December 16 in Washington, D.C. He will write the lyrics to such popular hits as "Ain't Misbehavin'"and "Honeysuckle Rose."

1896

POLITICS AND CIVIL RIGHTS

There are 77 recorded lynchings.

In *Plessy* v. *Ferguson* the Supreme Court decides that the practice of "separate but equal" accommodations is a "reasonable" solution to prevent the mingling of the races. It holds that the 14th Amendment was never intended to "abolish distinction based on color, or to enforce social as distinguished from political . . . equality."

Mary Church Terrell helps organize the National Association of Colored Women in Washington, D.C. The organization will sponsor many social reforms and educational programs.

Black militant Amy Jacques Garvey is born December 31 in Kingston, Jamaica.

RELIGION AND EDUCATION

At Tuskegee Institute, George Washington Carver is appointed director of agricultural research.

W. E. B. Du Bois establishes the Atlanta University Studies, a yearly series of scholarly conferences and publications on African-American life, considered to be the first sociological research undertaken in the South.

South Carolina State College is founded as the Colored Normal Industrial, Agricultural, and Mechanical College at Orangeburg.

Booker T. Washington receives an honorary master of arts degree from Harvard University, the first African American to do so.

LITERATURE AND JOURNALISM

W. E. B. Du Bois publishes *The Suppression of the African Slave Trade,* the first volume in the Harvard Historical Studies.

Paul Laurence Dunbar publishes his collection of verse *Lyrics of Lowly Life.*

The Atlanta University Press begins publishing books.

Writer Eslanda Robeson is born December 12 in Washington, D.C.

SCIENCE AND TECHNOLOGY

Pioneer physician May Chinn is born April 15.

The National Association of Colored Women

The National Association of Colored Women was founded in Washington, D.C., in 1896 when the National Federation of Afro-American Women and the Colored Women's League merged. The new organization had far-reaching social goals. It sent health teams into several states to educate poor people about hygiene as a means of preventive health care. In New Orleans the organization established a nurses' training school for African-American women. The association purchased land in Memphis on which to build a residence for the elderly. Among its more ambitious plans was a series of "Mothers' Congresses" to provide instruction to black women on child-rearing practices, domestic skills, and health care. Politically, the association wrote petitions for the repeal of Jim Crow laws and an end to racial segregation. At its conventions papers were read on such topics as the convict-lease system and the need for an equal moral standard for men and women. In five years the association had chapters in 26 states.

Contemporary Events, 1896 ■ Utah becomes a state. ■ William McKinley is elected president.

PERFORMING ARTS

Emile "Stale Bread" Lacoume, "Cajun," "Whiskey," "Warm Gravy," and "Slew Foot Pete" improvise original music with homemade instruments on street corners in New Orleans. Their efforts are an early example of the "spasm band."

Blues singer Ida Cox is born February 25 in Georgia.

Actor Evelyn Preer is born July 26 in Vicksburg, Mississippi.

Guitar player "Blind" Gary Davis is born April 30 in Laurens, South Carolina.

Singer and dancer Florence Mills is born in Washington, D.C., January 25. She will become the most popular African-American entertainer of the 1920s.

VISUAL ARTS

Henry O. Tanner wins an honorable mention at the Paris Salon for his painting *Daniel in the Lion's Den.*

Artist Malvin Gray Johnson is born in Greensboro, North Carolina.

SPORTS

Willie Simms wins the Kentucky Derby.

William Henry Lewis writes *How to Play Football.*

1897

POLITICS AND CIVIL RIGHTS

There are 123 recorded lynchings.

RELIGION AND EDUCATION

Alexander Crummell, an Episcopal clergyman, cofounds the American Negro Academy to encourage literature, art, science, and higher education.

Elijah Poole, later known as Elijah Muhammad, is born in Sandersville, Georgia, October 8. He will assist W. D. Fard, founder of the Nation of Islam, and become head of the movement.

LITERATURE AND JOURNALISM

James Edwin Campbell writes *Echoes from the Cabin and Elsewhere,* a

---

Contemporary Events, 1897 ■ The first subway is completed in Boston.

collection of poetry using Gullah dialect and depicting customs found on the offshore islands of South Carolina.

Novelist Rudolph Fisher is born May 9 in Washington, D.C.

SCIENCE AND TECHNOLOGY

Andrew J. Beard invents the "Jenny Coupler," an automatic system for coupling railroad cars.

PERFORMING ARTS

Storyville, the red-light district in New Orleans, opens. It will inspire many musicians, composers, and entertainers, whose work will spread New Orleans musical styles to other parts of the nation.

Composer Thomas Million Turpin's "Harlem Rag" is published.

Sidney Bechet, considered the most talented clarinet and soprano saxophone player in jazz, is born May 14 in New Orleans.

Lizzie "Memphis Minnie" Douglas, the most important and influential singer of country blues, is born June 3.

Stride pianist Willie "The Lion" Smith is born November 25 in Goshen, New York.

Blues singer and guitarist "Blind Lemon" Jefferson is born July 1 in Texas. He will be one of the first to use the term "rock 'n' roll," a sexual euphemism.

Tap dancer Willie Covan is born March 4 in Atlanta.

Bandleader and jazz pianist Fletcher Henderson is born December 18 in Cuthbert, Georgia.

VISUAL ARTS

Henry O. Tanner wins a medal at the Paris Salon for *The Raising of Lazarus*, which is purchased by the French government.

SPORTS

Jockey Willie Simms wins the Brighton Handicap.

1898

POLITICS AND CIVIL RIGHTS

There are 101 recorded lynchings during this year.

Contemporary Events, 1898 ■ The Spanish-American War begins and ends with Spain ceding Cuba, Puerto Rico, Guam, and the Philippines to the United States.

The American Negro Academy

The American Negro Academy was founded in 1897 in Washington, D.C., by African-American intellectuals; its presidents over the years were Alexander Crummell, W. E. B. Du Bois, Archibald Grimké, John W. Cromwell, and Arthur Schomburg. Established when blacks were being lynched, disfranchised, and legally segregated, the academy set out to counter the "scientific" racism of the day, to encourage proud consciousness of African-American culture and history, and to prove that blacks were as capable of scholarly achievement as whites.

The academy provided a forum for black intellectual discourse. It achieved recognition from its exhibitions of African-American books, and it supported Kelly Miller's efforts to have Howard University establish a special collection of African and African-American materials. Over the years the American Negro Academy published 5 monographs and 22 "occasional papers" from its own meetings. The first African-American learned society, it functioned until 1928.

The U.S. Supreme Court in *Williams* v. *Mississippi* decides that the poll tax does not violate the 14th Amendment.

Georgia begins a practice known as the "white primary," in which only whites may vote in Democratic primary elections, which, in the one-party South, in fact determine winning candidates.

Louisiana adds a "grandfather clause" to its state constitution, releasing poor whites from strict voting requirements. In effect, the clause exempts anyone whose grandfather voted on January 1, 1867, from having to fulfill the requirements for voter registration—an exemption African Americans obviously cannot fulfill. The number of blacks registered to vote in Louisiana will drop from 130,344 in 1896 to 5,320 in 1900.

Blanche K. Bruce, the first full-term black senator, dies March 17.

Lawyer and activist Sadie T. M. Alexander is born January 2 in Philadelphia.

Activist Audley "Queen Mother" Moore is born July 27 in Louisiana.

Activist Septima Clark is born May 3.

BUSINESS AND EMPLOYMENT

African-American investors found the North Carolina Mutual Life and Provident Association. By the 1990s the company, renamed the North Carolina Mutual Life Insurance Company, will be one of the most prosperous U.S. insurance and investment companies.

In Galveston, Texas, African-American longshoremen strike for higher wages and better working conditions.

Entrepreneur Otis J. Rene is born October 2 in New Orleans. He and his brother Leon will found Exclusive and Excelsior Records in the 1930s, with such clients as Nat "King" Cole and Johnny Otis.

RELIGION AND EDUCATION

Scholar and intellectual Alexander Crummell dies September 10 in Red Bank, New Jersey.

Historian Chancellor Williams is born December 22 in South Carolina.

LITERATURE AND JOURNALISM

Writer and educator Melvin B. Tolson is born February 6 in Moberly, Missouri. As poet laureate of Liberia, he will write the long poem *Libretto for the Republic of Liberia*.

PERFORMING ARTS

Composer Will Marion Cook and poet Paul Laurence Dunbar collaborate on the operetta *Clorindy; or, the Origin of the Cakewalk*, a work credited with blending the minstrel and the musical.

An early musical comedy by African Americans, *A Trip to Coontown*, written by Robert Cole and William F. Johnson, is produced.

Jazz musician Clarence Williams is born October 8.

Paul Robeson, actor, concert singer, athlete, and political activist, is born April 9 in Princeton, New Jersey. He will star in Shakespearean plays as well as Broadway musicals.

Drummer Arthur James "Zutty" Singleton is born May 14.

Blues singer Beulah Thomas, known as Sippie Wallace, is born November 11 in Houston, Texas.

Film actress Hattie McDaniel is born June 10 in Wichita, Kansas. She will be the first African-American woman to win an Oscar, for her role as "Mammy" in *Gone with the Wind*.

Bandleader Andy Kirk is born May 28.

Singer Jules Bledsoe is born December 29 in Waco, Texas.

Jazz pianist Lil Hardin Armstrong is born February 3 in Memphis.

THE MILITARY

During the Spanish-American War the 9th and 10th Calvaries help save Theodore Roosevelt's Rough Riders as Las Guasimas and participate in the charge up San Juan Hill. The 25th Infantry helps capture a Spanish fort at the Battle of El Caney.

SPORTS

Willie Simms wins the Kentucky Derby and the Brighton Handicap.

Marshall "Major" Taylor is declared national cycling champion, although the League of American Wheelmen refuses to recognize this and chooses another champion.

1899

POLITICS AND CIVIL RIGHTS

There are 85 recorded lynchings.

The National Afro-American Council, founded in 1898, calls for a day of fasting to protest lynchings and racial massacres.

Contemporary Events, 1899 ■ Filipino guerrilla fighters stage insurrections against the United States for the islands' independence. ■ The United States proposes an "Open Door" policy for China to prevent any nation from having exclusive trading privileges.

Diplomat Clifton R. Wharton, Sr., is born in Baltimore. He will be the first African American to head a European embassy (Romania).

Activist Anna Arnold Hedgeman is born July 5 in Marshalltown, Iowa.

LITERATURE AND JOURNALISM

Charles Waddell Chesnutt publishes two collections of stories, *The Conjure Woman* and *The Wife of His Youth.*

Baptist minister Sutton E. Griggs publishes *Imperium in Imperio,* a novel attacking whites and mulattoes, and advocating a separate African-American state.

SCIENCE AND TECHNOLOGY

L. C. Bailey receives a patent for a folding bed.

George F. Grant, an African-American dentist in Boston, receives a patent for a wooden golf tee.

PERFORMING ARTS

Bert Williams and George Walker begin their 10-year collaboration on ragtime musicals, starring in *The Policy Players.*

Eubie Blake composes his "Charleston Rag."

Thomas "Georgia Tom" Dorsey, blues performer and composer known as the "Father of Gospel," is born July 1 in Georgia. He will compose such classics as "Tight Like That" and "Precious Lord, Take My Hand."

Edward Kennedy "Duke" Ellington, one of the most important jazz musicians and composers, is born April 29 in Washington, D.C. He will compose and orchestrate over 1,500 songs, including "Sophisti-cated Lady," "Solitude," and "Mood Indigo," as well as longer pieces such as "Black, Brown, and Beige."

Musician Noble Sissle is born July 10 in Indianapolis.

Bluesman "Sleepy" John Estes is born January 25.

VISUAL ARTS

Painter Aaron Douglas, a leading artist of the Harlem Renaissance, is born May 26 in Topeka, Kansas.

1900

POLITICS AND CIVIL RIGHTS

There are 115 recorded lynchings.

The first bill to make lynching a federal crime is introduced in Congress by a representative from North Carolina, George H. White, the last African American elected during the Reconstruction era. The bill never gets out of committee.

In London, W. E. B. Du Bois is elected vice president of the first Pan-African Congress, whose objectives are to end Western imperialism and advance self-determination for colonized people.

BUSINESS AND EMPLOYMENT

The National Negro Business League is organized under the sponsorship of Booker T. Washington to encourage business ventures by African Americans. Washington is elected president of the league by 400 delegates, representing 34 states.

The American Federation of Labor begins to form local all-black labor unions in parts of the country where they will be tolerated.

RELIGION AND EDUCATION

Over 2,000 African Americans hold college degrees. Over 21,000 are schoolteachers.

Illiteracy among African Americans nationwide is 44.5%.

The German government requests graduates from Tuskegee Institute to teach West Africans how to grow cotton. Booker T. Washington sends a team to begin the project, which lasts for six years.

Theologian Howard Thurman is born November 18 in Daytona Beach, Florida. He will found the Church for the Fellowship of All Peoples in San Francisco and serve as dean of Marsh Chapel at Boston University.

LITERATURE AND JOURNALISM

Booker T. Washington publishes his autobiography *Up from Slavery*.

Charles Chesnutt publishes *The House Behind the Cedars*, a novel depicting the mulatto as an outcast from both black and white societies.

Contemporary Events, 1900 ■ William McKinley is elected for his second term as president, winning over William Jennings Bryan. ■ The territorial government of Puerto Rico is established after the United States captures the island in the Spanish-American War. ■ Hawaii is given territorial status.

Grandfather Clauses

In order to disfranchise African-American voters, southerners revised their state constitutions between 1895 and 1910, adding the infamous "grandfather clauses." The 15th Amendment, ratified in 1870, assured that no one would be denied the right to vote because of color or previous condition of servitude, but the grandfather clauses restricted the right to vote to those who had voted on January 1, 1867, and to the descendants of those who had the right to vote on that date. In effect, this disqualified African Americans, who could not vote prior to passage of the 15th Amendment. Grandfather clauses were enacted in Alabama, Georgia, Louisiana, North and South Carolina, Oklahoma, Maryland, and Virginia. In 1915 the United States Supreme Court declared these laws unconstitutional.

SCIENCE AND TECHNOLOGY

The Washington Society of Colored Dentists is founded in Washington, D.C., November 14, the first organization for African Americans in dentistry.

PERFORMING ARTS

The African-American song-and-dance team Bert Williams and George Walker opens in *Sons of Ham*, a musical comedy, which runs for two years in New York.

James Weldon Johnson writes the lyrics and his brother, J. Rosamond Johnson, composes the music for "Lift Every Voice and Sing."

Blues singer and actress Ethel Waters is born October 31 in Chester, Pennsylvania.

VISUAL ARTS

Painter and educator Hale A. Woodruff is born August 26 in Cairo, Illinois.

Sculptor and educator Selma Burke is born December 31 in Mooresville, North Carolina.

SPORTS

Marshall "Major" Taylor becomes the U.S. sprint champion in bicycle racing for the second consecutive year.

ADDITIONAL STATISTICS

The U.S. census counts 8,833,994 African Americans, making up 11.6% of the U.S. population. Almost 90% live in the South. A little more than one-fourth live in urban areas.

Life expectancy for African-American men and women is 34 years, compared with 48 years for white Americans.

Almost one-fourth of the black population are homeowners.

1901

POLITICS AND CIVIL RIGHTS

There are 130 recorded lynchings.

President Theodore Roosevelt takes a controversial step by inviting

---

Contemporary Events, 1901 ■ President McKinley is assassinated and is succeeded by Theodore Roosevelt. ■ Oil is found at Spindletop in Texas.

Booker T. Washington to be the first African American to dine at the White House.

George H. White from North Carolina ends his second term in the U.S. Congress. The next African American to serve in Congress will not be elected until 1928.

Racial violence breaks out in northern cities, as African Americans migrate north in search of better jobs.

Roy Wilkins is born August 30 in St. Louis. He will edit the NAACP's *Crisis* magazine for 15 years and later become executive director of the NAACP.

LITERATURE AND JOURNALISM

In Boston, civil rights activist William Monroe Trotter and George Washington Forbes found the *Guardian*, a newspaper boldly opposed to the accomodationist position of Booker T. Washington.

Writer, literary critic, and intellectual Sterling A. Brown is born in Washington, D.C. He will publish major studies of African-American literature.

PERFORMING ARTS

The Coleridge-Taylor Society is founded in Washington, D.C., to study and perform the music of England's most honored black composer, Samuel Coleridge-Taylor, whose worldwide reputation was established with his *Hiawatha's Wedding Feast*.

Music arranger and choir conductor Jester Hairston, who will arrange choral soundtracks for dozens of films, is born in Pennsylvania. He will appear in the television shows *Amos 'n' Andy* and *Amen*.

Bluesman "Blind" Willie McTell is born May 5 in Georgia.

Singer Adelaide Hall is born October 20 in Brooklyn, New York.

Louis ("Satchmo" or "Pops") Armstrong is born August 4 in New Orleans. Critics consider him the most influential African-American musician of the century.

VISUAL ARTS

Sculptor Richmond Barthé is born January 28 near New Orleans. He will become the first black sculptor in the National Academy of Arts and Letters.

Painter William H. Johnson is born March 18 in Florence, South Carolina. He will be the first modern African-American artist to be given a retrospective by the National Museum of American Art.

Painter Beauford Delaney is born December 31 in Knoxville, Tennessee.

SPORTS

"Jersey" Joe Walcott becomes the world's welterweight champion in boxing, and Joe Gans the world's lightweight champion.

1902

LITERATURE AND JOURNALISM

Writer Langston Hughes, called the "poet laureate of Harlem," is born February 1 in Joplin, Missouri.

Arna Bontemps, poet, novelist, and librarian, is born October 13 in Alexandria, Louisiana.

Harlem Renaissance poet Gwendolyn Bennett is born July 8.

PERFORMING ARTS

"Ma" Rainey, "Queen of the Blues," begins her singing career, which will last until her retirement in 1933.

In Dahomey, a musical by Paul Laurence Dunbar and Will Marion Cook, starring Bert Williams and George Walker, is a hit on Broadway and will later travel to London.

The Victor Talking Machine Company on October 21 records the first black music, the Dinwiddie Quartet, on records.

Contralto Marian Anderson is born February 17 in Philadelphia. An internationally acclaimed concert and opera singer, she will also serve on the U.S. delegation to the United Nations.

Jazz musician James "Jimmie" Lunceford is born in Seaside, Oregon.

Bluesman Eddie "Son" House, Jr., is born March 21.

Blues musician William "Peetie" Wheatstraw is born December 21.

VISUAL ARTS

Painter, printmaker, and educator James Lesesne Wells is born November 2 in Atlanta.

SPORTS

Jockey Jimmy Winkfield wins the Kentucky Derby, bringing the number of wins by African-American jockeys to 15 out of 28 races.

Contemporary Events, 1902 ■ The Bureau of the Census is formally established. ■ Alfred Stieglitz starts **Camera Works,** the first fine-arts photography magazine. ■ U.S. Army uniforms are switched from blue to olive for fear that blue is too easily seen.

POLITICS AND CIVIL RIGHTS

There are 99 recorded lynchings.

Civil rights activist Ella Baker is born in Norfolk, Virginia. She will be executive director of the Southern Christian Leadership Conference and help set up the Student Nonviolent Coordinating Committee.

BUSINESS AND EMPLOYMENT

The first woman U.S. bank president is Maggie Lena Walker, founder of Saint Luke Penny Savings Bank in Richmond, Virginia.

An African-American realtor begins to develop Manhattan's Harlem district into a predominantly black community.

RELIGION AND EDUCATION

John D. Rockefeller's donations to the General Education Board provide money to train African-American teachers for the South.

Minister and educator Francis Cardozo dies July 22 in Washington.

LITERATURE AND JOURNALISM

Poet Countee Cullen is born May 30 in Baltimore.

W. E. B. Du Bois publishes *The Souls of Black Folk*, presenting a daring alternative to the conciliatory policies of Booker T. Washington.

PERFORMING ARTS

Singer Jimmy Rushing is born August 26.

Earl "Fatha" Hines, "Father of Modern Jazz Piano," is born December 28 in Pennsylvania. He will develop and popularize the trumpet style of piano playing.

Actress Fredi Washington is born December 23 in Savannah.

Trumpeter "Bubber" Miley is born January 19.

Bluesman Whittaker Hudson, better known as "Tampa Red," is born December 15.

VISUAL ARTS

Meta Vaux Warrick exhibits her sculpture *The Wretched*, depicting seven types of anguish, at the Paris Salon.

Contemporary Events, 1903 ■ The longest motion picture to date, **The Great Train Robbery,** is made. It lasts 12 minutes. ■ Orville and Wilbur Wright fly the first powered airplane. ■ Henry Ford founds the Ford Motor Company. ■ The United States signs a treaty to build the Panama Canal.

A Credo

In October 1904 W. E. B. Du Bois published his "Credo" in the New York journal the **Independent.** His words were reprinted in a number of other publications. Many African Americans bought scrolls with Du Bois's "Credo" and hung these on their walls. In this statement of his beliefs, Du Bois declared, "I believe in Liberty for all men; the space to stretch their arms and their souls; the right to breathe and the right to vote, the freedom to choose their friends, enjoy the sunshine and ride on the railroads, uncursed by color; thinking, dreaming, working as they will in a kingdom of God and love."

1904

POLITICS AND CIVIL RIGHTS

There are 83 recorded lynchings.

A meeting of African-American leaders in Atlanta, financed by Andrew Carnegie, brings Booker T. Washington and W. E. B. Du Bois together in a brief alliance to promote black interests. Du Bois soon withdraws, however, over ideological and tactical differences with the moderate Washington.

In Statesboro, Georgia, a white mob seizes and burns two African Americans convicted of murdering a white family. The whites then terrorize the blacks in the town, beating a young mother and killing her husband, whipping others, and destroying property.

Diplomat Ralph J. Bunche is born August 7 in Detroit. He will win the Nobel Peace Prize in 1950 for his work in resolving conflicts in the Middle East.

RELIGION AND EDUCATION

Mary McLeod Bethune founds the Daytona Normal and Industrial School in Florida, now known as Bethune-Cookman College.

LITERATURE AND JOURNALISM

William Stanley Braithwaite publishes his first volume of poems, *Lyrics of Life and Love.*

SCIENCE AND TECHNOLOGY

Physician Charles Richard Drew, a creator of the plasma method of blood preservation and founder of the Blood Bank, is born June 3 in Washington, D.C.

PERFORMING ARTS

Bandleader William "Count" Basie is born August 21 in Red Bank, New Jersey. His music will help to popularize the big band movement in the 1930s and 1940s.

Tenor saxophonist Coleman Hawkins is born November 21 in St. Joseph, Missouri. He will become famous for his jazz recording of "Body and Soul."

Pianist and composer Thomas "Fats" Waller is born May 21 in New

Contemporary Events, 1904 ■ Theodore Roosevelt is elected president. ■ Fear of the "Yellow Peril" brings pressure on Congress to suspend Chinese immigration indefinitely. ■ The World Exhibition and the first American Olympics are held in St. Louis.

York. He will compose such popular songs as "Ain't Misbehavin'" and "Honeysuckle Rose."

Bluesman Clarence "Pine Top" Smith is born January 11.

Gospel singer Willie Mae Ford Smith is born June 23 in Rolling Fork, Mississippi.

SPORTS

The first African-American Olympic medal winner, George C. Poage, places third in the 400-meter hurdles in St. Louis.

Charles W. Follis formally signs on with the Shelby Athletic Association and becomes the first African-American professional football player.

1905

POLITICS AND CIVIL RIGHTS

There are 62 recorded lynchings.

The Niagara Movement begins in Canada with a conference called by W. E. B. Du Bois, William Monroe Trotter, and other African-American leaders. The meeting protests the systematic denial of civil and human rights. Opposed to the conciliatory policies of Booker T. Washington, the movement will give birth in 1909 to the National Association for the Advancement of Colored People.

The state of Georgia begins a movement to segregate public parks.

Robert N. C. Nix is born in South Carolina. The first black congressman elected from Pennsylvania, he will serve 11 terms.

BUSINESS AND EMPLOYMENT

The Industrial Workers of the World advocates the inclusion of all workers in labor unions, regardless of race, creed, or color.

Alonzo F. Herndon founds the Atlanta Life Insurance Company, the largest African-American-owned business in the nation.

RELIGION AND EDUCATION

Librarian and historian Dorothy Burnett Porter Wesley is born May 25 in Virginia. She will serve as founding curator of the Moorland-Spingarn Research Center at Howard University.

Contemporary Events, 1905 ■ President Theodore Roosevelt mediates the Treaty of Portsmouth, ending the Russo-Japanese War. ■ Labor leader "Big Bill" Haywood founds the Industrial Workers of the World, known as the "Wobblies."

LITERATURE AND JOURNALISM

Robert S. Abbott begins publishing the *Chicago Defender*. The newspaper will militantly attack racism and serve as a forum for distinguished writers, such as poet Gwendolyn Brooks.

Poet Frank Marshal Davis is born in Kansas. He will found the *Atlanta Daily World* in the early 1930s.

PERFORMING ARTS

The black-owned Pekin Theater opens in Chicago.

Singer Ivie Anderson is born July 10 in Los Angeles.

Blues singer Bertha "Chippie" Hill is born March 15 in Charleston, South Carolina.

VISUAL ARTS

Painter Lois Mailou Jones is born November 3 in Boston.

Painter and art historian James A. Porter, chair of the art department at Howard University, is born December 22 in Baltimore.

SPORTS

African Americans in Brooklyn found the Smart Set, an athletic club.

Bob Marshall, an athlete at the University of Minnesota, is chosen for the All-American football team.

1906

POLITICS AND CIVIL RIGHTS

There are 65 recorded lynchings.

The second Niagara conference meets at Harpers Ferry, West Virginia, from August 16 to 19, to commemorate John Brown's raid on the federal arsenal and to issue a strong statement demanding voting and civil rights, educational opportunities, and an end to racial violence and discrimination.

An incident involving racial slurs by a white citizen provokes a riot in Brownsville, Texas. African-American soldiers allegedly "shoot up the town." Without a fair trial, President Theodore Roosevelt gives three companies of black soldiers dishonorable discharges and bans them from future military or civil service.

Contemporary Events, 1906 ■ Upton Sinclair publishes **The Jungle,** an exposé of Chicago's food-packing industry. ■ Congress passes the first Pure Food and Drug Act. ■ The first radio program with voice and music is broadcast. ■ A major earthquake occurs in San Francisco.

Race riots in Atlanta take the lives of several African Americans and cripple the city for days. Many blacks emigrate. The Atlanta Civic League is formed to work for better race relations.

RELIGION AND EDUCATION

William J. Seymour leads the Azusa Street Revival in Los Angeles, the beginning of modern Pentecostalism.

LITERATURE AND JOURNALISM

During the Atlanta riots, violent whites force Jesse Max Barber, the editor of the *Voice of the Negro,* to leave town.

Poet Paul Laurence Dunbar dies in Dayton, Ohio, February 9.

Writer and educator Jay Saunders Redding is born in Wilmington, Delaware.

SCIENCE AND TECHNOLOGY

Aviator Willa Brown is born January 22 in Glasgow, Kentucky.

PERFORMING ARTS

The Shoofly Regiment by Bob Cole and J. Rosamond Johnson plays on Broadway.

Jazz alto saxophonist Johnny Hodges is born July 25.

Entertainer Josephine Baker is born June 3 in St. Louis. She will star in the Folies Bergère, serve as an Allied spy during World War II, and protest racial segregation in the postwar era.

Blues singer Victoria Spivey is born October 15 in Houston.

Bluesman Roosevelt Sykes is born January 30.

VISUAL ARTS

The Pennsylvania Academy of Fine Arts in Philadelphia exhibits *Portraits from Mirrors,* the sculpture of 28-year-old Meta Vaux Warrick.

1907

POLITICS AND CIVIL RIGHTS

There are 60 recorded lynchings.

A Supreme Court decision upholds the railroads' right to segregate

---

Contemporary Events, 1907 ■ Oklahoma becomes the 46th state. ■ The stock market falls, initiating a financial panic and depression. ■ The Ziegfeld Follies opens in New York.

The Bishops' Appeal

In 1908 in Washington, D.C., 25 bishops belonging to three churches—the Colored Methodist Episcopal, African Methodist Episcopal Zion, and African Methodist Episcopal—issued an appeal. They asked white Americans to stop the mob violence against African Americans and to bring an end to Jim Crow laws, the peonage and convict labor systems, and all the other violations of African Americans' rights under the U.S. Constitution. "We do not ask at your hands any special favors," the bishops pointed out, "we ask . . . nothing to which we are not entitled under the law and Constitution. We ask only for that which belongs to us as a right, for justice, for equality, for freedom of action and opportunity before the law and in the industrial life of the land, North and South alike."

passengers by race, even in interstate travel when the train is in a state where segregation is prohibited.

The first African-American cabinet member, Robert C. Weaver, is born in Washington, D.C. He will direct the Department of Housing and Urban Development under President Lyndon Johnson.

RELIGION AND EDUCATION

Alain Leroy Locke is the first African-American Rhodes Scholar.

LITERATURE AND JOURNALISM

Wendell P. Dabney founds the *Union*, a newspaper to foster greater unity among African Americans in Cincinnati.

Writer and activist Shirley Graham Du Bois is born November 11 in Indianapolis.

Novelist Dorothy West is born June 2 in Boston.

SCIENCE AND TECHNOLOGY

In New York, Harlem Hospital opens, a pioneer institution in providing health care for the black community.

PERFORMING ARTS

Cabell "Cab" Calloway is born December 25 in Rochester, New York. A popular singer, entertainer, and bandleader, Calloway will write and record "Minnie the Moocher."

Benny Carter, musician, bandleader, and arranger, is born August 8 in New York.

Actor Canada Lee is born May 3 in New York.

Blues pianist Lu Andrew Albert, better known as "Sunnyland Slim," is born September 5 in Vance, Mississippi.

Singer and pianist Gladys Bentley is born August 12.

VISUAL ARTS

Painter Charles Alston is born November 28 in Charlotte, North Carolina. He will depict the African-American contribution to medicine in the entrance lobby of Harlem Hospital in New York.

1908

POLITICS AND CIVIL RIGHTS

There are 97 recorded lynchings.

In Springfield, Illinois, a violent white mob lynches two African

Americans and drives many black residents from their homes, destroying their property. The governor calls in thousands of troops to quell the riot.

Thurgood Marshall is born July 8 in Baltimore. He will argue the groundbreaking Supreme Court case on segregation in 1954 and become the first black justice on the Supreme Court in 1967.

Adam Clayton Powell, Jr., civil rights activist, minister, and congressman from New York, is born in New Haven, Connecticut.

BUSINESS AND EMPLOYMENT

Developer Allen Allensworth files a plan for the all-black town of Allensworth in Tulare County, California, to allow blacks to develop industry and a lifestyle on their own equal to that of local whites.

RELIGION AND EDUCATION

The sorority Alpha Kappa Alpha for African-American college women is established at Howard University by Ethel Hedgeman and eight other students on January 15.

LITERATURE AND JOURNALISM

William Stanley Braithwaite publishes his poetry book *The House of Falling Leaves*.

Novelist Richard Wright, author of *Native Son* and *Black Boy*, is born September 4 in Natchez, Mississippi.

Novelist, critic, and short-story writer Ann Petry is born October 12 in Old Saybrook, Connecticut.

SCIENCE AND TECHNOLOGY

Martha M. Franklin founds the National Association of Colored Graduate Nurses to improve the status and working conditions of black nurses.

PERFORMING ARTS

Actor Frederick O'Neal is born in Brookville, Mississippi. He will found the New York American Negro Theater.

Trumpeter Oran "Hot Lips" Page is born January 28.

SPORTS

John Baxter "Doc" Taylor, the record-setting quarter miler from the

---

Contemporary Events, 1908 ■ William Howard Taft is elected president. ■ The first Model T Ford is produced.

University of Pennsylvania, is the first African American to win an Olympic gold medal, in the 4x400-meter medley in London. Taylor dies the same year of typhoid pneumonia, at the age of 26.

African-American boxer Jack Johnson knocks out Tommy Burns in Australia, winning the world heavyweight title. Later Burns will explain his loss by saying that "race prejudice. . . [and] hatred made me tense."

1909

POLITICS AND CIVIL RIGHTS

There are 82 recorded lynchings.

The National Association for the Advancement of Colored People (NAACP) is founded. Its first conference, in New York, attracts 300 participants, among them some of the nation's most distinguished progressives and intellectuals, both black and white.

George W. Crockett, Jr., the first African-American lawyer to serve in the U.S. Department of Labor (1943), is born in Florida.

LITERATURE AND JOURNALISM

On December 4 in New York, James Anderson founds the *Amsterdam News,* which will become a major newspaper for the African-American community.

Novelist Chester Himes, creator of the characters "Gravedigger Jones" and "Coffin Ed Johnson," is born in Jefferson City, Missouri.

PERFORMING ARTS

W. C. Handy writes "Memphis Blues" as a campaign song for that city's long-lived mayor Ed "Boss" Crump.

Tenor saxophonist Lester Young, one of the most influential musicians in the development of bop, is born August 27.

Composer Howard Swanson is born in Atlanta, Georgia.

Jazz vibraphonist Lionel Hampton is born April 12 in Louisville, Kentucky. He will be the first musician to feature the Vibes, now a major component in small jazz combos.

Dancer Katherine Dunham is born June 22 near Chicago.

Contemporary Events, 1909 ■ The Rockefeller Sanitary Commission is founded; later it will evolve into the Rockefeller Foundation.

VISUAL ARTS

Painter Norman Lewis is born July 23 in New York.

EXPLORATION

Explorer Matthew Henson, a member of Admiral Robert E. Peary's expedition, erects the American flag at the North Pole.

1910

POLITICS AND CIVIL RIGHTS

There are 76 recorded lynchings.

In Boston, William Monroe Trotter leads a protest against the racist play *The Clansman.*

An African-American graduate student in social work at Columbia University, George Edmund Haynes, and a white woman, Mrs. William H. Baldwin, Jr., found the Committee on Urban Conditions to address the problems of blacks in cities. It will be one of the groups to evolve into the National Urban League the following year.

City ordinances requiring segregation of black and white citizens begin to appear in southern and border state cities: first Baltimore, and then Norfolk, Richmond, Roanoke, Greensboro, St. Louis, Oklahoma City, Dallas, and Louisville.

Bayard Rustin is born in West Chester, Pennsylvania. A civil rights activist advocating pacifism and nonresistance, he will be influential in the Freedom Movement of the 1950s and 1960s.

RELIGION AND EDUCATION

There are 100 African-American colleges, almost all open to women, and 35,000 black churches, with about 3.5 million members.

Writer, lawyer, and theologian Pauli Murray, the first African-American woman priest ordained in the Episcopal Church, is born.

LITERATURE AND JOURNALISM

The NAACP's monthly journal, the *Crisis*, edited by W. E. B. Du Bois, begins publication in November with 1,000 copies. In eight years the magazine will have 100,000 subscribers. The first issue sets a militant tone opposing discrimination and segregation.

Contemporary Events, 1910 ■ Writer Mark Twain and philosopher William James die. ■ The Carnegie Endowment for International Peace is created. ■ The Boy Scouts of America is started.

PERFORMING ARTS

Bert Williams, the most popular vaudevillian of the day, signs a contract to perform with the Ziegfeld Follies.

Blues singer Chester Arthur Burnett is born June 10 in Mississippi. As "Howlin' Wolf," he will inspire British rock bands in the 1960s.

Blues guitarist Aaron "T-Bone" Walker is born May 28.

Musician William "Champion Jack" Dupree is born July 4.

Drummer Sidney "Big Sid" Catlett is born January 17 in Evansville, Indiana.

Saxophonist Leon "Chu" Berry is born September 13 in Wheeling, West Virginia.

Pianist Mary Lou Williams is born May 8 in Atlanta.

Pianist Art Tatum is born October 13 in Toledo, Ohio.

VISUAL ARTS

Painter and printmaker Wilmer Angier Jennings is born in Atlanta.

Artist Allan Rohan Crite is born in Boston.

SPORTS

After the Detroit Tigers are tied by the Havana Stars, a black Cuban baseball team (the score in the six-game series was 3 to 3), a ban is instituted to prevent black teams from playing against whites.

Boxer Jack Johnson knocks out James Jeffries in Reno to win the world's heavyweight championship.

Ralph Metcalfe, Olympic champion and later congressman from Illinois, is born in Atlanta.

ADDITIONAL STATISTICS

According to the U.S. Census Bureau, the African-American population is 9,827,763, or 10.7% of the U.S. population. Eighty-nine percent of African Americans live in the South. Just over half are engaged in farm work, and only 350,000 are employed in factories.

1911

POLITICS AND CIVIL RIGHTS

There are 67 recorded lynchings.

The National Urban League is founded to assist southern blacks migrating to urban centers in the North. The interracial league helps new arrivals adjust to city life and the demands of industrial jobs.

James B. Parsons, the first African American appointed to a lifetime federal judgeship (1961), is born in Kansas City, Missouri.

BUSINESS AND EMPLOYMENT

To protest the hiring of African-American firemen, white firemen strike at the Cincinnati, New Orleans, and Texas Pacific Railroad.

On June 28, Samuel J. Battle becomes New York's first African-American police officer.

RELIGION AND EDUCATION

The Negro Society for Historical Research is founded by John Edward Bruce and Arthur Schomburg.

The first African-American fraternity to be chartered as a national organization, Kappa Alpha Psi, is founded at Indiana University.

Librarian and children's storyteller Augusta Baker is born April 1.

LITERATURE AND JOURNALISM

Claude McKay publishes two poetry books: *Songs of Jamaica* and *Constab Ballads*.

Historian Frank Snowden is born in Virginia. His work will become a leading source on blacks in ancient history.

PERFORMING ARTS

Scott Joplin completes his folk opera *Treemonisha,* which he will stage without an orchestra or scenery in 1915.

Composer and popular minstrel performer James A. Bland dies.

Mahalia Jackson, "Queen of the Gospel Song," is born October 26 in New Orleans.

Robert Johnson, perhaps the finest performer of country blues, is born May 8.

Drummer Jo Jones is born October 7.

Actress Butterfly McQueen is born January 8 in Tampa, Florida.

David Roy Eldridge, the influential jazz trumpeter and instrumentalist, is born in Pittsburgh.

SPORTS

Pitcher Andrew "Rube" Foster, later known as the "Father of Black Baseball," forms the Chicago American Giants.

James A. Bland

When songwriter James A. Bland died on May 5, 1911, he left behind an international reputation and some 700 songs, many of which were the most popular songs of their day. Born in 1854, Bland became a famous minstrel entertainer, leaving for Europe in 1881, where he enjoyed fame for 20 years. Of the hundreds of songs he wrote, only 38 were copyrighted. Perhaps the most famous became the state song of Virginia in 1940, "Carry Me Back to Old Virginny."

Contemporary Events, 1911 ■ Edith Wharton publishes **Ethan Frome.** ■ Irving Berlin writes "Alexander's Ragtime Band," taking advantage of black ragtime music's popularity.

John Henry Lloyd switches to the New York Lincoln Giants, where he bats .475 and joins another African-American baseball great, "Smokey Joe" Williams.

1912

POLITICS AND CIVIL RIGHTS

There are 63 recorded lynchings.

The NAACP, the National Independent League, and the Colored National Democratic League support Woodrow Wilson for president. W. E. B. Du Bois's endorsement of Wilson as a fair, decent, and farsighted politician convinces many African Americans to vote for Wilson.

New York City theaters are desegregated.

Dorothy Height, who will become president of the National Council of Negro Women, is born in Richmond, Virginia, March 24.

BUSINESS AND EMPLOYMENT

Memphis real estate tycoon Robert R. Church, Sr., dies August 2.

RELIGION AND EDUCATION

Carter G. Woodson receives a Ph.D. from Harvard, the second African American to earn a doctorate in history.

LITERATURE AND JOURNALISM

James Weldon Johnson anonymously publishes *The Autobiography of an Ex-Colored Man*, a psychological novel, and a seminal work in the "new Negro movement."

The first edition of *The Negro Yearbook* is published.

Charlotta Bass buys and publishes the newspaper *California Eagle*.

Novelist Willard Motley is born in Chicago. His works will include *Knock on Any Door* and *Let No Man Write My Epitaph*.

PERFORMING ARTS

Blues guitarist Sam "Lightnin'" Hopkins is born March 15 in Texas.

Actress Nina Mae McKinney is born August 27 in Lancaster, South Carolina.

Contemporary Events, 1912 ■ New Mexico and Arizona become the 47th and 48th states. ■ Woodrow Wilson is elected president. ■ The **Titanic** sinks on its maiden voyage, drowning 1,513 passengers. ■ The F. W. Woolworth Company is founded.

VISUAL ARTS

Life magazine photographer and film director Gordon Parks, Sr., is born in Kansas.

Artist Romare Bearden is born September 2 in Charlotte, North Carolina.

POLITICS AND CIVIL RIGHTS

There are 52 recorded lynchings.

The first Congress to meet under the Democratic Woodrow Wilson administration is flooded with more anti-African-American bills than were ever before introduced in a single session.

President Wilson breaks the tradition of appointing African Americans as consuls to Haiti and Santo Domingo. He also rejects a proposal for a National Race Commission to study the status of blacks in the United States and begins segregating blacks and whites in government offices.

Underground Railroad conductor and women's rights advocate Harriet Tubman dies March 10.

Activist Rosa Parks is born February 4 in Alabama. Her refusal to give her bus seat to a white man in Montgomery in 1955 will launch a bus boycott and begin the modern Civil Rights Movement.

RELIGION AND EDUCATION

The African-American sorority Delta Sigma Theta is created by members of Alpha Kappa Alpha at Howard University. It will become a major institution for black college women, with 800 chapters and over 175,000 members.

Educator and missionary Fanny Jackson Coppin, one of the first African-American women to graduate from college (1865), dies January 21 in Philadelphia.

The first African-American president of the American Library Association, Clara Stanton Jones, is born in St. Louis.

LITERATURE AND JOURNALISM

Poet Robert E. Hayden is born August 4 in Detroit.

Contemporary Events, 1913 ■ The 16th Amendment introduces the federal income tax. ■ The U.S. Federal Reserve System is created. ■ The Armory Show in New York City, a groundbreaking art exhibit, introduces postimpressionism and cubism to the United States.

SCIENCE AND TECHNOLOGY

Daniel Hale Williams becomes a charter member of the American College of Surgeons.

The forerunner to the National Dental Association, the Tri-State Dental Association, is organized in Virginia. The fledgling effort will become the top professional organization for black dentists.

PERFORMING ARTS

Blues pianist Joe Willie "Pinetop" Perkins is born July 7.

SPORTS

Track and field star Jesse Owens, who will win four gold medals in the 1936 Berlin Olympics, is born in Alabama.

Boxing champion Archie Moore is born in Mississippi.

1914

POLITICS AND CIVIL RIGHTS

There are 55 recorded lynchings.

The NAACP initiates the Spingarn Medal, an achievement award presented annually to a leading African American.

Led by Alfred Sam, hundreds of African Americans from Oklahoma set sail for Africa.

RELIGION AND EDUCATION

African-American students found Phi Beta Sigma fraternity and incorporate Omega Psi Phi fraternity at Howard University.

In Baton Rouge, Louisiana, a group of 47 students and 9 teachers open a new campus of Southern University.

Jean Blackwell Hutson is born September 4 in Florida. She will serve as curator of the Schomburg Center for Research in Black Culture in New York City.

LITERATURE AND JOURNALISM

Writer Ralph Ellison is born in Oklahoma City. His 1952 novel, *Invisible Man*, will win the National Book Award.

Poet and dramatist Owen Dodson is born in Brooklyn, New York.

Contemporary Events, 1914 ■ World War I breaks out in central Europe. ■ The U.S. Federal Trade Commission is created to regulate interstate commerce.

SCIENCE AND TECHNOLOGY

Psychologist Kenneth B. Clark is born in Panama. His studies of the damage done to African-American children by segregation will be used to argue the desegregation case *Brown* v. *Board of Education*.

PERFORMING ARTS

Popular vaudevillian Bert Williams stars in *Darktown Jubilee*, one of the first movies to use an African-American actor, rather than white actors in blackface. The movie causes a riot in Brooklyn, New York.

W. C. Handy publishes his "St. Louis Blues."

Singer William Clarence "Billy" Eckstine is born July 8 in Pittsburgh.

Jazzman Herman "Sonny" Blount, who will be known as "Sun Ra," is born May 22 in Birmingham, Alabama.

Blues harmonica player John "Sonny Boy" Williamson is born March 30.

VISUAL ARTS

Sculptor William Ellisworth Artis is born in North Carolina.

Painter and illustrator Ernest Crichlow is born in Brooklyn.

SPORTS

Joseph Louis Barrow, the "Brown Bomber," is born in Alabama. As Joe Louis, the heavyweight boxer will hold a record of 68 wins, with 54 knockouts.

1915

POLITICS AND CIVIL RIGHTS

There are 69 recorded lynchings.

Fearing increased violence against blacks, the NAACP tries unsuccessfully to prevent the showing of D. W. Griffith's movie *Birth of a Nation*, which portrays African Americans in derogatory racial stereotypes and perpetuates the myth of "Negro rule" during Reconstruction. Civil rights activist William Monroe Trotter is arrested and jailed for picketing the film.

In *Guinn* v. *United States* the Supreme Court declares unconstitutional the "grandfather clause" in Oklahoma's and Maryland's state con-

Contemporary Events, 1915 ■ U.S. troops invade Haiti. ■ The first transcontinental telephone call is made between New York and San Francisco. ■ Congress creates the U.S. Coast Guard. ■ Edgar Lee Masters publishes the **Spoon River Anthology**.

The Revived Ku Klux Klan

The original Ku Klux Klan died out in the 1870s due to Reconstruction legislation and changing political alignments. But in the 1920s the Klan showed a resurgence, not just in the South, but in the North and Midwest. The Klan fought the "new Negro" and the new immigrants from southern and eastern Europe. Reborn in Georgia in 1915, the Klan reached a peak membership of 4.5 million people in 1924, self-described as "white male persons, native-born Gentile citizens." Primarily Democrats, the Klan often controlled politics, although in Indiana it dominated state politics through the Republican Party. By 1925 scandals discredited top officials in the Klan. Newspaper exposés, detailing widespread corruption, eventually caused membership to dwindle, and the Klan became less powerful.

stitutions. The "grandfather clause" exempted citizens from certain voter qualifications if their grandfathers voted, in effect disfranchising African Americans whose grandparents lived before the 15th Amendment was passed. This was the first important court victory sponsored by the NAACP.

The modern Ku Klux Klan begins in earnest when a local chapter in Fulton County, Georgia, is chartered.

Oklahoma becomes the first state to segregate phone booths.

Oscar DePriest becomes Chicago's first black alderman.

Civil rights activist Mifflin Wistar Gibbs dies. He was editor and publisher of *Mirror of the Times*, the first black newspaper in California, and the first black municipal judge in Little Rock, Arkansas.

BUSINESS AND EMPLOYMENT

The boll weevil plague in southern cotton fields and the growth of the war industries in the North spur a mass migration of southern blacks to northern cities in search of better jobs.

RELIGION AND EDUCATION

The Association for the Study of Negro Life and History is founded in Chicago by Carter G. Woodson and other scholars.

Founded in 1876, Meharry Medical College is incorporated in Nashville, Tennessee. It joins three other African-American medical schools: Howard University Medical School, Shaw Medical School, and the Medical Department of the University of West Tennessee.

Educator Booker T. Washington dies November 14 on the campus of Tuskegee Institute.

The first African-American minister appointed to a chaplaincy in the U.S. Army, Henry McNeal Turner, dies May 8 in Canada.

Bibliographer Ernest Kaiser is born December 5 in Virginia.

Gospel preacher C. L. Franklin is born January 22 in Mississippi.

LITERATURE AND JOURNALISM

Historian John Hope Franklin is born in Oklahoma.

Poet and novelist Margaret Walker is born July 7 in Birmingham. Among her works will be *For My People* and *Jubilee*.

SCIENCE AND TECHNOLOGY

Zoologist Ernest Everett Just is presented with the Spingarn Medal.

PERFORMING ARTS

Jelly Roll Morton publishes his "Jelly Roll Blues."

McKinley Morganfield, the blues singer known as "Muddy Waters," is born April 4 in Mississippi.

Singer Eleanora Fagan, better known as Billie Holiday ("Lady Day"), is born April 7 in Baltimore. More than any other modern singer, she will express the heart of the blues.

Songwriter, arranger, composer, and pianist William "Billy" Strayhorn is born November 29 in Dayton, Ohio. For 28 years he will work with Duke Ellington's band, writing such famous pieces as "Satin Doll" and "Take the 'A' Train."

Trumpeter Harry "Sweets" Edison is born October 10 in Columbus, Ohio.

Gospel singer "Sister" Rosetta Tharpe is born March 20 in Cotton Plant, Arkansas.

VISUAL ARTS

Painter Hughie Lee-Smith is born September 20 in Eustis, Florida.

Sculptor and printmaker Elizabeth Catlett is born April 15 in Washington, D.C.

Artist Claude Clark, Sr., is born in Georgia.

1916

POLITICS AND CIVIL RIGHTS

There are 54 recorded lynchings.

At a conference in Amenia, New York, leading African Americans come together and agree to work toward equal education, full voting rights, equal protection of civil liberties, and an end to the lawlessness of lynching.

The NAACP expands its operations into the South, with James Weldon Johnson as its field secretary.

Black nationalist Marcus Garvey arrives in the United States from Jamaica and inaugurates his "Back to Africa" movement. His Universal Negro Improvement Association will have many branches in the United States within the year.

U.S. Court of Appeals Judge Spottswood W. Robinson is born in Richmond, Virginia.

Contemporary Events, 1916 ■ Woodrow Wilson is reelected president. ■ Wilson appoints Louis Brandeis, the first Jewish justice to the Supreme Court. ■ The United States buys the Virgin Islands from Denmark for $25 million. ■ Jeannette Rankin, the first U.S. congresswoman, is elected.

BUSINESS AND EMPLOYMENT

Henry Green Parks, Jr., is born in Atlanta. He will found Parks Sausage Company of Baltimore, the first black-owned public company listed for trading on the over-the-counter market (in 1969).

LITERATURE AND JOURNALISM

Editor Carter G. Woodson publishes the first issue of the *Journal of Negro History*, which he edits until his death in 1950.

Novelist Frank Yerby is born in Augusta, Georgia. His popular historical novels will consistently make the best-seller lists.

Novelist, biographer, essayist, and screenwriter John Oliver Killens is born in Macon, Georgia.

Essayist Albert Murray is born in Alabama. His work will include *The Omni-Americans,* on the black experience and American culture.

PERFORMING ARTS

In New York Charles Gilpin founds the Lafayette Theater Company.

Angelina Grimké's play *Rachel* is first produced by the NAACP Drama Committee in Washington, D.C.

THE MILITARY

The highest-ranking African American in the U.S. Army, Lieutenant Colonel Charles Young, commands a squadron in Mexico in pursuit of Mexican revolutionary Francisco "Pancho" Villa.

SPORTS

Sophomore tackle and guard Paul Robeson is taken off the Rutgers football team after another university refuses to play Rutgers because of Robeson's race.

Fritz Pollard, a running back for Brown University's football team, becomes the first African American to play in the Rose Bowl.

1917

POLITICS AND CIVIL RIGHTS

There are 38 recorded lynchings.

The NAACP wins a battle against segregated housing in the U.S. Supreme Court decision *Buchanan* v. *Warley,* which states that it is unconstitutional for a law to require whites and blacks to live on separate streets, because it destroys an individual's right "to acquire, enjoy, and dispose of his property."

In East St. Louis, Illinois, a race riot kills anywhere from 40 to 200 African Americans. Martial law is declared. The NAACP defends 10 blacks accused of murder in the riot's aftermath and assists hundreds who are left wounded and homeless.

More than 10,000 African Americans protest lynchings and other racial abuses in a silent march led by the NAACP down New York City's Fifth Avenue.

Houston police spark a riot when they beat an African-American soldier. Seventeen whites and two blacks are killed. Over 100 African-American soldiers are charged with riot, 13 are summarily executed, and many others are given life imprisonment. For 20 years the NAACP will lobby on behalf of the imprisoned soldiers, until President Franklin Roosevelt releases the last prisoner in 1938.

Marcus Garvey founds the *Negro World*, which becomes a strong voice for militant black nationalism.

Civil rights activist Fannie Lou Hamer is born October 6 in rural Mississippi.

LITERATURE AND JOURNALISM

James Weldon Johnson publishes *Fifty Years and Other Poems*.

The socialist journal the *Messenger,* founded by A. Philip Randolph and Chandler Owen, begins publication.

Gwendolyn Brooks, the first African-American Pulitzer Prize winner for poetry (1950), is born June 17 in Topeka, Kansas.

PERFORMING ARTS

The red-light district of New Orleans, Storyville, where many African-American musicians play, is closed by the U.S. Navy. Jazz musicians move to Chicago and other northern cities.

The Jazz Age begins when the Original Dixieland Jazz Band debuts in New York with five white musicians from New Orleans.

Composer Harry T. Burleigh receives the Spingarn Medal for his contributions in the field of music.

In New York, a group of black actors present three one-act plays at Madison Square Garden.

Jazz musician John Birks "Dizzy" Gillespie, one of the great innovators of bop, is born October 21 in South Carolina.

Contemporary Events, 1917 ■ President Wilson asks Congress to make the world "safe for democracy" by declaring war on Germany. ■ Literacy becomes a requirement for U.S. citizenship.

Classical composer Ulysses Simpson Kay is born in Tucson, Arizona. He will be one of the first American composers to travel to the Soviet Union on a cultural exchange program.

Film and television actor, playwright, screenwriter, and director Ossie Davis is born in Georgia.

Singer, movie star, and civil rights advocate Lena Horne is born June 17 in Brooklyn, New York.

The first African-American prima ballerina at New York's Metropolitan Opera House, Janet Collins, is born in New Orleans.

Actress Claudia McNeil is born August 13 in Baltimore. She will play "Lena Younger" in stage and screen versions of *A Raisin in the Sun*.

Blues singer John Lee Hooker is born August 22 in Mississippi.

Bluesman "Hound Dog" Taylor is born April 12 in Natchez.

Jazz pianist and composer Thelonious Monk, considered the father of improvisation and a leader of the jazz revolution in the 1940s, is born October 11 in North Carolina.

VISUAL ARTS

Painter Jacob Lawrence, one of the major African-American artists of the century, is born September 7 in Atlantic City, New Jersey.

THE MILITARY

During World War I, over 300,000 African Americans will serve in the armed forces—1,400 as commissioned officers.

After initially opposing separateness, the NAACP successfully lobbies the U.S. Army to establish an officers' training camp for African Americans in Des Moines, Iowa. During the war, 678 black officers receive their commission from here.

Emmett J. Scott is appointed special assistant to the secretary of war with specific duties to maintain morale among African Americans, both civilian and military, and to investigate complaints of prejudicial treatment. W. E. B. Du Bois believes Scott covers up segregation and ill treatment.

1918

POLITICS AND CIVIL RIGHTS

There are 64 recorded lynchings.

LITERATURE AND JOURNALISM

Poet and literary critic William Stanley Braithwaite is awarded the

NAACP Spingarn Medal for his contributions in literature. His annual *Anthology of Magazine Verse*, published from 1913 to 1929, introduces many Americans to the works of such poets as Edgar Lee Masters, Vachel Lindsay, and Carl Sandburg.

Georgia Douglas Johnson publishes her poetry collection *The Heart of a Woman*.

Publisher John H. Johnson, founder of *Negro Digest*, *Ebony*, and *Jet*, is born January 19 in Arkansas.

PERFORMING ARTS

Bluesman Elmore James is born January 27.

Actress, singer, and entertainer Pearl M. Bailey is born March 29 in Newport News, Virginia. She will win acclaim for her roles in *Porgy and Bess*, *Carmen Jones*, *House of Flowers*, and an all-black production of *Hello, Dolly*.

Jazz singer Ella Fitzgerald is born April 25 in Newport News, Virginia. Discovered at an amateur contest at Harlem's Apollo Theater in 1934, she will be acclaimed for her easy improvisational ability and scat styling.

Musician Roy "Professor Longhair" Byrd is born December 19.

Jazz singer Joe Williams is born in Georgia. His most popular recording will be "Every Day I Have the Blues."

VISUAL ARTS

Sculptor John Rhoden is born in Birmingham, Alabama.

Painter Charles White is born April 2 in Chicago.

THE MILITARY

By the end of World War I, African Americans represent 11% of the American armed forces overseas.

The 369th Infantry is the first Allied unit to reach the Rhine, and the whole regiment is given the Croix de Guerre for heroism at Maison-en-Champagne.

Henry Johnson and Needham Roberts are the first African Americans to receive the Croix de Guerre for their heroic stand against a German raiding expedition, an encounter that will become known as the "Battle of Henry Johnson."

The 369th Infantry

During World War I, an African-American regiment, the 369th Infantry, displayed astounding heroism. The soldiers arrived in France in 1918 and were assigned to fight under French command. At Bois d'Hauza, they held off a German attack for two months. Eventually, fighting their way through other encounters, their detail reached the Rhine. In the course of their operations, they never retreated, nor were any of their command captured. The 369th Infantry was cited for bravery 11 times, and 171 of its members were awarded the French Legion of Honor. In addition to their bravery under fire, the 369th Regimental Band introduced jazz to Europe. Bandleader Lieutenant James Reese Europe conducted concerts for both French and American soldiers, in hospitals and on the battlefields, as well as for civilians in Paris.

Contemporary Events, 1918 ■ Woodrow Wilson proposes his "Fourteen Points" as a basis for world peace. ■ Daylight savings time begins in the United States. ■ Influenza kills about a half-million people in the United States.

Numerous soldiers from the 370th, 371st, and 372nd regiments win medals for bravery.

African-American investors support the war effort by buying $250 million worth of government bonds and stamps.

1919

POLITICS AND CIVIL RIGHTS

There are 83 recorded lynchings of African Americans.

In *State* v. *Young*, the Supreme Court decides that African Americans should be admitted to juries.

Over 25 major race riots occur across the country, leading James Weldon Johnson to characterize the season as "Red Summer."

The Chicago race riot begins on July 27 when four young African-American boys try to cross the traditional dividing line between the white and black beaches on Lake Michigan. A black swimmer is killed, and violence erupts for almost a week. The militia is called out; 38 blacks and whites are killed; and 537 people are injured.

W. E. B. Du Bois organizes the Pan-African Congress in Paris. Sixteen countries and colonies participate in this three-day meeting to work toward the full participation of Africans in their governments.

Civil rights leader William Monroe Trotter unsuccessfully argues at the Paris Peace Conference that the treaty to end World War I should also outlaw racial discrimination.

Archibald H. Grimké, one of the original founders of the NAACP, receives the Spingarn Award for his years of distinguished service as an attorney, U.S. consul to Santo Domingo, and president of the American Negro Academy.

Edward W. Brooke, attorney general of Massachusetts and the first African-American senator since Reconstruction, is born October 27 in Washington, D.C.

BUSINESS AND EMPLOYMENT

The American Federation of Labor votes to end racial discrimination in membership.

Madame C. J. Walker, the millionaire founder of the largest African-American cosmetics and hair-care company, dies May 25.

Contemporary Events, 1919 ■ The 18th Amendment passes, making it illegal to produce, sell, or drink alcoholic beverages. ■ Poet Carl Sandburg wins a precursor of the Pulitzer Prize for **Cornhuskers.**

RELIGION AND EDUCATION

Father Divine starts his congregation in Sayville, Long Island.

LITERATURE AND JOURNALISM

The Associated Negro Press is established by Claude A. Barnett. The organization will provide news releases for approximately 95% of all African-American newspapers.

Writer and teacher Kelly Miller publishes *History of the World War and the Important Part Taken by the Negroes.*

PERFORMING ARTS

The African-American-owned Lincoln Motion Picture Company releases its first major film, *A Man's Duty.*

Oscar Micheaux's movie company produces its first film, *The Homesteader,* based on Micheaux's autobiography.

In New York Charles Gilpin appears as "Rev. William Custis" in the play *Abraham Lincoln.*

The National Association of Negro Musicians holds its first convention in Chicago.

Singer, jazz pianist, and entertainer Nat "King" Cole is born in Montgomery, Alabama, March 17. He will be a founding member of the National Academy of Recording Arts and Sciences and one of the first African Americans to host a network television show (1956).

Bandleader Art Blakey is born October 11.

Jazz musician Charles Christian is born in Dallas. Christian will pioneer the single-string solo on the electric guitar.

VISUAL ARTS

Photographer and teacher Roy DeCarava is born in New York City. He will be the first African-American photographer awarded a Guggenheim fellowship.

THE MILITARY

Pearl Harbor hero Dorie Miller is born October 12 in Texas.

SPORTS

Fritz Pollard of the Akron Indians becomes the first African American to play professional football.

Baseball player Jackie Robinson is born in Georgia. In 1947 he will become the first African American to play with a major league baseball team, the Brooklyn Dodgers.

Harlem

The northward migration of African Americans leaving the South swelled the black populations of large urban areas, but nowhere did African-American culture and lifestyle dominate the national consciousness as dramatically as it did in New York City's Harlem. At the end of World War I, Harlem contained the largest black urban population in the world and quickly became the black cultural center, attracting immigrants from Cuba, Haiti, Puerto Rico, the British West Indies, and elsewhere, bringing with them their languages, religions, foods, music, and literature.

Religion in the Urban North

The migration of African Americans from the rural South to the urban North took its toll on church attendance during the 1920s. The Office of Race Activity for the Congregational Church Extension Boards reported that only 5 million of the 12 million African Americans in the United States attended church. Studies showed that almost two-thirds of the African-American populations in New York, Chicago, Washington, Detroit, Cleveland, Boston, and Buffalo were not affiliated with any church.

1920

POLITICS AND CIVIL RIGHTS

There are 61 reported lynchings.

Marcus Garvey's Universal Negro Improvement Association meets in Harlem with 3,000 delegates. Included in the order of business is a declaration to pass a bill of rights for blacks and the establishment of the Black Star Steamship Corporation to provide trade and transportation to Africa.

The Republican National Convention declares that African Americans must be admitted to state and district conventions.

James Weldon Johnson becomes the first African-American executive secretary of the NAACP.

The Ku Klux Klan operates in 27 states with over 100,000 members.

Activist James Farmer is born in Texas. In 1942 he will help found the Congress of Racial Equality (CORE).

BUSINESS AND EMPLOYMENT

The Brotherhood of Dining Car Employees, representing African-American workers, becomes a national union.

RELIGION AND EDUCATION

Two African-American bishops, Matthew W. Clair of Washington, D.C., and Robert E. Jones of New Orleans, are elected at the Methodist Episcopal Church Conference, held in Des Moines.

Founded at Howard University in 1914, Phi Beta Sigma fraternity is officially incorporated.

Leontine Turpeau Current Kelly, the first black woman to be appointed bishop of a major religious body, the United Methodist Church, is born March 5 in Washington, D.C.

LITERATURE AND JOURNALISM

W. E. B. Du Bois publishes *Darkwater,* a collection of essays.

PERFORMING ARTS

Actor Charles Gilpin stars in the opening of Eugene O'Neill's first successful play, *The Emperor Jones,* at the Provincetown Theater in

Contemporary Events, 1920 ■ Warren G. Harding is elected president. ■ The 19th Amendment gives American women the right to vote. ■ The United States Senate votes against joining the League of Nations, which comes into existence this year.

New York, and his performance wins him recognition as one of the 10 best actors of the year. Gilpin also stars in the Colored Players Film Corporation's *Ten Nights in a Barroom*.

Mamie Smith records "Crazy Blues," which is the first genuine blues recording.

Jazz pianist and composer John Lewis is born May 3 in Illinois. He will help initiate the Modern Jazz Quartet.

Charlie "Bird" Parker is born August 29 in Kansas City, Missouri. He will be perhaps the greatest instrumental soloist in jazz history and will have a New York nightclub, the Birdland, named in his honor.

Jazz pianist and singer Hazel Scott is born June 11 in Port of Spain, Trinidad.

Baritone William Warfield is born in Arkansas. He will play in *Set My People Free*, *Showboat*, and *Porgy and Bess*.

VISUAL ARTS

Leslie Rogers's comic strip "Bungleton Green" first appears in the *Chicago Defender*.

SPORTS

The National Negro Baseball League is organized January 4 and plays its first game in Indianapolis.

Boxing champion Walker Smith, Jr., better known as "Sugar Ray" Robinson, is born in Detroit.

ADDITIONAL STATISTICS

According to the U.S. Census Bureau, 10,463,131 African Americans live in the nation, making up 9.9% of the total population. Life expectancy for black men is 45.5 years, compared with 54.4 years for whites; black women live 45.2 years, compared with 55.6 years for white women.

1921

POLITICS AND CIVIL RIGHTS

There are 64 reported lynchings.

A major race riot breaks out in Tulsa, Oklahoma, leaving at least 30

Contemporary Events, 1921 ■ The Immigration Act of 1921 sets quotas based on national origins for incoming immigrants. ■ Nicola Sacco and Bartolomeo Vanzetti are found guilty of murder, but many feel that the immigrants are convicted solely for their anarchist beliefs.

people dead. National guardsmen are called in to restore order.

Reconstruction political leader from Louisiana P. B. S. Pinchback dies in Washington, D.C.

Civil rights leader Whitney M. Young, Jr., is born July 31 in Kentucky. He will lead the National Urban League and receive the Presidential Medal of Freedom.

Constance Baker Motley, Manhattan borough president and the first African-American woman to be appointed to a federal judgeship, is born September 14 in New Haven, Connecticut.

BUSINESS AND EMPLOYMENT

New York's police department appoints Wesley Redding to detective sergeant, the first African American to hold that rank.

Henry Pace founds the first African-American-owned record company, Pace Phonograph Company. Under the Black Swan label, it will record diverse musical styles from operatic arias to spirituals and blues.

LITERATURE AND JOURNALISM

Writer Alex Haley is born August 11 in Ithaca, New York. He will win a Pulitzer Prize for his historical novel *Roots*.

SCIENCE AND TECHNOLOGY

Bessie Coleman is the first African American worldwide to become a licensed airplane pilot. Her accreditation is from the Federation Aeronautique Internationale in France.

PERFORMING ARTS

The first recorded jazz piano solo, "Carolina Shout," is made by James P. Johnson for Okeh Records. Johnson is master of the stride piano technique popular in the 1920s in conjunction with rent parties, held to raise rent money.

Noble Sissle and Eubie Blake's *Shuffle Along*, an all-black musical, opens at the 63rd Street Theater in New York. It introduces singers Josephine Baker, Florence Mills, and Caterina Jarboro, and musicians William Grant Still and Hall Johnson.

The Spingarn Medal is awarded to Charles S. Gilpin for his performance in the title role of Eugene O'Neill's *Emperor Jones*.

Jazz pianist and bandleader Billy Taylor is born July 24 in Greenville, North Carolina. He will become jazz correspondent for CBS's *Sunday Morning*.

Jazz singer Jon Carl Hendricks is born in Newark, Ohio.

Erroll Garner, who will become the best-selling pianist in the world, is born June 15 in Pittsburgh.

VISUAL ARTS

The first large show of African-American artists is held at the 135th Street branch of the New York Public Library.

Printmaker Robert Blackburn is born in New York.

SPORTS

Football player Frederick "Duke" Slater at the University of Iowa is named Most Valuable College Player.

Baseball great Roy Campanella is born November 19 in Philadelphia. He will play for the Brooklyn Dodgers and be named the National League's Most Valuable Player three times.

1922

POLITICS AND CIVIL RIGHTS

There are 57 recorded lynchings.

Marcus Garvey is arrested and framed on a trumped-up charge of mail fraud by integrationist African Americans who resent his popular nationalism.

The Dyer Anti-Lynching Bill dies in the Senate after passing in the House of Representatives.

The Lincoln Memorial is dedicated in a segregated ceremony in which African Americans have to use separate washrooms and restaurants and stand in a special section roped off behind the white ticket holders.

Floyd McKissick, who will become national director of CORE in 1966, is born in Asheville, North Carolina.

Harold Washington, the first African-American mayor of Chicago, is born April 15 in Chicago.

The first African American elected to Congress from Maryland, Parren James Mitchell, is born April 29 in Baltimore.

RELIGION AND EDUCATION

The sorority Sigma Gamma Rho is founded in Indianapolis.

Contemporary Events, 1922 ■ Investigations into the Teapot Dome scandal begin. ■ Sinclair Lewis publishes his novel **Babbitt**.

The Dyer Anti-Lynching Bill

In 1921 Congressman L. C. Dyer of Missouri introduced into the U.S. House of Representatives a bill that would have made lynching a federal crime. In 1922 the bill passed the House, stating that any federal officer, whose job was to protect the lives of citizens attacked by mobs, must make "reasonable efforts to prevent the killing" or be fined and imprisoned. The bill also stated that anyone who participated in a mob murder was guilty of a felony, and the county where the murder occurred should pay the victim's family $10,000. The bill was introduced into the U.S. Senate three times, but it never passed.

LITERATURE AND JOURNALISM

Claude McKay publishes *Harlem Shadows*, a book of poetry.

Georgia Douglas Johnson publishes *Bronze*, a book of poetry.

James Weldon Johnson publishes an anthology, *The Book of American Negro Poetry*.

PERFORMING ARTS

Vaudeville and Ziegfeld Follies star Bert Williams dies March 5 in New York.

Jazz bassist Charlie Mingus is born April 22 in Nogales, Arizona. In the mid-1950s he will develop a liberating musical style based on atonalities and dissonance.

Actress Dorothy Dandridge is born November 9 in Cleveland.

Entertainer Carmen McRae is born April 8 in New York.

Tenor saxophonist "Big Nick" Nicholas is born August 2.

Theater director Lloyd Richards is born in Toronto. He will direct Lorraine Hansberry's *A Raisin in the Sun* on Broadway, head the Yale School of Drama, and direct August Wilson's plays.

THE MILITARY

The highest-ranking African American in the U.S. Army, Colonel Charles Young, dies January 8 in Nigeria.

Samuel L. Gravely, Jr., the first African American to become an admiral in the U.S. Navy, is born June 4 in Richmond, Virginia.

ADDITIONAL EVENTS

The Frederick Douglass Museum opens in Anacostia, Virginia, and Mary Burnett Talbert receives the Spingarn Medal for her efforts in establishing it.

1923

POLITICS AND CIVIL RIGHTS

There are 33 recorded lynchings.

Marcus Garvey is found guilty of mail fraud, fined, and sentenced to five years in prison.

Contemporary Events, 1923 ■ President Harding dies in office and is succeeded by Vice President Calvin Coolidge. ■ The first regularly scheduled air flights begin between Chicago and Cheyenne, Wyoming. ■ Cecil B. De Mille makes the first version of his film **The Ten Commandments.**

In *Moore* v. *Dempsey*, the U.S. Supreme Court decides that due process of law is violated if a trial is dominated or terrorized by mobs, or if witnesses are physically threatened or beaten, as occurs in many trials of African Americans accused of violent crimes.

Martial law is declared in Oklahoma with the governor decrying the rebellious activities of the Ku Klux Klan.

Civil rights activist Charles Evers is born September 11 in Decatur, Mississippi. He will head Mississippi's NAACP and become mayor of Fayette in 1969.

BUSINESS AND EMPLOYMENT

Ophelia DeVore-Mitchell is born August 12 in South Carolina. Her company, the Grace Del Marco Model Agency, will pave the way for African-American models to enter the industry.

RELIGION AND EDUCATION

Adam Clayton Powell, Sr., is pastor of the new Abyssinian Baptist Church, which is dedicated in Harlem.

Zeta Phi Beta Sorority, founded at Howard University in 1920, is officially incorporated.

LITERATURE AND JOURNALISM

Jean Toomer publishes his experimental novel *Cane*, now considered a masterpiece of the Harlem Renaissance.

The National Urban League begins publishing *Opportunity: A Journal of Negro Life*, edited by Charles S. Johnson.

SCIENCE AND TECHNOLOGY

Garrett A. Morgan, inventor of the gas mask, receives the patent on November 20 for the automatic traffic light, which he sells to General Electric for $40,000.

PERFORMING ARTS

Jelly Roll Morton is possibly the first black musician to record with a white band, the New Orleans Rhythm Kings.

Bessie Smith records "Down-Hearted Blues," her first for Columbia Records. The song, written by Alberta Hunter and Lovie Austin, will sell over a million copies.

The Ethiopian Art Theater of Chicago stages *The Chip Woman's Fortune* by Willis Richardson at the Frazee Theater.

On Broadway, Flournoy Miller and Aubrey Lyles's *Runnin' Wild* introduces the Charleston to a large audience.

The National Urban League

Sociologist Charles S. Johnson became director of research and investigation for the National Urban League in 1921. Two years later, its publication **Opportunity: A Journal of Negro Life,** became a major magazine reporting on African Americans. The league's annual conferences drew both black and white social workers, whose concerns reached far beyond the black communities. The league's training program prepared many young social workers for careers in a new field that was constantly being challenged by the growth of cities and industrialization.

Jazz guitarist Wes Montgomery is born in Indianapolis.

Trumpeter Theodore "Fats" Navarro is born September 24.

Vibraphonist Milt Jackson is born January 1 in Detroit.

Drummer "Philly Joe" Jones is born July 15 in Philadelphia.

VISUAL ARTS

The first African American to graduate from a four-year school of art, Charles Ethan Porter, dies March 6 in Connecticut.

SPORTS

The Rens become the first black professional basketball team.

1924

POLITICS AND CIVIL RIGHTS

There are 16 recorded lynchings.

Fifty African-American organizations attend the All-Race Sanhedrin Conference, headed by Kelly Miller, in Chicago.

The Democratic National Convention is held in New York, without segregation of the 13 African Americans who attend. The Republican Convention, however, continues to maintain segregated sections for blacks and whites.

The Ku Klux Klan continues to grow, reaching 4.5 million members.

The new immigration law excludes blacks of African descent from entry into the United States.

Shirley Chisholm, the first African-American woman elected to Congress, is born November 3 in New York City.

Patricia R. Harris is born May 3 in Mattoon, Illinois. As secretary of housing and urban development under President Carter, she will become the first African-American female cabinet member.

Civil and human rights activist Joseph E. Lowery is born October 6 in Huntsville, Alabama. He will serve as president of the Southern Christian Leadership Conference.

BUSINESS AND EMPLOYMENT

The National Negro Finance Corporation, an offshoot of the

Contemporary Events, 1924 ■ The National Origins Act greatly restricts immigration from southern and eastern Europe. ■ Calvin Coolidge wins the presidential election. ■ J. Edgar Hoover is appointed to head the organization that will become the Federal Bureau of Investigation.

National Negro Business League, is created with $1 million to foster African-American business expansion and investment.

The National Negro Bankers Association is organized.

LITERATURE AND JOURNALISM

Jessie Fauset publishes her novel *There Is Confusion*.

Walter White publishes his novel *The Fire in the Flint*.

Journalist John Edward "Bruce Grit" Bruce dies in New York.

Novelist and essayist James Baldwin is born in Harlem.

Writer John A. Williams is born in Jackson, Mississippi.

SCIENCE AND TECHNOLOGY

Cancer research biologist Jewel Plummer Cobb is born January 17 in Chicago. She will become president of Fullerton in the California state university system.

PERFORMING ARTS

Noble Sissle and Eubie Blake stage the musical *Chocolate Dandies*, featuring Josephine Baker and Johnny Hudgins.

Starring Florence Mills, *Dixie to Broadway* opens at the Broadhurst Theater in New York.

Scandal arises when a white actress, Marie Blair, stars opposite Paul Robeson in Eugene O'Neill's *All God's Chillun Got Wings*.

Singer Roland Hayes gives the first recital by an African American at Carnegie Hall and also receives the Spingarn Medal.

Actor Sidney Poitier is born February 20 in Miami. He will win an Academy Award in 1964 for *Lilies of the Field*.

Jazz and pop singer Sarah Vaughan, the "Divine One," is born March 27 in Newark. She will make her first record in 1945.

Gospel singer Clara Ward is born April 21 in Philadelphia.

Bluesman Clarence "Gatemouth" Brown is born April 18 in Louisiana.

Cabaret pianist Bobby Short is born September 15 in Illinois.

Singer "Big Maybelle" Smith is born May 1 in Jackson, Tennesee.

Actress Ruby Dee is born October 22 in Cleveland.

Rhythm and blues singer Dinah Washington is born August 29 in Tuscaloosa, Alabama.

VISUAL ARTS

Muralist John T. Biggers is born April 24 in North Carolina.

A. Philip Randolph

A. Philip Randolph was born to a minister and seamstress, both of whom had been slaves. He grew up in Florida and worked as an elevator operator, porter, and waiter in New York, where he attended City College at night. An outspoken advocate of nonviolent protest, Randolph joined the Socialist Party, went to jail in 1918 for criticizing American engagement in World War I, and in the 1920s became a persuasive and effective labor organizer. In 1917, with Chandler Owen, he founded the socialist magazine the **Messenger,** touted as "the only radical Negro magazine in America." In 1925, after fighting for a strong union in the Pullman Company for 12 years, he successfully founded and headed the Brotherhood of Sleeping Car Porters—one of the most influential African-American labor unions.

Landscape painter Richard Mayhew is born April 3 in Amityville, New York.

SPORTS

William DeHart Hubbard wins a gold medal in the long jump in the Paris Olympics.

The first world series of the Negro League teams is held.

1925

POLITICS AND CIVIL RIGHTS

There are 17 recorded lynchings.

The number of states with antilynching legislation is now 13.

Hailie Q. Brown, the president of the National Federation of Colored Women's Clubs, leads a walkout of over 2,000 delegates at a convention of the International Council of Women in Washington, D.C., when attempts are made to segregate the event.

Militant civil rights leader Malcolm Little, who will become Malcolm X, is born May 19 in Omaha, Nebraska.

BUSINESS AND EMPLOYMENT

A. Phillip Randolph organizes the Brotherhood of Sleeping Car Porters.

LITERATURE AND JOURNALISM

The *Chicago Defender* celebrates its 20th anniversary.

Alain Leroy Locke publishes *The New Negro*, an anthology of essays, stories, poems, and artwork defining the black experience and the Harlem Renaissance.

Countee Cullen's first collection of poetry, *Color*, is published.

Syndicated radio journalist Carl T. Rowan is born August 11 in Tennessee.

Novelist Rosa Guy is born September 1 in Trinidad.

PERFORMING ARTS

Playwright Garland Anderson's *Appearances* is produced at the Frolic Theater in New York.

Contemporary Events, 1925 ■ The Chrysler Corporation is founded by Walter P. Chrysler. ■ John Scopes is convicted of violating a Tennessee law that prohibits teaching the theory of evolution in public schools. ■ F. Scott Fitzgerald publishes his novel **The Great Gatsby.**

Paul Robeson makes his film debut in Oscar Micheaux's *Body and Soul* on November 9.

Josephine Baker dazzles Paris audiences in *La Revue Nègre*.

Florence B. Price receives the Wannamaker Award for her Symphony in E Minor.

Singer, dancer, and entertainer Sammy Davis, Jr., is born December 8 in New York.

Jazz drummer Max Roach is born January 10 in North Carolina.

Opera singer Mattiwilda Dobbs is born July 11 in Atlanta.

Jazz pianist Oscar Peterson is born August 15 in Montreal.

Blues guitarist Riley B. B. King is born September 16 in Indianola, Mississippi.

Zydeco musician Clifton Chenier is born June 25 in Louisiana.

1926

POLITICS AND CIVIL RIGHTS

There are 23 recorded lynchings.

Attorney Violette N. Anderson of Chicago is the first African-American woman admitted to practice before the U.S. Supreme Court.

In Washington, D.C., a law is passed to segregate all public bathing beaches.

Civil rights advocate Ralph David Abernathy is born March 11 in Alabama. He will succeed Martin Luther King, Jr., as head of the Southern Christian Leadership Conference.

Johnnie Tillmon Blackston, founder and director of the National Welfare Rights Organization, is born April 10 in Arkansas.

Mervyn Dymally, California legislator and the state's first black lieutenant governor, is born May 12 in Trinidad.

BUSINESS AND EMPLOYMENT

The *Chicago Defender* calls for the "opening up of all trades and trade unions to blacks as well as whites."

RELIGION AND EDUCATION

Carter G. Woodson, head of the Association for the Study of Negro

Contemporary Events, 1926 ■ The National Broadcasting Company is set up as a nationwide radio network. ■ Ernest Hemingway publishes his novel **The Sun Also Rises.**

Life and History, institutes Negro History Week for the study of the African-American heritage. In 1976 it will be expanded into Black History Month.

The Carnegie Corporation grants money to the New York Public Library to purchase Arthur A. Schomburg's library, a collection of works on African-American history, literature, and culture.

Mordecai W. Johnson is the first African-American president of Howard University.

LITERATURE AND JOURNALISM

The *Nation* publishes Langston Hughes's article "The Negro Artist and the Racial Mountain," urging African-American writers to draw on the black experience and not try to imitate white writers.

Langston Hughes publishes the first collection of his poems, *Weary Blues.*

Walter White publishes his novel *Flight.*

White writer Carl Van Vechten publishes the controversial *Nigger Heaven,* which glamorizes life in Harlem and creates a fad of white tourists visiting the area's cabarets, nightclubs, and jazz joints.

SCIENCE AND TECHNOLOGY

Pilot Bessie Coleman is killed in a plane crash in Florida.

PERFORMING ARTS

Gospel pianist and singer Arizona Dranes makes her first records.

The Eva Jessye Choir begins performing in New York City.

The revue *Blackbirds of 1926,* starring Florence Mills, plays to full houses in New York and then travels to London and Paris.

Actress Rose McClendon first gains critical attention for her role in *Deep River.* Later in the year she appears with Jules Bledsoe, Abbie Mitchell, and Frank Wilson in the Pulitzer-Prize-winning play *In Abraham's Bosom.*

W. C. Handy edits *Blues: An Anthology,* a collection of songs compiled from his travels in the South.

Actor Earle Hyman is born in North Carolina. He will appear at the American Shakespeare Festival as well as on Broadway and TV.

Jazz trumpeter Miles Davis is born May 25 in Alton, Illinois.

Composer and avant-garde jazz musican John Coltrane is born September 23 in Hamlet, North Carolina.

One of the original rock 'n' rollers, Chuck Berry is born October 18 in St. Louis.

Singer Willie Mae "Big Mama" Thornton is born December 11 in Montgomery, Alabama.

VISUAL ARTS

Palmer C. Hayden wins the first Harmon Foundation gold medal for painting.

Paul Revere Williams becomes the first African-American member of the American Institute of Architects.

Artist Betye Saar is born in California.

SPORTS

Boxer Theodore Flowers, the "Georgia Deacon," wins the world's middleweight championship.

1927

POLITICS AND CIVIL RIGHTS

There are 16 recorded lynchings.

In *Nixon* v. *Herndon*, the U.S. Supreme Court decides that state laws forbidding blacks from voting in primary elections are unconstitutional and in direct violation of the 14th Amendment.

In Memphis, the mayor categorically refuses to consider a petition from local blacks to open the fire and police departments to African Americans, or to allow blacks to enter the city parks, which are reserved for whites only.

Congress passes a bill conferring citizenship upon Virgin Islanders. About half the 23,000 inhabitants of the islands are black.

After serving half his prison sentence, Pan-Africanist Marcus Garvey is deported to Jamaica.

Activist Coretta Scott King is born April 27 in Marion, Alabama.

LITERATURE AND JOURNALISM

James Weldon Johnson publishes his sermon poems in *God's Trombones*, with illustrations by Aaron Douglas.

Langston Hughes publishes his book of poems *Fine Clothes to the Jews*.

Countee Cullen publishes two books of his own poems, *The Ballad of the Brown Girl* and *Copper Sun*, and edits an anthology, *Caroling Dusk*.

Langston Hughes on Black Pride

In his seminal essay "The Negro Artist and the Racial Mountain," published in 1926, poet Langston Hughes called for a bold, nonapologetic celebration of pride in being African American. His essay ends: "We . . . intend to express our individual dark-skinned selves without fear or shame. If white people are pleased, we are glad. If they are not, it doesn't matter. We know we are beautiful. And ugly too. . . . We build our temples for tomorrow, strong as we know how, and we stand on the top of the mountain, free within ourselves."

Contemporary Events, 1927 ■ Charles Lindbergh flies **The Spirit of St. Louis** from New York to Paris nonstop in 33.5 hours. ■ The Holland Tunnel, linking New York and New Jersey, opens.

PERFORMING ARTS

Composer William Grant Still's *Darker American* is performed by the Rochester Symphony Orchestra.

Duke Ellington opens at Harlem's Cotton Club.

Actor Frederick O'Neal helps found the Ira Aldridge Players.

In New York, the all-black musical *Rang Tang* opens, Ethel Waters appears in the revue *Africana,* and Rose McClendon and Frank Wilson star in the play *Porgy.*

Well-loved entertainer Florence Mills dies November 1 in New York. Over 150,000 crowd the streets at her Harlem funeral.

Folksinger and actor Harry Belafonte, Jr., is born in New York.

Internationally acclaimed opera singer Leontyne Price is born February 10 in Laurel, Mississippi.

VISUAL ARTS

Henry O. Tanner is the first African American elected to the National Academy of Design.

"The Negro in Art Week" show is held at the Art Institute of Chicago.

Portraitist Laura Wheeler Waring is awarded the Harmon Foundation gold medal.

SPORTS

The Harlem Globetrotters are organized as a performance rather than an athletic team, entertaining audiences with their amazing basketball feats.

Tennis star Althea Gibson, the first African American to win at Wimbledon, is born August 25 in South Carolina.

POLITICS AND CIVIL RIGHTS

Oscar DePriest, a Chicago Republican, is elected to Congress, the first African-American representative in the 20th century and the first ever from the North.

When the Paul Laurence Dunbar Apartments in Harlem, built by John D. Rockefeller, open as a low-income housing project, they are

Contemporary Events, 1928 ■ Herbert Hoover is elected president. ■ New York Governor Al Smith, the Democratic nominee for president, calls for the repeal of Prohibition. ■ The United States supports the Kellogg-Briand Pact, outlawing war as a means of national policy.

hailed as a revolutionary innovation in housing by the National Urban League.

Robert N. C. Nix, Jr., the first African American to serve on a state supreme court (Pennsylvania), is born in Philadelphia.

LITERATURE AND JOURNALISM

Novelist Charles Waddell Chesnutt is awarded the Spingarn Medal for "depicting the life and struggle" of African Americans.

Nella Larsen's novel *Quicksand* is published.

Claude McKay publishes his novel *Home to Harlem*.

An Autumn Love Cycle, a book of poems by Georgia Douglas Johnson, is published.

Rudolph Fisher's novel *The Walls of Jericho* is published.

Poet and essayist Maya Angelou is born April 4 in St. Louis.

SCIENCE AND TECHNOLOGY

Inventor Lewis H. Latimer dies December 11 in Flushing, New York.

PERFORMING ARTS

Bill "Bojangles" Robinson tap-dances in *Blackbirds of 1928*.

Frank Wilson's play *Meek Mose* is produced on Broadway.

Evelyn Preer, Edward Thompson, and Spencer Williamson appear in the sound film *The Melancholy Dame*.

Singer Eartha Kitt is born January 26 in South Carolina.

Rock 'n' roll singer Otha "Bo Diddley" McDaniels is born December 30 in Mississippi.

Rhythm and blues singer and pianist Antoine "Fats" Domino is born February 26 in New Orleans. Among his hits will be "Ain't That a Shame" and "Blueberry Hill."

Soul singer James Brown is born June 3 in Macon, Georgia.

Composer, bandleader, and pianist Horace Silver is born September 2 in Norwalk, Connecticut.

Jazz saxophonist and bandleader Julian "Cannonball" Adderley is born September 15 in Tampa, Florida.

Jazz and blues singer Ernestine Anderson is born November 11 in Houston, Texas.

Singer Ruth Brown is born January 30.

VISUAL ARTS

The first public Harmon show of African-American artists is held.

"Chicago Police Kill 16-Year-Old Boy in Own Home"

The above headline, which appeared in the **Negro Champion** on December 29, 1928, was followed by the story of Ernest Wickhurst, a 16-year-old who had barricaded himself, his younger brothers, a crippled sister, and an infant sister in their apartment when he heard that the Chicago police were pursuing him for breaking a plate glass window. Two hundred policemen surrounded the alley apartment and for five hours fired into it with machine guns, revolvers, automatics, shotguns, and rifles, and threw tear-gas bombs and hand grenades into a window. Wickhurst had one gun. Finally, the police stormed the apartment, a sergeant shot a bullet into Wickhurst's head, and other officers poured a volley of 30 bullets into the boy's body.

The work of Archibald J. Motley, Jr., is featured in the article "A Negro Artist Plumbs the Negro Soul" in the *New York Times Magazine*.

ADDITIONAL STATISTICS

On average, black men live 40.5 years and white males 54.1 years; black women live 42.3 years and white women 56.4 years.

1929

POLITICS AND CIVIL RIGHTS

There are seven recorded lynchings.

Martin Luther King, Jr., is born January 15 in Atlanta.

Congressman John Conyers, Jr., is born in Detroit.

BUSINESS AND EMPLOYMENT

African-American women workers in the dress industry are organized by the International Ladies Garment Workers Union.

Three major African-American-owned life insurance companies merge to form the Supreme Liberty Life Insurance Company with assets of $1.5 million.

RELIGION AND EDUCATION

The Atlanta University system is formed, joining Atlanta University, Morehouse College, and Spelman College. John Hope is president.

LITERATURE AND JOURNALISM

A number of important novels are published, including Nella Larsen's *Passing*, Claude McKay's *Banjo*, Jessie Fauset's *Plum Bun*, and Wallace Thurman's *The Blacker the Berry*.

Walter White publishes *Rope and Faggot: A Biography of Judge Lynch*.

Countee Cullen's *The Black Christ*, a book of poems, is published.

Born to Be, concert singer Taylor Gordon's autobiography, appears.

Novelist Paule Marshall, author of *Brown Girl, Brownstones*, is born April 9 in Brooklyn, New York.

PERFORMING ARTS

Wallace Thurman's play *Harlem* opens in New York City.

Contemporary Events, 1929 ■ The U.S. stock market collapses on Friday, October 29, and the world economic crisis begins. ■ The St. Valentine's Day massacre of Chicago gang members occurs.

Two Hollywood movies feature all-black casts: King Vidor's *Hallelujah* and *Hearts in Dixie*.

The musical *Hot Chocolates* opens in New York City. The musical numbers by Fats Waller and Andy Razaf include two songs that will become popular classics, "Ain't Misbehavin'" and "Black and Blue."

The Harlem Broadcasting Company opens its radio stations.

Jack L. Cooper's show "The All-Negro Hour" airs on the white radio station WSBC in Chicago.

POLITICS AND CIVIL RIGHTS

There are 20 recorded lynchings.

The NAACP successfully campaigns to defeat confirmation of Supreme Court nominee John H. Parker, who was on record in opposition to voting rights for African Americans.

The League of Struggle for Negro Rights is founded by the American Communist Party. Langston Hughes is elected president.

Mary McLeod Bethune, educator and civil rights activist, is cited as one of America's 50 leading women by historian Ida Tarbell.

Lawyer and jurist Clarence Pendleton, Jr., is born November 10 in Louisville, Kentucky. He will be the first African-American chairperson of the U.S. Civil Rights Commission in 1981.

Cardiss Robertson Collins is born September 24 in St. Louis. In 1973 she will be elected to the U.S. House of Representatives.

BUSINESS AND EMPLOYMENT

R. L. Mays, president of the Railway Men's International Benevolent Industrial Association, organizes a convention of black railway workers to fight discrimination in job appointments and promotions.

The Depression-related failure of four African-American banks severely affects the black community in Chicago.

RELIGION AND EDUCATION

Over two-thirds of all African Americans in professional jobs are teachers or ministers.

Contemporary Events, 1930 ■ Sinclair Lewis wins the Nobel Prize for literature. ■ Grant Wood paints **American Gothic**.

The Great Depression and Southern Blacks

During the Great Depression of the 1930s, southern blacks in agriculture suffered more economic adversity than any other American group, black or white. In 1930 there were 1,112,510 African Americans employed as agricultural laborers: two-thirds of all southern blacks. Ten years later, this number dropped to 780,312: a 30% reduction even though the affected population declined only 4%. In addition, the average wage earned by a southern black agricultural laborer in 1940 was less than half what it was in 1930. Black migration from the South to the North came to a virtual standstill during this period because northern whites were taking the unskilled jobs formerly left for migrating African Americans to fill.

Where public school segregation is legally mandated, $44.31 is spent annually on each white child and $12.57 on each black child.

LITERATURE AND JOURNALISM

Langston Hughes publishes his novel *Not Without Laughter*.

James Weldon Johnson publishes *Black Manhattan*.

In a gesture meant to convey respect, the *New York Times* on June 7 begins capitalizing the word "Negro."

Playwright Lorraine Hansberry, who will write *A Raisin in the Sun*, is born May 19 in Chicago.

PERFORMING ARTS

Richard B. Harrison stars as "De Lawd" in *The Green Pastures*, which opens on Broadway.

Blind Lemon Jefferson, the most influential African-American country blues singer of his time, freezes to death in a Chicago blizzard.

Bluesman Bobby "Blue" Bland is born January 27 in Tennessee.

Jazz trumpeter Richard "Blue" Mitchell is born March 13 in Miami.

Jazz saxophonist Ornette Coleman is born March 18 in Texas.

Jazz singer Betty Carter, popularly known as "Betty Bebop," is born May 16 in Flint, Michigan.

Ray Charles, jazz, soul, and pop singer, is born September 23 in Albany, Georgia. Blind by age six, he will become one of America's most-beloved performing artists, earning three Grammys.

Odetta Felious Gordon, the folksinger and activist known as "Odetta," is born December 31 in Birmingham, Alabama.

VISUAL ARTS

Painter William H. Johnson wins the Harmon gold medal for his expressionist landscapes.

Artist Faith Ringgold is born October 8 in New York.

SPORTS

At age 19, Josh Gibson joins the Pittsburgh Homestead Grays and begins a successful 15-year career as a catcher in various professional black baseball teams. He will achieve a .423 lifetime batting average and be inducted into the Baseball Hall of Fame in 1972.

ADDITIONAL STATISTICS

The U.S. Census Bureau reports that 11,891,100 African Americans live in the United States, 9.7% of the total population.

1931

POLITICS AND CIVIL RIGHTS

There are 12 recorded lynchings.

Police in Scottsboro, Alabama, arrest nine African-American youths for allegedly raping two white women who, like them, were riding a freight train. The subsequent conviction of the "Scottsboro Boys," based on hearsay evidence, will cause national and international protest and result in several appeals and retrials. Only by 1950 will all nine men be free, as a result of appeal, parole, or escape.

Walter F. White is named executive secretary of the NAACP; Roy Wilkins is appointed assistant secretary.

Ida B. Wells Barnett, journalist, antilynching crusader, and a founder of the NAACP, dies March 25 in Chicago.

William Lacy Clay, congressman from Missouri and chair of the Post Office and Civil Service Committee, is born April 30 in St. Louis.

Carrie Saxon Perry is born August 30 in Hartford, Connecticut, where in 1987 she will become the first African-American female mayor of a major city in the Northeast.

BUSINESS AND EMPLOYMENT

In 19 major U.S. cities with large African-American populations, at least 25% of all black men and women are unemployed. In Detroit 60% of black men and 75% of black women are unemployed.

Comer Cottrell is born December 7 in Mobile, Alabama. In 1973 he will found Pro-Line Corporation, and in 1989 he will become co-owner of the Texas Rangers.

LITERATURE AND JOURNALISM

George Schuyler publishes two books: *Slaves Today: A Story of Liberia*, comparing conditions in present-day Liberia to those in the antebellum South, and *Black No More*, a satire on U.S. race relations.

Jessie Fauset's novel *The Chinaberry Tree* is published.

Arna Bontemps publishes his novel *God Sends Sunday*.

A'Lelia Walker Robinson dies August 17 in New York. The daughter of millionaire Madame C. J. Walker, Robinson created Harlem's celebrated "Dark Tower," a salon where African-American writers, ar-

---

Contemporary Events, 1931 ■ In New York City, the Empire State Building is completed and construction on Rockefeller Center begins. ■ Pearl Buck publishes her novel **The Good Earth.**

tists, and philosophers mingled with members of New York society.

Toni Morrison, the first African American to win the Nobel Prize for literature, is born February 18 in Lorain, Ohio.

Literary critic Darwin Turner is born May 7 in Cincinnati, Ohio.

SCIENCE AND TECHNOLOGY

Daniel Hale Williams, heart surgeon and founder of Chicago's Provident Hospital, dies August 4 in Chicago.

PERFORMING ARTS

The Harlem Experimental Theater Group launches its first season at St. Philip's Parish House.

In Chicago Thomas Dorsey and Theodore Frye establish their gospel choir.

William Grant Still's *Afro-American Symphony* is performed by the Rochester Philharmonic Symphony.

Duke Ellington composes "Mood Indigo."

Buddy Bolden, considered the first man to play jazz, dies November 4 in a segregated Louisiana mental institution.

Tony-Award-winning actor James Earl Jones is born January 17 in Arkabutla, Mississippi.

Soprano and mezzo-soprano Shirley Verrett, who will become known for her performance in the title role of Bizet's *Carmen*, is born May 31 in New Orleans.

Pop and soul singer Brook Benton is born September 19 in Camden, South Carolina. His 16 gold records will include "A Rainy Night in Georgia."

James Cleveland, "King of Gospel," is born December 5 in Chicago. After singing with Mahalia Jackson and groups such as "The Caravans," he will start his own group, "The Gospel Chimes."

Singer and actress Della Reese is born July 6 in Detroit.

Child-prodigy pianist Philippa Schuyler is born August 2.

Dancer Carmen de Lavallade is born March 5 in Los Angeles.

VISUAL ARTS

Painter Horace Pippin finishes *The End of the War: Starting Home*, which is burned into an oak panel.

Artist Edwin A. Harleston dies May 5 in Charleston, South Carolina.

David C. Driskell, artist and art historian, is born June 7 in Eatonton, Georgia.

POLITICS AND CIVIL RIGHTS

There are six recorded lynchings.

The NAACP publishes "Mississippi River Slavery—1932" after investigating the conditions of African-American workers on federal flood-control projects. It will lead to a U.S. Senate investigation and to the setting of federal standards for minimum conditions and wages.

The Communist Party selects an African American, James W. Ford, as its vice-presidential candidate.

Civil rights leader Andrew Young is born March 12 in New Orleans. He will become the first African-American United Nations ambassador and mayor of Atlanta.

Yvonne Brathwaite Burke, the first African-American congresswoman from California and the first woman to chair the Congressional Black Caucus, is born October 5 in Los Angeles.

BUSINESS AND EMPLOYMENT

Ten blacks are killed when white employees of the Illinois Central Railroad try to prevent African Americans from working there.

RELIGION AND EDUCATION

Among the 117 African-American institutions of higher education, 36 are public, 81 are private (74 of which are church-affiliated), and 5 offer graduate-level instruction.

Howard University begins publishing the *Journal of Negro Education*.

LITERATURE AND JOURNALISM

Countee Cullen publishes his only novel, *One Way to Harlem*.

Wallace Thurman's novel *Infants of the Spring* is published.

Rudoph Fisher publishes *The Conjure Man Dies*, the first African-American detective novel.

Victor Daly's novel *Not Only War*, an attack on racism within the U.S. Army during World War I, is published.

The James Weldon Johnson Literary Guild conducts a nationwide poetry contest for African-American children. One winner is Margaret Walker of New Orleans with her poem "When Night Comes."

Contemporary Events, 1932 ■ Franklin D. Roosevelt is elected president on a campaign promising a "New Deal" for Americans stricken by the Depression. ■ The son of aviator Charles Lindbergh is kidnapped, resulting in a sensational manhunt and trial.

FDR and the Black Voter

Prior to 1932, African Americans had traditionally voted Republican, the party of Abraham Lincoln and Frederick Douglass. Franklin Delano Roosevelt's 1932 promise of a "New Deal for all Americans" caused only a slight shift toward the Democratic Party. Some blacks voted instead for the Communist Party, whose vice-presidential candidate was an African American, James W. Ford. By 1936 the voting picture had changed dramatically. Grateful for President Roosevelt's relief programs and record number of black appointments to high offices, as well as for First Lady Eleanor Roosevelt's advocacy of civil rights, blacks voted overwhelmingly Democratic—setting a pattern that continued into the future.

Poet Mari Evans is born July 16 in Toledo, Ohio. Her most famous works will include *I Am a Black Woman* and *Nightstar: 1973–1978*.

SCIENCE AND TECHNOLOGY

Aliene Carrington Ewell founds a society for black nurses, Chi Eta Phi, in Washington, D.C. It will expand to 72 chapters in 22 states.

PERFORMING ARTS

Bill Pickett, one of the most famous performing cowboys of his day, dies April 2. Publicly acclaimed by President Theodore Roosevelt, Pickett performed throughout Europe and the United States, where he was often assisted by two young whites, Tom Mix and Will Rogers.

Florence B. Price plays her piano concerto with the Chicago Symphony Orchestra, which will do her Symphony in E Minor in 1933.

Melvin Van Peebles, motion picture producer and director, is born August 21 in Chicago. His films will include *Watermelon Man, Sweet Sweetback's Baadasss Song,* and *Putney Swope*.

Comedian and civil rights activist Richard "Dick" Gregory is born October 12 in St. Louis.

Rhythm and blues singer "Little Richard" Penniman, a formative figure in rock 'n' roll music, is born December 25 in Macon, Georgia.

SPORTS

The New York Rens, a black professional basketball team, win the first world championship in any sport by beating the Boston Celtics.

At the Olympics, Eddie Tolan wins a gold medal in a record 100-meter dash; Ralph Metcalfe is a close second. Tolan also wins a gold in the 200-meter run, and Ed Gordon earns a gold in the long jump.

George "Kid Chocolate" Dixon wins the featherweight boxing championship, which he will hold through 1934.

1933

POLITICS AND CIVIL RIGHTS

There are 24 recorded lynchings.

President Franklin D. Roosevelt brings several prominent African Americans into government to serve in the "Black Cabinet," an advi-

---

Contemporary Events, 1933 ■ The 21st Amendment to the U.S. Constitution repeals Prohibition. ■ The United States recognizes the Soviet Union and resumes trade. ■ The Tennessee Valley Authority is created. ■ As secretary of labor, Frances Perkins becomes the first female cabinet member.

sory group. The most famous member is Mary McLeod Bethune.

The NAACP begins a widespread campaign against segregation by filing a suit on behalf of Thomas Hocutt against the University of North Carolina. The suit is lost.

Angelo Herndon, a 19-year-old Cincinnati native and member of the Communist Party, leads hunger marches in the South in an attempt to secure relief support due African Americans. He is arrested, convicted, and sentenced to 20 years on a chain gang.

To encourage white employers in New York to hire blacks, John Johnson organizes the Citizens League for Fair Play. Blacks quickly gain several hundred jobs, but tensions aggravated by league activities will lead to a riot in Harlem in 1935.

YMCA secretary Max Yergan receives the Spingarn Medal for his work as a missionary in South Africa.

The U.S. Housing Authority begins building low-cost housing, and African Americans occupy about a third of the units. The housing is segregated in the South and partly integrated in the North.

Solomon Lightfoot Michaux, religious leader, founds the Good Neighbor League in Washington, D.C., an organization that feeds 250,000 homeless and unemployed African Americans and later works to organize the black vote for Franklin Roosevelt.

BUSINESS AND EMPLOYMENT

More than 25% of urban African Americans are on relief, compared with about 12% of urban whites.

RELIGION AND EDUCATION

The Works Projects Administration initiates adult education programs that teach 400,000 African Americans to read and write.

Louis Eugene Walcott is born May 11 in New York. As Louis Farrakhan, he will become national representative of Elijah Muhammad's Nation of Islam, and on Muhammad's death, lead a faction of the movement.

LITERATURE AND JOURNALISM

Carter G. Woodson publishes *The Miseducation of the Negro*.

Leon H. Washington founds the *Los Angeles Sentinel*.

Tony Brown, producer and host of the Emmy-winning TV series *Black Journal*, is born April 11 in Charles Town, West Virginia.

SCIENCE AND TECHNOLOGY

Louis Wade Sullivan, founder of the Morehouse School of Medicine and President George Bush's secretary of health and human services, is born November 3 in Atlanta.

PERFORMING ARTS

Hall Johnson's folk drama *Run Little Chillun* opens on Broadway.

United Artists releases the movie *Emperor Jones,* starring Paul Robeson in his first leading role. It is also the first Hollywood movie to star an African American with white actors in supporting roles.

Benny Goodman, a white bandleader, begins using African-American musicians in recording sessions. In 1936 he will be the first major bandleader to have blacks and whites playing together for the public.

Katherine Dunham stars in Ruth Page's ballet *La Guiablesse.*

Choreographer Hemsley Winfield and his dance company appear in the Metropolitan Opera's production of *Emperor Jones,* although they are not listed in the program.

Soprano Sissieretta Jones, known as "Black Patti," dies June 14 in Providence, Rhode Island. She sang at Carnegie Hall, Madison Square Garden, and the White House.

Actress Cicely Tyson, winner of two Emmys, is born December 19 in New York City.

Singer Nina Simone, "High Priestess of Soul," is born February 21 in Tryon, North Carolina.

Trumpeter and record producer Quincy Delight Jones, winner of 20 Grammys, is born March 14 in Chicago.

VISUAL ARTS

E. Simms Campbell begins contributing cartoons and artwork to *Esquire* magazine.

Camille Billops, painter, sculptor, and filmmaker, is born August 12 in Los Angeles.

Artist Sam Gilliam is born November 30 in Tupelo, Mississippi.

POLITICS AND CIVIL RIGHTS

There are 15 recorded lynchings.

An antilynching bill fails in Congress due to lack of support from the Roosevelt administration.

Arthur W. Mitchell of Chicago is the first African-American Democrat elected to the U.S. House of Representatives.

W. E. B. Du Bois resigns from the NAACP, where he has edited the *Crisis* magazine, in a conflict over the value of voluntary segregation, which he supports. Roy Wilkins, assistant secretary of the NAACP, becomes the new editor of the *Crisis*.

Donald Payne, the first African American elected to the U.S. House of Representatives from New Jersey, is born July 16 in Newark.

Politician Edolphus Towns is born July 21 in Chadbourn, North Carolina. He will become Brooklyn borough president, U.S. representative from New York, and chair of the Congressional Black Caucus.

BUSINESS AND EMPLOYMENT

The American Federation of Labor rejects a resolution to end discrimination within its ranks and says no discrimination exists.

The percentage of the population on relief in major urban areas is 52% among blacks and 13% among whites in northern cities; 52% among blacks and 10% among whites in border-state cities; and 38% among blacks and 11% among whites in southern cities.

Maggie Lena Walker, the first African-American female bank president, dies December 15 in Richmond, Virginia.

RELIGION AND EDUCATION

William T. B. Williams, dean of Tuskegee Institute, receives the Spingarn Medal for his achievements in education.

Alain Leroy Locke founds the Associates in Negro Folk Education.

George Alexander McGuire, founding bishop of the African Orthodox Church, dies November 10 in New York.

LITERATURE AND JOURNALISM

The magazine *Challenge*, edited by Dorothy West, debuts. It is designed to stimulate interest among blacks in their African heritage.

Zora Neale Hurston's novel *Jonah's Gourd Vine* is published.

George W. Lee publishes *Beale Street: Where the Blues Began*.

Henry Dumas, author of *Ark of Bones and Other Stories*, is born July 20 in Sweet Home, Arkansas.

Sonia Sanchez, poet, playwright, and short-story writer, is born September 19 in Birmingham, Alabama.

Poet and essayist Audre Lorde is born in New York City.

Contemporary Events, 1934 ■ The most popular musical on Broadway is Cole Porter's **Anything Goes.** ■ FBI agents shoot John Dillinger, "Public Enemy Number 1."

Poet, playwright, and essayist LeRoi Jones, later known as Imamu Amiri Baraka, is born October 7 in Newark. He will become a leader of the Black Arts Movement in the 1960s.

PERFORMING ARTS

William Levi Dawson's *Negro Folk Symphony* is performed at Carnegie Hall by the Philadelphia Symphony Orchestra.

At a White House dinner hosted by President and Mrs. Franklin D. Roosevelt, Etta Moten Barnett sings songs from her roles in the movies *Golddiggers of 1933* and *Swing Low Sweet Chariot*.

On January 26 Harlem's Apollo Theatre stages its first live show.

The Hollywood movie *Imitation of Life* opens. It stars black actress Louise Beavers and white actress Claudette Colbert as two women who go into business together.

Actor Greg Morris is born September 27 in Cleveland. He will have a role in the popular TV series *Mission Impossible*.

VISUAL ARTS

Aaron Douglas completes his murals *Aspects of Negro Life* for the 135th Street branch of the New York Public Library.

Painter Malvin Gray Johnson dies October 4 in New York City. The Harmon Foundation will mount a memorial retrospective of his work in 1935.

SPORTS

Baseball player Henry "Hank" Aaron, who will break Babe Ruth's home-run record, is born February 5 in Mobile, Alabama.

Basketball player and coach William Felton "Bill" Russell, who will be named Most Valuable Player of the Year five times, is born in Monroe, Louisiana.

Track star Rafer Johnson is born August 18 in Hillsboro, Texas. He will win a gold medal in the decathlon at the 1960 Rome Olympics.

1935

POLITICS AND CIVIL RIGHTS

There are 18 recorded lynchings.

The NAACP issues statements chastising President Roosevelt for not proposing or supporting civil rights legislation.

The International Council of Friends of Ethiopia is founded in New York to protest Italy's invasion of that country. Willis N. Huggins, council president, pleads Ethiopia's cause before the League of Nations.

Mary McLeod Bethune organizes the National Council of Negro Women. Later in the year she receives the Spingarn Medal.

The U.S. Supreme Court upholds a Texas law that keeps African Americans from voting in Democratic primaries.

Tensions arising from racial discrimination and poverty fuel a riot in Harlem that kills three African Americans and causes over two million dollars in property damage.

BUSINESS AND EMPLOYMENT

After the American Federation of Labor (AFL) rejects proposals to unionize unskilled labor and to end discrimination, the Congress of Industrial Organizations (CIO) is organized. It creates integrated unions in various industries, including the United Mine Workers.

The National Association of Negro Business and Professional Women's Clubs is founded.

RELIGION AND EDUCATION

A survey of elementary and secondary schools in 10 southern states reveals that an average of $17.04 is spent on each black student as opposed to an average of $49.30 on each white student.

LITERATURE AND JOURNALISM

George W. Henderson publishes his novel *Ollie Miss*.

Writer Alice Moore Dunbar-Nelson dies in Philadelphia.

Earl G. Graves, publisher of *Black Enterprise* magazine, is born January 9 in Brooklyn, New York.

SCIENCE AND TECHNOLOGY

Chemist Percy Julian develops physostigmine, a drug for the treatment of the eye disease glaucoma.

Namahyoke Sokum Curtis, leader of 32 African-American nurses who aided yellow-fever victims in the Spanish-American War, dies November 25 and is interred with honors in Arlington National Cemetery.

PERFORMING ARTS

Following a triumphal tour of Europe, contralto Marian Anderson

---

Contemporary Events, 1935 ■ President Franklin D. Roosevelt signs the U.S. Social Security Act. ■ Huey Long, U.S. senator from Louisiana, is assassinated in the Louisiana Capitol Building.

The Federal Theater Project

Founded by the Works Progress Administration, a New Deal relief agency, the Federal Theater Project's Negro Unit was the main source of work for people involved in black drama all during the 1930s. New York City's Lafayette Theater offered such plays as Orson Welles's adaptation of **Macbeth,** set in Haiti; Frank Wilson's **Walk Together Children;** and Rudolph Fisher's **The Conjure Man Dies.** In Los Angeles, Hall Johnson's **Run Little Chillun** was performed; and in Seattle, Theodore Browne's **Natural Man.** Congress stopped supporting the Federal Theater Project in 1939.

performs at Town Hall in New York, prompting the *New York Times* music critic to call her "one of the great singers of our time."

Todd Duncan stars as "Porgy," Ann Brown as "Bess," and John Bubbles as "Sportin' Life" in *Porgy and Bess,* George Gershwin's "folk opera," at the Alvin Theater on Broadway.

Langston Hughes's long-running play *Mulatto,* with Rose McClendon and Morris McKinney, opens on Broadway. Another play by Hughes, *Little Ham,* is also staged on Broadway.

The WPA launches the Federal Theater Project in Harlem, which produces such works as J. Augustus Smith's *Turpentine* and W. E. B. Du Bois's *Haiti.*

Blues singer Cora "Koko Taylor" Walton is born September 28.

Sam Cooke, popular singer during the 1960s, is born January 22.

Actress and singer Carol Diahann Johnson, known as Diahann Carroll, is born July 17 in the Bronx. She will earn an Oscar nomination as best actress for her work in the movie *Claudine.*

Singer Johnny Mathis is born September 30 in San Francisco. He will earn more than 50 gold and platinum records.

Lou Rawls, jazz and blues singer, is born December 1 in Chicago. He will record over 30 albums.

"Little" Esther Phillips, singer best known for the songs "And I Love Him" and "Release Me," is born December 23 in Galveston, Texas.

VISUAL ARTS

The Harlem Artists Guild is formed to voice black artists' concerns.

Sargent Johnson creates his sculpture *Forever Free,* which wins the San Francisco Art Association medal.

The Whitney Museum of American Art purchases *African Dancer* and two other sculptures by Richmond Barthé.

Under the WPA program Charles Alston and other African-American artists paint the Harlem Hospital murals.

Sculptor Richard Hunt is born September 7 in Chicago.

SPORTS

Joe Louis defeats Primo Carnera, a white boxer, at Yankee Stadium in New York and launches his meteoric boxing career.

Boxer John Henry Lewis becomes the light heavyweight champion of the world. He will keep the title until he retires, the first American-born boxer to do so.

Boxer Floyd Patterson is born January 4 in Waco, North Carolina.

He will become the first Olympic gold medalist (1952) to win a world professional boxing title.

1936

POLITICS AND CIVIL RIGHTS

There are eight recorded lynchings.

The NAACP prompts the case of *Gibbs* v. *Board of Education of Montgomery County, Maryland,* which sets a precedent for offering equal salaries to black and white schoolteachers.

The American Communist Party establishes the Negro People's Committee to Aid Spanish Democracy when the Spanish Civil War breaks out.

A U.S. senator from South Carolina and the mayor of Charleston walk out of the Democratic National Convention in protest when an African-American minister offers a prayer at the opening of a session. Later, the South Carolina delegation officially protests the presence of blacks at the convention.

Mary McLeod Bethune becomes director of the Division of Negro Affairs in President Roosevelt's National Youth Administration.

Barbara Jordan, three-term U.S. representative, is born February 21 in Houston. She will become the first African American to make the keynote speech at the Democratic National Convention.

Political activist Bobby Seale is born October 22 in Dallas. He will cofound the Black Panther Party with Huey P. Newton.

Activist Betty Shabazz, who will marry Malcolm X, is born May 28 in Detroit.

BUSINESS AND EMPLOYMENT

The National Negro Congress is organized in Chicago to work for better business and economic opportunities for African Americans. The 817 delegates from more than 500 organizations elect A. Philip Randolph of the Brotherhood of Sleeping Car Porters as president.

RELIGION AND EDUCATION

The NAACP presents the Spingarn Medal posthumously to John Hope, president and founder of the Atlanta University system.

Contemporary Events, 1936 ■ Franklin D. Roosevelt is elected by a landslide to a second term as U.S. president. ■ Margaret Mitchell's novel **Gone with the Wind** is published. ■ Boulder (later, Hoover) Dam is completed, blocking the Colorado River to create Lake Mead, the world's largest reservoir.

Educator Marva Collins is born August 31 in Monroeville, Alabama. She will start Westside Preparatory School in one of Chicago's poorest neighborhoods.

Educator Johnnetta Betsch Cole is born October 19 in Jacksonville, Florida. She will be the first African-American female president of Spelman College.

LITERATURE AND JOURNALISM

Arna Bontemps's novel *Black Thunder*, based on the 1800 slave revolt led by Gabriel Prosser, is published and hailed by the *Crisis* as "the best historical novel written by an American Negro."

Louis E. Martin founds the *Michigan Chronicle*, a black newspaper.

Virginia Hamilton, author of juvenile fiction such as *M.C. Higgins the Great* and *Sweet Whispers, Brother Rush*, is born March 12 in Yellow Springs, Ohio.

PERFORMING ARTS

Composer William Grant Still is guest conductor of the Los Angeles Symphony Orchestra in the Hollywood Bowl, the first African American to lead a major symphonic orchestra.

The movie version of *The Green Pastures* is released, featuring Eddie "Rochester" Anderson and Rex Ingram as "De Lawd."

The movie *The Big Broadcast of 1937* is widely criticized for showing a white pianist on screen while Teddy Wilson, a black pianist, plays the music off screen. Critics feel Wilson's talent is being exploited.

Count Basie makes his first appearance in New York City at the Roseland Ballroom.

Langston Hughes's *Troubled Island* opens on Broadway.

Actress Rose McClendon dies July 12 in New York. Famous for her roles in *Deep River*, *In Abraham's Bosom*, and *Porgy*, she helped found the Negro People's Theater and the Rose McClendon Players.

Dancer Alvin Ailey is born January 5 in Rogers, Texas.

Jazz tenor saxophonist Roland Kirk is born August 7 in Columbus, Ohio. He will become famous for making his own instruments and playing more than one at a time.

SPORTS

Jesse Owens wins four gold medals in track events at the Berlin Olympics. Other African Americans earning gold medals are John Woodruff in the 800-meter run and Archie Williams in the 400-meter run.

Football player Jim Brown is born February 17 on St. Simons Island, Georgia. A record-breaking offensive back for the Cleveland Browns, he will later star in films and found the Negro Industrial and Economic Union.

Basketball player and coach Wilt Chamberlain is born August 21 in Philadelphia. He will be widely regarded as the best offensive player in basketball history.

ADDITIONAL STATISTICS

The average annual income per family is: in the urban North, $1,227 for blacks, $2,616 for whites; in the urban South, $635 for blacks, $2,019 for whites; in the rural South, $556 for blacks, $1,535 for whites.

1937

POLITICS AND CIVIL RIGHTS

William Hastie is the first African American appointed to be a federal judge, in the Virgin Islands.

The U.S. Supreme Court rules that picketing is a legal means for blacks to protest or express grievances.

A breakthrough law in Pennsylvania denies certain state services to any union that discriminates against African Americans.

The NAACP successfully pressures the Boy Scouts of America to allow African-American scouts to join the national Scout Jamboree in Washington, D.C.

The NAACP honors Walter F. White, writer and civil rights leader, for his work in lobbying for federal antilynching legislation.

An antilynching bill passes in the U.S. House of Representatives, but is killed by a southern filibuster in the Senate.

Eleanor Holmes Norton is born June 13 in Washington, D.C. She will chair the U.S. Equal Opportunity Commission and serve as delegate to Congress from the District of Columbia.

BUSINESS AND EMPLOYMENT

The International Brotherhood of Red Caps, a union of black railway workers, is established in Chicago. It will evolve into the United

Jesse Owens

In 1936 Jesse Owens from Ohio State University won four gold medals at the Berlin Olympics and infuriated German Chancellor Adolf Hitler, who preached the mental and physical supremacy of Aryan whites over all other racial types. Archie Williams was another African-American gold medalist at the 1936 Olympics. In 1981, he reminisced about that experience for an **Oakland Tribune** reporter: "When I came back home people asked me, 'How did those dirty Nazis treat you?' To which I always replied, 'Well, over there at least we didn't have to ride in the back of the bus.'" Recalling that the Germans didn't seem familiar with blacks, he said, "I think they wanted to see if the black would come off if they rubbed our skin. Jesse Owens might have been snubbed by Hitler, but he was a hero in the eyes of the Germans. They followed him around the streets like he was the Pied Piper."

Contemporary Events, 1937 ■ Walt Disney's animated feature **Snow White and the Seven Dwarfs** premieres. ■ Amelia Earhart disappears while flying over the Pacific Ocean. ■ The **Hindenburg** dirigible explodes while attempting to land in Lakehurst, New Jersey.

Transport Service Employees of America. Willard S. Townsend (later the first vice president of the newly combined AFL-CIO) is elected president.

Among blacks, 26% of men and 33% of women are unemployed. Among whites, 18% of men and 24% of women are unemployed.

In southern states, 40% of African Americans over age 65 do not qualify for social security payments due to their low-paying employment history.

RELIGION AND EDUCATION

Issac Lane, a bishop of the Colored Methodist Episcopal Church and founder of Lane College in Tennessee, dies July 2.

LITERATURE AND JOURNALISM

Richard Wright assumes editorship of *Challenge* magazine, changes its title to *New Challenge*, and issues a manifesto calling for articles and fiction with more "social realism."

Zora Neale Hurston publishes her novel *Their Eyes Were Watching God*.

Waters Turpin's *These Low Grounds*, a fictional version of an African-American family chronicle, is published.

Sterling A. Brown's studies *The Negro in American Fiction* and *Negro Poetry and Drama* are published.

George W. Lee publishes his novel *River George*.

William Melvin Kelley, novelist and short-story writer, is born in New York City.

PERFORMING ARTS

The film company Negro Marches On is founded by Jack and David Goldberg to make movies for black audiences. It will have imitators over the next 15 years, but remain the largest and highest-quality production company of its kind.

Eddie "Rochester" Anderson makes his first appearance on Jack Benny's radio show.

Bessie Smith, "Empress of the Blues," dies September 26 in Clarksville, Mississippi, from injuries in an automobile accident. She is considered not only the greatest of the urban blues singers, but one of the great voices of modern times.

Nancy Wilson, jazz and pop singer, is born February 20 in Ohio.

TV and film actor Billy Dee Williams is born April 6 in New York. He will star in the movie *Lady Sings the Blues* and in two *Star Wars* films.

Entertainer William "Bill" Cosby is born July 12 in Philadelphia.

Actor Morgan Freeman is born June 1 in Greenwood, Mississippi. He will receive an Obie award and three Oscar nominations.

Woodie King, Jr., dramatist, critic, and producer, is born July 27 in Detroit. As artistic director of the New Federal Theater, he will adapt Langston Hughes's *Weary Blues* for the stage.

Jazz saxophonist Archie Shepp is born May 24 in Fort Lauderdale.

Olly Wilson, classical composer, is born September 7 in St. Louis.

VISUAL ARTS

Augusta Savage opens the Harlem Community Arts Center.

Self-taught sculptor William Edmondson is the first African American to have a solo show at New York's Museum of Modern Art.

Painter Henry Ossawa Tanner dies May 25 in Paris.

Sculptor Melvin Edwards is born May 4 in Houston.

THE MILITARY

Approximately 80 African Americans join voluntary American forces fighting on the Republican side of the Spanish Civil War. Oliver Law from Chicago gains fame as commander of the "Lincoln Brigade."

General Colin L. Powell is born April 5 in New York. He will become the first African-American chairman of the Joint Chiefs of Staff.

SPORTS

Joe Louis defeats James J. Braddock and becomes heavyweight boxing champion of the world.

1938

POLITICS AND CIVIL RIGHTS

There are six recorded lynchings.

Crystal Bird Fauset is the first African-American woman elected to serve in a state legislature, Pennsylvania's House of Representatives.

In Harlem, the Greater New York Coordinating Committee for Employment, chaired by Adam Clayton Powell, Jr., compels employers to hire staffs that are at least one-third African American and to provide equal advancement opportunities for blacks and whites.

Oliver Law and the Lincoln Brigade

The first group of 550 Americans to fight in the Spanish Civil War (on the Republican side, against the Fascists) formed the Lincoln Brigade. Only 10 were African American, but one became the brigade's leader in 1937: Oliver Law of Chicago, a career man in the U.S. Army. As far as military historians can establish, it was the first time a black American commanded a mostly white American military unit. Law was killed in action July 13, 1937. A total of about 80 African Americans joined the war effort, including Harry Heywood, who served as assistant commissar of the 15th Brigade; Milton Herndon of the U.S. Young Communist League, who was killed heading a machine-gun crew in 1937; and Solaria Kee, a nurse.

Contemporary Events, 1938 ■ Thornton Wilder wins the Pulitzer Prize for his play **Our Town.** ■ Orson Welles causes widespread panic with his realistic radio broadcast of H. G. Wells's **War of the Worlds.**

The NAACP appoints Thurgood Marshall special counsel for its legal cases.

Fortune magazine reports that 84.7% of African Americans support President Franklin D. Roosevelt.

Maynard Jackson is born March 23 in Dallas. He will be elected three times as mayor of Atlanta (1974, 1982, 1989).

Maxine Waters is born in St. Louis. She will become a U.S. representative from Los Angeles.

RELIGION AND EDUCATION

The U.S. Supreme Court rules that Missouri cannot compel Lloyd L. Gaines, an African-American law student, to attend an out-of-state school, but must supply equal educational facilities for blacks and whites within the state borders.

In Philadelphia, Marion Turner Stubbs founds Jack and Jill of America, Inc., an organization offering educational and cultural programs to African-American children. It will expand to 180 chapters across the country.

Historian and civil rights advocate Mary Frances Berry is born February 17 in Nashville. She will become chancellor of the University of Colorado and a member of the U.S. Commission on Civil Rights.

Niara Sudarkasa, educator and anthropologist, is born August 14 in Fort Lauderdale, Florida. She will become the first woman president of Lincoln University, Pennsylvania.

Theologian James Cone is born August 5 in Fordyce, Arkansas. He will become the major spokesperson for Black Theology.

LITERATURE AND JOURNALISM

Richard Wright's novel *Uncle Tom's Children* is published.

Poet and novelist Ishmael Reed is born February 22 in Chattanooga, Tennessee.

PERFORMING ARTS

For a performance of jazz at Carnegie Hall, white bandleader Benny Goodman overrides management's reservations and insists on having two black musicians in his group, Teddy Wilson (piano) and Lionel Hampton (vibraphone).

The musicians Meade Lux Lewis, Albert Ammons, and Pete Johnson perform at Carnegie Hall, starting a "Boogie-Woogie" craze.

Jazz singer Billie Holiday makes her first appearance with Artie Shaw's band.

Contralto Marian Anderson is awarded an honorary doctorate by Harvard University.

The Harlem Suitcase Theatre launches its first season with Langston Hughes's *Don't You Want to Be Free?*, starring Robert Earl Jones, father of actor James Earl Jones.

Joe "King" Oliver, pioneer jazz cornetist and bandleader, dies April 10 in Savannah, Georgia. He was an important early influence on Louis Armstrong and on the shape of early jazz.

Country singer Charley Pride is born March 18 in Mississippi.

Baritone Simon Estes, who will become known for singing lead roles in Wagnerian operas, is born February 2 in Centerville, Iowa.

Trumpeter and bandleader Frederick Dewayne Hubbard is born April 7 in Indianapolis. He will win a Grammy for his album *Straight Life*.

VISUAL ARTS

Jacob Lawrence completes his *Toussaint L'Ouverture* series, which will be exhibited in its own room at the 1939 Baltimore Museum show.

Horace Pippin's work is included in the show "Masters of Popular Painting—Artists of the People" at the Museum of Modern Art in New York.

Painter Emilio Cruz is born March 15 in New York.

SPORTS

Joe Louis retains his title as world heavyweight boxing champion by defeating German boxer Max Schmeling, a Nazi hero and proclaimed exemplar of Aryan superiority. Blacks and whites hail the match as a victory for democracy as well as for the black race.

Henry Armstrong wins both the welterweight and the lightweight boxing championship. Having already won the featherweight championship, he holds all three titles concurrently.

Basketball player Oscar "The Big O" Roberston is born November 24 in Charlotte, Tennessee. With Kareem Abdul-Jabbar, he will lead the Milwaukee Bucks to a 1971 NBA championship.

1939

POLITICS AND CIVIL RIGHTS

There are two recorded lynchings.

Jane Bolin is named to New York City's domestic relations court, the first African-American female judge.

Joe Louis

More than any other individual during the 1930s, Joe Louis was regarded by African Americans as a symbol of black power and achievement. He was born Joseph Louis Barrow May 13, 1914, in rural Alabama, where his parents were tenant farmers. When he was still a boy, he and his family moved to Detroit. He dropped out of school to start boxing and, after winning the national amateur light heavyweight championship in 1934, turned professional. In a 1936 match, he was knocked out by Max Schmeling, a German boxer who symbolized Aryan supremacy. It was a crushing defeat in the eyes of all Americans, black and white. A year later, however, Louis defeated James J. Braddock to become world heavyweight champion. In 1938 he fought Schmeling again and knocked him out in the first round, causing celebration across the country. Called the "Brown Bomber" by some of his fans, Louis successfully defended his title 24 times and retired undefeated in 1949. He fought 71 matches between 1934 and 1949 and won every match, except for his 1936 loss to Schmeling.

The NAACP creates the Legal Defense and Educational Fund to fight discriminatory laws throughout the United States. It is headed by Thurgood Marshall.

The New Jersey Supreme Court rules that segregation of New Jersey beaches is illegal.

In Miami, Florida, the Ku Klux Klan wages a strong but ultimately unsuccessful campaign to prevent African Americans from voting in a city election.

A back-to-Africa bill is introduced in the U.S. Senate by segregationist Senator Theodore C. Bilbo from Mississippi.

Activist Marion Wright Edelman, founder of the Children's Defense Fund, is born June 6 in Bennettsville, South Carolina.

BUSINESS AND EMPLOYMENT

There are nearly 30,000 black-owned retail stores and restaurants. They employ some 43,000 African Americans and generate about $71 million in sales (0.02% of total national sales).

The WPA employs, or provides relief for, over one million African Americans.

RELIGION AND EDUCATION

The NAACP initiates nine court cases claiming the right of African Americans to attend tax-supported colleges and universities in their home states.

Morgan State College is founded in Baltimore, developed from Morgan State Biblical College.

Of the 774 libraries in the 13 southern states, 99 admit African Americans.

Kelly Miller, dean of Howard University, dies December 29 in Washington, D.C.

LITERATURE AND JOURNALISM

Arna Bontemps publishes his historical novel about Haiti, *Drums at Dusk*.

Waters Turpin's novel *O, Canaan* is published.

Jay Saunders Redding's anthology of poems and essays *To Make a Poet Black* is published.

Contemporary Events, 1939 ■ The World's Fair opens in New York. ■ The United States declares its neutrality when war breaks out in Europe. ■ John Steinbeck's **The Grapes of Wrath** wins a Pulitzer Prize. ■ Pan-American Airways begins regularly scheduled commercial flights to Europe.

Toni Cade Bambara, author of the novels *Gorilla* and *The Salt Eaters*, is born March 25 in New York.

Writer and artist Barbara Chase-Riboud, author of *Sally Hemings,* is born June 26 in Philadelphia.

PERFORMING ARTS

Denied permission to sing in Washington, D.C.'s Constitution Hall by the Daughters of the American Revolution, contralto Marian Anderson performs April 9 on the steps of the Lincoln Memorial for 75,000 people.

On September 19, the Dixie Hummingbirds, a male gospel quartet, record for the first time.

Hollywood releases *Way Down South*, an interracial movie, written by Langston Hughes and starring Clarence Muse.

Ethel Waters stars as "Hagar" in the *Mamba's Daughters* on Broadway.

Singer Annie Mae Bullock is born November 26 in Tennessee. As Tina Turner, she will have a successful R&B career as lead singer in the Ike and Tina Turner Revue and, later, on her own.

Singer Marvin Gaye is born April 2 in Washington, D.C.

Pop singer Roberta Flack is born February 10 in Asheville, North Carolina. Her hits will include "The First Time Ever I Saw Your Face" and "Killing Me Softly with His Song."

VISUAL ARTS

The Baltimore Museum of Art mounts a major exhibition, "Contemporary Negro Art," featuring the works of Richmond Barthé, Aaron Douglas, Jacob Lawrence, and others.

Painter Hale Woodruff creates murals of the *Amistad* mutiny for Talladega College in Alabama and is named professor of art at Atlanta University.

Augusta Savage completes her sculpture *Lift Every Voice and Sing,* commissioned by the New York World's Fair.

Jerry Pinckney, children's book illustrator and postage stamp designer, is born December 22 in Philadelphia.

THE MILITARY

The U.S. Army includes 3,640 African-American men.

SPORTS

Jackie Robinson helps the UCLA football team score an undefeated season and, in the same year, is the top scorer in the Pacific Coast Conference for basketball.

"One of the Great Singers . . ."

Marian Anderson debuted with the New York Philharmonic in 1925. From 1930 to 1935, she performed in Europe, where concert opportunities were greater and racial discrimination less severe. Returning in triumph to the United States, she was signed by Sol Hurok to sing at Town Hall in New York on December 30, 1935. She was soon performing some 70 recitals annually across the United States. When Hurok tried to book her into Washington, D.C.'s Constitution Hall in 1939, the Daughters of the American Revolution, who owned the hall, told him all requested dates were taken. Later, posing as a white performer's agent, he was told those same dates were available. He publicly charged the DAR with prejudice. First Lady Eleanor Roosevelt resigned from the DAR in protest, and U.S. Secretary of the Interior Harold L. Ickes arranged for Anderson to sing on the steps of the Lincoln Memorial on Easter Sunday. Some 75,000 people attended the historic outdoor concert and millions more listened on national radio. Photographs and films of the event became potent symbols for the soon-to-emerge modern Civil Rights Movement.

1940

POLITICS AND CIVIL RIGHTS

There are four recorded lynchings.

The U.S. Supreme Court, in *Hansberry* v. *Lee*, rules that blacks cannot be restricted from buying homes in white neighborhoods.

Mass meetings, sponsored by African Americans of West Indian descent, are held in New York City to protest the transfer of the West Indian islands to the United States.

Pan-Africanist Marcus Garvey dies June 10 in London.

Only 5% of eligible African Americans in the South are registered to vote.

Activist Anne Moody, author of the autobiography *Coming of Age in Mississippi*, is born September 15 in Mississippi.

BUSINESS AND EMPLOYMENT

The U.S. Supreme Court upholds a New York law forbidding union discrimination.

Unemployment among U.S. blacks is 19.4% for men and 35.9% for women. Among whites, it is 12.4% for men and 23.8% for women.

RELIGION AND EDUCATION

In *Alston* v. *School Board of the City of Norfolk* (Virginia), a federal court rules that black and white teachers must receive equal pay.

Jesse E. Moorland, who worked on behalf of black YMCAs and donated his African-American library to Howard University, dies April 30 in Washington, D.C.

LITERATURE AND JOURNALISM

Richard Wright's novel *Native Son* is published.

Langston Hughes publishes *The Big Sea*.

Heart Shape in the Dusk, the first collection of poetry by Robert Hayden, is published.

Cultural critic Alain Locke publishes *The Negro in Art*.

Robert Sengstacke Abbott, newspaper editor and publisher of the *Chicago Defender*, dies February 29 in Chicago. His nephew, John

---

Contemporary Events, 1940 ■ Franklin D. Roosevelt is reelected to an unprecedented third term as president of the United States. ■ Ernest Hemingway's novel **For Whom the Bell Tolls** is published. ■ Hollywood releases Alfred Hitchcock's **Rebecca**.

Sengstacke, helps found the National Newspaper Publishers Association in Washington, D.C.

Bernard Shaw is born May 22 in Chicago. He will become one of the main anchors for Cable News Network.

SCIENCE AND TECHNOLOGY

Louis T. Wright is awarded the Spingarn Medal for his "contribution to the healing of mankind." He was the first African American surgeon at Harlem Hospital and chairman of the board of directors of the NAACP.

PERFORMING ARTS

Hattie McDaniel becomes the first African American to win an Academy Award for her role as "Mammy" in *Gone with the Wind*.

Frederick O'Neal, Abram Hill, and the Rose McClendon Players establish the American Negro Theatre in Harlem.

Theodore Ward's play *The Big White Fog* is produced at the Lincoln Theater in Harlem. *New York Times* critic Brooks Atkinson calls it "the best serious play by Negro authorship about race problems."

Ethel Waters and Todd Duncan star in *Cabin in the Sky* on Broadway.

Musicians like Dizzie Gillespie, Thelonius Monk, and Charlie Parker are playing "bop" music at Minton's Play House in Harlem.

The Cotton Club, Harlem nightspot famous for classic jazz, closes.

Singer "Little" Anthony Gourdine is born January 8 in Brooklyn.

William "Smokey" Robinson is born February 19. He will become lead singer for the R&B and pop group "The Miracles."

Dionne Warwick, popular singer of Burt Bacharach and Hal David songs, is born December 12 in East Orange, New Jersey.

Jazz composer and bandleader Herbie Hancock is born April 12 in Chicago.

Richard Pryor, comedian, recording artist, and movie star, is born December 1 in Peoria, Illinois.

VISUAL ARTS

Sargent Johnson creates his popular lithograph *Singing Saints*.

Elizabeth Catlett's *Mother and Child* wins first prize at the American Negro Exposition in Chicago.

Multimedia artist Lev T. Mills is born December 11 in Tallahassee, Florida. His work will include mosaics for the Atlanta subway system and the floor of Atlanta's City Hall.

Sculptor John T. Scott is born June 30 in New Orleans.

To Be or Not to Be

Hattie McDaniel was criticized by many blacks and liberal whites for playing a stereotypical black maid, "Mammy," in the 1939 movie **Gone with the Wind.** When she won an Academy Award for that role in 1940, the criticism escalated. A commentator in the black newspaper **Louisville Defender** said, "This award tells all Negro Americans, 'You just be Uncle Tom and we'll be nice to you.'" McDaniel's supporters countered that "Mammy" was not a stereotype but a strong, intelligent woman with an independent spirit. McDaniel herself had the final word, indicating, "I'd sure rather play a maid than be one."

Charles Drew

Charles Richard Drew's innovative work to develop systems for mass blood donation saved tens of thousands of lives during World War II. Prior to the war, he had established the first successful blood plasma bank at Presbyterian Hospital in New York. In 1940 Great Britain, already embroiled in the war, hired him to lead a mass-volume "plasma project" that became a model for blood banks throughout Europe. A year later, he was assigned to create a similar system for American GIs. Unfortunately, he had no control over segregation policies in the U.S. Armed Services, where blood collected from blacks—even his own blood—could not be transfused to whites.

THE MILITARY

The NAACP launches a campaign to desegregate the U.S. Armed Forces, sending a seven-point manifesto to President Roosevelt. Roosevelt promises to create more job opportunities for blacks in the army, but insists that troops will not be integrated because that would "produce situations destructive to morale."

Benjamin O. Davis, Sr., becomes a brigadier general in the U.S. Army, the highest rank held to date by an African American.

Among the 230,000 men in the army, fewer than 5,000 are black.

Brigadier general Sherian Grace Cadoria is born January 26 in Marksville, Louisiana.

SPORTS

Runner Wilma Rudolph is born June 23 in Clarksville, Tennessee. In Rome she will become the first American woman to win three gold medals in a single Olympics.

ADDITIONAL STATISTICS

The African-American population of the United States reaches 12,866,000, representing 9.8% of the total.

Life expectancy for U.S. men is 62.1 years for whites, 51.5 years for blacks; for U.S. women, 66.6 years for whites, 54.9 years for blacks.

ADDITIONAL EVENTS

The Booker T. Washington postage stamp is issued, the first stamp to honor an African American.

1941

POLITICS AND CIVIL RIGHTS

There are four recorded lynchings.

The U.S. Supreme Court rules that railroad accommodations must be "substantially equal" in quantity and quality for both blacks and whites.

Civil rights activist and presidential candidate Jesse Jackson is born October 8 in Greenville, South Carolina. He will found People to Save Humanity (PUSH) and form the Rainbow Coalition.

Contemporary Events, 1941 ■ Following the Japanese attack on Pearl Harbor, the United States declares war on Japan and, later, on Germany and Italy, bringing the United States into World War II.

BUSINESS AND EMPLOYMENT

A four-week boycott by African-American patrons forces New York City bus companies to begin hiring black drivers and mechanics.

The NAACP makes its strongest alliance with industrial labor unions to date by working with the striking United Auto Workers to secure equal rights for blacks at the Ford Motor Company.

RELIGION AND EDUCATION

Chester Lovelle Talton, first African-American Episcopal bishop in the West (Los Angeles), is born September 22 in Arkansas.

LITERATURE AND JOURNALISM

Sterling Brown publishes *Negro Caravan*, a major anthology of African-American writing.

John Edgar Wideman, author of the novels *Hurry Home* and *Philadelphia Fire*, is born June 14 in Washington, D.C.

Ed Bradley, Emmy-winning co-anchor of CBS's news program *60 Minutes*, is born June 22 in Philadelphia.

SCIENCE AND TECHNOLOGY

After having established a pioneer blood bank operation at New York City's Presbyterian Hospital, Charles R. Drew is named professor of surgery at Howard University. He establishes donor banks in many states to collect blood for the U.S. Armed Forces.

PERFORMING ARTS

Operatic coach Mary Caldwell Dawson and coloratura Lillian Evanti establish the National Negro Opera Company in Pittsburgh.

A dramatic version of Richard Wright's novel *Native Son* opens on Broadway.

At New York's Carnegie Hall, the *Cafe Society* concert features jazz performers Albert "Jug" Ammons, Hazel Scott, Art Tatum, and Lena Horne in her debut performance.

Natural Man by Theodore Browne becomes the first play produced by the American Negro Theatre in Harlem.

Duke Ellington's orchestra records "Take the 'A' Train" on February 15.

Dean Dixon conducts the New York Philharmonic.

Ferdinand "Jelly Roll" Morton, pianist and composer who claimed to have invented jazz, dies July 10 in Los Angeles.

Musician Otis Redding is born September 9 in Macon, Georgia.

Ernest Evans, who will gain rock 'n' roll fame as "Chubby Checker," father of the twist, is born October 3 in Philadelphia.

VISUAL ARTS

The groundbreaking exhibit "American Negro Art: 19th and 20th Century" opens at New York's Downtown Gallery.

Fortune magazine publishes 26 of Jacob Lawrence's panels for his *Migrants* series.

Charles White paints his mural *Five Great American Negroes* for the Chicago Public Library.

THE MILITARY

A. Philip Randolph threatens to organize a mass march on Washington, D.C., protesting discrimination in the military and in the defense industry. After government pressure fails to change Randolph's plans, President Roosevelt issues Executive Order 8802, banning federal discrimination, and the march is cancelled.

On the USS *Arizona* Dorie Miller, a Navy messman with no weapons training downs four Japanese fighter planes during the attack on Pearl Harbor. He is later awarded the Navy Cross.

The 99th Pursuit Squadron, the first all-black unit of the army air corps, is formed in Tuskegee, Alabama. It will fly more than 500 missions during one year of World War II, before being joined with the 332nd Fighter Group.

At Freeman Field, Indiana, over 100 African-American military officers are locked in the stockade after entering a whites-only officers' club.

1942

POLITICS AND CIVIL RIGHTS

There are six recorded lynchings.

James Farmer and students at the University of Chicago form the Congress of Racial Equality (CORE), a nonviolent protest group based on Gandhi's principles of passive resistance.

A riot erupts in Detroit when 1,200 whites bearing knives, clubs, and firearms try to prevent three black families from moving into the

---

Contemporary Events, 1942 ■ The U.S. government places over 100,000 Japanese Americans living on the West Coast in inland labor camps. ■ General Douglas MacArthur is appointed Commander in Chief in the Far East. ■ The first computer is developed in the United States.

new 200-unit Sojourner Truth Settlement, designated as black housing by the U.S. Housing Authority. After scores of injuries and arrests, occupancy is postponed.

William L. Dawson of Chicago is elected to the U.S. House of Representatives. He will serve in that body until 1970, earning the title "Dean of Black Congressmen."

Activist Stokely Carmichael, later known as Kwame Toure, is born in Trinidad. He will coin the expression "Black Power" in 1966.

BUSINESS AND EMPLOYMENT

Richard Parsons is born April 4 in New York. He will become CEO of Dime Savings Bank.

The *Booker T. Washington* is launched at Wilmington, Delaware, commanded by Hugh Mulzac, the first African-American captain of a U.S. merchant ship.

RELIGION AND EDUCATION

Historian Nell I. Painter is born August 2 in Houston.

LITERATURE AND JOURNALISM

The Department of Justice threatens to sue several African-American newspapers for sedition because they have attacked the government's racial policies in the military. The NAACP prevents the suits by issuing editorial guidelines that appease department officials.

John H. Johnson publishes *Negro Digest* in Chicago. He will later add *Ebony* and *Jet* to his publishing empire.

Langston Hughes's book of poems *Shakespeare in Harlem* appears.

Margaret Walker wins the Yale University Younger Poets Award for her collection *For My People*.

Poet and literary critic Don Lee, later known as Haki Madhubuti, is born February 23. He will found the Third World Press.

PERFORMING ARTS

NAACP president Walter White meets with heads of the Hollywood movie studios to complain about the perpetuation of negative black stereotypes in American films.

On October 24, *Billboard*, the major newspaper of the music industry, begins a new feature, "Harlem Hit Parade," a sales and popularity ratings chart devoted to black recordings. In 1949 the feature will be renamed "Rhythm and Blues." In 1969 it will be called "Soul Music" and in 1982 renamed "Black Music." In 1990 the chart will again be called "Rhythm and Blues."

Blues and gospel singer Aretha Franklin, who will earn the title "Queen of Soul," is born March 25 in Memphis.

Nicholas Ashford is born May 4 in Fairfield, South Carolina. In collaboration with his wife, Valerie Simpson, he will become a hit songwriter ("Ain't No Mountain High Enough") and performer.

Issac Hayes, singer and composer of the award-winning score for the movie *Shaft*, is born August 20 in Covington, Tennessee.

Rock guitarist and vocalist Johnny "Jimi" Hendrix is born November 27 in Seattle.

Singer and songwriter Curtis Mayfield is born June 3 in Chicago.

Musician "Taj Mahal" is born May 17 in New York.

VISUAL ARTS

Atlanta University begins its annual show of African-American art.

THE MILITARY

In Fort Huachuca, Arizona, the U.S. Army establishes the 93rd Infantry, the first African-American division created during World War II. It is sent on combat duty to the South Pacific.

In the South Pacific, General Douglas MacArthur is one of the few army generals to accept black troops for combat duty. Most generals dissolve black combat units or reassign them to service duty.

Bernard W. Robinson, a medical student at Harvard University, becomes an ensign in the Naval Reserve, making him the first African American to receive a commission in the U.S. Navy.

African-American women are declared eligible to join the newly formed Women's Army Auxiliary Corps.

Almost 500,000 African Americans are now in the army. However, only 4.8% of the combat units are black, compared to 20.7% of the service units. In the navy, blacks are only allowed to serve on-shore.

SPORTS

Cassius Marcellus Clay, Jr., is born January 17 in Louisville, Kentucky. Later known as Muhammad Ali, he will become one of the most popular world heavyweight boxing champions in history.

1943

POLITICS AND CIVIL RIGHTS

There are three recorded lymchings.

African Americans in Detroit riot to protest their exclusion from civilian defense-related jobs. Federal troops are summoned after 34 people are killed.

In a Mobile, Alabama, shipyard, the assignment of black welders to work alongside white welders triggers a riot causing extensive property damage and injury. The shipyard remains closed until Governor Chauncey Sparks orders 7,000 black workers at the shipyard and elsewhere to stay home for the day.

A riot erupts in Harlem after a white policeman shoots a black soldier. Five African Americans are killed and hundreds wounded. Figures for property damage run into several million dollars.

CORE conducts its first sit-in to protest segregation at a restaurant in Chicago.

Edwin Barclay, president of Liberia, visits President Roosevelt at the White House. It is the first official visit by an African head of state to an American president.

H. Rap Brown, chairman of the Student Nonviolent Coordinating Committee (SNCC), is born October 4 in Baton Rouge.

Faye Wattleton, president of Planned Parenthood, is born July 8 in St. Louis.

BUSINESS AND EMPLOYMENT

Eta Phi Beta, national professional sorority for businesswomen, is founded in Detroit.

Through various constitutional and organizational maneuvers, 30 AFL unions deny membership to African Americans, including the unions for airline pilots, plumbers, railroad telegraphers, and glassworkers.

LITERATURE AND JOURNALISM

The *Sun-Reporter* is started in San Francisco.

Artist and art historian James A. Porter publishes *Modern Negro Art*.

Poet Nikki Giovanni is born June 7 in Knoxville.

Poet and biographer Quincy Troupe is born July 23.

SCIENCE AND TECHNOLOGY

George Washington Carver, scientist, teacher, and nutritionist, dies January 5 in Tuskegee, Alabama.

"We Who Have Known Deprivation . . ."

On September 9, 1943, Lester B. Granger of the National Urban League sent a contribution from a committee of 77 African Americans to the United Jewish Appeal. Here is an excerpt from the letter he wrote to accompany the contribution:

"We who have known deprivation and suffering in our native land, America, stand aghast at the maniacal fury and bestial atrocities practiced against the Jewish people by Hitler and his foul associates. Those crimes of Nazi leadership constitute one further reason why Negroes must remain wholeheartedly committed to this war until the last vestige of Nazism is driven from the earth."

Contemporary Events, 1943 ■ President Roosevelt meets with Winston Churchill at the Casablanca Conference in Morocco. ■ Richard Rodgers and Oscar Hammerstein's musical **Oklahoma** opens on Broadway. ■ A "jitterbug" craze, based on a black dance, sweeps the United States.

PERFORMING ARTS

Hollywood releases *Panama Hattie,* with Lena Horne in her first important movie role; *Stormy Weather,* starring Lena Horne, Fats Waller, Cab Calloway, and Bill Robinson; and *Cabin in the Sky,* featuring Eddie Robinson, Ethel Waters, Duke Ellington, and Louis Armstrong.

Othello opens on Broadway with Paul Robeson in the title role. It runs 296 performances, a record for a Shakespeare play.

The all-black musical *Carmen Jones,* with Muriel Rahn and Muriel Smith alternating in the title role, opens on Broadway.

Fats Waller, pianist and composer ("Ain't Misbehavin'," "Honeysuckle Rose," and "Stormy Weather"), dies December 15 in Kansas City, Missouri.

Jazz guitarist and vocalist George Benson is born March 22 in Pittsburgh.

Singer and actress Leslie Uggams is born May 25 in New York City.

Singer and dancer Lola Falana is born September 11 in Philadelphia.

VISUAL ARTS

Selma Burke designs the portrait of Franklin Roosevelt that is used in minting the dime.

Artist Howardena Pindell is born April 14 in Philadelphia.

Fashion designer Stephen Burrows is born September 15 in Newark, New Jersey.

THE MILITARY

William Hastie, a former federal judge and law school dean, resigns his position as aide to U.S. Secretary of War Henry Stimson to protest discriminatory practices in the armed forces. He later wins the NAACP's Spingarn Medal.

The 99th Pursuit Squadron performs its first combat mission by attacking Axis forces on the Italian island of Pantelleria.

The navy launches the destroyer escort USS *Harmon,* named for Mess Attendant First Class Leonard Harmon, recipient of the Navy Cross.

African-American women are eligible to join the newly formed Women's Naval Corp (WAVES).

SPORTS

Tennis star Arthur Ashe, the first African American to win the men's singles at the U.S. Open and Wimbledon, is born April 10 in Richmond, Virginia.

Chicago Bears running back Gale Sayers is born May 30 in Wichita. He will be the youngest player elected to the Football Hall of Fame.

1944

POLITICS AND CIVIL RIGHTS

The U.S. Supreme Court, in *Smith* v. *Allwright,* rules that African Americans cannot be excluded from voting in primary elections.

Minister and civil rights activist Adam Clayton Powell, Jr., is elected to the U.S. House of Representatives from Harlem, the first African-American representative from the Northeast.

Activist Angela Davis is born January 26 in Birmingham, Alabama.

Sharon Pratt Dixon Kelly is born January 30 in Washington, D.C. In 1990 she will become the capital's first woman mayor.

BUSINESS AND EMPLOYMENT

The CIO under the leadership of Sidney Hillman begins integrating African-American workers into its political structure.

When the Fair Employment Practices Commission, a federal agency, directs the Philadelphia Transportation Company to hire African Americans, 4,500 white employees strike in protest. Rioting breaks out in many areas of the city, prompting President Roosevelt to order an army takeover of the Philadelphia transit system and to announce his personal support of the commission's directive.

RELIGION AND EDUCATION

The United Negro College Fund is founded by Frederick Douglass Patterson, president of Tuskegee Institute, to coordinate fund-raising efforts for historically black private colleges.

LITERATURE AND JOURNALISM

Harry S. McAlpin, reporter for Atlanta's *Daily World,* becomes the first African American given credentials to attend White House press conferences.

Frank Yerby wins the O. Henry Award for his first published short story, "Health Card."

Poet Melvin P. Tolson publishes a collection, *Rendezvous with America.*

Contemporary Events, 1944 ■ Franklin Delano Roosevelt is elected to his fourth term as president of the United States. ■ General George Patton leads U.S. forces across France, routing the Germans. ■ Tennessee Williams completes his first play, **The Glass Menagerie.**

Novelist, poet, and essayist Alice Walker is born February 9 in Eaton-ton, Georgia. She will win the American Book Award and the Pulit-zer Prize for her novel *The Color Purple*.

PERFORMING ARTS

The NAACP bestows its first awards to motion picture actors whose roles advance the image of African Americans. Among the recipients are Rex Ingram for *Sahara*, Lena Horne for *As Thousands Cheer*, and Dooley Wilson for *Casablanca*.

The play *Anna Lucasta*, starring Hilda Simms and Frederick O'Neal, opens on Broadway.

Dancer Pearl Primus makes her Broadway debut in a show combining African and traditional American dance patterns.

Singer Diana Ross is born March 26 in Detroit.

Singer Patricia Louise Holte, better known as "Patti LaBelle," is born May 24 in Philadelphia.

Singer Gladys Knight is born May 28 in Atlanta.

VISUAL ARTS

Printmaker Stephanie Pogue is born September 27 in Shelby, North Carolina.

THE MILITARY

The 92nd Division of the U.S. Army becomes the first African-American unit sent into combat duty in Europe.

The 761st Tank Battalion plays a major role in the D-Day invasion in Normandy. It is the first African-American armored unit in combat.

At Anzio Beach, Italy, the 387th Separate Engineer Battalion, consisting of 500 African Americans, engages in heavy combat, even though it is not a combat unit. Fifteen men die and 61 are seriously injured. Three members are later awarded Silver Stars for gallantry.

The War Department calls for an end to segregation in U.S. Army recreation and transportation facilities. The announcement is met with widespread white protest and noncompliance.

The U.S. Navy removes restrictions that prevent African Americans from serving at sea. It also begins allowing African Americans into the Marine Corps and the Coast Guard, and starts integrating its training, mess, and recreational facilities.

In Port Chicago, California, the explosion of an ammunitions depot kills 320 navy men, including 202 African Americans. When 258 African Americans subsequently refuse to work at the depot, the "Port Chicago Mutiny" trial is held. Fifty African Americans are convicted.

EXPLORATION

Congress awards Matthew Henson a medal for his participation with Commander Robert Peary on the 1909 expedition to the North Pole. It is the first official recognition of Henson's contribution.

SPORTS

Bob Montgomery wins the world lightweight boxing championship. He will hold the title through 1947.

POLITICS AND CIVIL RIGHTS

There are seven recorded lynchings.

The NAACP sends a representative to the United Nations conference in San Francisco to propose the abolition of colonialism throughout the world.

Congress refuses to fund the Fair Employment Practices Commission, thereby discontinuing it.

Ralph Bunche is appointed division head in the U.S. Department of State.

President Harry S Truman names Irwin C. Mollison to the U.S. Customs Court.

In New York, the legislature creates the State Commission Against Discrimination, the first such state commission in U.S. history.

Kathleen Cleaver, who will later become the highest-ranking woman in the Black Panther Party, is born May 13 in Dallas.

Jewell Jackson McCabe is born August 2 in Washington, D.C. As president of the Coalition of 100 Black Women, she will build a network among leading African-American women.

RELIGION AND EDUCATION

In Gary, Indiana, 1,000 white students in public schools boycott classes to protest racial integration.

LITERATURE AND JOURNALISM

Richard Wright's autobiographical novel *Black Boy* is published.

Chester Himes publishes his first novel, *If He Hollers Let Him Go.*

Contemporary Events, 1945 ■ President Franklin D. Roosevelt dies, and Vice President Harry S Truman assumes the presidency. ■ The United States drops atomic bombs on Hiroshima and Nagasaki, killing or wounding over 200,000 people.

Battles on the Home Front

World War II meant many new unskilled labor opportunities in defense-related industries, most of which were based in northern and western cities. Poor blacks from the South migrated to these areas in record numbers. In the years between 1941 and 1945, more than 50,000 African Americans moved to Detroit alone. Many white residents of these northern and western cities resented black competition for jobs, but also opposed black families living in their neighborhoods and seeking admission to public schools. The result was a dramatic increase throughout northern and western cities in the number and intensity of white race riots.

Gwendolyn Brooks publishes her first collection of poems, *A Street in Bronzeville*.

The first issue of *Ebony* magazine is published by John H. Johnson in Chicago.

Stanley Crouch, poet and *Village Voice* journalist, is born December 14 in Los Angeles.

PERFORMING ARTS

Todd Duncan debuts as "Tonio" in the New York City Opera's production of *Il Pagliacci*, making him the first African American to sing a leading role with a major U.S. opera company.

Sarah Vaughan makes her first record, "I'll Wait and Pray," with Billy Eckstine.

Freda Payne, pop singer famous for the hit "Band of Gold," is born September 19 in Detroit.

Donny Hathaway is born October 1 in Chicago. He will become a major R&B recording artist during the 1970s.

VISUAL ARTS

The Albany, New York, Institute of History and Art holds a major exhibit, "The Negro Artist Comes of Age: A National Survey of Contemporary American Artists."

The documentary *We've Come a Long Way*, charting the progress of African Americans in U.S. history, is released.

Photographer Anthony Bonair is born March 7 in Trinidad.

Photographer Fern Logan is born July 7 in Jamaica, New York. Her *Artists Portrait Series* will feature images of African-American artists.

THE MILITARY

By the end of World War II in August, when the Japanese surrender, over a million African Americans have served in the U.S. Armed Forces. The U.S. Navy has about 165,000 African-American men. Only 53 are officers, and 95% are messmen, due to discrimination that prevents them from filling other roles.

Colonel Benjamin O. Davis, Jr., assumes command of Godman Field in Kentucky, becoming the first African American to command an air force base.

The Army Nurse Corps begins admitting black nurses after protests from the National Association of Colored Nursing Graduates.

On March 8, Phyllis Mae Daley becomes the first African American to receive a commission from the U.S. Navy Nurse Corps.

SPORTS

The Brooklyn Dodgers hire Jackie Robinson and send him to their top farm club, the Montreal Royals.

Walt Frazier, basketball player for the New York Knicks, is born March 29 in Atlanta.

1946

POLITICS AND CIVIL RIGHTS

There are six recorded lynchings.

President Truman creates the Presidential Committee on Civil Rights to study federal policies and practices affecting civil rights.

As the first African-American governor of the Virgin Islands, William Hastie becomes the first African American to govern a U.S. state or territory since Reconstruction.

The U.S. Supreme Court, in *Morgan* v. *Commonwealth of Virginia*, rules that segregation in interstate bus travel is unconstitutional.

A federal district court rules against an amendment to the Alabama state constitution that calls for a literacy test to limit African-American voter registration.

In Columbia, Tennessee, a race riot ends in two deaths and a number of serious injuries.

Thurgood Marshall is awarded the Spingarn Medal for his "distinguished service as a lawyer."

BUSINESS AND EMPLOYMENT

Anthony Overton, prominent cosmetics manufacturer, banker, and publisher, dies in Chicago.

RELIGION AND EDUCATION

Mississippi Valley State University is established in Itta Bena.

LITERATURE AND JOURNALISM

Frank Yerby's novel *The Foxes of Harrow* is published and becomes a nationwide bestseller.

Ann Petry publishes her novel *The Street,* which will sell over a million copies.

Contemporary Events, 1946 ■ British Prime Minister Winston Churchill delivers his "Iron Curtain" speech in Fulton, Missouri. ■ Benjamin Spock publishes his best-selling **Common Sense Book of Baby and Child Care.**

Poet Owen Dodson publishes his collection *Powerful Long Ladder*.

Poet Countee Cullen dies January 10 in New York.

SCIENCE AND TECHNOLOGY

The American Nurses Association begins admitting African-American nurses, allowing them to join the national organization if the local chapter refuses membership.

Charles F. Bolden, Jr., astronaut on several space missions, including the 1992 voyage of the space shuttle *Atlantis,* is born August 19 in Columbia, South Carolina.

PERFORMING ARTS

The musical *St. Louis Woman*, featuring Pearl Bailey, opens on Broadway. Bailey later wins the Donaldson award for the most promising new performer.

Ruby Dee debuts in the Broadway play *Jeb.*

Abram Hill's *Walk Hard,* starring Maxwell Glanville, opens in Harlem and moves to Broadway.

Jazz singer Sarah Vaughan wins *Downbeat* magazine's Female Vocalist of the Year Award. She will continue to win this award every year through 1952.

Jazz pianist Erroll Garner records "Laura," which will sell half a million copies.

Tap dancer and actor Gregory Hines is born February 14 in New York City.

Al Green, soul, pop, and gospel singer, is born April 13 in Arkansas.

Actress Marla Gibbs, known for her roles on TV in *The Jeffersons* and *227,* is born June 14 in Chicago.

Ben Vereen, dancer, singer, and actor, is born October 10 in Miami.

VISUAL ARTS

In Brussels, Josef Nassy, a Dutch-born African-American artist, exhibits work he made while held in a Nazi concentration camp.

THE MILITARY

Only 1 of 776 generals in the U.S. Army is an African American; only 7 of 5,200 colonels are African Americans; and only 818 of 22,672 second lieutenants are African Americans.

SPORTS

Joe Louis successfully defends his world heavyweight boxing championship for the 23rd time.

Boxer Jack Johnson dies in Raleigh, North Carolina. In 1908 he became the first African-American heavyweight boxing champion.

Reginald "Reggie" Jackson, star baseball player for the Oakland A's and the New York Yankees, is born May 18 in Pennsylvania.

ADDITIONAL EVENTS

Emma Clarissa Clement, mother of Rufus E. Clement, president of Atlanta University, becomes the first African-American woman to be named "Mother of the Year" by the Golden Rule Foundation.

1947

POLITICS AND CIVIL RIGHTS

The NAACP claims that 1946 was "one of the grimmest years" in African-American history, with "blowtorch killing and eye-gouging of Negro veterans freshly returned from a war to end torture and racial extermination."

The NAACP submits to the United Nations a scathing report on racism, "Statement on the Denial of Human Rights to Minorities in the Case of Citizens of Negro Descent in the U.S.A."

The President's Committee on Civil Rights issues a study, "To Secure These Rights," that condemns racial discrimination and prejudice in the United States.

The U.S. Supreme Court, in the case of *United Public Workers* v. *Mitchell*, rules against discrimination in the federal civil service.

To test compliance with the 1946 Supreme Court ban on segregating interstate buses, CORE sends the first bus of black and white "Freedom Riders" on a trip through the South.

The Southern Regional Council reports that only 12% (around 600,000) of African Americans living in the South are eligible to register to vote. Statistics from Louisiana, Alabama, and Mississippi show that not even 3% are eligible.

Carol Moseley Braun is born August 16. She will be the first black woman elected to the U.S. Senate.

RELIGION AND EDUCATION

In St. Louis, Archbishop Joseph E. Ritter threatens to excommuni-

---

Contemporary Events, 1947 ■ Thanks to grants offered under the GI Bill of Rights, over one million World War II veterans enter college. ■ U.S. Secretary of State George Marshall announces a massive aid program to help Europe recover from World War II. It becomes known as the Marshall Plan.

cate any Roman Catholic who protests against the integration of parochial schools.

Texas Southern University is founded in Houston.

LITERATURE AND JOURNALISM

John Hope Franklin publishes the first edition of his historical study *From Slavery to Freedom*.

Langston Hughes publishes his collection of poems *Fields of Wonder*.

Willard Motley's novel *Knock on Any Door* is published.

Science fiction writer Octavia E. Butler is born June 22 in California.

SCIENCE AND TECHNOLOGY

Percy Julian, research chemist, is awarded the Spingarn Medal for pioneering work in the area of human reproduction.

PERFORMING ARTS

Langston Hughes writes the lyrics for Kurt Weill's work *Street Scene*, which opens on Broadway.

Theodore Ward's play *Our Lan'* opens on Broadway.

In a concert at Town Hall in New York City, Dizzy Gillespie introduces Afro-Cuban drummer Chano Pozo, inspiring widespread enthusiasm for Afro-Cuban-flavored jazz.

VISUAL ARTS

Palmer C. Hayden completes his *John Henry* series of paintings, which are shown in New York City.

Artist and photographer Harrison Branch is born in New York City.

SPORTS

Jackie Robinson signs a professional baseball contract April 11, becoming the first African American to play for a major league club, the Brooklyn Dodgers. Other blacks hired by major league clubs during the year include Larry Doby by the Cleveland Indians, Dan Bankhead by the Brooklyn Dodgers, and Willard Brown and Henry Thompson by the St. Louis Browns.

Ferdinand Lewis Alcindor, Jr., later known as Kareem Abdul-Jabbar, is born April 16 in New York. A star basketball player for UCLA, the Milwaukee Bucks, and the Los Angeles Lakers, he will become the leading scorer in the National Basketball Association.

ADDITIONAL STATISTICS

Average annual income among American men is $2,357 for whites and $1,279 for blacks; among American women, $1,269 for whites and $432 for blacks.

1948

POLITICS AND CIVIL RIGHTS

President Harry S Truman calls upon the U.S. Congress to pass civil rights legislation, with antilynching, fair employment, and anti-poll-tax provisions.

President Truman signs Executive Order 9981 calling for an end to segregation and discrimination in the armed forces and all other areas of federal employment.

The U.S. Supreme Court, in the case *Shelley* v. *Kraemer*, rules that courts cannot uphold segregation clauses in housing covenants.

A federal district court rules that the Democratic Party of South Carolina cannot require members to take an oath upholding segregation and opposing fair employment practices. This oath had effectively prevented African Americans from joining.

The California Supreme Court rules that the state's miscegenation law is unconstitutional.

Attempts by African Americans to vote stir a wave of violence in the South. In Montgomery, Georgia, NAACP President D. V. Carter is beaten for leading African Americans to the polls. In Vidalia, Georgia, Richard Mallard is lynched for voting. At Tougaloo College in Mississippi, William Bender is held prisoner at gunpoint to keep him from voting.

The newly formed Progressive Party, which nominates Henry Wallace for president, makes an effort to enlist African-American support. It fails, but compels the Democratic Party to be more responsive to black issues.

When the Democratic National Convention adopts a civil rights plank, several Alabama, Mississippi, and South Carolina delegates walk out. They form the nucleus of the States' Rights or "Dixiecrat" Party, which nominates Strom Thurmond for president and wins four states in the national election.

Ralphe Bunche is appointed chief assistant to the UN mediator in Palestine.

Ralph J. Bunche

In 1948, when Ralph Bunche was appointed chief assistant to the United Nations mediator in the Palestine crisis, it was the turning point of an outstanding career in international statesmanship. Two years later, he won the Nobel Peace Prize for arranging an Arab-Israeli cease-fire, becoming the first African American to win this award. He was acclaimed throughout the world and welcomed as a hero when he returned to the United States.

Bunche was born August 7, 1904, in Detroit and educated at UCLA and Harvard, where he received a doctorate. During World War II, he was assigned to the African section of the Office of Strategic Services and helped draw up boundary lines for the new postwar territories and trusteeships that emerged in Africa. He became undersecretary for special political affairs at the United Nations in 1955 and undersecretary-general in 1967, playing a significant role in molding that organization. He died in 1971, only a few weeks after he retired from the UN.

Contemporary Events, 1948 ■ Democratic nominee Harry S Truman upsets favored Republican nominee Thomas E. Dewey to become president of the United States. ■ Alfred Kinsey's landmark study **Sexual Behavior in the Human Male** is published. ■ The long-playing record is invented.

William T. Coleman is appointed clerk to the U.S. Supreme Court, the first African American to be so honored.

RELIGION AND EDUCATION

The U.S. Supreme Court, in the case *Sipuel* v. *Oklahoma State Board of Regents,* rules that a state must afford African Americans "equal opportunity" to study law at a state institution.

The University of Arkansas opens its professional schools to African-American students.

LITERATURE AND JOURNALISM

Jonathan Henderson Brooks's collection *The Resurrection and Other Poems* is published posthumously.

Writer Ntozake Shange is born October 18 in Trenton, New Jersey.

Bryant Gumbel is born September 29 in New Orleans. He will join NBC's *Today Show* and become the first African-American co-anchor of a national network morning news program.

PERFORMING ARTS

Actors Equity and the League of New York Theaters combine to boycott the National Theater in Washington, D.C., for practicing racial discrimination. The theater closes and will remain closed for five years.

Oscar Micheaux releases his last film, *The Betrayal.*

Fashion model Naomi Sims is born March 30 in Oxford, Mississippi.

Soprano Kathleen Battle is born August 13 in Portsmouth, Ohio.

Singer and actor Nell Carter is born September 13 in Alabama.

Singer Donna Summer, known as "Queen of Disco," is born December 31 in Boston.

VISUAL ARTS

Willi Smith, fashion designer and creator of "Willi Wear Ltd.," is born April 29 in Philadelphia.

THE MILITARY

First Lieutenant Nancy Leftenant is the first African American to be admitted into the regular army nursing corps.

SPORTS

Charles Fonville breaks the world record for the shotput.

In the London Olympics, Alice Coachman wins a gold medal for the high jump, becoming the first African-American woman to earn an

Olympic gold medal. Other gold medalists include Harrison Dillard (100-meter dash), Mal Whitfield (800-meter run), and William Steele (long jump).

Joe Louis retires from boxing after fighting 25 championship bouts since 1937.

Of all the boxers listed in *Ring* magazine's directory, almost one-half are African Americans.

ADDITIONAL EVENTS

Botanist George Washington Carver is honored on a postage stamp.

POLITICS AND CIVIL RIGHTS

Federal legislation takes effect prohibiting racial discrimination in the federal civil service.

New Jersey becomes the first state to end discrimination in all public accommodations. Later in the year, Connecticut follows suit, and also becomes the first state to legislate against discrimination in public housing.

Congressman William L. Dawson assumes the chair of the House Expenditures Committee, becoming the first African American to chair a standing congressional committee.

African Americans form the Atlanta Negro Voters' League to focus the black vote on candidates favorable to black issues.

CORE organizes a sit-in campaign to protest segregated public accommodations in St. Louis.

In a closely watched New Jersey trial, six African-American men, the "Trenton Six," are convicted on questionable evidence of murdering a white man. The NAACP successfully files suit for a retrial.

RELIGION AND EDUCATION

The U.S. Supreme Court rules that the University of Kentucky must allow African Americans into its graduate school.

LITERATURE AND JOURNALISM

Writer Jamaica Kincaid is born May 25 in Antigua.

Contemporary Events, 1949 ■ William Faulkner wins the Nobel Prize for literature. ■ The North Atlantic Treaty Organization (NATO) is established. This event and the first testing of an atomic bomb by the USSR spark much discussion of a new "cold war" between the Soviets and the Western world.

SCIENCE AND TECHNOLOGY

Peter Murray Marshall of New York City is appointed to the American Medical Association's House of Delegates.

PERFORMING ARTS

Hollywood releases several films with strong appeals for racial tolerance, including *Intruder in the Dust* and *Home of the Brave*.

The first African-American-owned radio station, WERD in Atlanta, begins broadcasting.

William Grant Still's opera *Troubled Island* premieres at the New York City Opera, and Robert McFadden debuts in the starring role. It is the first opera written by an African American to be performed by a major opera company.

On Broadway, Juanita Hall plays "Bloody Mary" in *South Pacific*. For this role, she will be the first African American to win a Tony Award.

An outdoor singing performance by Paul Robeson in Westchester County, New York, turns into a riot triggered by agitators protesting Robeson's affiliation with the Communist Party. A later concert scheduled in nearby Peekskill is also disrupted by rioting.

Singer and songwriter Lionel Richie is born June 20 in Alabama.

Comedian and actress Caryn Johnson, better known as Whoopi Goldberg, is born November 13 in New York.

VISUAL ARTS

Robert Blackburn founds the Printmaking Workshop in New York.

THE MILITARY

Wesley A. Brown is the first African American to graduate from the U.S. Naval Academy at Annapolis.

African Americans represent 9.6% of enlistees and 1.7% of officers in the army, 4.5% of enlistees and less than 0.5% of officers in the navy, 2.1% of enlistees and less than 0.5% of officers in the marines, and 5.1% of enlistees and 0.06% of officers in the air force.

SPORTS

Jackie Robinson of the Brooklyn Dodgers becomes the National League batting champion (.342 average) and is named the National League's Most Valuable Player.

The Dayton (Ohio) Rens, formerly based in New York, play their last basketball game, against the Denver Nuggets.

Ezzard Charles defeats "Jersey" Joe Walcott to become heavyweight boxing champion of the world.

1950

POLITICS AND CIVIL RIGHTS

The National Emergency Civil Rights Conference is held in Washington, D.C., attracting over 4,000 delegates from 100 national organizations.

Ralph Bunche becomes the first African American to receive the Nobel Peace Prize. It is awarded for his achievement as a United Nations mediator in Palestine.

In *Henderson* v. *the United States* the Supreme Court rules that dining cars on interstate trains cannot be segregated.

Edith Sampson becomes the first African American to serve on the U.S. delegation to the United Nations.

The NAACP launches an investigation of Communist activity within its ranks. As a result, charters of some branches or groups are withdrawn, and new anti-Communist branches or groups are chartered to replace them.

RELIGION AND EDUCATION

The U.S. Supreme Court orders law schools at the University of Texas, University of Virginia, and Louisiana State University to admit African-American students. It also declares that the University of Oklahoma cannot segregate a black student within the school.

The James Weldon Johnson Collection, featuring the papers of many of the leading writers in the Harlem Renaissance, is created at Yale University by Carl Van Vechten.

Carter G. Woodson, the "Father of Black History," dies April 3 in Washington, D.C.

LITERATURE AND JOURNALISM

Poet Gwendolyn Brooks is the first African American to win a Pulitzer Prize, for her book *Annie Allen*.

William Demby's novel *Battlecreek*, about a white man's doomed efforts to be accepted by the local black community, is published.

Writer Gloria Naylor is born January 25 in Brooklyn, New York.

Cultural critic Henry Louis Gates, Jr., is born September 16 in Keyser, West Virginia.

Contemporary Events, 1950 ■ Senator Joseph McCarthy accuses the State Department of being riddled with Communist sympathizers and urges Congress to pass the McCarran Act, restricting Communist activity. ■ North Korean forces invade South Korea, beginning the Korean War.

SCIENCE AND TECHNOLOGY

African-American delegates are seated at the American Medical Association's national convention for the first time.

Charles Drew, hematologist and blood bank pioneer, is killed in an automobile accident on April 1 in Washington, D.C.

Alexa Canady, the first African-American female neurosurgeon, is born November 7 in Lansing, Michigan.

PERFORMING ARTS

The Council on Harlem Theater is formed to support black playwrights and actors. Among the plays it helps to produce are Julian Mayfield's *The Other Foot* and Ossie Davis's *Alice in Wonderland*.

Ethel Waters stars in *Member of the Wedding* on Broadway.

Composer Howard Swanson's *Short Symphony* is performed by the New York Philharmonic.

Jazz musician Bobby McFerrin, most famous for his 1989 Grammy winner, "Don't Worry, Be Happy," is born March 11 in New York.

Steveland Judkins Morris, the singer better known as Stevie Wonder, is born May 13 in Saginaw, Michigan.

THE MILITARY

African-American troops of the U.S. Army's 24th Infantry Regiment help recapture Yechon in Korea, which represents the first victory in the Korean War.

The White House Committee on Equality of Treatment and Opportunity in the Armed Forces finds that President Truman's order banning segregation in the military has received widespread compliance. However, blacks continue to be kept from 198 of the 490 specialties in the army.

SPORTS

The Boston Celtics pick Charles "Chuck" Cooper, making him the first African American drafted by a National Basketball Association team. The first African American actually to play in an NBA game is Earl Lloyd of the Washington Capitols, later this year against the Rochester Royals.

At Forest Hills, Althea Gibson becomes the first African American to be accepted for competition in the National Tennis Championship.

Jackie Robinson of the Brooklyn Dodgers becomes the first African American to appear on the cover of *Life* magazine, which has been publishing for 13 years.

Julius Erving, basketball star of the Philadelphia 76ers, is born February 22 in Roosevelt, New York.

ADDITIONAL STATISTICS

According to the 1950 census, there are 15,042,286 African Americans living in the United States, who represent 10% of the total U.S. population.

Among black families living in the United States, 60.6% have an income of less than $3,000; among white families, 28.4%.

1951

POLITICS AND CIVIL RIGHTS

President Truman creates a White House committee to investigate compliance with antidiscrimination provisions in government contracts.

The New York City Council passes a bill that outlaws discrimination in city housing.

In Washington, D.C., the municipal court of appeals rules against segregation in restaurants. One of the principal leaders in the anti-segregation effort is Mary Church Terrell.

After entertainer Josephine Baker complains of being refused service at New York's Stork Club, the NAACP pickets the club. The city's special investigation team declares the charges groundless, but NAACP attorney Thurgood Marshall calls the declaration "a complete and shameless whitewash."

Serious rioting breaks out in Cicero, Illinois, over a black family's attempt to move into an all-white area, causing Governor Adlai Stevenson to call in the National Guard.

Harry T. Moore, a leader in the Florida state branch of the NAACP, and his wife, also a civil rights activist, are killed by a bomb in their Mims home. The bombing is apparently a retaliation against the campaign to expand the black vote in Florida and to desegregate the University of Florida.

A committee led by Paul Robeson and William L. Patterson submits a petition to the U.S. government accusing it of having a policy of genocide against African Americans.

Mary Church Terrell

Mary Church Terrell's lifetime extended from the year of the Emancipation Proclamation (1863), when she was born the child of newly liberated slaves, to the year of the **Brown** decision barring public school segregation (1954). During that lifetime, she campaigned tirelessly against racial discrimination and segregation. She became a member of the Washington, D.C., board of education in 1895 and, in the following year, founded the National Association of Colored Women. A courageous and eloquent speaker as well as an ardent feminist, she remarked in 1940, "A white woman has one handicap to overcome: that of sex. I have two—both sex and race." A tireless fighter, she, more than any other single person, is responsible for seeing that public accommodations in the nation's capital were finally desegregated, setting a model for desegregation in other cities throughout the United States.

Contemporary Events, 1951 ■ J. D. Salinger's **Catcher in the Rye** is published. ■ Electric power is produced from atomic energy in Idaho. ■ Color TV makes its first appearance in the United States. ■ The 22nd Amendment is passed, limiting presidents to two terms.

Oscar DePriest, the first black congressperson since Reconstruction, dies May 12 in Chicago.

BUSINESS AND EMPLOYMENT

American Express executive Kenneth I. Chenault is born June 2 in Mineola, New York.

RELIGION AND EDUCATION

The NAACP mounts an attack on segregation in public schools by filing suits to integrate elementary and secondary schools in five school districts, in Delaware, Kansas, South Carolina, Virginia, and Washington, D.C. This campaign will culminate in the historic 1954 Supreme Court decision in *Brown* v. *Board of Education of Topeka*.

The University of North Carolina admits its first African-American student.

LITERATURE AND JOURNALISM

Langston Hughes publishes his poems in the collection *Montage of a Dream Deferred*.

Jet magazine debuts in Chicago.

Best-selling novelist Terry McMillan is born October 18 in Port Heron, Michigan.

SCIENCE AND TECHNOLOGY

The Spingarn Medal is awarded by the NAACP to Mabel Keaton Staupers for her outstanding work as a nurse and an advocate for integration in the nursing profession.

PERFORMING ARTS

Janet Collins debuts in *Aida* as the first African-American principal dancer at the Metropolitan Opera House in New York.

Harry Belafonte, singing folk ballads, opens at the Village Vanguard in New York.

Oscar Micheaux, founder of the African-American film company that bears his name, dies April 1 in Charlotte, North Carolina.

Luther Vandross, R&B and pop singer, is born April 20 in New York.

VISUAL ARTS

Fashion designer Jeffrey Banks is born in Washington, D.C.

THE MILITARY

The Congressional Medal of Honor is awarded to Private William Thompson of Brooklyn, who was killed in combat during the

Korean War. He is the first African American to receive this award since the Spanish-American War.

The 24th Infantry Regiment is deactivated in Korea, bringing to an end the tradition of all-black units that was first authorized by Congress in 1866.

SPORTS

Hosea Richardson becomes the first African-American jockey licensed to ride on the Florida circuit.

"Jersey" Joe Wolcott defeats Ezzard Charles to become heavyweight boxing champion of the world.

Roy Campanella of the Brooklyn Dodgers is named the National League's Most Valuable Player of the Year.

Tennis star Althea Gibson becomes the first African American to play at Wimbledon.

David Winfield, baseball star for the San Diego Padres, the New York Yankees, and the California Angels, is born October 3 in St. Paul, Minnesota.

ADDITIONAL EVENTS

George Washington Carver National Monument opens in Joplin, Missouri, the first national park to honor an African American.

1952

POLITICS AND CIVIL RIGHTS

For the first time in the 71 years it has been keeping records, Tuskegee Institute reports that there is no known lynching of an African American.

A civil rights bill is repeatedly "kept in committee" in Congress, never coming to the floor for a vote.

In the southern states, only 28% of African Americans eligible to vote are registered.

Through legal action, the NAACP desegregrates various types of public facilities, including a swimming pool in Kansas City, Missouri; a golf course in Louisville, Kentucky; and Ford's Theater in Baltimore, Maryland.

Contemporary Events, 1952 ■ The Revised Standard Version of the Bible is issued. ■ Norman Vincent Peale's best-seller **The Power of Positive Thinking** is published. ■ The United States explodes the first hydrogen bomb (or H-bomb) at Eniwetok Atoll in the Pacific Ocean.

The Progressive Party nominates Charlotta A. Bass, publisher of the *California Eagle*, for vice president of the United States.

In the presidential election that brings Dwight David Eisenhower to the White House, only 21% of voting blacks cast their ballots for Eisenhower. The low percentage is perceived as a retaliation for Eisenhower's testimony against desegregating the army in the early years of Truman's presidency.

President-elect Eisenhower meets with NAACP officials and says he opposes federal aid to segregated schools, but he would not intervene to enforce desegregation.

The Southern Regional Council reports "an alarming increase" in racist-related bombings across the nation.

The Spingarn Medal is awarded to Harry T. Moore, murdered Florida state director of the NAACP, for his work toward civil rights.

BUSINESS AND EMPLOYMENT

NAACP campaigns lead to the desegregation of the Philco Corporation and to the inclusion of an antidiscrimination clause in United Auto Workers contracts.

RELIGION AND EDUCATION

The U.S. Supreme Court agrees to hear the cases challenging segregated schools that the NAACP initiated in 1951.

The University of Tennessee admits its first black student.

Historian Marcia R. Sawyer is born August 11 in Pittsburgh.

LITERATURE AND JOURNALISM

Ralph Ellison's novel *Invisible Man* wins the National Book Award.

Jay Saunders Redding publishes his landmark study of the psychological effects of racism, *On Being a Negro in America*.

Rita Dove, who will become poet laureate of the United States, is born August 28 in Akron, Ohio.

PERFORMING ARTS

Singer and actress Eartha Kitt debuts in the musical *New Faces* on Broadway and will appear in the film *New Faces* in 1953.

Actor Canada Lee, who first gained fame playing "Bigger Thomas" in the 1941 play *Native Son*, dies May 9 in New York.

Fletcher Henderson, bandleader and "Father of the Big Band," dies December 29 in New York.

Fashion model Grace Jones is born May 19 in Jamaica.

VISUAL ARTS

To show the work of painter Ellis Wilson, the Louisville, Kentucky, Art Center Association decides to change its whites-only policy.

SPORTS

At the Helsinki Olympics, eight African Americans win gold medals, including individual medalists Jerome Biffle (long jump), Mal Whitfield (800-meter run), Harrison Dillard (110-meter hurdles), Andrew Stanfield (200-meter run), and Floyd Patterson (middleweight boxing).

ADDITIONAL STATISTICS

Personal income for African Americans totals $11.4 billion; for whites, $194.1 billion. Median incomes are: black men, $2,038; black women, $814; white men, $3,507; white women, $1,976.

1953

POLITICS AND CIVIL RIGHTS

The NAACP announces its "Fight for Freedom" campaign, intended to remove all racial discrimination by 1963, the 100th anniversary of the Emancipation Proclamation.

The NAACP and other African-American groups complain when Governor James F. Byrnes of South Carolina, U.S. delegate to the United Nations, is appointed the spokesperson on human rights. Accused of holding racist views, Byrnes is replaced by Frances Bolton, congressperson from Ohio.

The U.S. Supreme Court rules in favor of the desegregation of Washington, D.C., restaurants.

President Eisenhower creates the Government Contract Compliance Committee to monitor compliance with antidiscrimination provisions in government contracts.

Citizens of Baton Rouge boycott city buses to protest segregation.

In Chicago, white rioting begins when black families move into Trumbull Park, a housing project. It will persist for over three years.

Hulan Jack becomes the first African American to be elected Manhattan borough president in New York.

Contemporary Events, 1953 ■ The Korean War ends when an armistice is signed at Panmunjom. ■ Congress creates a new cabinet position: secretary of health, education, and welfare. ■ Movie theaters are adapted for CinemaScope projection.

The NAACP succeeds in reversing the conviction of Matt Ingram, a North Carolina farmer who had been accused of assault "by leering" at a white woman.

BUSINESS AND EMPLOYMENT

Under pressure from the NAACP, General Motors permits African Americans to apply for skilled jobs in the Fisher Body Division and the Electromotive Diesel Division.

RELIGION AND EDUCATION

Joseph H. Jackson, minister of Olivet Baptist Church in Chicago, is elected president of the National Baptist Convention.

Fisk University receives a chapter of the scholastic honor society Phi Beta Kappa.

Atlanta University president Rufus E. Clement is elected to the Atlanta board of education.

LITERATURE AND JOURNALISM

Gwendolyn Brooks's novel *Maud Martha* is published.

James Baldwin publishes his first novel, *Go Tell It on the Mountain*.

Ann Petry publishes her novel *The Narrows*.

SCIENCE AND TECHNOLOGY

Dillard University president Albert W. Dent is elected president of the National Health Council.

PERFORMING ARTS

Louis Peterson's play *Take a Giant Step* opens on Broadway, featuring Frederick O'Neal, Helen Martin, and Maxwell Glanville.

VISUAL ARTS

The Spingarn Medal is awarded to architect Paul Williams for his contributions to building design.

THE MILITARY

The Department of Defense orders racial desegregation of all schools on military bases and in Veterans hospitals.

SPORTS

Larry Doby is signed by the Cleveland Indians baseball team, making him the first African American to play in the American League.

Don Barksdale of the Boston Celtics is the first African American to play in the National Basketball Association All-Star game.

1954

POLITICS AND CIVIL RIGHTS

President Eisenhower orders the desegregation of the Washington, D.C., fire department, but refuses requests to support civil rights legislation.

President Eisenhower appoints J. Ernest Wilkins as assistant secretary of labor.

Charles H. Mahoney becomes the first African American to be appointed a permanent delegate to the United Nations.

Ralph Bunche is named undersecretary for special political affairs at the United Nations, a post he will assume on January 1, 1955.

Charles C. Diggs, Jr., of Detroit becomes the first African American elected to the U.S. House of Representatives from Michigan. Altogether, three black representatives are elected to Congress during this year, the largest number so far in the 20th century. The other two are reelected: William Dawson of Chicago and Adam Clayton Powell, Jr., of New York.

Ignoring protests from black and liberal white groups, the Federal Housing and Home Finance Agency continues to subsidize the building of segregated communities, and the Department of Health, Education, and Welfare continues to aid segregated hospitals.

Mary Church Terrell, prominent civil rights leader and educator, dies July 24 in Annapolis, Maryland.

Activist Al Sharpton is born in Brooklyn, New York.

RELIGION AND EDUCATION

The U.S. Supreme Court, in the landmark case of *Brown* v. *Board of Education of Topeka*, rules that "separate but equal" educational facilities are "inherently unequal" and therefore segregation in public education is unconstitutional. Chief Justice Earl Warren writes the unanimous decision, and Thurgood Marshall heads the NACCP's legal team.

The Supreme Court rules that the University of Florida must admit black students despite any "public mischief" the action might cause.

Reports of public education expenditures in the South show that white students consistently receive more support than black students:

From the Brown Decision:

"Liberty under law extends to the full range of conduct which an individual is free to pursue, and it cannot be restricted except for a proper governmental objective. Segregation in public education is not reasonably related to any proper governmental objective."

Contemporary Events, 1954 ■ Senator Joseph McCarthy runs a televised congressional hearing on Communist infiltration of the army. Protests against this witch-hunt lead to his censure by the Senate. ■ Jonas Salk develops the polio vaccine. ■ The first Newport Jazz Festival is held in Rhode Island.

Mississippi spends $98 per white student, $43 per black student; Louisiana spends $165 per white student, $122 per black student; and Florida spends $176 per white student, $160 per black student.

Public school integration begins September 7 in Washington, D.C.

LITERATURE AND JOURNALISM

John Oliver Killens publishes his autobiographical novel *Youngblood*.

Richard Wright's *Black Power* is published.

Philosopher and writer Alain Locke dies June 9 in New York.

SCIENCE AND TECHNOLOGY

Peter Murray Marshall becomes the president of the New York County Medical Society, making him the first African American to lead a unit of the American Medical Association.

The Spingarn Medal is awarded to Theodore Lawless for his work on skin diseases.

PERFORMING ARTS

Pearl Bailey and Diahann Carroll star in Truman Capote's play *House of Flowers*, which opens on Broadway.

The play *Mrs. Patterson*, by Charles Sebree and Greer Johnson, opens at the National Theater in Washington, D.C.

Dorothy Dandridge plays the lead role in the film *Carmen Jones* and will receive an Academy Award nomination for best actress.

The Chords debut on the R&B chart on July 3 with "Sh-Boom."

Thelonius Monk records "Bag's Groove" with the Miles Davis All-Stars.

Oprah Winfrey, actress, talk-show host, and TV and film producer, is born January 29 in Kosciusko, Mississippi.

Actor Denzel Washington is born December 28 in Mount Vernon, New York.

VISUAL ARTS

Fashion designer Patrick Kelly is born September 24 in Mississippi.

THE MILITARY

A report commissioned by the Defense Department concludes that there are no longer any all-black military units, but that some bases have continued to "evade integration."

Benjamin O. Davis, Jr., is appointed the first African-American general in the United States Air Force.

SPORTS

Willie Mays of the New York Giants is the National League's batting champion (.345 average) and Most Valuable Player.

Hank Aaron joins the Milwaukee Braves and begins his major league baseball career.

POLITICS AND CIVIL RIGHTS

On December 1 Rosa Parks of Montgomery, Alabama, refuses to give her bus seat to a white man. Her subsequent arrest prompts formation of the Montgomery Improvement Association, which organizes a bus boycott. A local Baptist minister, Martin Luther King, Jr., is elected president of the association.

Lynchings begin again in the South, including the murder of Emmett Till near Money, Mississippi. A 14-year-old boy visiting from Chicago, Till was accused of having made suggestive remarks to a white woman.

The Interstate Commerce Commission bans segregated buses and bus station facilities involved in interstate travel.

The U.S. House of Representatives defeats a bill introduced by New York's Adam Clayton Powell, Jr., to deny federal funds to segregated schools.

E. Frederic Morrow becomes administrative aide to President Eisenhower, making him the first African American to hold an executive position on a White House staff.

The Supreme Court outlaws segregation in public recreational facilities in Baltimore.

Robert C. Weaver becomes New York State rent commissioner, the highest New York post achieved to date by an African American.

NAACP executive Walter White dies March 21 in New York. He is succeeded by Roy Wilkins.

BUSINESS AND EMPLOYMENT

The NAACP, the Committee on Government Contracts, and the CIO Oil Workers Union successfully fight to allow the hiring of blacks in the oil-refining industry.

The Montgomery Bus Boycott

When Montgomery, Alabama, citizen Rosa Parks boarded the Cleveland Avenue bus on December 1, 1955, she had no idea that she was taking the first step in a long Civil Rights Movement that would culminate in the civil rights legislation of the 1960s. In addition to making Martin Luther King, Jr., a national leader, the Montgomery bus boycott popularized the use of nonviolent protest to oppose racial discrimination and injustice.

Contemporary Events, 1955 ■ President Eisenhower has a heart attack. ■ The U.S. Air Force Academy opens in Colorado.

Chuck Berry

The release of Chuck Berry's record "Maybelline" in 1955 introduced black rhythm 'n' blues music to a vast audience of white teenagers who were hungry for a new sound. They loved it, called it "rock 'n' roll," and gave Chuck Berry 10 other top-10 hits between 1955 and 1961, including "Roll Over Beethoven" and "Johnny B. Goode." Dave Marsh, reporter for **Rolling Stone** magazine, later cited Berry's enormous influence on popular musicians ranging from Fats Domino to the Beatles and claimed, "Chuck Berry is to rock what Louis Armstrong was to jazz." Berry was awarded a Grammy for lifetime achievement in 1984 and was inducted into the Rock and Roll Hall of Fame in 1986.

A. Philip Randolph and William S. Townsend are elected vice presidents of the newly merged AFL-CIO.

RELIGION AND EDUCATION

The U.S. Supreme Court orders all U.S. school boards to inaugurate desegregation plans with "all deliberate speed."

Desegregation of public schools proceeds fairly quickly in most states, with the exception of the South. The Georgia state board of education resolves to revoke the license of any teacher who conducts an integrated class. In this same year Mississippi establishes a government agency to maintain public school segregation.

Mary McLeod Bethune, educator and civil rights activist, dies May 18 in Daytona Beach, Florida.

LITERATURE AND JOURNALISM

Richard Wright publishes *White Man, Listen!* and *Pagan Spain*.

Carl Murphy receives the Spingarn Medal for his achievements as publisher of the *Afro-American*.

PERFORMING ARTS

Marian Anderson becomes the first African American to sing at the Metropolitan Opera House in New York when she performs in Verdi's *A Masked Ball*.

Carmen de Lavellade is signed to dance with the Metropolitan Opera Company in New York, and Arthur Mitchell appears as a principal dancer with the New York City Ballet.

Chuck Berry records his first number-one R&B hit, "Maybelline."

Jazz musician Charlie "Bird" Parker dies March 12 in New York.

VISUAL ARTS

Geoffrey Holder has the first New York exhibit of his paintings at the Garone Gallery and wins a Guggenheim fellowship.

Normal Lewis's painting *Migrating Birds* receives the popular prize at the Pittsburgh International Exhibition at the Carnegie Institute.

SPORTS

Sugar Ray Robinson becomes world middleweight boxing champion, a rank he holds until 1957 and again from 1958 through 1960.

ADDITIONAL STATISTICS

African Americans represent 12.2% of the population of New York City; 11.3% of Los Angeles, 22% of Detroit, and 18% of Chicago.

POLITICS AND CIVIL RIGHTS

Senator Harry Byrd of Virginia delivers the "Southern Manifesto" to the U.S. Supreme Court, protesting its 1954 *Brown* decision on school desegregation. It is signed by over 100 southern congresspeople. Among nonsigning senators from the South are Estes Kefauver and Albert Gore, Sr., of Tennessee and Lyndon B. Johnson of Texas.

Martin Luther King, Jr., and 100 other participants in the Montgomery bus boycott are indicted for conspiracy to conduct an illegal boycott and sentenced to prison. Ultimately, the cases are settled by the payment of $100 fines.

The U.S. Supreme Court rules that segregation of buses is unconstitutional, and the Montgomery bus boycott ends in victory for the protestors.

The Birmingham, Alabama, home of civil rights leader Fred L. Shuttlesworth is bombed, sparking mass civil disobedience among African Americans regarding segregation on city buses.

Alabama prohibits the NAACP from operating in that state after the NAACP refuses to open its books to state examiners. The NAACP suspends all activities in Alabama for the next two years.

After a six-month boycott by African Americans, buses in Tallahassee, Florida, are desegregated.

In a successful presidential election campaign, President Dwight Eisenhower wins 40% of the African-American vote. Experts attribute this sharp increase in Eisenhower's popularity among blacks to the 1954 desegregation ruling issued by the Supreme Court, led by an Eisenhower appointee, Earl Warren.

The Eisenhower administration proposes the Civil Rights Act of 1957, which includes the provision that the Justice Department can sue on behalf of any African American who is denied the right to vote. The House of Representatives passes the bill and sends it to the Senate, where it is stalled.

RELIGION AND EDUCATION

Across the United States, 1,000 school districts with about 400,000 black children are newly desegregated. However, about 2.4 million

Contemporary Events, 1956 ■ The United States arranges for a cease-fire in the Suez Canal crisis. ■ John F. Kennedy publishes his Pulitzer-Prize-winning biography, **Profiles in Courage.** ■ **My Fair Lady** opens on Broadway. ■ Elvis Presley releases his first number-one rock 'n' roll hit, "Hound Dog."

black children still attend segregated schools; and there are no desegregated districts in Virginia, North Carolina, South Carolina, Georgia, Florida, Alabama, Mississippi, or Louisiana.

A mob of white protestors blocks the enrollment of African-American students at Mansfield High School in Mansfield, Texas.

The University of Alabama admits its first African American, Autherine J. Lucy, in February. She is expelled within a month for making "false and outrageous" statements about the university.

Mordecai Johnson retires as president of Howard University, a position he has held since 1926.

Sociologist and Fisk University president Charles S. Johnson dies October 27 in Louisville, Kentucky.

LITERATURE AND JOURNALISM

Historian John Hope Franklin publishes his study *Militant South*.

James Baldwin's autobiographical novel about a black homosexual, *Giovanni's Room*, is published.

Poet Gwendolyn Brooks's *Bronzeville Boys and Girls* is published.

L. R. Lautier is the first African American admitted to the National Press Club.

SCIENCE AND TECHNOLOGY

Astronaut Mae C. Jemison is born October 17 in Decatur, Alabama.

PERFORMING ARTS

Singer Nat "King" Cole is attacked by white supremacists while performing in Birmingham, Alabama.

The Nat King Cole Show debuts on November 11. It is the first nationally broadcast TV variety series hosted by an African American.

Geoffrey Holder begins dancing for the Metropolitan Opera Company in New York.

Alice Childress's *Trouble in Mind* wins an Obie award for the best original Off-Broadway play.

Sammy Davis, Jr., debuts on Broadway in *Mr. Wonderful.*

The Platters hit number one on the pop charts with "My Prayer."

Jazz trumpeter Clifford Brown, founder of the Brown-Roach Quintet, is killed June 26 in a car accident on the Pennsylvania Turnpike.

VISUAL ARTS

Painter Jacob Lawrence completes his series *Struggle: From the History of the American People.*

SPORTS

At the Olympics in Melbourne, Australia, a number of African Americans win gold medals, including individual medals for Gregory Bell (long jump), Lee Calhoun (110-meter hurdles), Milton Campbell (decathlon), Charles Dumas (high jump), Charles Jenkins (400-meter run), and Mildred McDaniel (high jump).

Floyd Patterson wins the world's heavyweight boxing championship.

Hank Aaron of the Milwaukee Braves wins the National League batting championship.

The Spingarn Medal is awarded to Jackie Robinson for his "conduct on and off the baseball field."

Boxer "Sugar" Ray Charles Leonard is born May 17 in Wilmington, South Carolina.

POLITICS AND CIVIL RIGHTS

The Civil Rights Act of 1957 protecting the right to vote passes the U.S. Senate and becomes law, but only after strong school integration provisions are deleted. It is the first significant civil rights legislation since 1875.

Martin Luther King, Jr., Bayard Rustin, and black ministers form the Southern Christian Leadership Conference (SCLC) to link diverse nonviolent protest groups that support civil rights.

In Tuskegee, Alabama, African Americans boycott white merchants to protest the gerrymandering of local electoral districts to reduce black voting power.

Over 25,000 African Americans, led by Martin Luther King, Jr., gather at the Lincoln Memorial in Washington, D.C., in a "Prayer Pilgrimage" to demonstrate support for black voting rights.

In Birmingham, Fred Shuttlesworth is attacked by protestors as he attempts to enroll his children in an all-white school.

In Nashville, Tennessee, a bomb set by an integration protestor destroys an elementary school.

New York passes the first fair housing practice ordinance in the United States, prohibiting discrimination in private housing.

Contemporary Events, 1957 ■ Jack Kerouac publishes his novel **On the Road.** ■ The USSR launches the first space satellite, **Sputnik,** prompting concern among Americans about U.S. inferiority in science, technology, and education. ■ The Brooklyn Dodgers move to Los Angeles.

Crisis in Little Rock

In 1957 Central High School in Little Rock, Arkansas, was ready to begin admitting black students on the first day of the school term, September 3. But on September 4, Arkansas Governor Orval Faubus, previously silent on racial matters, surprised everyone by calling in the National Guard "to preserve order." In fact, the guardsmen only turned away black students seeking admission. President Eisenhower tried for most of the month to end the stand-off diplomatically, but Faubus refused to permit integration. On September 24, Eisenhower ordered 1,000 federal troops into Little Rock, federalized 10,000 Arkansas National Guardsmen, and insisted that the nine black students still seeking admission should be allowed to register. From that day forward, Central High School held integrated classes. The federal troops stayed until November 27 to ensure a peaceful transition. Intensive TV coverage, including direct addresses from President Eisenhower explaining his determination to enforce integration, brought the injustice of racial discrimination to the attention of millions of whites.

Oregon, Washington, Massachusetts, and New Jersey pass laws prohibiting discrimination in public housing.

Archibald Carey is appointed head of the President's Committee on Government Employment Policy.

African Americans celebrate when Ghana becomes the first African nation to be decolonized. Ghana's independence ceremony is attended by Ralph Bunche, A. Philip Randolph, Adam Clayton Powell, Jr., and Martin Luther King, Jr.

BUSINESS AND EMPLOYMENT

The District of Columbia Bar Association admits black members for the first time.

African Americans are admitted for the first time into the International Brotherhood of Electrical Workers and the Bricklayers, Masons, and Marble Masons Protective Association.

The 14 African-American banks have total assets of $46,789,607.

RELIGION AND EDUCATION

A mob of white protestors harass 18 black students who seek admission to Central High School in Little Rock, Arkansas. President Eisenhower sends in paratroopers to enforce integration.

Tennessee passes legislation to desegregate its state universities starting in 1958.

Among Americans age 25 to 29, the average number of years spent in school is: black women, 10.3; white women, 12.3; black men, 9.4; white men, 12.3.

LITERATURE AND JOURNALISM

Richard Wright publishes *White Man, Listen!* and *Pagan Spain.*

Sociologist E. Franklin Frazier publishes *Black Bourgeoisie.*

SCIENCE AND TECHNOLOGY

In Los Angeles, the Sickle Cell Disease Research Center is founded. It will grow to be a national organization devoted to the detection and treatment of sickle cell anemia, a genetic illness that most commonly afflicts African Americans.

PERFORMING ARTS

Lena Horne stars in the musical *Jamaica,* which opens on Broadway.

Langston Hughes's play *Simply Heavenly* opens on Broadway.

Fats Domino records "I'm Walkin'" on January 3.

Filmmaker Spike Lee is born March 20 in Atlanta.

THE MILITARY

Robert Ming is elected chairperson of the American Veterans Committee, becoming the first African American to lead a national veterans group.

SPORTS

Hank Aaron of the Milwaukee Braves becomes home-run champion for the year and is named the National League's Most Valuable Player.

Althea Gibson is the first African-American tennis champion at Wimbledon, where she wins the women's singles and, with Darlene Hard, a white athlete, the doubles. In the same year she also wins the women's singles at Forest Hills.

Jim Brown becomes the National Football League's All-League fullback, a title he holds until he retires from pro football in 1966.

Charles Sifford wins the Long Beach Open, the first major golf tournament win by an African American.

ADDITIONAL STATISTICS

The average annual income for nonwhite families is $2,764; for white families, $5,166.

POLITICS AND CIVIL RIGHTS

African-American voter registration in the South begins to increase, to 72% registration in Tennessee, 39% in Florida, and 36% in North Carolina and Texas. But in Mississippi registration remains at 3%.

The Supreme Court, in *NAACP* v. *Alabama,* rules that Alabama's attempts to drive the NAACP out of operation in that state are unconstitutional.

In Oklahoma City, the NAACP Youth Council begins sit-in demonstrations to desegregate lunch counters.

Clifford R. Wharton, Sr., becomes minister to Romania, the first African American to head an American embassy in Europe.

Martin Luther King, Jr., is stabbed in New York by an apparently deranged woman. His wound is serious, but he recovers.

Contemporary Events, 1958 ■ The United States establishes the National Aeronautics and Space Administration (NASA) and launches its first space satellite, **Explorer I.** ■ James Agee's **A Death in the Family** wins the Pulitzer Prize.

The Brown *Decision and the White Backlash*

The Supreme Court's historic 1954 ruling in **Brown** v. **Board of Education** that school segregation is unconstitutional overturned a "separate but equal" policy that had legalized school segregation since the **Plessy** decision of 1896. After the **Brown** decision, many racist antidesegregation groups sprang up among outraged whites. The largest and most demonstrative was the White Citizens Council, which gained over 80,000 members in hundreds of localized units within the next two years.

African-American leaders have a summit meeting with President Eisenhower, where he is criticized for urging them to "be patient" about civil rights.

Dorothy I. Height begins serving on New York State's Social Welfare Board.

Two African-American boys in Monroe, North Carolina, are sentenced to reform school because they were kissed by a white girl with whom they were playing.

BUSINESS AND EMPLOYMENT

The national unemployment rate is 14.4% among blacks (the highest level in 11 years) and 6.9% among whites.

Anheuser-Busch Breweries and the Teamsters Union adopt nondiscriminatory policies, allowing African Americans to apply for union jobs in the brewing industry.

Boeing Aircraft and National Cash Register allow blacks into their apprentice training programs.

RELIGION AND EDUCATION

Jackie Robinson, Harry Belafonte, A. Philip Randolph, and over 10,000 African-American students participate in the Youth March for Integrated Schools in Washington, D.C.

Orval Faubus, governor of Arkansas, evades the Supreme Court school desegregation ruling by closing the public schools in Little Rock and reopening them as private, segregated schools.

Ernest Green is the first African American to graduate from Central High School in Little Rock, and the only African American among the 601 graduates.

The University of Florida integrates.

The Spingarn Medal is awarded to the nine students who integrated Little Rock's Central High School and to Daisy Bates, leader of the NAACP's Little Rock branch.

LITERATURE AND JOURNALISM

Willard Motley publishes his novel *Let No Man Write My Epitaph*.

Jay Saunders Redding's *The Lonesome Road: The Story of the Negro's Part in America* is published.

Julian Mayfield publishes his novel *The Long Night*.

PERFORMING ARTS

Alvin Ailey founds his own company, the Alvin Ailey American Dance Theater.

Hollywood releases the movie *Anna Lucasta*, starring Eartha Kitt and Sammy Davis, Jr.

Sidney Poitier is nominated for an Oscar for best actor for his performance in *The Defiant Ones*.

W. C. Handy, "Father of the Blues," dies April 10 in New York.

Anita Baker, jazz and R&B singer, is born February 26 in Toledo, Ohio.

Singer Michael Jackson is born August 29 in Gary, Indiana.

Musician Prince Rogers Nelson, better known as just Prince, is born June 6 in Minneapolis.

SPORTS

Ernie Banks of the Chicago Cubs is named the Most Valuable Player in the National League.

Roy Campanella is paralyzed from the waist down and retires from the Brooklyn Dodgers.

Bill Russell of the Boston Celtics is named the National Basketball Association's Most Valuable Player.

Willie O'Ree, playing for the Boston Bruins, is the first African American in the National Hockey League.

ADDITIONAL EVENTS

In honor of the 100th anniversary of Booker T. Washington's birth, the U.S. Postal Service issues a stamp bearing the likeness of the cabin in which he was born.

1959

POLITICS AND CIVIL RIGHTS

In the first reported lynching since 1955, Mack Charles Parker is murdered in Poplarville, Mississippi, for allegedly raping a white woman.

California passes legislation prohibiting discrimination in public housing and overturning miscegenation laws.

In Memphis, a major voting drive adds over 15,000 African Americans to the roster of registered voters.

Contemporary Events, 1959 ■ Alaska becomes the 49th and Hawaii the 50th state. ■ The Guggenheim Museum, designed by Frank Lloyd Wright, opens in New York. ■ The musicals **Gypsy** and **The Sound of Music** open on Broadway.

In Washington Parish, Louisiana, 1,377 of the 1,517 African Americans who are registered to vote are removed from the list because of technicalities.

Ross Barnett is elected governor of Mississippi. The White Citizens Council, a militant anti-integration group, is instrumental in his campaign, and there is speculation that Barnett himself is a member of the WCC.

A U.S. district court overturns an Arkansas law making it illegal for government agencies to hire a member of the NAACP.

BUSINESS AND EMPLOYMENT

In the United States there are 272,541 African-American farm owners, compared with 926,000 in 1920. Cotton and tobacco continue to be the most significant crops produced by these farmers.

A. Philip Randolph attacks the AFL-CIO for not having eliminated discrimination within union ranks.

RELIGION AND EDUCATION

Prince Edward County, Virginia, discontinues its public school system in order to avoid having to comply with order for racial integration.

Five states have still not made any moves toward desegregating their schools: South Carolina, Georgia, Alabama, Mississippi, and Louisiana.

Schools in Little Rock that had been converted from public to private schools for the purpose of avoiding integration are converted back to public schools by a newly elected board of education, and integration begins to take place.

LITERATURE AND JOURNALISM

Paule Marshall's novel *Brown Girl, Brownstones* is published.

Frank London Brown publishes his novel *Trumbull Park*.

PERFORMING ARTS

Lorraine Hansberry's *A Raisin in the Sun* opens on Broadway, starring Sidney Poitier. It wins the New York Drama Critics Circle Award for best play on April 7.

Berry Gordy, Jr., establishes Motown Records, and the Tamla label, in Detroit.

Ella Fitzgerald and Count Basie are the first African Americans to win Grammy awards.

James Cleveland starts his group the Gospel Chimes.

Folksinger Odetta gives her first major concert at Town Hall in New York.

Nina Simone launches her career with her recording of "I Loves You, Porgy."

Hollywood releases the film *Porgy and Bess,* starring Dorothy Dandridge and Sidney Poitier.

The movie *Odds Against Tomorrow,* with a screenplay by John Oliver Killens, is released, starring Harry Belafonte.

The Spingarn Medal is awarded to Edward Kennedy "Duke" Ellington for his contributions as composer, pianist, and bandleader.

Jazz saxophonist Lester Young dies March 15 in New York.

Blues singer Billie Holiday dies July 17 in New York.

THE MILITARY

Brigadier General Benjamin O. Davis, Jr., of the U.S. Air Force is promoted to major general, the highest military rank yet achieved by an African American.

SPORTS

Wilt Chamberlain is the National Basketball Association's scoring champion.

Earvin "Magic" Johnson, basketball star for the Los Angeles Lakers and AIDS spokesperson, is born August 14 in Lansing, Michigan.

Sprinter Florence Griffith Joyner is born December 21 in Los Angeles. She will win three gold medals and one silver at the 1988 Olympics in Seoul.

1960

POLITICS AND CIVIL RIGHTS

President Eisenhower signs the Civil Rights Act of 1960 into law. It strengthens the 1957 act by making the federal government more responsible in cases of civil rights violations.

College students stage a sit-in at an F. W. Woolworth lunch counter in Greensboro, North Carolina, inspiring a wave of sit-ins throughout the South.

Contemporary Events, 1960 ■ The United States admits to aerial spy flights after American Gary Powers's U-2 airplane is shot down over Soviet territory. ■ Harper Lee's Pulitzer-Prize-winning novel **To Kill a Mockingbird,** about racial prejudice, is published.

Words about A Raisin in the Sun

Lorraine Hansberry expressed the mission of her 1959 play, **A Raisin in the Sun,** in a letter to her mother: "I think it will help a lot of [white] people to understand how we are just as complicated as they are—and just as mixed up—but above all, that we have among our miserable and downtrodden ranks—people who are the very essence of human dignity."

The Student Nonviolent Coordinating Committee (SNCC) is organized in Raleigh, North Carolina.

The NAACP sponsors voter registration drives in southern cities, including Jacksonville, Tampa, Savannah, and Memphis.

The Supreme Court, in the case of *United States* v. *Raines*, rules that the names of over 1,300 black voters in Washington Parish, Louisiana, who were dropped from the registration list after "dubious challenges" must be reinstated.

San Antonio desegregates all city lunch counters, the first large southern city to do so.

After segregationists bomb the Nashville home of Z. Alexander Looby, legal counsel for sit-in demonstrators, over 2,000 African Americans march in protest to city hall.

At a New York rally, Elijah Muhammad of the Nation of Islam calls for the creation of an all-black nation within the United States.

In the first case involving voting rights under the Civil Rights Act of 1957, a federal court lifts antiblack voting restrictions in Fayette County, Tennessee.

In Jacksonville, Florida, a sit-in ends in a riot, in which many black and white protestors are beaten. Photographs of the victims are widely publicized, drawing increased national attention to police brutality.

In the middle of the presidential election campaign, Democratic nominee John F. Kennedy calls Coretta Scott King to offer his personal support after her husband, Martin Luther King, Jr., is arrested during an Atlanta sit-in. The day after Kennedy's call, which is immediately followed by his brother Robert's visit to King's attorney, King is released on bond.

President-elect John F. Kennedy appoints Andrew Hatcher his associate press secretary.

BUSINESS AND EMPLOYMENT

Frustrated by the slow progress of desegregation within the AFL-CIO, A. Philip Randolph founds the Negro American Labor Council.

In Philadelphia a series of targeted boycotts led by 400 African-American ministers pressures Sun Oil, Gulf Oil, Tastee Baking, and Pepsi-Cola to hire over 600 blacks for administrative and managerial positions.

The unemployment rate for black men is 10.7% compared with 4.8% for white men; for black women, 9.5%, compared with 5.3% for white women.

RELIGION AND EDUCATION

Houston desegregates its public school system.

In the first case of its kind in the North, African-American parents file suit to end *de facto* school segregation in New Rochelle, New York.

The Nation of Islam has an estimated membership of 100,000 in 33 temples across the United States. Its increasing popularity is attributed in part to the zeal of minister Malcolm X.

The Mississippi legislature passes constitutional amendments that make the state's public school system "permissive" rather than "mandatory." This means the federal government cannot order the reopening of public schools closed to avoid racial integration.

In New Orleans, school integration is enforced by the federal government after the legislature closes the public school system. U.S. deputy marshals escort black students to two white elementary schools and demand that the schools begin conducting classes. For the rest of the term, the public school system is boycotted by most white students.

South Carolina, Georgia, Alabama, and Mississippi have still not made any efforts to desegregate public schools.

LITERATURE AND JOURNALISM

Gwendolyn Brooks's book of poetry *The Bean Eaters* is published.

LeRoi Jones begins editing *Yugen*, a "beat" poetry magazine.

The Spingarn Award is presented to Langston Hughes, "the poet laureate of the Negro race."

Richard Wright, novelist and essayist, dies November 28 in Paris.

PERFORMING ARTS

Harry Belafonte wins the first Emmy Award awarded an African American for his television special "Tonight with Harry Belafonte."

Alvin Ailey presents his first version of *Revelations,* choreographed to African-American spirituals.

Soprano Camilla Williams sings at a special performance at the White House.

Ray Charles records his number-one hit "Georgia on My Mind."

Chubby Checker launches a new dance craze with his number-one hit record "The Twist."

Jazz saxophonist Branford Marsalis is born August 26 in New Orleans.

Freedom in Africa

In 1957 Ghana gained its independence, and during the 1960s colonial rule ended in many other countries in Africa, causing much celebration among African Americans. The newly freed countries included formerly French-held Mauritania, Senegal, Gambia, Ivory Coast (now Côte d'Ivoire), Mali, Upper Volta (now Burkina Faso), Dahomey (now Benin), Togo, Niger, Chad, Ubangui-Shari (now Central African Republic), Cameroon, Gabon, the French Congo (now Congo), and Madagascar; formerly British-held Nigeria, Kenya, Sierra Leone, Tanzania, Uganda, and Zambia; formerly Belgian-held Belgian Congo (now Zaire); and formerly Italian-held Somalia.

VISUAL ARTS

Painter Jean-Michel Basquiat is born in Brooklyn, New York.

Artist-photographer Lorna Simpson is born in Brooklyn, New York.

SPORTS

A number of African Americans win gold medals at the Rome Olympics, including individual medalists Ralph Boston (long jump), Lee Calhoun (110-meter hurdles), Cassius Clay (light heavyweight boxing), Otis Davis (400-meter run), Rafer Johnson (decathlon), and Wilma Rudolph (100- and 200-meter dashes). Rudolph is also on the team of four black women who win the 400-meter relay.

ADDITIONAL STATISTICS

According to the U.S. Census Bureau, 18,871,831 blacks live in the United States, which is 10.5% of the total population. It is the first time in the nation's history that over 50% of African Americans live outside of the South and that a northern state, New York, has a larger black population than any southern state.

Women head 21% of black households with children under 18, compared with 6% of white households.

1961

POLITICS AND CIVIL RIGHTS

CORE sends several buses of Freedom Riders through the South to test compliance with federal laws integrating bus stations. On several occasions, they are arrested and attacked. In Montgomery, U.S. Attorney General Robert Kennedy is forced to send in 600 federal marshals to keep the peace.

In Rock Hill, North Carolina, students arrested while protesting racial discrimination refuse to pay fines and request jail sentences instead. Responding to this incident, SNCC calls for "Jail, No Bail" campaigns across the South.

Robert C. Weaver becomes administrator of the Housing and Home Finance Agency, the highest federal job held to date by an African American.

Clifton R. Wharton, Sr., is named ambassador to Norway.

Contemporary Events, 1961 ■ The United States breaks off diplomatic relations with Fidel Castro's Cuba and sponsors an abortive invasion at the Bay of Pigs. ■ Congress investigates the John Birch Society, a white supremacist organization. ■ Alan Shepard makes the first U.S. manned space flight.

Adam Clayton Powell, Jr., becomes chair of the House Education and Labor Committee.

Judge James B. Parsons is named to the District Court of Northern Illinois, becoming the first African American to receive such an appointment in the continental United States.

Thurgood Marshall is named to the U.S. Circuit Court of Appeals.

Atlanta adopts plans for desegregating restaurants and other public gathering places.

In Albany, Georgia, Martin Luther King, Jr., leads over 700 civil rights demonstrators in five mass marches on city hall. He and many other demonstrators are arrested.

In Baton Rouge, police use tear gas and attack dogs to disperse 1,500 peaceful civil rights demonstrators.

RELIGION AND EDUCATION

Riots at the University of Georgia result in the suspension of two black students, Charlayne Hunter and Hamilton Holmes. A federal court orders their reinstatement. Hunter (later, Hunter-Gault) will become known as a reporter on PBS-TV's *MacNeil/Lehrer News Hour*.

A federal judge orders New Rochelle, New York, to integrate its public school system.

In Atlanta, Dallas, Tampa, and Memphis public schools are integrated without trouble.

LITERATURE AND JOURNALISM

James Baldwin's book of essays *Nobody Knows My Name* is published.

John A. Williams's *Night Song*, a novel based on the life of jazz great Charlie Parker, is published.

LeRoi Jones publishes his first volume of poetry, *Prelude to a 20-Volume Suicide Note.*

SCIENCE AND TECHNOLOGY

The American Dental Association orders its branches to remove discriminatory provisions from their bylaws.

The Spingarn Medal is awarded to psychologist Kenneth B. Clark for groundbreaking studies that helped explain the causes and effects of racial prejudice, and influenced the 1954 Supreme Court ruling on school desegregation.

PERFORMING ARTS

Ossie Davis's play *Purlie Victorious*, starring Davis and his wife, Ruby Dee, opens on Broadway.

Langston Hughes's musical *Black Nativity* opens on Broadway with gospel singer Marion Williams and the Stars of Faith.

Soprano Leontyne Price debuts at New York City's Metropolitan Opera House in *Il Trovatore*.

Soprano Grace Bumbry debuts at West Germany's Bayreuth Festival singing the role of "Venus" in Wagner's *Tannhauser*.

Godfrey Cambridge wins Off-Broadway's Obie award for best actor for his performance in Jean Genet's *The Blacks*.

Dick Gregory launches his career as a comedian at the Chicago Playboy Club.

The Vibrations debut on the charts with "The Watusi."

The Shirelles have their first number-one hit with "Will You Love Me Tomorrow?" The next year they will have an even bigger hit with "Soldier Boy."

On November 11 Ray Charles's "Hit the Road, Jack" is the number one R&B single.

The Marvelettes make their chart debut September 11 with "Please, Mr. Postman."

Comedian and movie star Eddie Murphy is born April 3 in Brooklyn, New York.

Jazz trumpeter Wynton Marsalis is born October 18 in New Orleans.

VISUAL ARTS

Sculptor Elizabeth Catlett's speech "The Negro People and American Art," published in the journal *Freedomways,* calls for shows of African-American art and prompts many black artists to form groups to discusss their special concerns.

THE MILITARY

Fred Moore is the first African-American sentry appointed to guard the Tomb of the Unknown Soldier.

SPORTS

College football's Heisman Trophy is awarded to Ernie Davis, a halfback for Syracuse University, the first time the trophy has been given to an African American.

Isiah Thomas, basketball star for the Detroit Pistons, is born April 30 in Chicago.

ADDITIONAL STATISTICS

Average annual incomes for wage and salary workers are: black women, $1,302; black men, $3,015; white women, $2,538; white men, $5,287.

1962

POLITICS AND CIVIL RIGHTS

In the Albany Movement, Martin Luther King, Jr., returns to Albany, Georgia, with prominent civil rights leaders from SNCC, CORE, and the NAACP to conduct a massive sit-in and marching campaign against segregation. King is once again arrested, along with many other protestors.

In Leesburg, Georgia, white supremacists set fire to Shady Grove Baptist Church, burning it to the ground. Within a month, eight more African-American churches are burned down in southern Georgia.

Two Freedom Riders on a voter registration drive are wounded by shotgun blasts in Ruleville, Mississippi, prompting James Forman of SNCC to call for a special White House Conference on safeguarding voter registration in the South.

President Kennedy signs an executive order outlawing racial discrimination in federally financed housing.

A. Leon Higginbotham, Jr., is appointed to the Federal Trade Commission, the first African American to sit on the commission.

California voters elect Augustus Hawkins to the U.S. House of Representatives, the first African American from California to sit in the House. He will serve in Congress until 1990.

Edward W. Brooke is elected attorney general of Massachusetts.

BUSINESS AND EMPLOYMENT

The Kennedy administration orders the desegregation of the southern paper mill industry.

At Pepsico, Harvey Clarence Russell, Jr., becomes the first African American to serve at a vice-presidential level within a major U.S. corporation.

RELIGION AND EDUCATION

Riots erupt at the University of Mississippi when James Meredith

Contemporary Events, 1962 ■ President Kennedy reveals that the USSR has missile installations in Cuba and pressures Premier Nikita Khrushchev to remove them. ■ In South Vietnman a U.S. military council investigates the need for military aid. ■ John Steinbeck wins the Nobel Prize for literature.

New Face at Ole Miss

When James Meredith sought to enroll as the first African-American student at the University of Mississippi in September 1962, Governor Ross Barnett physically blocked Meredith's way into the admissions office, saying to a national TV audience that he would die before allowing a black man into "Ole Miss." Subsequent rioting, with white students chanting "Kill the nigger!" resulted in the deaths of two whites, one of them a French reporter. James Meredith, finally allowed to enroll and start classes with an escort of federal troops, commented, "It's more for America than for me."

tries to enroll as its first black student. About 12,000 federal troops are sent in to maintain order and to ensure Meredith's admission.

Demonstrations against *de facto* public school segregation continue in the North. In Chicago four black mothers are arrested at an elementary school sit-in. Suits are filed in federal courts to end *de facto* segregation in Englewood, New Jersey, and Rochester, New York.

Roman Catholic Archbishop Joseph Rummel excommunicates three Louisiana segregationist leaders for opposing his orders to integrate parochial schools in New Orleans.

Throughout the 12 southern states, 5 border states, and the District of Columbia, only 7.6% of black public school students attend racially integrated classes.

The Episcopal Church consecrates John M. Burgess as suffragan bishop of Massachusetts.

LITERATURE AND JOURNALISM

James Baldwin's novel *Another Country* is published.

William Melvin Kelley publishes his novel *A Different Drummer.*

Robert Hayden publishes a collection of his poems entitled *A Ballad of Remembrance.*

Mal Goode is hired as a news commentator by ABC-TV, the first African American to appear in this capacity on a national network.

PERFORMING ARTS

The Supremes make their chart debut December 29 with "Let Me Go the Right Way."

Ray Charles's "I Can't Stop Loving You" stays at the top of Billboard's Hot 100 for five weeks.

Ebony magazine cites Johnny Mathis, popular singer, as the only entertainer among 35 African-American millionaires.

Diahann Carroll wins a Tony Award for her performance in *No Strings,* which composer Richard Rodgers wrote for her.

Ellen Stewart founds LaMama Experimental Theater Club, an avant-garde performance space, in New York.

Film star Louise Beavers dies October 26 in Los Angeles.

VISUAL ARTS

John T. Biggers completes his book of drawings *Ananse: The Web of Life in Africa.*

Sculptor Augusta Savage dies March 26 in New York.

THE MILITARY

Lieutenant Commander Samuel L. Gravely, Jr., is appointed captain of the navy destroyer escort USS *Falgout*, becoming the first African American to command a U.S. warship.

In the U.S. Army, 12% of the enlisted men and 3% of the officers are black; in the U.S. Navy, 5% of the enlisted men and 3% of the officers are black.

The Kennedy administration orders military commanders to take "active opposition" to discriminatory practices in the armed forces.

SPORTS

Wilt Chamberlain, basketball star of the Philadelphia 76ers, scores 100 points against the New York Knicks. He achieves the same high score once again in his career, but no other NBA player ever matches it.

Jackie Robinson, the first African American to play in baseball's major leagues, is inducted into the National Baseball Hall of Fame.

Sonny Liston knocks out Floyd Patterson to become the world's heavyweight boxing champion.

Bill Russell, basketball star of the Boston Celtics, is named Player of the Year.

Jacqueline Joyner (later, Joyner-Kersee), Olympic track star, is born March 3 in East St. Louis, Illinois.

1963

POLITICS AND CIVIL RIGHTS

A round of protests throughout the South in observance of the Emancipation Centennial begins in Greenwood, Mississippi, with a march against discrimination and a voter registration drive.

The National Guard is summoned to quell a race riot in Cambridge, Maryland.

In Savannah, several mass civil rights demonstrations ultimately force business and civic leaders to agree to desegregate hotels, bowling alleys, and most theaters.

Over 250,000 participate in the March on Washington at the Lin-

---

Contemporary Events, 1963 ■ President Kennedy is assassinated in Dallas, Texas. ■ At the Guggenheim Museum in New York, Pop Art is given its first major show. ■ Joan Baez and Bob Dylan achieve popularity as folksingers. ■ Betty Friedan publishes **The Feminine Mystique.**

"I Have a Dream . . ."

"I have a dream that one day this nation will rise up, live out the true meaning of its creed: 'We hold these truths to be self-evident, that all men are created equal.'

"I have a dream that one day . . . sons of former slaves and sons of former slave-owners will be able to sit down together at the table of brotherhood. . . .

"I have a dream that . . . little children will one day live in a nation where they will not be judged by the color of their skin but by the content of their character.

"I have a dream that one day . . . little black boys and black girls will be able to join hands with little white boys and white girls as brothers and sisters."

—Martin Luther King, Jr., from his "I Have a Dream" address at the Lincoln Memorial, August 28, 1963

coln Memorial, the largest protest assembly in U.S. history. Martin Luther King, Jr., delivers his "I Have a Dream" speech.

President Kennedy declares segregation to be morally wrong in the strongest statement on the subject ever made by a U.S. president. He adds, "It is time to act in the Congress, in your state and local legislative body, and . . . in all of our daily lives." He proposes civil rights legislation to Congress, but no action is taken.

In Birmingham, Alabama, four young African-American girls are killed on September 15 when segregationists bomb the 16th Street Baptist Church.

Medgar Evers, NAACP field secretary and civil rights leader, is assassinated June 12 by a segregationist at his home in Jackson, Mississippi.

President Kennedy announces that Ralph J. Bunche and Marian Anderson are the first recipients of the Medal of Freedom, an honor he has just created.

In his inaugural address, Alabama Governor George C. Wallace declares, "Segregation now, segregation tomorrow, segregation forever."

Martin Luther King, Jr., leads a peaceful protest demonstration in Birmingham. Televised coverage of Police Chief Eugene "Bull" Connor and his officers using water hoses and police dogs against the protestors raises an outcry of indignation across the country.

After President Kennedy's assassination, Lyndon B. Johnson, the newly sworn president, vows to support strong civil rights legislation.

W. E. B. Du Bois, intellectual, civil rights pioneer, and founder of the NAACP, dies August 27 in Accra, Ghana, where he has made his home after abandoning the United States.

BUSINESS AND EMPLOYMENT

A. Philip Randolph formally criticizes the AFL-CIO for not endorsing the March on Washington.

RELIGION AND EDUCATION

The University of Alabama is integrated by the admission of two black students. Governor George C. Wallace personally tries to block their entrance into the administration building, but National Guardsmen sent by President Kennedy ensure their entry.

To protest *de facto* segregation, about 3,000 black students boycott Boston public schools. Later in the year, over 220,000 African-American students boycott Chicago public schools.

LITERATURE AND JOURNALISM

James Baldwin's collection of essays *The Fire Next Time* is published.

LeRoi Jones publishes his study of music *Blues People*.

John Oliver Killens's novel *And Then We Heard the Thunder* is published and nominated for a Pulitzer Prize.

Ebony magazine's commemorative issue for the 100th anniversary of the Emancipation Proclamation sells over a million copies.

PERFORMING ARTS

Sidney Poitier stars in *Lilies of the Field* and in 1964 receives the Academy Award for best actor for his performance. It is the first time an African-American male has been awarded an Oscar.

Pianist Andre Watts makes his debut at age 16 with the New York Philharmonic.

Number-one hits on the pop music charts include the Chiffons' "He's So Fine" and 12-year-old Stevie Wonder's "Fingertips Part 2."

Singer Whitney Houston is born August 9 in Newark, New Jersey.

Rapper M. C. Hammer is born March 30 in Oakland, California.

Vanessa Williams, the first black Miss America, is born in Tarrytown, New York. She will later become a singing and recording star.

VISUAL ARTS

In New York, African-American artists form the group Spiral, dedicated to defining the special problems faced by African-American artists and to linking art with social responsibility. Among the founders are Charles Alston, Romare Bearden, Norman Lewis, and Hale Woodruff.

SPORTS

Arthur Ashe is the first African American named to the U.S. Davis Cup tennis team, although he plays only as a substitute this year.

Michael Jeffrey Jordan, Olympic and professional basketball star, is born February 17 in Brooklyn, New York.

1964

POLITICS AND CIVIL RIGHTS

Under heavy pressure from President Lyndon Johnson, Congress passes a Civil Rights Bill, banning discrimination in public accommodations, education, and employment.

The Council of Federated Organizations (SNCC, CORE, SCLC, and NAACP) sponsors the Mississippi Summer Project, in which over 1,000 black and white volunteers help African Americans in Mississippi register to vote.

In Philadelphia, Mississippi, three civil rights demonstrators—one black man and two white men—are murdered. Among the suspects is the sheriff of the county where the murders took place. There are several arrests but no convictions.

Spontaneous protest-related rioting breaks out in Harlem, resulting in one death, 140 serious injuries, and over 500 arrests. Similar riots follow in Brooklyn and Rochester, New York; Paterson, Jersey City, and Elizabeth, New Jersey; Philadelphia, Pennsylvania; and Dixmoor, Illinois.

Referring to the wave of riots, Roy Wilkins of the NAACP calls attention to a split in the Civil Rights Movement between nonviolent protestors and what he calls "criminal elements."

Alabama Governor George Wallace, a segregationist, wins the highest percentage of votes in several Democratic primaries for the presidential nomination, including Indiana (30%) and Maryland (43%).

In Alabama, K. L. Buford and Stanley Smith are elected to the Tuskegee City Council, the first African Americans in the 20th century to hold public office in Alabama.

Carl T. Rowan is appointed director of the U.S. Information Agency.

The 24th Amendment to the U.S. Constitution outlaws the poll tax, commonly employed in the South to keep blacks from voting.

In Indiana, Wyoming, and 17 southern and border states, marriages between blacks and whites are still illegal.

Martin Luther King, Jr., is awarded the Nobel Peace Prize on December 10.

President Johnson presents the Medal of Freedom to Leontyne Price and A. Philip Randolph.

BUSINESS AND EMPLOYMENT

The Independence Bank of Chicago is founded.

The National Labor Relations Board refuses to recognize unions that have discriminatory admissions policies or practices.

Contemporary Events, 1964 ■ Lyndon B. Johnson is elected president. ■ New York hosts a World's Fair. ■ Discotheques are popular, featuring such black-inspired dances as the Watusi and Frug. ■ Congress passes the Tonkin Gulf Resolution, allowing the president to take military action in Vietnam.

RELIGION AND EDUCATION

Malcolm X breaks with the Nation of Islam and founds the Organization for Afro-American Unity.

The passage in Congress of the Economic Opportunity Act, part of President Johnson's "War on Poverty," benefits many African Americans through such programs as Head Start for preschoolers, the Upward Bound program for high school students, and work-study financial aid incentives for college students.

In New York and Cleveland, hundreds of thousands of African-American students boycott public schools to protest poor facilities.

LITERATURE AND JOURNALISM

Ralph Ellison's collection of essays *Shadow and Act* is published.

LeRoi Jones's poetry collection *The Dead Lecturer* is published.

Owen Dodson's novel *A Bent House* is published.

Kristin Hunter publishes *God Bless the Child*.

SCIENCE AND TECHNOLOGY

The American Medical Association adopts a resolution opposing discrimination in membership, privileges, or responsibilities in all county, state, and regional medical societies and associations.

PERFORMING ARTS

Sammy Davis, Jr., stars in the musical *Golden Boy* on Broadway.

Lorraine Hansberry's play *The Sign in Sidney Brustein's Window* opens on Broadway.

James Baldwin's play *Blues for Mr. Charlie* opens on Broadway.

LeRoi Jones's play *Dutchman* is produced Off-Broadway.

The Four Tops debut on the charts August 15 with "Baby, I Need Your Loving."

Louis Armstrong's recording of "Hello, Dolly!" is a number one hit, earning the largest amount of money ever by an African-American recording.

The Supremes' "Where Did Our Love Go" becomes number one on the pop charts August 23. They follow it up with the hit "Baby Love" on October 3.

Actor Frederick O'Neal becomes the first African-American president of the union Actors' Equity.

VISUAL ARTS

The Museum of African Art is established in Washington, D.C.

"More So Than Any Other Time"

"This generation, especially of our people, have a burden, more so than any other time in history. The most important thing we can learn to do today is think for ourselves."

—Malcolm X, 1964

247

On to Selma

The 1965 march to Selma to protest the denial of black voting rights exposed the depth of discrimination in the South and inspired a generation of college students to take action against it. Martin Luther King, Jr., and 500 followers first attempted the march on March 7, but were attacked and repulsed by 200 state troopers acting under direct orders from Governor George Wallace. On March 9, President Lyndon Johnson condemned the police action, stating that he was sure all Americans "joined in deploring the brutality with which a number of black citizens in Alabama were treated when they sought to dramatize their deep and sincere interest in attaining the precious right to vote." That same day 1,500 demonstrators tried to march again but were restrained by federal order until a ruling could be made. Finally, on March 21, about 3,000 civil rights demonstrators completed the march, armed with a federal warrant that allowed them to march and forced Governor Wallace to provide them with police protection. On March 25, some 40,000 civil rights supporters gathered at a mass protest rally.

Sculptor Geraldine McCullough is awarded the George D. Widener Gold Medal at the Pennsylvania Academy of Fine Arts Exhibition.

SPORTS

Cassius Clay knocks out Sonny Liston to win the world's heavyweight boxing championship. Later this same year, he converts to Islam and adopts the name Muhammad Ali.

In the Tokyo Olympics, Bob Hayes wins a gold medal for the 100-meter dash. Other African-American gold medalists include Henry Carr (200-meter dash), Joe Frazier (heavyweight), Hayes Jones (110-meter hurdles), Edith McGuire (200-meter dash), and Wyomia Tyus (100-meter dash).

1965

POLITICS AND CIVIL RIGHTS

Martin Luther King, Jr., begins an extended campaign to register black voters in Selma, Alabama. Three white ministers are beaten for participating in this voter registration campaign. James J. Reeb dies of his injuries. Three white segregationists are indicted for his murder but later acquitted.

To protest opposition from local officials to his voter registration campaign, Martin Luther King, Jr., and thousands of supporters conduct a five-day, 54-mile march from Selma to Montgomery that is sanctioned by the federal government. A previous attempt to march was thwarted by local police using tear gas, nightsticks, whips, and cattle prods.

Viola Gregg Liuzzo, a white civil rights advocate from Detroit, is killed by gunfire following the Selma–Montgomery protest march. Four Ku Klux Klan members are arrested. Three are later convicted of conspiracy in the murder.

Jimmie L. Jackson, a black civil rights demonstrator, is killed by state troopers in Marion, Alabama.

Constance Baker Motley is elected Manhattan borough president, the highest elective office held to date by an African-American woman in a major U.S. city.

Martin Luther King, Jr., leads a three-mile march protesting discrim-

---

Contemporary Events, 1965 ■ College students demonstrate to protest the American bombing of North Vietnam. ■ Pope Paul VI visits New York and addresses the United Nations. ■ The northeastern United States suffers an electrical blackout when a relay switch near Niagara Falls malfunctions.

ination in Boston, after which he addresses a crowd of 20,000 on Boston Common.

Mass antidiscrimination demonstrations and marches in Chicago lead to the arrest of hundreds of civil rights advocates, including comedian Dick Gregory and CORE leader James Farmer.

In Bogalusa, Louisiana, protest marches are subjected to police brutality and gunfire attacks from segregationists. The U.S. Department of Justice intervenes to set up peace negotiations.

Thurgood Marshall becomes solicitor general of the United States, the first African American to receive such an appointment.

President Johnson signs the Voting Rights Act of 1965, letting federal agents register black voters if state agents refuse to do so.

The most severe race-related rioting so far in U.S. history takes place over six days in the predominantly black area of Watts in Los Angeles. Over 30 people are killed, some 1,000 are seriously injured, and property damage exceeds $46 million.

The House Un-American Activities Committee begins investigating the Ku Klux Klan.

Patricia R. Harris is appointed ambassador to Luxembourg, the first African-American woman named an ambassador.

BUSINESS AND EMPLOYMENT

Seaway National Bank of Chicago is founded.

RELIGION AND EDUCATION

On February 21, Malcolm X is assassinated at a rally in the Audubon Ballroom in New York, apparently by members of the Nation of Islam.

The Johnson administration sets a deadline of fall 1967 for the integration of all grade levels of public schools seeking federal funds.

In Brooklyn, black students riot and stage a one-day boycott of public schools.

The pope appoints Harold R. Perry as the first black Roman Catholic bishop in the United States in the 20th century. Perry replaces John Patrick Cody as bishop of New Orleans when Cody, a white civil rights advocate, is named archbishop of Chicago, the nation's most populous Roman Catholic see.

Vivian Malone is the first African American to graduate from the University of Alabama.

Father Divine, founder of the Peace Mission Movement, dies September 10 in Philadelphia.

LITERATURE AND JOURNALISM

The Autobiography of Malcolm X (as told to Alex Haley) is published.

Claude Brown's autobiography *Manchild in the Promised Land* is published.

John Oliver Killens's account of the Civil Rights Movement, *The Black Man's Burden*, is published.

John A. Williams's travelogue *This Is My Country, Too* is published.

Chester Himes publishes his novel *Cotton Comes to Harlem*.

Novelist William Melvin Kelley publishes *A Drop of Patience*.

Playwright Lorraine Hansberry dies January 12 in New York.

PERFORMING ARTS

James Baldwin's play *The Amen Corner* opens on Broadway.

LeRoi Jones's plays *The Toilet* and *The Slave* open Off-Broadway.

In Stratford, Connecticut, Ruby Dee is the first African-American actress to play major roles at the American Shakespeare Festival.

Martina Arroyo debuts as "Aida" at the Metropolitan Opera House.

Dancer Judith Jamison debuts with Alvin Ailey's dance troupe.

Muhal Richard Abrams founds the Association for the Advancement of Creative Musicians.

On the pop music charts, the Supremes have their fourth consecutive number-one hit with "Stop! In the Name of Love." The Temptations have their first number-one hit with "My Girl," written by William "Smokey" Robinson; the Four Tops also have their first number-one hit with "I Can't Help Myself (Sugar Pie, Honey Bunch)."

Singer Nat "King" Cole dies February 15 in Santa Monica, California.

Actress Dorothy Dandridge, nominated for an Oscar in *Carmen Jones*, dies September 8 in Hollywood.

Jazz saxophonist Earl Bostic dies October 28 in Rochester, New York.

THE MILITARY

Major General Benjamin O. Davis, Jr., of the U.S. Air Force is named lieutenant general, the highest rank achieved to date by an African American.

SPORTS

Satchel Paige is named all-time outstanding player by the National Baseball Congress on January 30.

Gale Sayers of the Chicago Bears breaks the NFL's touchdown record and is named Rookie of the Year.

Mike Garrett, running back for the University of Southern California, wins the Heisman Trophy. He will later play for the Kansas City Chiefs and the San Diego Chargers.

ADDITIONAL STATISTICS

According to the Social Security Administration, nonwhites represent 34% of the population living below the poverty level.

1966

POLITICS AND CIVIL RIGHTS

Robert C. Weaver becomes head of the Department of Housing and Urban Development, the first African American appointed to serve in a presidential cabinet.

Constance Baker Motley becomes the first African-American woman appointed a federal judge.

Stokely Carmichael assumes leadership of SNCC and speaks for more militant civil rights activists by advocating Black Power.

Vernon Dahmer, a black civil rights advocate, is killed by a fire bomb in Hattiesburg, Mississippi.

James Meredith, the first black to enroll at the University of Mississippi, is shot by a white segregationist during a voting rights march from Memphis, Tennesee, to Jackson, Mississippi. He is seriously injured but recovers.

President Johnson appoints Andrew Brimmer governor of the Federal Reserve Board.

CORE adopts a resolution endorsing the more militant concept of Black Power, but the NAACP disassociates itself from the slogan.

Martin Luther King, Jr., starts a campaign to make Chicago an "open city" by addressing a rally of 45,000 at Soldiers Field. Rioting breaks out on Chicago's West Side two days later, killing two blacks and injuring many others. Sporadic violence continues throughout the year.

President Johnson holds a White House Conference on Civil Rights, attended by 2,400 prominent whites and blacks. It is boycotted by SNCC and CORE.

Rioting in Cleveland kills 4, injures nearly 50, and causes extensive

Contemporary Events, 1966 ■ Color television becomes available to a nationwide mass market.
■ The National Organization for Women is founded, with Betty Friedan as president.

property damage. Major race-related riots also erupt in Milwaukee, Atlanta, San Francisco, Lansing (Michigan), Waukegan (Illinois), and other cities.

The Black Panther Party is founded in Oakland, California, by Huey P. Newton and Bobby Seale.

Edward Brooke, a Republican, is elected to the U.S. Senate from Massachusetts, the first black senator since Reconstruction.

Julian Bond is denied a seat in the Georgia House of Representatives because of his opposition to the Vietnam War, but many believe that a critical factor against Bond is his role as communications director of SNCC. The U.S. Supreme Court later rules that Bond must be seated.

BUSINESS AND EMPLOYMENT

Investigations find that the Civil Rights Act of 1964 has not prevented the following industries from continuing discriminatory unions: railroads, steamships, paper and pulp manufacturing, chemicals and oil refining, printing, skilled metal trades, tobacco manufacturing, Great Lakes shipping, and building and construction.

Senator Robert F. Kennedy of New York announces the formation of two groups of black community business leaders in the New York City area: the Bedford-Stuyvesant Renewal and Rehabilitation Corporation, and the Development and Services Corporation.

RELIGION AND EDUCATION

In the South, 15.9% of African-American students attend integrated schools. State figures range from a high of 44.9% in Texas to a low of 2.5% in Mississippi.

LITERATURE AND JOURNALISM

LeRoi Jones's collection of essays *Home* is published, offering his strongest antiwhite statements to date.

James Baldwin publishes his short stories *Going to See the Man*.

Samuel Delany publishes *Babel-17,* which wins the Nebula Award of the Science Fiction Writers of America.

The Spingarn Medal is awarded to John H. Johnson, publisher of *Negro Digest, Jet,* and *Ebony,* for enhancing the self-image of African Americans.

SCIENCE AND TECHNOLOGY

Samuel Nabrit is the first African American to serve on the Atomic Energy Commission.

The Charles R. Drew Postgraduate Medical School, later known as the Charles R. Drew University of Medicine and Science, is founded in Los Angeles.

PERFORMING ARTS

Bill Cosby wins the Emmy Award for best actor in a TV series (*I Spy*).

Andre Watts performs as the principal soloist in the Philharmonic Stravinsky Festival in New York.

Leontyne Price opens both the opera season and the new Metropolitan Opera House at Lincoln Center when she sings the lead role in *Antony and Cleopatra,* which was written for her by Samuel Barber.

Singer and actress Janet Jackson is born May 16 in Gary, Indiana.

VISUAL ARTS

African-American painters and sculptors form the largest delegation of visual artists to exhibit at the first World Festival of Black Arts in Dakar, Senegal. William Majors, an engraver, wins a first prize.

THE MILITARY

Martin Luther King, Jr., deplores the Vietnam War, calling it "a sordid military adventure."

In the Vietnam War, Milton L. Olive III dies while catching a grenade and saving his comrades. He is posthumously awarded the Congressional Medal of Honor for his heroism.

SPORTS

Emmett Ashford becomes the first African-American umpire in baseball's major leagues.

Bill Russell joins the coaching staff of basketball's Boston Celtics, becoming the first African American to coach a major professional athletic team.

Frank Robinson of the Baltimore Orioles baseball team is the American League's batting and home-run champion and the Most Valuable Player of the Year.

ADDITIONAL STATISTICS

Among all Americans living in cities of over a million people, African Americans make up 26%.

ADDITIONAL EVENTS

Maulana Karenga creates the festival of Kwanza (celebrated annually between Christmas and New Year's Day) "to restore and reaffirm our African heritage and culture."

Kwanza

Created in 1966 by a professor of African-American studies, the holiday of Kwanza (from the Swahili **matunda ya kwanza,** "first fruits") runs from December 26 through January 1 and celebrates African-American culture and community with feasting, storytelling, and symbolic activities. Each day is dedicated to one of seven principles:

1. **umoja** (unity)
2. **kujichangulia** (self-determination)
3. **ujima** (collective work and responsibility)
4. **ujamaa** (cooperative economics)
5. **nia** (purpose)
6. **kuumba** (creativity)
7. **imani** (faith)

1967

POLITICS AND CIVIL RIGHTS

U.S. Representative Adam Clayton Powell, Jr., is expelled from Congress for "misuse of public funds." After unsuccessfully fighting the expulsion (and winning a special runoff election in his district), he begins a two-year exile on the Bahamian island of Bimini.

Civil rights demonstrations in Louisville, Kentucky, prompt rioting and force county and city leaders to hold bargaining sessions.

President Lyndon Johnson asks Congress to pass civil rights legislation regarding the sale and renting of housing.

Martin Luther King, Jr., leads thousands of marchers protesting the Vietnam War to the United Nations building in New York City. Later, he forms the group Negotiation Now to secure one million signatures on a peace petition to be delivered to the president.

In Jackson, Mississippi, Benjamin Brown, a black delivery man, is shot to death on the campus of Jackson State College. Angry demonstrations follow, causing the governor to call in 1,000 National Guardsmen.

H. Rap Brown succeeds Stokely Carmichael as head of SNCC.

Rioting breaks out in the Roxbury section of Boston after black welfare mothers barricade themselves in a building to protest discrimination. Over 90 people are seriously injured.

President Johnson appoints Thurgood Marshall to the Supreme Court, the first African American to sit on the bench.

Nine civil rights leaders, including Martin Luther King, Jr., announce their intention to help relieve racial disharmony in Chicago, which they say has reached "crisis proportions." J. Edgar Hoover, director of the FBI, criticizes King for issuing an "open invitation" to violence.

The "long, hot summer" of race riots erupts in Newark with the biggest race-related insurrection since the 1965 Watts riot. Serious riots also occur in New York City, Atlanta, Buffalo, Detroit, Milwaukee, New Haven, Cambridge (Maryland), and other cities.

James Meredith leads a new March Against Fear in Mississippi to "expose and oppose" discrimination.

Contemporary Events, 1967 ■ The United States manned space program is temporarily suspended after three astronauts die during a fire on a launching pad. ■ Billie Jean King wins the women's singles tennis competitions at both Forest Hills and Wimbledon. ■ The musical **Hair** opens in New York.

The first National Conference on Black Power is held in Newark, consisting of representatives of nearly 50 different activist groups. Among those attending are SNCC's H. Rap Brown and SCLC's Jesse Jackson.

President Johnson forms a Special Advisory Committee on Civil Disorders to investigate racial disturbances and propose remedies.

President Johnson names Walter E. Washington to lead the newly reconstituted government of Washington, D.C., making him the first African American to govern a major U.S. city. Later, Carl Stokes is elected mayor of Cleveland and Richard Hatcher is elected mayor of Gary, Indiana.

The U.S. Supreme Court rules that a Virginia state law prohibiting racially mixed marriages is illegal.

Ralphe J. Bunche is promoted to undersecretary-general at the United Nations, the highest rank held so far by an American within the organization.

BUSINESS AND EMPLOYMENT

The Equal Opportunities Commission accuses the American pharmaceutical industry of widespread discrimination and demands the immediate hiring of blacks and upgrading of black-held positions.

The Ford Motor Company, the Michigan Bell Telephone Company, and the Chrysler Corporation open more jobs to African Americans in Detroit and launch programs to recruit black job prospects.

RELIGION AND EDUCATION

A federal court in Montgomery, Alabama, orders the governor and the state board of education to integrate all public schools this year. It is the first case of an entire state being placed under a single federal desegregation injunction.

Benjamin Mays retires as president of Morehouse College, a position he has held since 1940.

There are 113 African-American colleges and universities in the United States.

The Anacostia Museum, designed to reflect the contributions of African Americans to the social and cultural history of the United States, opens in Washington, D.C.

LITERATURE AND JOURNALISM

William Melvin Kelley's novel *Dem*, a critique of white American society, is published.

John A. Williams publishes his novel *The Man Who Cried I Am*.

LeRoi Jones's collection of short stories *Tales* is published. During the year Jones changes his name to Imamu Ameer Baraka (later Amiri Baraka).

John Oliver Killens's novel *Sippi* is published.

Stokely Carmichael and Charles V. Hamilton publish *Black Power: The Politics of Liberation in America.*

Haki Madhubuti starts the Third World Press in Chicago.

Langston Hughes dies May 22 in New York. His poetry collection *The Panther and the Lash* is published posthumously.

SCIENCE AND TECHNOLOGY

Astronaut Robert H. Lawrence is chosen to be on the crew of a staffed orbiting laboratory, becoming the first African American to be selected for the U.S. space program. He dies, however, in an airplane accident.

PERFORMING ARTS

On Broadway, the musical *Hello, Dolly* features an all-black cast, starring Pearl Bailey and Cab Calloway. Bailey will receive a special Tony Award for her performance.

Leslie Uggams stars in the Broadway musical *Hallelujah Baby* and will win a Tony Award for this role.

Hollywood releases *Guess Who's Coming to Dinner?* with Katharine Hepburn and Spencer Tracy as parents of a daughter who is engaged to marry a black man, played by Sidney Poitier.

The Negro Ensemble Company is formed in New York.

When Aretha Franklin records "Respect," written by Otis Redding, it goes to number one on the charts.

Entertainer Otis Redding dies December 10 in a plane crash. His recording of "(Sittin' On) The Dock of the Bay" will be a posthumous hit, topping the charts for four weeks in 1968.

John Coltrane, jazz composer and saxophonist, dies July 17.

VISUAL ARTS

Over 250,000 people attend an exhibition of African-American artists at the City University of New York.

The Organization of Black American Culture paints the *Wall of Respect* in Chicago.

SPORTS

After refusing to be drafted into the U.S. Army for religious reasons,

Muhammad Ali is stripped of his world heavyweight boxing championship by the World Boxing Association and the New York Athletic Association.

For the second year Wilt Chamberlain is the National Basketball Association's Most Valuable Player. He will be chosen again in 1968.

Civil rights groups discuss whether to boycott the 1968 Olympics in Mexico City to protest racial discrimination in the United States.

1968

POLITICS AND CIVIL RIGHTS

On a speaking tour of California college campuses, Adam Clayton Powell, Jr., urges blacks and whites to join "the black revolution." Later, he tells his Abyssinian Baptist congregation in Harlem that nonviolence is no longer the most effective civil rights strategy.

In Orangeburg, South Carolina, three black students are shot to death by police during a race riot at South Carolina State College.

President Johnson's National Advisory Committee on Civil Disorders (the Kerner Commission) issues its report on the causes of the many 1967 race riots in U.S. urban areas. It cites the major cause as the existence of two unreconciled groups in America—"one black, one white, separate and unequal"—and blames white racism for most of the trouble.

The Civil Rights Bill of 1968, including nondiscriminatory housing measures and antirioting provisions, is signed into law.

Martin Luther King, Jr., leads a protest march in support of striking African-American sanitation workers in Memphis. It turns violent, resulting in the death of a black teenager. King is rushed to a nearby motel before the march can be completed.

Martin Luther King, Jr., is assassinated April 4 by white segregationist James Earl Ray in Memphis a few days after a disrupted protest march for striking sanitation workers. The nation mourns, and violence erupts in the black sections of many U.S. cities, including Baltimore, Chicago, and Washington, D.C. A total of 41 blacks and 5 whites are killed.

The Poor People's Campaign brings thousands of African Americans to Washington, D.C., to protest racial discrimination. Under

"A Drum Major for Peace"

After Martin Luther King, Jr.'s assassination in Memphis, on April 4, 1968, his body was placed on public view at Ebenezer Baptist Church in Atlanta. On April 9, a message that he tape-recorded shortly before his death, clearly indicating that he suspected he would one day be killed, was played at his funeral. It contained the words: "Say . . . that I tried to love and serve humanity . . . say that I was a drum major for peace . . . for righteousness." His coffin was then carried through the streets of Atlanta on a farm wagon pulled by two Georgia mules to a gravesite in South View Cemetery.

Contemporary Events, 1968 ■ President Johnson declines to run for a second term. Richard Nixon, the Republican nominee, is elected president on a promise to end the Vietnam War. ■ Violent crimes in the United States have increased 50% since 1960.

the leadership of Ralph Abernathy, Martin Luther King, Jr.'s successor as head of SCLC, protestors create a temporary shantytown near the Lincoln Memorial dubbed "Resurrection City." Coretta Scott King, the widow of Martin Luther King, Jr., leads a march of welfare mothers from 20 U.S. cities.

Senator Robert Kennedy is assassinated in Los Angeles after he wins the California Democratic primary. Coretta Scott King joins Kennedy's widow, Ethel, on the plane that returns Kennedy's body to New York.

A race riot in the Glenville section of Cleveland causes the deaths of eight blacks and three whites. Mayor Carl Stokes ends the riot by calling in 3,000 National Guardsmen.

In Miami, rioting, looting, and firebombing devastate the black district. Police kill three African-American men.

At a rally outside the Democratic National Convention in Chicago, Ralph Abernathy of SCLC attacks Democratic officials, including presidential nominee Hubert Humphrey, for offering little attention or support for African Americans, especially during the Poor People's Campaign. Later, a march on the convention hall led by comedian Dick Gregory is stopped by police using tear gas. TV coverage of the disturbance shocks viewers across the nation.

Channing Phillips, an African-American minister from Washington, D.C., is put forward as a candidate for the Democratic presidential nomination. Julian Bond, legislator from Georgia, is proposed as a vice-presidential nominee.

Huey P. Newton of the Black Panthers is convicted of manslaughter in the 1967 shooting of a white police officer. He is sentenced to 2 to 15 years in prison. Coverage of the trial focuses national attention on the Black Panthers for the first time.

Ten African American are elected to Congress. Shirley Chisholm of the Bedford-Stuyvesant section of Brooklyn is the first African-American woman elected to the House of Representatives. Voters in Harlem reelect Adam Clayton Powell, Jr., to the House.

At the University of California's Berkeley campus, Eldridge Cleaver, a leading member of the Black Panthers, is invited to deliver a series of lectures. Conservatives, including Governor Ronald Reagan, object strongly, while liberals support Cleaver's right to speak. Ultimately, Cleaver is allowed to give one lecture, "The Roots of Racism."

Eldridge Cleaver becomes a fugitive from the law when he violates parole in San Francisco to attend an international anti–Vietnam War conference in Montreal.

Police in Jersey City arrest three Black Panthers for attacking a police station with machine guns. The case creates unfavorable publicity for the Black Panthers.

The *New York Times* reports that 59% of African Americans who were polled prefer to be called "Afro-American" or "black" rather than "Negro."

BUSINESS AND EMPLOYMENT

According to *Fortune* magazine, the African-American consumer market in the United States amounts to $30 billion a year.

The Ford Foundation, led by McGeorge Bundy, grants money to two African-American business development agencies: $520,000 to the Negro Industrial and Economic Union of Cleveland, and $400,000 to the Bedford-Stuyvesant Development and Services Corporation in Brooklyn.

The National Business League reports that there are over 50,000 black-owned or black-controlled businesses.

RELIGION AND EDUCATION

The Roman Catholic Church in the United States issues a "declaration of war on racism."

The U.S. Supreme Court orders all U.S. public schools to draw up desegregation plans immediately. Thirteen years previously, the court had ordered schools to do the same thing "with all deliberate speed."

Teachers in the New York City public school system strike for several weeks. Racial discrimination in hiring, wages, and facilities is a major complaint of many strikers.

Howard University students take over the administration building, demanding a more black-oriented curriculum.

Elder Solomon Lightfoot Michaux, charismatic evangelist, dies October 20 in Washington, D.C.

LITERATURE AND JOURNALISM

Eldridge Cleaver's collection of autobiographical essays, *Soul on Ice*, is published.

Life magazine runs a four-issue series on African-American history, including interviews with Jesse Jackson, Eldridge Cleaver, Dick Gregory, and Julian Bond.

Science fiction writer Samuel R. Delany publishes the last volume in his *Fall of the Towers* trilogy.

Nikki Giovanni publishes her poetry collections *Black Feeling, Black Talk,* and *Black Judgment.*

William H. Grier and Price M. Cobbs, two African-American psychiatrists, publish their study *Black Rage*.

PERFORMING ARTS

Henry Lewis is hired as director of the New Jersey Symphony, the first African American to lead a major U.S. symphony orchestra.

Diahann Carroll stars on NBC in her TV comedy series *Julia*.

One Life to Live becomes the first TV soap opera to feature an African-American character. Ellen Holly, primarily a Shakespearean actress, plays a black woman who is passing for white.

The Spingarn Medal is awarded to entertainer Sammy Davis, Jr., who is cited for his "many-faceted talent."

Blues singer Ida Cox dies November 10 in Knoxville, Tennessee.

Rap artist L. L. Cool Jay is born James Todd Smith January 14 in New York.

Gary Coleman, star of the TV series *Diff'rent Strokes,* is born February 8 in Zion, Ohio.

VISUAL ARTS

The Studio Museum in Harlem, a major exhibition space for African-American art, opens in New York.

The group AfriCobra (African Commune of Bad Relevant Artists) forms in Chicago to promote Afrocentric art.

THE MILITARY

Ruth A. Lucas is the first African-American woman to become a colonel in the U.S. Air Force.

African Americans represent 9.8% of all troops stationed in Vietnam, 20% of the combat troops, and 14.1% of the troops killed in action.

The reenlistment rate for blacks in the U.S. Army is three times the rate for whites, reflecting limited job opportunities for African Americans in the economy.

SPORTS

Joe Frazier wins the world's heavyweight boxing championship.

At Forest Hills, tennis star Arthur Ashe is the first African American to win the U.S. Open men's singles championship.

At the Mexico City Olympics, Wyomia Tyus wins a gold medal in the 100-meter race—the first person to do so in two consecutive Olympics. Other track gold medalists include Bob Beamon (long jump), Willie Davenport (110-meter hurdles), Lee Evans (400-meter run), Jim Hines (100-meter dash), and Tommie Smith (200-meter dash). At the awards ceremony Smith and John Carlos raise their fists in a Black Power salute to call international attention to the movement. They are then suspended from the U.S. Olympic team.

O. J. Simpson, running back for the University of Southern California, wins football's Heisman Trophy.

Over half of all professional basketball players are African American, as are almost a third of major league baseball and football players.

ADDITIONAL EVENTS

The first Miss Black America pageant is held in Atlantic City. Saundra Williams is the winner.

1969

POLITICS AND CIVIL RIGHTS

In Charleston, South Carolina, Ralph Abernathy of SCLC, joined by Coretta Scott King, leads over 700 hospital workers striking to protest racial discrimination in a march through the downtown area. National Guardsmen are summoned and over 200 people are arrested.

Race-related rioting, firebombing, and sniping breaks out in Hartford, Connecticut, resulting in a dusk-to-dawn curfew.

The U.S. Commission on Civil Rights issues a report censuring the Nixon administration for a slow, misguided desegregation policy.

Black Panther leader Bobby Seale is one of the "Chicago 8" tried for conspiracy to incite a riot during the 1968 Democratic National Convention in that city. After criticizing the judge, Seale is gagged and chained. His case is separated from the others (now the "Chicago 7"), and he is later sentenced to four years in prison for contempt of court. He will serve two years before the charges are rescinded.

Police in Chicago raid the headquarters of the Black Panthers, killing two leaders in their beds and wounding four others. A grand jury investigation finds the raid "excessive."

The Supreme Court declares that the expulsion of Adam Clayton Powell, Jr., from the House of Representatives was unconstitutional.

Contemporary Events, 1969 ■ The first U.S. troops are withdrawn from Vietnam. ■ U.S. astronaut Neil Armstrong becomes the first man to set foot on the moon. ■ The Woodstock Music Festival attracts a crowd of over 400,000.

Charles Evers, brother of the assassinated civil rights leader Medgar Evers, is elected mayor of Fayette, Mississippi.

BUSINESS AND EMPLOYMENT

The U.S. Department of Justice pressures Cannon Mills, a southern textile company, to integrate company-owned housing facilities. It is the first time the federal government has taken such an action with a manufacturer.

In Pittsburgh, several hundred black construction workers close five construction sites to protest discriminatory hiring practices. Several hundred white workers stage a counterprotest. The standoff is not resolved until U.S. Secretary of Labor George Schultz intervenes with the so-called Philadelphia Plan, requiring contractors on federally funded projects to hire a certain percentage of African-American workers.

Johnson Products Company, the largest maker of African-American hair-care products, is incorporated. In 1971 it will be the first black-owned company listed on the American Stock Exchange.

RELIGION AND EDUCATION

African-American students, concerned about racial attacks on campus, stage an armed takeover of the student center at Cornell University. After unsuccessful counterattacks, the administration yields to their demands, and the students withdraw peacefully.

The U.S. Department of Health, Education, and Welfare decides that Antioch College can sponsor a "blacks only" black studies program. It advises Antioch that whites can be excluded only because their background is not "relevant to the course," not because of arbitrary distinctions based on race.

The Washington Square United Methodist Church in New York sends $15,000 to James Forman of the National Black Economic Development Conference. It is the first mainly white church to respond to Forman's demand for $500 million in reparations from American churches for their role in perpetuating slavery.

The U.S. Department of Justice sues the state of Georgia to end public school segregation. It is the first time the federal government has filed a desegregation suit against an entire state. Governor Lester G. Maddox vows to "win the war against these tyrants."

The mainly white American Baptist Convention chooses an African American, Thomas Kilgore of Los Angeles, as its president.

Clifton R. Wharton, Jr., is named president of Michigan State University, the first African-American president of a large, predominantly white university since Patrick Healy headed Georgetown University in the late 19th century.

At North Carolina A&T College, National Guardsmen fire on African-American demonstrators and kill one student.

Harvard University establishes an Afro-American Studies program, which inspires other universities to do the same.

The Amistad Research Center is established to collect source materials on the history of ethnic minorities.

LITERATURE AND JOURNALISM

In Boston, the Black Academy of Arts and Letters is founded.

Novelist Paule Marshall publishes *The Chosen Place, the Timeless People*.

Darwin Turner edits the anthology *Black American Literature*.

The journal *Black Scholar* begins publication.

Pearl Bailey publishes her first autobiography, *Raw Pearl*.

Activist H. Rap Brown publishes *Die Nigger Die!*

SCIENCE AND TECHNOLOGY

The National Association of Health Services Executives is created to ensure better-quality health care to disadvantaged minority groups.

PERFORMING ARTS

James Earl Jones wins Broadway's Tony Award for best actor for his portrayal of boxer Jack Johnson in *The Great White Hope*.

Charles Gordone's play *No Place to Be Somebody* opens Off-Broadway. It will win the 1970 Pulitzer Prize for drama.

The Bill Cosby Show debuts on TV. In the same year Cosby wins his fourth Emmy for a TV variety special.

Della Reese hosts her own TV show.

Rupert Crosse plays "Ned McCaslin" in the film *The Reivers*. For this role, he will receive an Oscar nomination for best supporting actor.

Hollywood releases Gordon Parks's *The Learning Tree*, the first major post–World War II film directed by an African American.

The Fifth Dimension hits number one with "Aquarius/Let the Sun Shine In," which will win a Grammy for best record.

Arthur Mitchell cofounds the Dance Theater of Harlem.

Gospel singer Roberta Martin dies January 18 in Chicago.

VISUAL ARTS

In the SoHo district of New York, Romare Bearden, Norman Lewis,

"Who Are the Real Outlaws . . . ?"

As head of the Student Nonviolent Coordinating Committee, H. Rap Brown had stirred up controversy with his militancy. In his autobiographical protest book, **Die Nigger Die!,** he was equally outspoken. "Who are the real outlaws in this country?" he demanded, asking how African Americans could be expected to obey laws when they were not "represented in making those laws." Throughout his book he called for defiance. Yet he directly countered the media claims that he was teaching hate—pointing out, "Hate, like love, is a feeling. How can you teach a feeling? If Black people hate white people, it's not because of me, it's because of what white people do to Black people."

and Ernest Crichlow establish the Cinque Gallery to promote African-American artists.

The Frederick Douglass Institute and the National Collection of Fine Arts sponsor a 90-piece retrospective of Henry Ossawa Tanner's work. The show tours several major museums.

Elizabeth Catlett completes her linocut *Malcolm Speaks for Us,* which will win first prize at the National Print Salon in Mexico.

Moneta Sleet, Jr., of *Ebony* magazine wins the Pulitzer Prize for photography. Among his many dramatic photographs is one of Coretta Scott King at her husband's funeral.

Several important exhibits are mounted in New York: "New Black Artists" at the Brooklyn Museum, "Harlem on My Mind" at the Metropolitan Museum of Art, "Invisible America: Black Artists of the Thirties" at the Studio Museum in Harlem, and "30 Contemporary Black Artists" at the IBM Gallery.

Artist James V. Herring, founder of the Howard University Art Gallery, dies May 29 in Washington, D.C.

THE MILITARY

General Leonard F. Chapman, Jr., commander of the Marine Corps, orders an end to discrimination against African Americans in all Marine Corps policies and procedures.

SPORTS

John B. McLendon becomes the first black ABA coach when he joins the Denver Nuggets' coaching squad.

ADDITIONAL EVENTS

The U.S. Postal Service issues a stamp commemorating W. C. Handy, "Father of the Blues."

1970

POLITICS AND CIVIL RIGHTS

Many states and schools across the nation hold ceremonies to observe Martin Luther King, Jr.'s birthday. In Atlanta, Coretta Scott King announces the creation of the Martin Luther King, Jr., Center for Nonviolent Social Change.

Contemporary Events, 1970 ■ The first Earth Day is celebrated April 22. ■ In Ohio, four student antiwar demonstrators are killed by the National Guard on the Kent State University campus. ■ The U.S. census shows the smallest ratio of males to females (94.8 to 100) in history.

J. Edgar Hoover, director of the FBI, claims that black militant groups in the United States are infiltrated by "foreign influences" and says that 1969 saw 100 serious attacks on police by "extremist, all-Negro, hate-type organizations such as the Black Panther Party."

Yielding to pressure from civil rights groups, the U.S. Senate rejects the nomination of G. Harrold Carswell to the U.S. Supreme Court. In 1948, Carswell had expressed a "firm, vigorous belief in the principles of white supremacy."

President Nixon signs a bill to keep the Civil Rights Act of 1965 in force until 1975.

Six African Americans are killed during a riot in Augusta, Georgia. Race-related riots occur in a number of places including Miami, Florida; Asbury Park, New Jersey; Hartford, Connecticut; New Orleans, Louisiana; Henderson, North Carolina; and Daytona Beach, Florida.

An African Peoples Convention in Atlanta, designed as a forum for discussing national and international black pride, draws over 2,000 delegates from groups in the United States, Africa, the Caribbean, South America, and Australia.

In a courtroom shootout in San Rafael, California, Jonathan Jackson tries to liberate several African Americans on trial. Jackson, two defendants, and the presiding judge are all killed. A nationwide search is conducted for Angela Davis, a UCLA professor who had been fired for being a Communist Party member, as she is believed to have supplied the gun. The FBI lists her as one of the nation's 10 most wanted criminals, and she is eventually arrested in New York.

In New Haven, Black Panther Lonnie McLucas is convicted of conspiring to murder Alex Rackley, a one-time Black Panther alleged to be an FBI informant. Charges are ultimately dropped against all other defendants in the case.

Congressional elections result in a record 12 African Americans in Congress, including 5 new representatives: Ronald Dellums (California), Parren Mitchell (Maryland), Ralph Metcalfe (Illinois), George Collins (Illinois), and Charles Rangel (New York), who defeats Adam Clayton Powell, Jr., ending Powell's long political career.

Kenneth Gibson is elected mayor of Newark, New Jersey, the first African American to lead the government of a major northeastern city. James McGhee becomes the first black mayor of Dayton, Ohio.

In Atlanta, African Americans gain significant power in city government after five blacks are elected to the 18-member city council and Benjamin E. Mays is made head of the school board.

A 100-mile civil rights march ends in Atlanta with a protest rally. Coretta Scott King, Senator George McGovern, and SCLC leader Ralph Abernathy speak out against racism, police brutality, and the Vietnam War.

The 1968 conviction of Black Panther leader Huey P. Newton for manslaughter is reversed by a California court of appeals.

BUSINESS AND EMPLOYMENT

A federal court orders Roadway Express Company, America's third-largest trucking outfit, to launch an equal opportunity employment program.

Among over 3,000 senior officers at the top 50 U.S. corporate firms, only three are African Americans: Thomas A. Wood of Chase Manhattan Bank, Clifton R. Wharton, Jr., of the Equitable Life Assurance Society, and Robert C. Weaver of the Metropolitan Life Insurance Company.

RELIGION AND EDUCATION

The Department of Health, Education, and Welfare announces that 61% of black students and 65.5% of white students are attending segregated public schools.

Governors of four southern states—Florida, Georgia, Alabama, and Louisiana—vow to fight any order to bus public school students to achieve integration.

A U.S. district court rules that the IRS cannot grant tax-exempt status to any new segregated private schools created in Mississippi. It had been Mississippi Governor John Bell Williams's plan to encourage more segregated private schools as a means of avoiding public school integration.

In Ann Arbor, a peaceful strike by University of Michigan students persuades university officials to increase the enrollment of African-American students.

In Columbus, Ohio, students at Ohio State University protest, demanding the enrollment of more African-American students. The National Guard is called in to restore peace.

In Denver, segregationists dynamite one-third of the buses intended to be used to transport public school students.

The Commission on Civil Rights blasts President Nixon's desegregation policy as "inadequate, overcautious, and indicative of possible retreat." Later, the NAACP sues the Department of Health, Education, and Welfare, charging it with default in enforcing school integration.

In Washington, D.C., Hugh S. Scott becomes the first African American superintendent of schools in a major U.S. city.

John M. Burgess is elected bishop of the Episcopal diocese of Massachusetts.

LITERATURE AND JOURNALISM

Toni Morrison's first novel, *The Bluest Eye*, is published.

Bobby Seale publishes *Seize the Time*, about the Black Panthers.

Black Enterprise and *Essence* magazines begin publishing.

Louis E. Lomax, author and columnist, dies July 30 in Santa Rosa, New Mexico.

PERFORMING ARTS

The Flip Wilson Show, a comedy and variety series, debuts on NBC-TV.

Hollywood releases *Cotton Comes to Harlem*, produced by Ossie Davis and starring Godfrey Cambridge and Raymond St. Jacques. Cambridge also stars in the film *Watermelon Man*, directed by Melvin Van Peebles.

On the pop charts, the Jackson Five reach number one with "I Want You Back" on January 31 and have three more top hits during the year. Diana Ross's "Ain't No Mountain High Enough" becomes number one on September 19. Smokey Robinson and the Miracles also hit number one with "The Tears of a Clown."

Duke Ellington conducts a historic concert of sacred music at St. Sulpice Church in Harlem.

Rock guitarist Jimi Hendrix dies September 18 in London.

VISUAL ARTS

The Spingarn Medal is awarded to Jacob Lawrence for his "eminence among American painters."

THE MILITARY

Pentagon figures show that the proportion of African-American troops being killed in Vietnam has gone down from 1969. In early 1970 blacks represent 10% of the troops and 8.5% of the fatalities, compared to 9.5% of the troops and 13.5% of the fatalities in 1969.

Benjamin O. Davis, Sr., the first African-American general in the U.S. Armed Forces, dies November 26 in Chicago.

SPORTS

Joe Frazier wins the world's heavyweight boxing championship.

Body-builder Chris Dickerson is the first black Mr. America.

On the Move

In 1971 the National Urban Coalition's Committee on Cities noted that the percentage of African Americans living in the downtown areas of major American cities was increasing at a dramatic rate, not only because blacks were moving in to take advantage of greater employment and welfare opportunities, but also because whites were moving out to avoid living in heavily black communities. The coalition referred to this phenomenon as "white flight" and predicted that America's inner cities would be "black, brown, and bankrupt" by 1980 if nothing were done to address the trend.

As the decade continued, another population shift took place. For the first time since the Civil War, more blacks were moving into the South (mostly to urban areas) than leaving the region. In 1970 blacks accounted for 49% of the South's population; by 1980 they accounted for 53%. The shift was motivated primarily by increasing economic prosperity in the "New South" as the economic situation in the North steadily worsened.

Basketball star Willis Reed of the New York Knicks is named Most Valuable Player of the year, the All-Star game, and the playoffs.

ADDITIONAL STATISTICS

According to the Census Bureau, 22,600,000 African Americans live in the United States and constitute 11.1% of the total population.

ADDITIONAL EVENTS

Cheryl Adrienne Brown is crowned Miss Iowa, thus becoming the first African American to compete in the Miss America pageant.

1971

POLITICS AND CIVIL RIGHTS

The Congressional Black Caucus is created. President Nixon meets with the caucus and fails to support their demands, although he does promise to push for stronger enforcement of civil rights laws. The caucus later expresses its unanimous disappointment on a nationwide television broadcast.

President Nixon's State of the Union address is boycotted by 12 African-American congresspeople, who cite his "consistent refusal" to respond effectively to the needs of African Americans.

A race riot in Wilmington, North Carolina, results in two deaths. Other riots erupt in New York (the Brownsville section); Chattanooga, Tennessee; Jacksonville, Florida; and Columbus, Georgia.

Civil rights leader Benjamin Chavis and nine other people are arrested in Wilmington, North Carolina, and charged with burning a store. The case of the "Wilmington 10," who receive stiff sentences, will be taken up by Amnesty International and other groups. Only in 1980 will the convictions be overturned.

In Memphis, 17-year-old Elton Hayes is killed by law enforcement officers, sparking a five-day riot. Later, nine policemen, one of whom is black, are charged with murder.

The U.S. Supreme Court rules that a community does have the constitutional right to close public recreational facilities rather than desegregate them.

The "Soledad Brothers," three African Americans whose conviction

---

Contemporary Events, 1971 ■ The United States conducts heavy bombing raids over North Vietnam. ■ Lieutenant William Calley, Jr., is found guilty of premeditated murder in the My Lai massacre trial. ■ The movie **Patton** receives an Academy Award for best picture.

is being protested by Angela Davis and other activists, reportedly attempt to escape from Soledad Prison in California. One of them, George Jackson, is shot in the back and killed. The other two are later acquitted of charges that they killed a white guard.

In Attica, New York, a group of predominantly black and Puerto Rican convicts riot at the Attica correctional facility to demand an end to discrimination and an improvement in prison conditions. Over 1,000 state troopers, guards, and policemen storm the prison and over 40 people, including several guards being held as hostages, are killed. It is the worst prison riot in U.S. history.

After traveling through Africa, Vice President Spiro Agnew attacks African Americans who have "arrogated unto themselves the positions of black leaders and spend their time in querulous complaint and constant recrimination against the rest of society instead of undertaking constructive action." He refuses to offer specific names.

Julian Bond, a representative in the Georgia legislature, conducts a highly publicized voter registration tour through predominantly black areas of Georgia.

Black Panther Party cofounder Bobby Seale is tried for ordering the murder of Alex Rackley, an allegedly disloyal Black Panther Party member. The judge dismisses the case after a mistrial is declared.

In Mississippi, 11 members of the Republic of New Africa, a black separatist group, are charged with the murder of a white policeman involved in an FBI-assisted raid of their headquarters.

In Chicago, Jesse Jackson organizes People United to Save Humanity (PUSH).

In Washington, D.C., eight African-American civil servants file suit in a federal court claiming that the Civil Service entrance examination is discriminatory.

At the Leadership Conference on Civil Rights in Washington, D.C., leaders from 126 civil rights groups denounce President Nixon's housing desegregation policies as "disastrous and chaotic."

The House Internal Security Committee reports that the Black Panther Party does pose a danger to U.S. law enforcement officers, but is incapable of overthrowing the U.S. government by violence.

After the longest-running trial in New York City history (nine months), 13 Black Panthers are acquitted of 156 conspiracy charges relating to the bombing of police stations and department stores.

Dick Gregory, entertainer and 1968 presidential candidate, calls for African Americans to produce more children in order to counteract the "genocidal" effects of white policies and attitudes.

African-American Artists Speak Out

In **Black Artists on Art,** a publication intended to "promote change," Samella Lewis and Ruth Waddy brought together the words and images of African-American artists working in diverse styles. The second volume, which came out in 1971, included this statement from Elizabeth Catlett: "Within the past few years I have gradually reached the conclusion that art is important only to the extent that it helps in the liberation of our people. . . . It must answer a question, or wake somebody up, or give a shove in the right direction—our liberation."

"Jersey" Joe Walcott, former heavyweight boxing champion, is elected sheriff of Camden, New Jersey.

Whitney M. Young, Jr., executive director of the National Urban League, drowns in Lagos, Nigeria, on March 11. He is succeeded by Vernon E. Jordan, Jr.

Ralph Bunche, winner of the Nobel Peace Prize, dies December 9 in New York. Earlier this year, he retired from his position as undersecretary-general of the United Nations.

BUSINESS AND EMPLOYMENT

Leon Sullivan is elected to General Motors' board of directors, the first African American to gain such a position in the U.S. automobile industry.

Under pressure from civil rights organizations, Bethlehem Steel adopts a quota system to ensure fair hiring, training, and promotion of African Americans.

In Chicago, "Black Expo," a four-day exhibition run by Jesse Jackson and designed primarily to stimulate interest and investment in African-American enterprises, is attended by over 800,000 people.

The U.S. Supreme Court rules that companies cannot use tests as a means of qualifying or disqualifying employees if these tests are not specifically related to job ability. The ruling is meant to minimize the common and discriminatory use of general education tests to screen out black job applicants.

James O. Plinton, Jr., is the first African American to head a major airline, Eastern.

RELIGION AND EDUCATION

The U.S. Supreme Court rules that busing students is a constitutionally valid means of achieving the integration of public schools.

More public school desegregation occurs during this year than in any year since 1954, when the Supreme Court issued its first desegregation order.

President Nixon signs into law a $5 billion education appropriation bill, the most ambitious bill of its kind ever instituted, but draws criticism from civil rights advocates for not tying the granting of funds to desegregation measures.

The Ford Foundation in New York City creates a $100-million, six-year program of scholarships to aid black private colleges.

In Pontiac, Michigan, whites protesting integration set fire to 10 school buses and block drivers from using other buses.

In Georgia, Howard Jordan, Jr., president of Savannah State College, becomes vice chancellor of the Georgia State Board of Regents, the highest office in the Georgia state educational system held to date by an African American.

At the University of Florida at Gainesville, an estimated 2,000 black and white students protest the school's racist policies and low enrollment of African-American students. After the administration refuses to grant the student demands, about 100 black students withdraw from the university.

LITERATURE AND JOURNALISM

Maya Angelou publishes her first book of poetry, *Just Give Me a Cool Drink of Water 'fore I Diiie*.

Two volumes of Gwendolyn Brooks's poetry are published, *Family Pictures* and *Aloneness*, as well as a collection of her major works, *The World of Gwendolyn Brooks*.

Nikki Giovanni publishes *Spin a Soft Black Song: Poems for Young People*.

The anthology *Cavalcade: Negro American Writing from 1760 to the Present*, edited by Andrew B. Davis and J. Saunders Redding, is published.

John Oliver Killens's novel *The Cotillion* is published.

Ernest J. Gaines publishes his novel *The Autobiography of Miss Jane Pittman*, which will later be made into a television movie.

PERFORMING ARTS

The movie *Sweet Sweetback's Baadaass Song*, written, produced, directed, and distributed by Melvin Van Peebles, who also stars in it, grosses $15 million, a record for a black-oriented film. *Shaft*, directed by Gordon Parks and debuting Richard Roundtree, is another high-grossing, black-oriented film released this year.

Issac Hayes's recording "Theme from *Shaft*" is a number-one pop hit and will win an Academy Award for best song.

Louis Armstrong, influential jazz trumpeter, singer, and bandleader, dies July 6 in Queens, New York.

VISUAL ARTS

Gordon Parks's book of photographs and poems, *Whispers of Intimate Things*, is published.

"Contemporary Black Artists in America," an exhibit of 58 painters and sculptors, opens at the Whitney Museum of American Art in New York. Among the artists exhibited are Jacob Lawrence, Alma Thomas, and David Driskell.

Romare Bearden has a one-person show at the Museum of Modern Art in New York.

THE MILITARY

Samuel L. Gravely, Jr., is promoted to admiral in the U.S. Navy, the highest rank yet achieved by an African American.

The U.S. Army promotes three African Americans to the rank of brigadier general—Alvin W. Dillard, James F. Hamlet, and Roscoe C. Cartwright.

SPORTS

The U.S. Supreme Court overturns boxer Muhammad Ali's conviction for draft evasion.

Joe Frazier, world heavyweight boxing champion, becomes the first African American to speak before the South Carolina legislature since Reconstruction.

Basketball star Lew Alcindor, who changes his name to Kareem Abdul-Jabbar, is the NBA's top scorer and Most Valuable Player.

Baseball star Vida Blue of the Oakland A's is named the American League's Most Valuable Player.

Satchel Paige, pitcher for 25 years in the Negro Leagues as well as the major leagues, is inducted into the Baseball Hall of Fame. His induction sets a Baseball Hall of Fame policy for including players in the Negro Leagues "with full honors," rather than assigning them a separate and subordinate classification.

Elgin Baylor of the Los Angeles Lakers retires after 14 years in the National Basketball Association. His lifetime score of 23,149 points is the third highest ever achieved.

ADDITIONAL STATISTICS

The U.S. Bureau of Labor Statistics reports that African Americans are still far behind whites in economic prosperity. The average black income is three-fifths of the average white income; and 50% of all black rural housing units are substandard, compared to 8% of white rural housing units.

1972

POLITICS AND CIVIL RIGHTS

An African-American political convention is held in Gary, Indiana, attracting 3,000 delegates and 5,000 others from across the nation. The NAACP breaks away from the convention in protest after it takes a stand against busing and the state of Israel (a gesture in support of the Palestinians).

In Baton Rouge, Louisiana, two black teenagers and two deputy sheriffs are killed during a shootout. In another incident in Baton Rouge, two young African Americans are killed as a result of demonstrations on the Southern University campus.

Benjamin L. Hooks, a lawyer from Memphis, is appointed to the Federal Communications Commission.

H. Rap Brown, former leader of SNCC, is sentenced to five years in prison for a weapons charge dating from 1968.

In San Jose, California, on June 4, activist Angela Davis is acquitted of charges that she aided and abetted a courtroom shootout in 1970. Later, she announces plans to form a national defense organization to help "black and brown prisoners of the government."

In Washington, D.C., security guard Frank Wills interrupts a break-in at the Democratic National Committee office, starting a chain of events that will lead to the Watergate scandal that forces President Nixon to resign.

The U.S. Supreme Court rules that the death penalty is unconstitutional. The decision has a race-related dimension since more than half of the 600 convicts on death row are African Americans.

James E. Baker is appointed an officer at the U.S. embassy in South Africa, the first African-American diplomat posted to that country.

The U.S. Supreme Court rules that residents in segregated housing developments have the right to sue for integration.

African-American delegates make up 15% of the Democratic National Convention, as opposed to 4.2% of the Republican National Convention. Senator George McGovern of South Dakota, an outspoken advocate of civil rights, is nominated for president. U.S. Representative Shirley Chisholm of Bedford-Stuyvesant, New York, receives 152 votes (out of 2,000) for president.

President Nixon wins the presidential election with only 21% of the black vote and 67% of the white vote. Senator McGovern, the Democratic nominee, receives 79% of the black vote and 33% of the white vote. A Louis Harris poll shows that the greatest division in the election returns is according to race.

Sixteen African Americans are elected to Congress, including An-

"The Time Has Come to Change America"

In her 1970 book, **Unbought and Unbossed,** U.S. Congresswoman Shirley Chisholm declared, "What we need is more women in politics . . . and not just to stuff envelopes, but to run for office." In 1972 she took up her own challenge and made a bid for president. As she later explained to Brian Lanker in his book **I Dream a World,** "I had gone into a number of states and said, 'The time has come to change America. Someday, somewhere, somehow, someone other than a white male could be President.'" But she was unprepared for the criticism she encountered. "I have met far more discrimination as a woman than being black in the field of politics," she told Lanker. Nevertheless, she said, "I went to the Democratic convention in 1972 and did my thing and began to open the way for women to think that they can run."

Contemporary Events, 1972 ■ Governor George C. Wallace of Alabama is shot by a mentally unbalanced white man. Wallace remains partially paralyzed. ■ Hollywood releases **Cabaret** and **The Godfather.** ■ President Nixon visits the People's Republic of China.

drew Young of Georgia, the first black congressperson from the South since the Reconstruction era, and two black women, Yvonne Brathwaite Burke of California and Barbara Jordan of Texas.

Adam Clayton Powell, Jr., minister, politician, and civil rights leader, dies April 4 in Miami.

BUSINESS AND EMPLOYMENT

Jerome H. Holland becomes the first African American to sit on the board of directors of the New York Stock Exchange.

William Lucy becomes secretary-treasurer of the State, County, and Municipal Employees union.

The NAACP charges that black membership in the building trade unions is shrinking rather than expanding, despite federal programs designed to facilitate black membership.

The National Black MBA Association is founded to help African Americans enter and progress in the business world.

The unemployment rate among African Americans is 9.9%, the highest since the Depression in the 1930s.

RELIGION AND EDUCATION

According to Department of Health, Education, and Welfare statistics, only 9.2% of southern black students are still in segregated schools, compared with 68% in 1968.

James M. Rodger, Jr., of Durham, North Carolina is named National Teacher of the Year, the first African American to be so honored.

President Nixon orders a moratorium on all court-imposed busing of public school children until July 1973.

W. Sterling Cary is elected president of the National Council of Churches, a first for an African American.

Horace Mann Bond, former president of Lincoln University in Pennsylvania, dies December 21 in Atlanta.

LITERATURE AND JOURNALISM

Nikki Giovanni's book of poetry *My House* is published.

Blackspirits: A Festival of New Black Poets in America, edited by Woodie King, is published. It anthologizes the works of 30 poets who participated in a major New York City poetry festival in 1971.

Ishmael Reed publishes *Conjure: Selected Poems 1963–1970,* which is nominated for a National Book Award, and his novel *Mumbo Jumbo.*

Historian Lerone Bennett, Jr., publishes *The Challenge of Blackness.*

Darwin Turner edits the anthology *Voices from the Black Experience.*

SCIENCE AND TECHNOLOGY

Federal health officials reveal that African Americans were used as test subjects in a 40-year study of syphilis.

William Shockley, winner of a Nobel Prize for physics, is denied permission to teach a course at Stanford University because of his pronouncements that blacks are genetically inferior to whites.

PERFORMING ARTS

Hollywood releases *Lady Sings the Blues*, a screen biography of jazz singer Billie "Lady Day" Holiday, with Diana Ross in the title role. Ross's performance will earn her an Academy Award nomination for best actress.

Cicely Tyson and Paul Winfield star in the film *Sounder*, which earns an Academy Award nomination for best picture and best actress. Tyson is the National Society of Film Critics' choice for best actress.

Melvin Van Peebles's play *Don' Play Us Cheap* opens Off-Broadway.

Micki Grant's musical *Don't Bother Me I Can't Cope* opens in New York, receiving Drama Desk and Obie awards.

On TV, Redd Foxx debuts as "Fred Sanford" in *Sanford and Son*.

Sixty-one years after publication, Scott Joplin's ragtime opera *Treemonisha* is given a full production in Atlanta.

James Brown, popular soul singer, is arrested for disorderly conduct in Knoxville, Tennessee. Brown threatens to sue the city for false arrest, claiming he was only talking with schoolchildren about the dangers of drugs. The mayor of Knoxville concedes that the arrest apparently resulted from a misunderstanding.

Sammy Davis, Jr., is widely criticized among blacks and liberal whites for endorsing President Nixon's policies and for allowing widespread distribution of a photograph showing him hugging Nixon.

Major civil rights groups form the Coalition Against Blax-ploitation to protest the number of Hollywood films aimed at the African-American market that perpetuate harmful self-images (such as *Super Fly*, the year's top-grossing black-oriented film). A press release says, "The transformation from the stereotype 'Stepin Fetchit' to 'Super Nigger' on the screen is just another form of cultural genocide."

On the pop charts, Roberta Flack's "The First Time Ever I Saw Your Face" stays at the top for six weeks and will win a Grammy. Michael Jackson has his first solo number-one hit with "Ben." Johnny Nash also hits number one, with "I Can See Clearly Now."

Mahalia Jackson, the greatest of the gospel singers, dies January 27 in Evergreen Park, Illinois.

VISUAL ARTS

In New York, African-American and Hispanic youths cover walls, subways, and urban rubble with spray-paint "graffiti" art. Some consider it vandalism, others view it as lively artistic expression.

Painter Charles White is the second African American (after Henry O. Tanner) elected to the National Academy of Design.

Painter Alma Thomas has major shows at the Whitney Museum in New York and the Corcoran Gallery of Art in Washington, D.C.

The Spingarn Medal is awarded to Gordon Parks for his achievements as a photographer, filmmaker, and writer.

THE MILITARY

Major General Frederic E. Davidson is placed in command of the Eighth Infantry Division stationed in Germany, the first African American to lead a division.

A racial conflict flares on the aircraft carrier *Kitty Hawk* stationed off the North Vietnamese coast, injuring 46 black and white servicemen.

The USS *Jesse L. Brown* is launched in Louisiana. It is the first U.S. navy ship named for an African-American naval officer. Brown was killed in action during the Korean War.

A federally commissioned biracial panel of military officers and civilian experts reports that "systematic and intentional discrimination" against African Americans continues within the U.S. Armed Forces.

Sergeant Major Edgar R. Huff retires after the longest Marine Corps career of any African American to date—30 years.

SPORTS

At the Munich Olympics, American black athletes draw criticism for supporting African black athletes in their protest of the participation of Rhodesia, a racist British colony. Three African Americans win individual gold medals: Vince Matthews (400-meter run), Rod Milburn (110-meter hurdles), and Randy Williams (long jump).

Wilt Chamberlain of the Los Angeles Lakers becomes the first basketball player in the NBA to score 30,000 points in his career.

Johnnie Rodgers, halfback for the University of Nebraska, wins college football's Heisman Trophy. A controversial choice because of a prior conviction for armed robbery, Rodgers declares, "I just missed getting into some scrapes when I was growing up and so did everybody else from the ghettoes."

Jackie Robinson, first African American to play baseball in the major leagues, dies October 24 in Stamford, Connecticut.

ADDITIONAL STATISTICS

A record 31.8% of African-American families are headed by women.

ADDITIONAL EVENTS

Esther Hunt Moore is named "Mother of the Year," the second African American to be so honored. She was the first black woman to register to vote in Hickory, North Carolina.

POLITICS AND CIVIL RIGHTS

African-American mayors are elected in major U.S. cities, including Thomas Bradley in Los Angeles, Maynard Jackson in Atlanta, and Coleman Young in Detroit. In Taft, Oklahoma, Lelia Smith Foley becomes the first African-American woman mayor of a U.S. city.

Ralph Abernathy resigns as president of SCLC, complaining of low funding and inadequate staffing. When SCLC refuses to accept the resignation and promises to rectify the complaints, Abernathy announces he will remain as president.

Vernon Jordan of the National Urban League accuses the Nixon administration of sabotaging the progress made for civil rights during the Johnson administration, an era that he calls the "Second Reconstruction."

Illinois declares Martin Luther King, Jr.'s birthday a holiday, the first state to do so.

Alabama Governor George C. Wallace recants much of his former segregationism and is invited to address the National Conference of Black Mayors.

In New York City, Eleanor Holmes Norton and Margaret Sloan help found the National Black Feminist Organization to fight sexist attitudes among black males.

Marian Wright Edelman sets up the Children's Defense Fund.

BUSINESS AND EMPLOYMENT

Comer Cottrell founds Pro-Line Corporation, the largest black-owned business in the Southwest.

Responding to a suit by the Federal Equal Employment Opportuni-

In Children's Defense

In her best-selling 1992 book, **The Measure of Our Success,** Marian Wright Edelman describes the legacy that led to her founding of the Children's Defense Fund in 1973. Most important were the lessons she learned fighting for civil rights in Mississippi and for Head Start programs in the mid-1960s. As she puts it, "I . . . learned that critical civil and political rights would not mean much to a hungry, homeless, illiterate child and family if they lacked the social and economic means to exercise them. And so children . . . became the passion of my personal and professional life. For it is they who are God's presence, promise, and hope for humankind."

Contemporary Events, 1973 ■ The Nixon administration is rocked by the Watergate investigation and Vice President Spiro Agnew's resignation. Gerald Ford becomes the new vice president. ■ The U.S. Supreme Court rules that states may not prohibit abortions during the first six months of pregnancy.

ties Commission, AT&T agrees to pay $15 million in back wages and to award $23 million in raises to employees who experienced discrimination.

Jesse W. Lewis, founder of Industrial Bank, dies in Washington, D.C.

RELIGION AND EDUCATION

Alonzo A. Crim becomes the first African-American superintendent of schools in Atlanta.

In Oakland, California, Marcus A. Foster, superintendent of schools, is killed by gunshot. A member of the Symbionese Liberation Army is convicted.

A federal court finds the city of Memphis guilty of cutting its school transportation budget in an effort to avoid busing students to achieve integration.

The Spingarn Medal is awarded to Wilson C. Riles, California state superintendent of public instruction.

LITERATURE AND JOURNALISM

Alice Walker publishes *In Love and Trouble: Stories of Black Women.*

John Edgar Wideman's novel *The Lynchers* is published.

Alice Childress publishes her novel *A Hero Ain't Nothin' But a Sandwich.*

Leon Forrest's first novel, *There Is a Tree More Ancient Than Eden,* is published.

Arna Bontemps, writer and educator, dies June 4 in Nashville.

SCIENCE AND TECHNOLOGY

George Washington Carver is elected to New York University's Hall of Fame of Great Americans.

PERFORMING ARTS

The National Black Network, America's first black-owned radio news network, begins broadcasting to 40 affiliates nationwide.

The musical *Raisin,* based on Lorraine Hansberry's play *A Raisin in the Sun,* opens on Broadway. Debbie Allen stars as "Beneatha Younger."

Douglas Turner Ward's *The River Niger* opens on Broadway.

Paul Robeson is honored by a tribute from Rutgers University on his 75th birthday, a gesture that helps to restore his reputation after years of being ostracized as a Communist sympathizer.

Redd Foxx receives the NAACP's Entertainer of the Year Award.

Blues singer B. B. King receives an honorary doctorate from Tougaloo College in Mississippi.

Bernice J. Reagon forms the group Sweet Honey in the Rock, which gives its first concert at Howard University.

Gladys Knight and the Pips hit number one on the pop charts with "Midnight Train to Georgia." Stevie Wonder also hits number one with "Superstition," followed by "You Are the Sunshine of My Life."

Actor Rupert Crosse dies March 5 in the West Indies.

VISUAL ARTS

Painter Lois Mailou Jones is given a retropective cosponsored by the Boston Museum of Fine Arts and the National Center of Afro-American Artists.

Dana Chandler receives a citation from the mayor of Boston for his murals in the Roxbury section of the city.

Palmer Hayden, one of the artists of the Harlem Renaissance, dies February 18 in New York.

THE MILITARY

Daniel James, Jr., is promoted to lieutenant general, becoming the highest-ranking African American in the U.S. Armed Forces.

SPORTS

Willie Mays, centerfielder for the New York Mets, retires from baseball after nearly 25 years, most of them spent with the New York and San Francisco Giants. He is honored in a special ceremony at Shea Stadium attended by 55,000 fans.

Reggie Jackson of baseball's Oakland Athletics is named the World Series' Most Valuable Player.

O. J. Simpson of football's Buffalo Bills gains a record-breaking 2,003 yards for the season, in addition to scoring 12 touchdowns. He is named NFL Player of the Year and wins the Jim Thorpe trophy.

George Foreman beats Joe Frazier to win the world heavyweight boxing championship.

ADDITIONAL EVENTS

Governor Jimmy Carter orders a portrait of Martin Luther King, Jr., mounted in the rotunda of the Georgia State Capitol in Atlanta.

Henry Ossawa Tanner, the first African-American artist to become a member of that National Academy of Design, is honored in a commemorative stamp issued by the U.S. Postal Service.

1974

POLITICS AND CIVIL RIGHTS

The second National Black Political Convention is held in Little Rock. It calls for the creation of an African-American "united fund," for cutting military aid to Israel, and for support of African liberation movements.

A federal court in San Francisco rules that local law enforcement officers violated the civil rights of approximately 600 African-American men who were stopped for questioning during the hunt for the "Zebra" killers. Later, four black men are indicted for the killings.

Two African Americans—John Conyers of Michigan and Barbara Jordan of Texas —are appointed to the House Judiciary Committee determining whether to recommend impeachment of President Nixon.

Mrs. Martin Luther King, Sr., and Edward Boykin are shot to death during a service at Ebenezer Baptist Church. Marcus Chennault, a deranged black man, is convicted for the murders.

Harold Ford is elected to the House of Representatives from Memphis, the first African-American congressperson from Tennessee.

BUSINESS AND EMPLOYMENT

A federal court orders the American Tobacco Company to cease discrimination against black employees by allowing them fair precedence over white employees with less seniority.

The national unemployment rate is 9%; the unemployment rate for blacks, 15%.

RELIGION AND EDUCATION

The Department of Health, Education, and Welfare approves plans submitted by Maryland, Virginia, North Carolina, Georgia, Florida, Arkansas, Pennsylvania, and Oklahoma for the desegregation of their university systems.

A federal court orders Boston public schools to integrate, using busing as one of the means. When protest marches and rioting interfere with busing, the National Guard is summoned to restore order.

Rabbi Balfour Brickner, speaking for the New York Federation of

Contemporary Events, 1974 ■ Richard Nixon is forced to resign as president of the U.S. to avoid impeachment proceedings stemming from the Watergate scandal. ■ Barbra Streisand's record "The Way We Were" goes to number one on the pop charts.

Reform Synagogues, pleads for blacks and Jews to close the widening gap between them and to live in political and social cooperation as they did during the 1960s.

C. Shelby Rooks becomes the first African-American president of the Chicago Theological Seminary.

Lawrence W. Bottoms, a minister from Decatur, Georgia, becomes the first African-American moderator of the General Assembly of the United Presbyterian Church.

The United Negro College Fund receives the largest endowment ever bestowed by a black group: $132,000 from Links, Inc., a black women's association.

In Washington, D.C., Eugene A. Marino becomes the first African-American Roman Catholic auxiliary bishop in the United States.

LITERATURE AND JOURNALISM

Maya Angelou publishes the second volume of her autobiography, *Gather Together in My Name.*

James Baldwin publishes his novel *If Beale Street Could Talk.*

Toni Morrison's novel *Sula* is published.

Reader's Digest publishes excerpts from Alex Haley's forthcoming novel *Roots.* The novel itself will be published in 1976.

Frank L. Stanley, Sr., *Louisville Defender* owner, dies October 12.

SCIENCE AND TECHNOLOGY

An anthropologist at the University of Pennsylvania publishes a study indicating that whites perform better than blacks on intelligence tests due to environmental factors rather than biological differences. Her study further suggests that most intelligence tests have content that is biased toward whites: i.e., that favors test takers who have grown up in a white environment.

PERFORMING ARTS

The soundtrack of the movie *The Sting* revives interest in the ragtime music of composer Scott Joplin. The American Society of Composers, Authors, and Publishers (ASCAP) places a monument on Joplin's neglected grave in Queens, New York.

Emmys are awarded to Cicely Tyson for best actress in a TV special and for best actress in a TV drama (*The Autobiography of Miss Jane Pittman*), and to Richard Pryor for best writer (with others) of Lily Tomlin's TV special "Lily."

Hollywood releases *Claudine*, starring Diahann Carroll and James Earl Jones, and *Uptown Saturday Night*, starring Sidney Poitier, Bill

Duke Ellington

When Duke Ellington, the great jazz pianist, bandleader, and composer, died May 24, 1974, the NAACP commented, "The Duke claimed the hearts of a wide range of followers, black and white, rich and poor. He was indomitable." Indeed, most critics regard him as a genius of popular American music and one of the most influential artists in the history of jazz.

Born Edward Kennedy Ellington in Washington, D.C., in 1899, he earned the nickname "Duke" for his sophisticated manner and clothing as a bandleader. In 1923 he and his orchestra secured a berth in Harlem's Cotton Club. His compositions, recordings, and radio performances gained him a large following. Over the years, Ellington's bands supported and influenced such outstanding jazz performers as Cootie Williams, Johnny Hodges, Oscar Pettiford, Ray Nance, Juan Tizol, and Harry Carney. His compositions included not only popular jazz classics like "Take the 'A' Train," "Satin Doll," and "Don't Get Around Much Anymore," but also tone poems, concert pieces, and operas that incorporated the jazz idiom.

Cosby, and Harry Belafonte. Carroll receives an Academy Award nomination for best actress.

"The Ruby Dee and Ossie Davis Story Hour" airs on television.

Charles Fuller's first play, *In the Deepest Part of Sleep*, is produced by the Negro Ensemble Company.

Stevie Wonder's album *Inversions* receives a Grammy for best album of 1973. His 1974 release, *Fulfillingness' First Finale*, will also win the best album award.

Edward Kennedy "Duke" Ellington, composer and bandleader, dies May 24 in New York.

VISUAL ARTS

The National Center for Afro-American Artists in Boston receives a grant from the Ford Foundation, becoming the first African-American cultural organization to do so.

Jacob Lawrence has a retrospective of his paintings at the Whitney Museum in New York, and the show then travels to museums in St. Louis, Birmingham, Seattle, Kansas City, and New Orleans.

THE MILITARY

Claiming racial discrimination and mistreatment, about 50 African-American sailors decline to report for duty on the USS *Midway*.

Jill Brown of the navy becomes the first African-American woman pilot in the U.S. Armed Forces.

SPORTS

Muhammad Ali beats George Foreman to become, once again, world heavyweight boxing champion. He will win the Associated Press's Athlete of the Year Award, indicating his widespread acceptance despite his having refused induction into the army in 1968 for religious reasons.

Hank Aaron of the Atlanta Braves hits his 715th home run, breaking Babe Ruth's major-league record.

Lee Elder, professional golfer, wins the Monsanto Open in Pensacola, Florida, thus becoming the first African American to qualify for the Masters Tournament.

Frank Robinson becomes manager of the Cleveland Indians, the first African-American baseball team manager in the major leagues.

The University of Georgia's marching band announces it will no longer play "Dixie" at football games, to avoid offending African Americans.

ADDITIONAL EVENTS

Beverly Johnson becomes one of the top high-fashion models and appears on the cover of *Vogue* magazine, a first for an African-American model.

In its annual list of America's 40 most highly respected women, *Good Housekeeping* magazine includes 5 African-American women: Congresswomen Yvonne Brathwaite Burke of California, Shirley Chisholm of New York, and Barbara Jordan of Texas; TV and movie star Cicely Tyson; and civil rights activist Coretta Scott King.

POLITICS AND CIVIL RIGHTS

After a trial watched by civil rights advocates as well as feminist groups, Joan Little is acquitted of charges that she murdered her white jailor in 1974 when he made sexual advances toward her.

The nation's press reveals that the FBI and the CIA have frequently conducted intensive spy campaigns—including wiretapping, surveillance, and background investigation—on prominent black people and groups. Among the most aggressively pursued targets were Martin Luther King, Jr., the Black Panthers, and singer Eartha Kitt.

After seven years of exile abroad, former Black Panther leader Eldridge Cleaver returns to the United States to face attempted murder charges stemming from a 1968 shootout with Oakland law enforcement officers.

President Gerald Ford appoints William T. Coleman secretary of transportation.

James B. Parsons is named chief judge of the U.S. district court in Chicago, the first African American to hold such a position.

BUSINESS AND EMPLOYMENT

The NAACP's annual convention calls attention to the worsening economic situation for African Americans, with over 12% of adults and almost 40% of eligible youth unemployed.

Harvard University contracts $47 million in group life insurance with the two largest black-owned life insurance companies in the United States: North Carolina Mutual Life and Atlanta Life.

Contemporary Events, 1975 ■ The United States withdraws all troops and civilians from South Vietnam as the Communists take over. ■ Michael Bennett's musical **A Chorus Line** opens on Broadway.

In Kansas City, Missouri, the Swope Parkway National Bank, a black-operated bank, fails; however, it is reopened by the Federal Deposit Insurance Corporation under receivership in recognition of its "practical and symbolic importance" to the black community.

Wallace "Wally" Amos, Jr., launches Famous Amos Chocolate Chip Cookies.

RELIGION AND EDUCATION

The NAACP files suit in federal court to force the U.S. government to impose the same desegregation measures in northern and western public school districts that it does in southern ones.

The W. E. B. Du Bois Institute for Afro-American Research is established at Harvard University.

Samuel Du Bois Cook becomes president of Dillard University in New Orleans.

The Anacostia Museum in Washington, D.C., sponsors a traveling exhibit on African-American history to celebrate the nation's bicentennial (1975–76).

Elijah Muhammad, head of the Nation of Islam, dies February 25 in Chicago. He is succeeded by his son, Wallace Muhammad, who opens the Nation of Islam to members of all races.

LITERATURE AND JOURNALISM

The National Association of Black Journalists is founded.

Maya Angelou publishes her collection of poetry *Oh Pray My Wings Are Going to Fit Me Well*.

Gwendolyn Brooks's collection of poetry *Beckonings* is published.

Samuel R. Delany publishes his science fiction work *Dhalgren*.

Frank Yerby's novel *Tobias and the Angel* is published.

J. Mason Brewer, a collector of African-American folklore, dies January 24 in Commerce, Texas.

Emory O. Jackson, editor of the *Birmingham World*, dies August 10 in Birmingham, Alabama.

SCIENCE AND TECHNOLOGY

Archeologists find evidence that Africans, rather than Europeans, may have been the first overseas explorers of the North American continent. Gravesites and statues suggest that seafarers from West Africa may have come to North America as early as 4000 B.C.

Chemist Percy Julian, known for his early synthesis of cortisone drugs, dies April 18.

PERFORMING ARTS

The Wiz, an all-black musical version of *The Wizard of Oz*, directed by Geoffrey Holder, opens on Broadway.

Ntozake Shange's play *For Colored Girls Who Have Considered Suicide/When the Rainbow Is Enuf* opens at Joseph Papp's Public Theater in New York. In 1976 it will move to Broadway, where it will become the most successful black-oriented play since Lorraine Hansberry's 1959 *A Raisin in the Sun*.

Hollywood releases *Mahogany*, starring Diana Ross.

Adam Wade hosts the network television game show *Musical Chairs*, becoming the first black game show host.

In Detroit WGPR-TV is the first black-owned television station in the United States.

The TV series *The Jeffersons* premieres.

The Staple Singers have a number-one hit on the pop charts, with "Let's Do It Again," written by Curtis Mayfield.

Entertainer Josephine Baker dies April 12 in Paris.

Julian "Cannonball" Adderley, jazz saxophonist and bandleader, dies August 8 in Gary, Indiana.

Noble Sissle, pioneer jazz composer, dies December 17 in Tampa.

Jackie "Moms" Mabley, singer and comedian, dies May 23 in White Plains, New York.

VISUAL ARTS

At the Museum of African Art in Washington, D.C., the U.S. Postal Service sponsors an exhibit "Black Americans on U.S. Postage Stamps." It issues a commemorative stamp honoring poet Paul Laurence Dunbar.

THE MILITARY

Daniel "Chappie" James, Jr., becomes a four-star general and commander-in-chief of the North American Air Defense Command.

Lieutenant Donna Davis is the first African-American doctor to serve in the U.S. Naval Medicine Corps.

SPORTS

Tennis star Arthur Ashe wins the men's singles at Wimbledon.

Archie Griffin of Ohio State becomes the first college football player to win the Heisman Trophy twice.

At a New York city press conference, Jesse Jackson of PUSH accuses the National Collegiate Athletic Association of racism. Among his

Theaters of Freedom

During the second half of the 1970s, many theater companies were formed expressly for the purpose of dramatizing black liberation. Their model was the Free Southern Theater of Atlanta, founded by SNCC in 1962 as a guerrilla theater, which toured the South to support the freedom marches and voter registration drives of the middle and late 1960s. In February 1975, the Free Southern Theater was revived after a six-year hiatus for a tour of the play **If Opportunity Scratches, Itch It,** and its revival sparked the development of other, similar organizations across the United States, including the Fire Company in Birmingham, the Ku Mba Workshop in Chicago, the Karamu House Theater in Cleveland, the Rapa House in Detroit, the Black Theater Troupe in Phoenix, and the Mafandi Institute and Performing Arts Society in Los Angeles.

criticisms are that colleges in the NCAA do not hire black head coaches or include more than a few token blacks in the selection committees for bowl games.

The Spingarn Medal is awarded to Hank Aaron for his overall sportsmanship.

Ezzard Charles, former world heavyweight boxing champion, dies May 27 in Chicago.

POLITICS AND CIVIL RIGHTS

Rubin "Hurricane" Carter and John Artis are released from prison after serving nine years for supposedly murdering three people in a tavern. The Supreme Court of New Jersey rules that evidence beneficial to their defense was suppressed during their trial. The case had long been infamous as an example of racial prejudice and persecution, inspiring celebrities like Muhammad Ali and Bob Dylan (who wrote a song "Hurricane") to plead for a reversal of Carter's and Artis's convictions.

The Supreme Court rules that predominantly white suburbs can be ordered to provide low-cost public housing for minorities even if those suburbs are not guilty of racial discrimination in housing.

Barbara Jordan is the first African American to make the keynote speech at the Democratic National Convention, which nominates Georgia Governor Jimmy Carter, a champion of civil rights, for the presidency. The convention ends with the singing of the civil rights anthem "We Shall Overcome" and a benediction delivered by Martin Luther King, Sr.

Earl L. Butz, U.S. agriculture secretary, is forced to resign after calling blacks "lazy and shiftless."

African Americans play a critical role in electing Carter to the presidency. Seventeen blacks, a record number, are elected to Congress.

President-elect Carter appoints Representative Andrew Young of Georgia as U.S. ambassador to the United Nations, and Patricia R. Harris as U.S. secretary of housing and urban development.

Benjamin Hooks succeeds Roy Wilkins as NAACP executive director.

Contemporary Events, 1976 ■ The United States celebrates its bicentennial as an independent nation. ■ Saul Bellow wins the Nobel Prize for literature. ■ The Episcopal Church approves the ordination of women as priests. ■ Hollywood releases **All the President's Men** and **Rocky.**

Newark Mayor Kenneth Gibson becomes president of the U.S. Conference of Mayors, the first African American to hold the post.

RELIGION AND EDUCATION

In Boston, white opposition to federally imposed desegregation by means of busing continues. Among other demonstrations, 2,000 anti-integrationists fight police outside South Boston High School, injuring 50 officers. The U.S. Supreme Court refuses to review the 1975 federal court ruling that mandated the busing.

The U.S. Supreme Court rules that private schools cannot deny admission to African-American students solely on the basis of race.

Joseph Evans becomes president of the United Church of Christ.

Richard Allen Chapelle is elected general conference secretary of the African Methodist Episcopal Church.

As chancellor of the University of Colorado, Mary Frances Berry becomes the first African-American woman to head a major research university.

College enrollment among African Americans has risen from 282,000 in 1966 to 1,062,000.

Vivian W. Henderson, president of Clark College in Georgia, dies January 28 in Atlanta.

Mordecai Johnson, first black president of Howard University, dies September 10 in Washington, D.C.

LITERATURE AND JOURNALISM

Alex Haley's *Roots* is published. It will win the National Book Award and the Pulitzer Prize.

Ishmael Reed publishes his novel *Flight to Canada*.

Alice Walker's novel *Meridian* is published.

June Jordan publishes her poems in *Things That I Do in the Dark*.

Albert Murray publishes his study of blues music, *Stomping the Blues*.

PERFORMING ARTS

Two musicals—*Bubbling Brown Sugar*, with music by Duke Ellington, Cab Calloway, and Eubie Blake, and *Your Arm's Too Short to Box with God*, with music and lyrics by Alex Bradford and Micki Grant—open on Broadway.

Melba Moore wins both an Emmy and a Peabody Award for her PBS children's series *Big Blue Marble*.

Soul singer Aretha Franklin performs a historic concert at Lincoln Center in New York.

Paul Robeson

Paul Robeson's death in 1976 ended one of the most remarkable lives in U.S. history. Born April 9, 1898, he went to Rutgers, where he was named one of football's All-Americans in 1917 and 1918. After earning a law degree from Columbia University, he debuted on Broadway in 1922. He was soon acting in Eugene O'Neill's plays **Emperor Jones** and **All God's Chillun Got Wings** and singing in the musicals **Show Boat** and **Porgy and Bess.**

From 1928 to 1939, Robeson toured the world. Perceiving an absence of racial prejudice in the Soviet Union, he developed Communist sympathies. Robeson returned to America and won praise for his lead performance in the 1943 Broadway production of **Othello.** He also appealed to President Truman for civil rights legislation, helped found the Progressive Party, and spoke out against America's treatment of blacks. In 1950 the government revoked his passport, claiming he had refused to sign an anti-Communism oath. In 1958, when his passport was restored, he gave a triumphant concert at Carnegie Hall. On that day, his 60th birthday, celebrations were held throughout the world, where he was hailed as one of the greatest men of his time.

Richard Pryor wins a Grammy for his comedy album *Bicentennial Nigger.*

The Spingarn Medal is awarded to Alvin Ailey for his achievements in the field of dance.

Paul Robeson, athlete, singer, actor, and civil rights activist, dies January 23 in Philadelphia.

Godfrey Cambridge, actor and comedian, dies November 29 in Los Angeles.

VISUAL ARTS

A landmark exhibit, "Two Centuries of Black American Art," opens at the Los Angeles County Museum of Art. Among other prominent painters, sculptors, and printmakers, it features the work of Henry Ossawa Tanner, Charles White, and Elizabeth Catlett.

THE MILITARY

In testimony before the House Armed Services Committee, two former Marine Corps recruiters admit that they were ordered to limit the number of African Americans they enlisted.

The U.S. Army enhances its college scholarship program as part of a plan to double the number of African Americans participating in ROTC by 1986.

Vice Admiral Samuel L. Gravely, Jr., is appointed commander of the U.S. Third Fleet.

SPORTS

At the Montreal Olympics, Edwin Moses wins a gold medal in the 400-meter hurdles, while Arnie Robinson earns a gold medal in the long jump.

Tommy Dorsett, running back for the University of Pittsburgh, wins the Heisman Trophy.

Bill Lucas, former player for the Milwaukee and Atlanta Braves, is named director of player personnel for the Atlanta Braves, the highest administrative position in professional baseball attained to date by an African American.

Elgin Baylor, who starred with the Minneapolis and Los Angeles Lakers, is inducted into the Basketball Hall of Fame.

ADDITIONAL STATISTICS

According to a report released by the National Urban League, the average black family income is only 58% of the average white family income—a decline of 61% since 1969.

1977

POLITICS AND CIVIL RIGHTS

In Washington, D.C., Black Muslim militants, protesting the premiere of the "racist and distorted" movie *Mohammad, Messenger of God,* take hostages at B'nai B'rith offices, an Islamic center, and city hall. One hostage is killed and eleven are injured before law enforcement officers resolve the incident.

Joseph E. Lowery succeeds Ralph Abernathy as president of the Southern Christian Leadership Conference.

Mabel Murphy Smythe is appointed U.S. ambassador to the Republic of Cameroon.

Ernest N. Morial is elected mayor of New Orleans.

Randall Robinson establishes TransAfrica, a lobbying organization, to influence U.S. foreign policy affecting Africa and the Caribbean.

Karen Farmer, who traces her ancestry to Revolutionary War soldier William Hood, is the first African American admitted into the Daughters of the American Revolution.

RELIGION AND EDUCATION

Joseph Lawson Howze becomes Roman Catholic bishop of the diocese of Biloxi, Mississippi.

Clifford R. Wharton, Jr., is chosen as chancellor of the State University of New York.

In Holly Springs, Mississippi, students at all-black Rust College demonstrate to protest the "dictatorial" activities of the president, W. A. McMillan.

Black colleges and universities experience a major increase in enrollment, producing the largest student bodies to date. The top three schools are Howard University in Washington, D.C., with 9,752; Texas Southern University in Houston, with 9,552; and Southern University in Baton Rouge, Louisiana, with 9,002.

In Washington, D.C., the Afro-American Historical and Genealogical Society is founded.

LITERATURE AND JOURNALISM

The U.S. Senate passes a resolution honoring Alex Haley, author of

Contemporary Events, 1977 ■ President Carter announces an "energy crisis" that imposes upon Americans "the moral equivalent of war." ■ Elvis Presley dies in Memphis. ■ Woody Allen and Diane Keaton star in Allen's film **Annie Hall.**

A Voice That Captivated the Nation

In 1977 Barbara Jordan, U.S. Representative from Houston, explained her retirement from politics as follows: "The longer you stay in Congress, the harder it is to leave. . . . I didn't want to wake up one fine sunny morning and say there is nothing else to do."

Jordan entered Congress in 1972, after having been the first African American to serve as president pro tempore of the Texas state senate. She became nationally prominent during the 1974 impeachment hearings for President Richard Nixon, when she delivered an eloquent and powerful address supporting the U.S. Constitution and censuring the president's role in the Watergate scandal. Two years later, she gave a historic keynote address at the Democratic National Convention, urging all Americans to join in a "great healing of the national heart and soul."

Roots, for "exceptional achievement." In this same year Harold Courlander, who claims that his novel *The African* was plagiarized for parts of *Roots*, is granted an out-of-court settlement.

Toni Morrison's novel *Song of Solomon* is published.

James Baldwin publishes *Little Man, Little Man: A Story of Childhood*.

Richard Wright's novel *American Hunger* is published posthumously.

Michael S. Harper's *Images of Kin: New and Selected Poems* is published.

Philip Butcher publishes his critical study *The Minority Presence in American Literature*.

Mildred D. Taylor's 1976 novel *Roll of Thunder, Hear My Cry* wins the Newberry Medal for children's literature.

PERFORMING ARTS

Over 130 million Americans watch ABC's televised version of Alex Haley's *Roots*. The final episode of the eight-night miniseries earns the highest ratings of any television program to date, breaking a record previously set by the first televising of the movie *Gone with the Wind*. The miniseries earns a record nine Emmys.

Pearl Bailey receives an honorary doctorate from Georgetown University in Washington, D.C.

James Earl Jones is the voice of "Darth Vader" in the film *Star Wars*.

Soprano Kathleen Battle makes her debut at the Metropolitan Opera House in New York, singing the role of the shepherd in Wagner's *Tannhauser*.

Singer Martina Arroyo sings at a White House dinner marking the signing of the Panama Canal Treaty.

Tenor Roland Hayes dies January 1 in Boston.

Jazz pianist Erroll Garner dies January 2 in Los Angeles.

Actor Eddie "Rochester" Anderson dies February 28.

Singer and actress Ethel Waters dies in Chatsworth, California.

VISUAL ARTS

African-American artists form the largest foreign delegation to the Second World Festival of Black and African Art, which is held in Lagos, Nigeria.

American Heritage magazine publishes the oldest known photographs of African-American slaves. The daguerrotypes, taken in Columbia, South Carolina, by photographer J. T. Zealy, date from 1850.

Painter Ellis Wilson dies January 2.

Painter and muralist Charles Alston dies April 27 in New York.

THE MILITARY

Clifford Alexander, Jr., becomes the first African American appointed secretary of the army.

Currently, 16% of the all-volunteer armed forces is African American, as opposed to 8% of the armed forces in 1960, when the draft was still in effect.

SPORTS

Reggie Jackson of the New York Yankees hits a record three home runs in a single World Series game. The Yankees win the series against the Los Angeles Dodgers.

Walter Payton, running back for the Chicago Bears, runs a record 275 yards in one game. He will be named the National Football League's Most Valuable Player for 1977.

Gale Sayers is the youngest player elected to the Football Hall of Fame.

ADDITIONAL STATISTICS

A study conducted at Case Western University in Cleveland reveals that homicide is the leading cause of death among African-American men between ages 25 and 34.

1978

POLITICS AND CIVIL RIGHTS

Testifying before the House Select Committee on Assassinations, two FBI agents claim that the FBI's intensive "spy campaign" on Martin Luther King, Jr., was based solely on FBI Director J. Edgar Hoover's "hatred" of King and could not otherwise be justified.

U.S. Representative Charles C. Diggs, Jr., of Michigan, an original member of the Congressional Black Caucus, is convicted in a federal court of using the mails to defraud. He is later reelected to Congress despite the conviction.

Faye Wattleton becomes president of Planned Parenthood.

Five new African Americans are elected to the House: Julian Dixon of California, George Leland of Texas, Bennett Stewart of Illinois, William Gray III of Pennsylvania, Melvin Evans of the Virgin Islands.

Contemporary Events, 1978 ■ Some 120 million Americans watch the TV miniseries **Holocaust.** ■ Disco music and dancing achieves mainstream popularity. ■ Isaac Bashevis Singer wins the Nobel Prize for literature.

BUSINESS AND EMPLOYMENT

In a case initiated by the Bell Telephone System, which challenged the legality of racial quotas in hiring and promotions, the U.S. Supreme Court rules that racial quotas are constitutional and a "viable means" of ending discrimination.

Joshua I. Smith founds Maxima Corporation, a computer systems and management firm that will grow into one of the largest U.S. companies owned by an African American.

RELIGION AND EDUCATION

The U.S. Supreme Court rules that the federal government is not liable for any of the costs associated with court-ordered busing to achieve public school desegregation.

The first mainly black medical school in over a century is founded at Morehouse College in Atlanta.

In Jonestown, Guyana, a religious community founded by white California prophet Jim Jones, over 900 persons, many of them African Americans, commit mass suicide.

The U.S. Supreme Court in the "Bakke decision" rules that the special admissions program favoring minority students at the University of California at Davis Medical College is unconstitutional. The college is ordered to admit Allan P. Bakke, an unsuccessful white applicant, to correct what is termed "reverse discrimination."

The Mormon Church puts an end to its policy of excluding African Americans from the priesthood.

Thomas W. Turner, founder of the Federation of Colored Catholics, dies April 17 in Washington, D.C.

LITERATURE AND JOURNALISM

James Alan McPherson wins the Pulitzer Prize for his collection of short stories *Elbow Room.*

Frank Yerby's novel *Hail the Conquering Hero* is published.

Nikki Giovanni publishes her volume of poetry *Cotton Candy on a Rainy Day.*

Audre Lorde's *The Black Unicorn: Poems* is published.

Ishmael Reed publishes his collection of essays *Shrovetide in Old New Orleans* and his book of poetry *A Secretary to the Spirits.*

The Diaries of Willard Motley are published.

Max Robinson becomes an anchor on ABC's *World News Tonight.* He is the first African-American anchor on a network television news program.

SCIENCE AND TECHNOLOGY

Frederick D. Gregory, Ronald McNair, and Guion S. Bluford, Jr., become U.S. astronauts.

A study released by Beverly Howze, research psychologist at the University of Michigan, reveals that suicides among African Americans have risen 97% over the past 20 years. The main age group affected is 15 to 34 years, which Howze suggests reveals increasing despair and low self-esteem among young African Americans.

PERFORMING ARTS

Ain't Misbehavin', based on the music of Fats Waller, opens on Broadway. It will win the Tony Award for best musical. Other black-oriented musicals that open are *Timbuktu*, directed by Geoffrey Holder; a variation of *Kismet*, starring Eartha Kitt; and *Eubie*, a tribute to composer Eubie Blake.

Billy Dee Williams plays the title role in the TV movie *Scott Joplin*.

Hollywood releases *Stir Crazy*, directed by Sidney Poitier and starring Richard Pryor and Gene Wilder.

VISUAL ARTS

The Studio Museum in Harlem shows Richard Mayhew's landscapes.

THE MILITARY

Amid increasing charges from civil rights groups that black enlistees are more likely to receive punishments and discharges than white enlistees, soldiers at Fort Stewart-Hunter near Savannah, register over 30 complaints of "abusive treatment" with the SCLC. The army promises an investigation.

General Daniel "Chappie" James, Jr., the first black four-star general, dies February 25 at the Air Force Academy in Colorado.

SPORTS

In a historic upset, Leon Spinks defeats Muhammad Ali to win the world heavyweight boxing championship. In a rematch later this same year, Ali beats Spinks, becoming the first boxer to win the championship three times.

Billy Simms, running back for the University of Oklahoma, wins the Heisman Trophy.

ADDITIONAL EVENTS

The U.S. Postal Service issues a stamp commemorating the abolitionist Harriet Tubman.

"By Choice, I Continued to Identify . . ."

"Unfortunately, but by birth, I come from the ranks of those who have known and identified with some level of oppression in the world. . . . By choice, I continued to identify with what would be called in Biblical terms 'the least of these my brethren.' . . . I could not say that given the same situation, I wouldn't do it again, almost exactly the same way."

—Andrew Young, referring to his unauthorized 1979 meeting with a representative of the Palestine Liberation Organization, a controversial event that forced him to resign as U.S. ambassador to the United Nations

1979

POLITICS AND CIVIL RIGHTS

Patricia R. Harris, formerly U.S. secretary of housing and urban development, becomes secretary of health, education, and welfare.

Andrew Young is forced to resign as U.S. ambassador to the United Nations after complaints about his unauthorized meeting with representatives of the Palestine Liberation Organization. Another African American, Donald McHenry, takes Young's position.

The Congressional Black Caucus sets up an "action alert communications network" to win the cooperation of white congresspeople representing districts with large black populations.

The NAACP announces that it will seek closer affiliation with groups in African and Latin American nations in order to help give black people internationally a stronger voice in world affairs.

In Greensboro, North Carolina, five people are killed when members of the Ku Klux Klan open fire on anti-Klan demonstrators. A study reveals that Klan membership in 22 states has grown from 8,000 to 10,000 over the past two years.

Congress votes to place a bust of Martin Luther King, Jr., in the Capitol rotunda, the first black American so honored.

The FBI admits starting a rumor in 1970 that the white actress Jean Seberg, an advocate of the Black Panther Party, was pregnant by a Black Panther. The rumor was designed to discredit her support. Seberg subsequently committed suicide.

Amalya Kearse is the first woman and second African American appointed to the U.S. Court of Appeals for the Second Circuit.

BUSINESS AND EMPLOYMENT

The U.S. Supreme Court, in *Weber* v. *Kaiser Aluminum and Chemical Corporation*, rules that unions as well as management have the constitutional right to create programs designed to help African Americans get jobs and promotions in situations where there is a "manifest racial imbalance."

The Small Business Administration publishes a study revealing that one out of every five recipients of federal aid for minority-owned businesses is, in fact, a front for a white-owned business.

Contemporary Events, 1979 ■ At Three Mile Island, Pennsylvania, a major nuclear disaster is narrowly averted. ■ Islamic militants seize the U.S. embassy in Iran, taking 90 hostages. ■ President Carter and Soviet Premier Brezhnev agree to the SALT II treaty, providing big cuts in nuclear armaments.

Franklin A. Thomas becomes president of the Ford Foundation, the first African American to serve as chief executive of a major charitable foundation.

In Bayonne, New Jersey, Loren Moore becomes the first "longshorewoman" to fish the Eastern seaboard.

Asa Philip Randolph, labor leader and civil rights activist, dies May 16 in New York.

RELIGION AND EDUCATION

James Patterson Lyke becomes auxiliary Roman Catholic bishop of Cleveland.

Arthur Lewis, a professor at Princeton University, wins the Nobel Prize for economics.

In Washington, D.C., the Bethune Museum and Archives, named for the civil rights pioneer Mary McLeod Bethune, is founded as a center for African-American women's history.

The U.S. Civil Rights Commission reports that 46% of African-American students still attend segregated public schools.

LITERATURE AND JOURNALISM

Maya Angelou's volume of poetry *And Still I Rise* is published.

James Baldwin publishes his novel *Just Above My Head.*

Lerone Bennett, Jr., publishes *Wade in the Water: Great Moments in Black History.*

Alice Childress's novel *A Short Walk* is published.

SCIENCE AND TECHNOLOGY

Walter Massey is appointed director of the Argonne National Laboratory.

PERFORMING ARTS

ABC airs the miniseries *Roots: The Next Generation,* with a teleplay by Alex Haley.

The Off-Broadway revue *One Mo' Time,* created by Vernel Bagneris, opens. It will become one of the longest-running cabaret-style shows in New York theatrical history.

Samm-Art Williams's play *Home* is produced by the Negro Ensemble Company in New York and wins a Drama Desk Award. Later, it will move to Broadway, where it will be nominated for two Tonys.

Robert Guillaume wins TV's Emmy Award for best actor, for his work on the satirical nighttime soap opera *Soap.*

Tenor Philip Creech debuts with the Metropolitan Opera in New York, singing the role of "Beppe" in Leoncavallo's *Pagliacci*.

Diana Ross signs a record $2.52 million contract to do 72 shows at the Resorts International Casino in Atlantic City.

Donna Summer has two number-one pop hits in succession, "Hot Stuff" and "Bad Girls."

Katherine Dunham, dancer and choreographer, is honored in a special program of her work at New York City's Carnegie Hall. She also receives the Albert Schweitzer Music Award.

Actor Clarence Muse appears in his 219th film, *Black Stallion*. He dies October 13 in Perris, California.

VISUAL ARTS

In New York, Lois Alexander opens the Black Fashion Museum to showcase African-American designers, photographers, and models.

Just Above Midtown/Downtown Alternative Art Center opens in the TriBeCa section of New York City to encourage and exhibit contemporary African-American artists.

Painter Charles White dies in Los Angeles.

THE MILITARY

Frank E. Petersen becomes the first African American to hold the rank of general in the U.S. Marine Corps.

Five African Americans are made generals in the U.S. Army: John Michael Brown, John Forte, Arthur Holmes, Edward Honor, and Colin Powell.

Second Lieutenant Marcella Hayes is the first African-American woman to become a pilot in the U.S. Armed Forces.

The American Civil Liberties Union files suit against the U.S. Navy for using a quota system against black recruitment. In response, the navy orders all commanders to "use their full powers to deal effectively with racist activity."

SPORTS

Charles White, running back for the University of Southern California, wins college football's Heisman Trophy.

Wilt Chamberlain is elected to the Basketball Hall of Fame.

ADDITIONAL EVENTS

The U.S. Postal Service issues a commemorative stamp of Martin Luther King, Jr.

POLITICS AND CIVIL RIGHTS

The Congressional Black Caucus labels President Jimmy Carter's proposed budget, which spends more for the military and less for domestic programs, "an unmitigated disaster" for African Americans.

Some 1,000 African-American leaders meet to discuss political and social issues at the first National Conference for a Black Agenda, sponsored by various black groups including the NAACP and the National Urban League.

After four policemen in Dade County, Florida, are acquitted of charges that they beat to death Arthur McDuffie, a black insurance executive, a riot breaks out in Miami's Coconut Grove district. The National Guard is called in to restore order, but about 15 people are killed and 165 seriously injured. It is the most serious racial disturbance since the 1960s.

In Fort Wayne, Indiana, Vernon E. Jordan, Jr., president of the National Urban League, is shot and severely wounded in what the FBI later calls "an apparent conspiracy to deprive Vernon Jordan of his civil rights."

After the U.S. Supreme Court declines to review previous charges of mail fraud against him, U.S. Representative Charles C. Diggs, Jr., of Michigan resigns from Congress, where he has served for 26 years.

Ronald Reagan, the front runner for the Republican presidential nomination, refuses to speak at the NAACP convention. Later, NAACP leader Benjamin Hooks is invited to address the Republican National Convention after African-American delegates threaten to walk out in protest against the Republican Party's indifference to black issues.

The Supreme Court rules that a local election system cannot be declared unconstitutional for violating the civil rights of voters unless intentional discrimination can be proven. The case behind the ruling involved the "at large" election system used in Mobile, Alabama, a city where blacks represent over one-third of the total population but where no black has ever been elected to public office.

In Philadelphia, 1,000 delegates from 25 states create the National Black Independent Party.

Occupations of African Americans in 1980

According to the U.S. Census Bureau, these are the percentages of the total African-American working population in each major occupational category in 1980 compared with 1970:

	1970	1980
White collar	**27.9**	**38.2**
professionals	9.1	12.4
managers and officials	1.6	4.2
clerical staff	13.2	17.9
sales staff	2.1	2.8
Blue collar	**42.2**	**42.2**
crafters and supervisors	8.2	16.9
operatives	23.7	18.6
nonfarm laborers	10.3	6.7
Service	**26.0**	**17.9**
private household workers	7.7	0.3
service workers	18.3	17.6
Farm	**3.9**	**1.7**
farmers and managers	1.0	0.3
laborers and supervisors	2.9	1.4

Contemporary Events, 1980 ■ The United States boycotts the 1980 Olympic Games in Moscow to protest the Soviet Union's invasion of Afghanistan. ■ John Lennon, pop musician, is shot to death outside his New York apartment building by a crazed fan.

Citing President Carter's history of "broken promises," civil rights leaders Ralph Abernathy and Hosea Williams endorse Republican presidential candidate Ronald Reagan.

Ku Klux Klan activity revives in the South with marches and cross burnings. Commentators call it the biggest resurgence of the Klan since the 1960s.

Ronald Reagan, a political conservative, is elected president by a landslide, thanks in part to an unofficial boycott of the polls by black voters, who feel they can't support either Reagan or Carter. In addition, conservatives gain control of the Senate, causing many civil rights groups to be concerned about the future for minorities.

President-elect Reagan names Samuel R. Pierce, Jr., secretary of housing and urban development.

The U.S. Justice Department charges Yonkers, New York, with intentionally segregating its schools and housing for 40 years.

BUSINESS AND EMPLOYMENT

Amoco Oil Company of Indiana is fined an unprecedented $200,000 civil penalty for discriminating against minorities in approving credit cards.

The U.S. Supreme Court rules that Congress can impose racial quotas to counteract discrimination against African-American contractors in federal jobs programs.

A federal court finds Republic National, the largest bank in the South, guilty of discrimination against African Americans in hiring, salaries, and promotions.

Wally "Famous" Amos, the creator of a $250 million cookie business, is asked to donate his trademark panama hat to the Americana Collection in the National Museum of American History. It is the first exhibit requested from an African-American businessperson.

RELIGION AND EDUCATION

Speaking on behalf of black Roman Catholics in America, 10 African-American bishops write a pastoral letter underlining both the contributions of African Americans to the church and the struggles they face within the church.

After eight years of controversy and strife, the St. Louis public school system is finally integrated peacefully with the busing of over 16,000 students.

The Congressional Black Congress issues a statement advising African Americans to take action against the antiminority positions and rhetoric of increasingly powerful evangelical Christian organizations.

As part of the first annual Black College Day, 18,000 black students conduct a march on Washington, D.C. The event is designed to attract attention and support to African-American colleges and universities across the nation.

Marva Collins, creator of the innovative, predominantly black Westside Preparatory School in one of the poorest sections Chicago, is named Educator of the Year by Phi Delta Kappa.

In New York, the Schomburg Center for Research in Black Culture dedicates a new, $4 million facility. It houses the world's largest collection of materials by and about people of African descent.

LITERATURE AND JOURNALISM

Nikki Giovanni's *Vacation Time: Poems for Children* is published.

Frank Yerby publishes his novel *Floodtide*.

June Jordan's *Passion: New Poems 1977–1980* is published.

Sidney Poitier, actor and director, publishes his autobiography, *This Life*.

Black Family magazine starts publishing.

Bernard Shaw begins his carer as Washington anchor for Cable News Network (CNN).

Robert E. Hayden, poet, consultant to the Library of Congress, and educator, dies February 25 in Ann Arbor, Michigan.

SCIENCE AND TECHNOLOGY

Levi Watkins, Jr., is the first surgeon to implant an automatic defibrillator in the human heart, a device that corrects arrhythmia, or a failure of the heart to pump blood properly.

Charles F. Bolden, Jr., is selected to be a U.S. astronaut.

PERFORMING ARTS

The cable-TV network Black Entertainment Television (BET) is founded by Robert L. Johnson. In 1991 it will become the first company owned by an African American to be listed on the New York Stock Exchange.

The first black public-broadcasting TV station, WHMM, begins broadcasting from Howard University in Washington, D.C.

Eddie Murphy debuts on TV's *Saturday Night Live*.

Hollywood releases *The Blues Brothers*, spotlighting artists Aretha Franklin, James Brown, and Cab Calloway.

Actor Billie Thomas, best known for his role as "Buckwheat" in the *Our Gang* film series, dies October 11 in Los Angeles.

VISUAL ARTS

Sam Gilliam is commissioned by the Atlanta Airport Terminal to design an artwork for public viewing. One of the largest airports in the world, it is also the first to install work by contemporary artists.

The Studio Museum in Harlem shows Betye Saar's works.

THE MILITARY

General Hazel W. Johnson of the U.S. Army Nurse Corps is appointed brigadier general, the highest rank yet achieved by a black woman.

SPORTS

Larry Holmes wins the world heavyweight boxing championship.

Willie Davenport and Jeff Gadley, part of a four-man bobsled team, are the first African Americans to compete in the Winter Olympics.

Maury Wills becomes manager of the Seattle Mariners baseball team, making him the third black manager of a major league club.

Track star Jesse Owens dies in Tucson, Arizona.

ADDITIONAL STATISTICS

According to the Census Bureau, there are 26,495,070 African Americans—11.2% of the total U.S. population. Among the black population, 22,594,061 are considered urban dwellers. Cities of over 300,000 residents with the largest percentage of blacks are: Washington, D.C., 70%; Atlanta, 67%; Detroit, 65%; New Orleans, 55%; and Memphis, 40%.

1981

POLITICS AND CIVIL RIGHTS

In Atlanta, the Martin Luther King, Jr., Library is established by Coretta Scott King. It holds a large collection of materials relating to the U.S. Civil Rights Movement.

John Jacob assumes the presidency of the National Urban League.

President Reagan fires Arthur S. Fleming as chairman of the U.S. Civil Rights Commission, reportedly due to Fleming's support of affirmative action, voting rights legislation, and busing to achieve school desegregation. Reagan replaces Fleming with Clarence

---

Contemporary Events, 1981 ■ The remaining 46 U.S. hostages held by Iranian terrorists are released after 14 months of captivity. ■ The first U.S. space shuttle, **Columbia,** conducts a successful mission. ■ Sandra Day O'Connor is confirmed as the first female justice on the Supreme Court.

Pendleton, Jr., a political conservative, and the first African American to chair the commission.

Roy Wilkins, civil rights leader and former executive secretary of the NAACP, dies September 8 in New York.

BUSINESS AND EMPLOYMENT

The U.S. Department of Labor announces an easing of antidiscrimination rules affecting contractors involved in federal jobs. Widely criticized by civil rights groups, the move is defended by Secretary of Labor Raymond Donovan as a means of reducing confrontations and helping to stimulate the economy.

The U.S. Department of Justice announces it will no longer demand that employers maintain affirmative action programs or hire according to numerical racial quotas. President Reagan argues that this policy is necessary to bring about "economic emancipation" for all Americans, black and white; but his argument is universally attacked by liberal politicians and commentators.

RELIGION AND EDUCATION

Ruth B. Love is selected as Chicago's superintendent of schools, the first African American to hold the post.

An 18-month report issued by the Southern Regional Council finds that public school education offered in predominantly black districts in the South is, in general, markedly inferior to that offered in predominantly white districts. To correct this problem, the council recommends mandatory state and federal standards and school boards with a black majority.

The U.S. Department of Justice announces it will no longer enforce busing as a means to counteract desegregation in public schools. It labels busing "ineffective and unfair."

Twelve U.S. Senators, including Edward M. Kennedy of Massachusetts, submit a letter to Congress criticizing the conservative trend toward deregulating school desegregation. The letter complains that the trend is discriminatory and unconstitutional.

Luther H. Foster retires after 28 years as president of Tuskegee Institute. He is replaced by Benjamin F. Payton.

LITERATURE AND JOURNALISM

Toni Morrison's novel *Tar Baby* is published. *Newsweek* publishes a cover story on Morrison, calling her "the best of the black writers today." She is elected to the American Institute of Arts and Letters.

Ntozake Shange publishes poetry and stage works in *Three Pieces*.

Toni Morrison

During the 1980s, Toni Morrison gained recognition as one of America's most original and talented writers. Her 1981 novel **Tar Baby** became standard reading in contemporary literature courses at U.S. colleges. Her 1987 novel **Beloved,** about an escaped slave who would rather kill her child than see her grow up in slavery, was so well received by critics and readers alike that there was a cry of outrage when it failed to win the National Book Award for fiction. In 1988 **Beloved** was awarded the even more prestigious Pulitzer Prize, as well as the Elmer Holms Bobst Award in Arts and Letters from New York University.

Born in Lorain, Ohio, February 19, 1931, Morrison published her first novel, **The Bluest Eye,** in 1970. Critics praised its sensual, lyrical imagery and its sophisticated plot structure. Her third novel, **Song of Solomon** (1977), won the National Book Critics Circle Award. She was equally lauded for **Jazz** (1992). Her achievement as the leading American writer was confirmed by her receiving the Nobel Prize for literature in 1993.

David Bradley publishes *The Chaneysville Incident,* which receives the PEN/Faulkner Award for best novel.

Maya Angelou's third autobiographical volume, *The Heart of a Woman,* is published.

Alice Walker publishes her poetry collection *You Can't Keep a Good Woman Down.*

Short-story writer James McPherson is awarded a five-year grant by the McArthur Foundation for his "exceptional talent."

In Ithaca, New York, Pam McAllister Johnson becomes publisher of the *Ithaca Journal,* the first African-American woman in charge of a non-black-oriented mass circulation newspaper.

On television, Bryant Gumbel coanchors ABC's *Today* show.

Hoyt J. Fuller, former editor of *Black World,* dies May 11 in Atlanta.

William Otis Walker, publisher of the *Cleveland Call & Post,* dies October 29.

SCIENCE AND TECHNOLOGY

James W. Mitchell, chemist, receives the Percy L. Julian Outstanding Research Award for his analyses of trace elements.

Samuel L. Kountz, an internationally acclaimed kidney-transplant surgeon, dies.

PERFORMING ARTS

The musical *Dreamgirls* opens on Broadway. Charting the rise of a black singing trio modeled closely on the Supremes, it will earn Tony awards for its stars Jennifer Holliday and Cleavant Derrick and for its choreographer Michael Peters.

The musical revue *Sophisticated Ladies,* featuring the work of Duke Ellington, opens on Broadway.

Lena Horne stars in a one-woman show, *Lena Horne: The Lady and Her Music,* on Broadway. She receives a special Tony Award for her performance.

Charles Fuller's *A Soldier's Play* is produced by the Negro Ensemble Company in New York City. It will win both the New York Drama Critics Award for best play and the Pulitzer Prize.

Isabel Sanford receives an Emmy Award for best actress in a TV comedy series, *The Jeffersons.*

The movie *Ragtime* stars Howard E. Rollins, Moses Gunn, and Debbie Allen. Rollins will win an Oscar nomination for best supporting actor.

Harry Belafonte ends a seven-year self-imposed retirement by appearing in a TV special, "Grambling's White Tiger," releasing an album, *Loving You Is Where I Belong*, and conducting a tour of the United States, Europe, and Australia.

Diana Ross and Lionel Richie's recording of "Endless Love" stays number one on the pop charts for nine weeks.

Jazz drummer William R. "Cozy" Cole dies in Columbus, Ohio.

Jazz pianist Mary Lou Williams dies in Durham, North Carolina.

Comedian Dewey "Pigmeat" Markham dies December 23.

THE MILITARY

Under pressure from civil rights groups, the U.S. Air Force Academy in Colorado Springs abandons its policy of not accepting applicants with a genetic predisposition to sickle cell anemia. Since blacks are far more susceptible to the disease than whites, the policy was widely viewed as discriminatory.

The Veterans Administration reports that the unemployment rate among black veterans of the Vietnam War is five times as high as the unemployment rate among white veterans.

SPORTS

The National Collegiate Athletic Association chooses its first African-American president, James Frank, president of Lincoln University, Jefferson City, Missouri.

Marcus Allen, tailback for the University of Southern California, wins football's Heisman Trophy.

Julius "Dr. J." Erving of the Philadelphia 76ers is named Most Valuable Player of the Year in the National Basketball Association.

Heavyweight champion Joe Louis dies in Las Vegas.

ADDITIONAL EVENTS

Over a period of almost two years, 28 young black males are murdered in Atlanta, causing a wave of fear and anger. Finally, William B. Williams, a black self-styled "talent scout," is arrested and charged with two of the killings. Later, he will be convicted and sentenced to two consecutive life terms in prison.

1982

POLITICS AND CIVIL RIGHTS

Andrew Young becomes mayor of Atlanta.

Hundreds of civil rights supporters join a 140-mile march through

1982 Family Income

	Black	White
Under $50,000	88%	69%
$50,000 to $74,999	9%	19%
$75,000 to $99,999	2%	7%
$100,000 and over	1%	5%

Alabama, from Carrolton through Selma to Montgomery, to protest the voting fraud convictions of two political activists.

The National Urban League reports that its top-priority concerns are (1) teenage pregnancies among blacks, (2) poverty-level households headed by single women, (3) crime and violence, and (4) voting registration.

U.S. Representative Shirley Chisholm of New York's Bedford-Stuyvesant area announces her retirement after 14 years in Congress, complaining of the "hopelessly conservative" trend in national politics.

President Reagan appoints Clarence Thomas chairperson of the Equal Employment Opportunity Commission. Reagan was forced to withdraw his original nominee, William Bell, after civil rights groups protested Bell's lack of experience for the position.

The American Civil Liberties Union issues a report attacking southern states for continuing to discriminate against African-American voters despite the Civil Rights Act of 1965, which guarantees voting rights. The ACLU also urges the federal government to be "more responsible and diligent" in enforcing compliance with the act.

Congress votes to extend the Civil Rights Act of 1965 (also called the Voting Rights Act), in spite of North Carolina Senator Jesse Helms's vehement opposition and lengthy filibuster.

Loretta Glickman is elected mayor of Pasadena, California, making her the first African-American woman to head the government of a major American city.

The United Nations honors Martin Luther King, Jr., with a posthumous award for his efforts to fight apartheid in South Africa. King campaigned for an international boycott of South Africa in 1965.

Rioting erupts in the Overtown district of Miami after a black man thought to be looting is shot and killed by a police officer. Two people are killed, 27 are wounded, and scores of homes and businesses are destroyed.

Amzie Moore, a civil rights advocate famous for leading voter registration drives in Mississippi during the 1960s, dies February 7.

BUSINESS AND EMPLOYMENT

The Reagan administration proposes "Urban Enterprise Zones" to stimulate business investment in the inner cities by means of tax

Contemporary Events, 1982 ■ Huge antinuclear demonstrations occur in major U.S. cities as the United Nations holds a disarmament conference. In New York and Washington, D.C., they are the largest demonstrations ever held. ■ Hollywood releases the film **E.T.**

incentives. The proposal draws fire from civil rights advocates, who say that instead of benefitting the poor people in inner cities, the program will simply disregard and displace them.

RELIGION AND EDUCATION

The U.S. Supreme Court rules unconstitutional Washington's state-wide vote to prohibit the busing of students to public schools to achieve desegregation. In 1977 Seattle passed a plan to bus 7,000 students. The next year, a statewide vote disallowed such busing. In its ruling, the Supreme Court accuses statewide voting of imposing an "unfair burden on minority groups."

A 10-year review of national tests to measure academic achievement in the public schools shows that black students have achieved an overall 12% increase in average scores, compared with an overall 5% increase among white students.

LITERATURE AND JOURNALISM

Julius Lester publishes *This Strange New Feeling*, love stories of newly emancipated black slaves.

Audre Lorde publishes *Chosen Poems, Old and New* and *Zami: A New Spelling of My Name.*

Sterling D. Plumpp's collection of poems *The Mojo Hands Call, I Must Go* is published.

PERFORMING ARTS

James Earl Jones stars in an acclaimed Broadway production of Shakespeare's *Othello.*

Leslie Uggams appears in the Broadway revue *Blues in the Night.*

Bass-baritone Simon Estes debuts at the Metropolitan Opera House. To do so, he must cancel his engagement to sing the national anthem at the opening of the major league baseball season.

Soprano Myra Merritt debuts at the Metropolitan Opera House.

Opera singers Grace Bumbry and Shirley Verrett give a historic "Tribute to Marian Anderson" concert at New York's Carnegie Hall.

August Wilson's play *Ma Rainey's Black Bottom* is accepted at the National Playwrights Conference. It will later be performed by the Yale Repertory Theater and become Wilson's first play on Broadway.

Quincy Jones earns five Grammy awards for his album *The Dude.*

Jazz pianist Thelonious Monk dies February 17 in New Jersey.

Calvin Simmons, conductor of the Oakland Symphony Orchestra, drowns August 21 in Lake Placid, New York.

THE MILITARY

The NAACP reports that Patsy Moore, an equal employment officer, was wearing a Ku Klux Klan costume during visits to four U.S. Army Engineers offices in Europe. The secretary of the army orders an investigation.

SPORTS

Henry "Hank" Aaron, National League baseball star, is elected to the Baseball Hall of Fame.

Herschel Walker, running back for the University of Georgia, wins football's Heisman Trophy.

Welterweight boxer Sugar Ray Robinson announces he is retiring from the sport due to an eye injury incurred during a world championship bout.

Leroy "Satchel" Paige, the first African-American pitcher to play in baseball's American League, dies June 8.

ADDITIONAL EVENTS

As part of its "Black Heritage" series, the U.S. Postal Service issues stamps commemorating Ralph Bunche, U.S. statesman, and Jackie Robinson, the first black player in major league baseball.

1983

POLITICS AND CIVIL RIGHTS

Martin Luther King, Jr.'s birthday, January 15, is declared a federal holiday.

Jesse Jackson launches a bid to become the Democratic nominee for president. He will win several primaries but fail to secure the nomination. Nevertheless, he will increase his power within the party to lobby on African-American issues.

Harold Washington is elected the first African-American mayor of Chicago, and W. Wilson Goode is elected the first African-American mayor of Philadelphia.

President Reagan and Congress agree to support a newly reorganized Commission on Civil Rights. Reagan had earlier fired several members who disagreed with his antibusing policy, prompting con-

---

Contemporary Events, 1983 ■ President Reagan orders U.S. troops to invade the Caribbean island of Grenada. ■ The movie **Gandhi** wins an Academy Award as the best picture of 1982. ■ Astronaut Sally Ride is the first woman in space.

cern from Congress that the commission could no longer remain "independent and fair."

BUSINESS AND EMPLOYMENT

The National Urban League issues a report stating that this year's business recession is hurting blacks far more than whites. It recommends more black-targeted job creation and jobs training programs.

The Martin Luther King, Jr., Nonviolent Peace Prize is established by the Martin Luther King, Jr., Center for Nonviolent Social Change. The first recipients are Martin Luther King, Sr., and Richard Attenborough, the British director of the film *Gandhi*, based on the life of the Indian political activist whose passive resistance movement influenced Martin Luther King, Jr.

RELIGION AND EDUCATION

The U.S. Supreme Court rules that private schools practicing racial segregation or discrimination cannot be given tax exemptions.

Chicago finally resolves its long-standing dilemma in desegregating public schools by adopting a plan calling for no school to be more than 70% white and by creating a system of "magnet" schools and voluntary transfers.

At the University of Mississippi in Oxford, black students complain about the widespread display of the Confederate flag, the singing of "Dixie" at athletic games, and the "Rebels" nickname. The administration agrees to discontinue using the Confederate flag as a "semi-official" symbol. But it refuses to disallow the singing of "Dixie," the "Rebels" nickname, or the "spontaneous and individual" waving of the Confederate flag on campus or at school-related events.

Nelson W. Trout becomes bishop of the South Pacific district (based in California) of the American Lutheran Church, the first African American to hold full-time office in the denomination.

Purdue University in West Lafayette, Indiana, sponsors the Conference on the Study and Teaching of Afro-American History. It is attended by over 600 historians and students from across the nation.

Mary Hatwood Futrell is elected president of the National Education Association. She will hold this position throughout the 1980s, establishing and administrating the Operation Rescue program to cut the high number of public school dropouts.

LITERATURE AND JOURNALISM

Alice Walker's novel *The Color Purple*, published in 1982, wins the Pulitzer Prize.

Robert C. Maynard

When Robert C. Maynard, editor of the **Oakland Tribune** in California, purchased the paper in 1983, he was widely hailed as the first black owner of a major mainstream daily newspaper. Maynard, however, claimed he was more excited that he was the first person—black or white—to engineer a management-leveraged buyout of a U.S. newspaper. He paid $22 million, without spending a cent of his own money.

A high school dropout at age 16, Maynard began his career in journalism in 1961, as a reporter for the **York Gazette** in Pennsylvania. By 1967 he was a star reporter for the **Washington Post.** During the 1970s, he rose to the editorship of the **Oakland Tribune,** making its staff one of the most talented and ethnically diverse in the country. He also founded the Institute for Journalism Education, which trained hundreds of minority journalists.

Despite the **Oakland Tribune'**s reputation for innovative, high-quality reporting, Maynard was forced by the 1992 economic recession to sell the paper. When he died of cancer later that year, he was eulogized as "The Little Engine That Could," a title he had given himself.

Gloria Naylor's novel *The Women of Brewster Place* is published and wins the American Book Award.

Maya Angelou publishes her collection of poems *Shaker, Why Don't You Sing?*

Nikki Giovanni's poetry collection *Those Who Ride the Night Winds* is published.

Ntozake Shange publishes a book of poems, *A Daughter's Geography.*

The poetry collection *Confirmation: An Anthology of African-American Women,* edited by Amiri Baraka and Amina Baraka, is published.

Activist Angela Davis publishes *Women, Race, and Class.*

Robert C. Maynard purchases the *Oakland Tribune,* making him the first African-American publisher of a major city's daily newspaper.

SCIENCE AND TECHNOLOGY

Guion S. Bluford, Jr., participates in a mission of the space shuttle *Challenger,* making him the first African American in space.

PERFORMING ARTS

Louis Gossett, Jr., receives an Oscar for best supporting actor for his performance in the 1982 film *An Officer and a Gentleman.*

Soprano Jessye Norman debuts at the Metropolitan Opera House in New York, singing the role of "Cassandra" in Berlioz's *Les Troyens.*

Michael Jackson releases his pop record album *Thriller.* It will sell over 40 million copies, the best-selling album in music history.

Diana Ross conducts a concert in New York's Central Park to raise money to build a children's playground. The scheduled performance is rained out, and the follow-up performance is plagued by gang warfare. When it is later revealed that the city earned nothing for the playground and, in fact, lost almost half a million dollars on the event, Ross presents the city with a personal check for $250,000.

A Nielson survey reveals that blacks spend 35% of their time watching TV, compared with 28% among whites. The TV show most watched by blacks is the nighttime soap opera *Dynasty;* the TV show most watched by whites is the news magazine program *60 Minutes.*

Ragtime musician Eubie Blake dies February 12 in New York.

VISUAL ARTS

Painter Jacob Lawrence is elected to the American Academy of Arts and Letters.

Artist Faith Ringgold makes her first painted story quilts.

THE MILITARY

Brigadier General Hazel W. Johnson, the first black woman to reach that rank and to command the Army Nurse Corps, retires from the U.S. Army.

SPORTS

Julius Erving of the Philadelphia 76ers scores the 25,000th point in his basketball career.

Herschel Walker, 1982 recipient of the Heisman Trophy, signs a three-year, $8 million contract with the U.S. Football League's New Jersey Generals. It is the largest contract to date in the history of football.

ADDITIONAL EVENTS

Scott Joplin, ragtime and jazz musician and composer, is the subject of a commemorative stamp issued by the U.S. Postal Service.

Vanessa Williams of New York State is crowned Miss America on September 17, the first African American to win the pageant. In 1984 she will be forced to resign after it is revealed that she once posed for nude photos. She will later regain national attention as a popular recording artist.

1984

POLITICS AND CIVIL RIGHTS

Robert N. C. Nix, Jr., becomes chief justice of the Pennsylvania Supreme Court, making him the first African-American leader of a state supreme court.

Numerous demonstrations take place throughout the United States to protest South Africa's policy of apartheid and to encourage various boycotts against South Africa. Among prominent African American who participate in the demonstrations are politician Jesse Jackson, singer Stevie Wonder, and tennis star Arthur Ashe.

After both the Republican and the Democratic parties fail to consider an African-American woman candidate for U.S. vice president, ex-Congresswoman Shirley Chisholm helps found the National Political Congress for Women.

Contemporary Events, 1984 ■ Ronald Reagan and George Bush are reelected U.S. president and vice president by one of the biggest margins in history: 58% of the vote, compared with 41% for the Democratic presidential nominee Walter Mondale and his running mate Geraldine Ferraro.

The Spingarn Medal is awarded to Tom Bradley, four-term mayor of Los Angeles.

Martin Luther King, Sr., minister and civil rights leader, dies November 11 in Atlanta.

BUSINESS AND EMPLOYMENT

Johnson Publishing Company, publisher of *Ebony* and *Jet* magazines, heads *Black Enterprise* magazine's list of the 100 leading black firms in the United States. Its assets are estimated to exceed $135 million.

RELIGION AND EDUCATION

The first nationwide telethon for the United Negro College Fund raises $14.1 million to support 40 historically black colleges and universities. It will become an annual event.

Benjamin Mays, former president of Morehouse College and civil rights leader, dies March 28 in Atlanta.

C. L. Franklin, famous for his preaching on nationwide radio, dies July 27 in Detroit. He was the father of Aretha Franklin.

LITERATURE AND JOURNALISM

Amiri Baraka publishes *Daggers and Javelins: Essays, 1974–1979.*

Jill Boyer's book of poetry *Breaking Camp* is published.

Ntozake Shange publishes *From Okra to Greens: Poems.*

Alice Walker's *Horses Make a Landscape More Beautiful,* a book of poems, is published.

The anthology, *3000 Years of Black Poetry,* edited by Alan Lomax and Raoul Abdul, is published. Beginning with ancient African chants, it features the poetry of blacks from around the world.

John Edgar Wideman publishes his autobiographical work *Brothers and Keepers.*

PERFORMING ARTS

NBC premieres *The Cosby Show,* starring Bill Cosby and Phylicia Ayers-Allen (later, Rashad). It will evolve into one of the most commercially successful and critically acclaimed TV comedy series.

Michael Jackson wins a record eight Grammy awards for his 1983 album *Thriller.* He also signs a $1 million contract with Doubleday for his autobiography, *Moonwalk,* to be edited by Jacqueline Onassis.

Prince's *Purple Rain* album, featuring music from his movie of the same name, is number one on the rock music charts, and contains Prince's first number one singles: "When Doves Cry" and "Let's Go Crazy."

Aretha Franklin releases her hit single "Freeway of Love." This same year she is scheduled to make her Broadway debut in a musical *Sing, Mahalia, Sing*, based on the life of gospel singer Mahalia Jackson. Her fear of flying leads to cancellation of the project, for which she must pay $234,000 in breach-of-contract charges.

Eddie Murphy stars in the movie *Beverly Hills Cop*, creating the popular character "Axel Foley."

Hollywood releases *Beat Street*, director Stan Lathan's movie about the break-dance phenomenon; *The Cotton Club*, a big-budget musical about the popular jazz nightspot in Harlem during the 1920s and 1930s; and *Purple Rain*, starring rock musician Prince.

Jazz bandleader William "Count" Basie dies April 26 in Hollywood, Florida.

Blues singer Alberta Hunter dies October 17 in New York.

VISUAL ARTS

The National Conference of Artists, the longest-standing organization of African-American artists, sponsors its first international conference in Dakar, Senegal.

The exhibit "African-American Art" is held at the High Museum of Art in Atlanta.

THE MILITARY

Jesse Jackson negotiates the release from a Syrian prison of U.S. Navy Lieutenant Robert O. Goodman, whose plane was shot down during a 1983 American air strike.

SPORTS

Decathlon star Rafer Johnson lights the torch at the Los Angeles Olympics, where Carl Lewis wins four gold medals in various track and field events. Other track and field golds go to Evelyn Ashford (100-meter dash), Alonzo Babers (400-meter run), Valerie Brisco-Hooks (200- and 400-meter runs), Benita Fitzgerald-Brown (100-meter hurdles), Al Joyner (triple jump), Roger Kingdom (110-meter hurdles), and Edwin Moses (400-meter hurdles).

In a dramatic comeback, Sugar Ray Leonard returns to professional boxing after a two-year absence and risks further damage to his eyes by fighting Kevin Howard. He knocks Howard out, to win the match.

The Georgetown Hoyas basketball team wins the National Collegiate Athletic Association championship, making John Thompson the first African-American coach of a championship team.

Marcus Allen, running back for the Los Angeles Raiders, is named

Most Valuable Player of the Super Bowl, where he helped the Raiders defeat the Washington Redskins.

ADDITIONAL STATISTICS

Washington D.C.'s Center for the Study of Social Policy reports that the income gap between blacks and whites is as wide in 1984 as it was in 1960.

1985

POLITICS AND CIVIL RIGHTS

The U.S. Supreme Court rules that affirmative action plans for state employment are constitutional.

U.S. Representative William H. Gray III becomes chair of the House Budget Committee, the highest post in Congress yet achieved by an African American.

The U.S. General Accounting Office is compelled to pay $3.5 million in back salaries to black employees who experienced discrimination in the granting of promotions.

Reuben V. Anderson becomes the first African-American judge to sit on the Mississippi Supreme Court.

U.S. District Judge Leonard Sand finds Yonkers, New York, liable for intentionally segregating its schools and housing.

Philadelphia police and firefighters destroy two city blocks when they bomb the headquarters of MOVE, a radical African-American group. Eleven people, almost half children, die, and 300 people are left homeless. Mayor W. Wilson Goode apologizes for the assault.

BUSINESS AND EMPLOYMENT

Tony Brown, syndicated columnist on black issues and host/producer of TV's *Tony Brown's Journal,* creates the Buy Freedom Campaign to assist African-American businesses. Noting that 95% of black consumer spending goes to nonblack firms and professionals, Brown calls for African Americans to support their own firms and professionals more conscientiously.

According to the Census Bureau, the number of black-owned businesses in the United States has risen to about 350,000.

Contemporary Events, 1985 ■ A TWA jet is skyjacked to Beirut, where the 39 Americans on board are held hostage by Shiite terrorists. One American is killed. ■ Movie star Rock Hudson dies of complications resulting from AIDS, bringing the disease to the forefront of national attention.

Julius Erving, former basketball great, and J. Bruce Llewellyn purchase Philadelphia's Coca Cola Bottling Company, which becomes the fourth largest black-owned business in the United States.

LITERATURE AND JOURNALISM

The anthology *Ancient Black Youth and Elders Reborn: The Poetry, Short Stories, Oral Histories, and Deeper Thoughts of African American Youths and Elders*, edited by Linda Cousins, is published.

Thulani Davis publishes her poems *Playing the Changes*.

Michael S. Harper's poetry collection *Healing Songs for the Inner Ear* is published.

June Jordan's poetry collection *Living Room* is published.

Ntozake Shange publishes her novel *Betsey Brown*.

Octavia E. Butler's science fiction novella *Bloodchild* wins the Nebula, Hugo, and Locust awards.

Publisher John H. Johnson launches *EM*, a lifestyle magazine for African-American men.

SCIENCE AND TECHNOLOGY

John P. Moon, a pioneer in personal computer technology, is appointed chief of Apple Computer's peripheral devices division, and starts working on the revolutionary new disk drive for the Macintosh computer.

PERFORMING ARTS

The Metropolitan Opera Company in New York stages an acclaimed production of *Porgy and Bess*, starring Simon Estes as "Porgy" and Grace Bumbry as "Bess."

James Earl Jones is inducted into the Theater Hall of Fame.

The movie *The Color Purple*, based on Alice Walker's novel, premieres. It stars Whoopi Goldberg, Danny Glover, Willard Pugh, Adolph Caesar, Oprah Winfrey, and Margaret Avery.

The film *White Nights* features the black and white modern-dance combo of Gregory Hines (tap) and Mikhail Baryshnikov (ballet).

Rock singer Tina Turner wins three Grammys, including Record of the Year for *What's Love Got to Do with It?* and has a starring role in the film *Mad Max III: Beyond Thunderdome*.

Shirley Caesar wins two Grammys for best gospel album and best gospel duo (with Al Green). This same year, the NAACP honors Caesar with its Image Achievement Award.

In Harlem, the Apollo Theater, for 50 years one of the major show-

The Apollo Theater

When Harlem's Apollo Theater reopened after 15 months to celebrate its 50th anniversary on May 5, 1985, more than 1,500 people crammed inside to enjoy the gala hosted by Bill Cosby, while another 2,000 crowded outside. They were overjoyed at the survival of America's best-known and most-loved showcase for African-American entertainers. Among the hundreds of singers, dancers, and comedians who launched their careers here—many on "Amateur Night"—were "Moms" Mabley, "Pigmeat" Markham, Ella Fitzgerald, Sarah Vaughan, Leslie Uggams, the Shirelles, Stevie Wonder, Patti LaBelle, and Gregory Hines.

cases for African-American musical talent, reopens after a $10 million, 15-month renovation.

Lena Horne wins a Kennedy Center Honors Award for Lifetime Achievement.

Pop singer Stevie Wonder receives a special humanitarian award from the United Nations on his 35th birthday.

As a fundraiser for African famine relief, the song "We Are the World" is written by Lionel Richie and Michael Jackson, produced by Quincy Jones, and recorded by a cast of popular entertainers.

Emmy Awards are earned by Robert Guillaume (best actor, in "Benson") and *The Cosby Show* (best comedy series).

Lincoln Theodore Andrew Perry, the actor known as Stepin Fetchit, dies November 19 in Woodland Hills, California.

VISUAL ARTS

The Bellevue Art Museum in Bellevue, Washington, and the Art Museum Association of America launch a tour of African-American art entitled "Hidden Heritage: Afro-American Art, 1850–1950."

The Washington Project for the Arts in D.C. holds the exhibit "Art in Washington and Its Afro-American Presence: 1940–1970."

THE MILITARY

Sherian Grace Cadoria becomes the first African-American female brigadier general in the regular army.

SPORTS

Eddie Robinson, football coach of Grambling University, becomes the longest-winning football coach in history.

Lou Brock, outfielder for the St. Louis Cardinals, is inducted into the Baseball Hall of Fame.

Mike Garrett is inducted into the National Football Hall of Fame.

ADDITIONAL EVENTS

The U.S. Postal Service issues a stamp commemorating Mary McLeod Bethune, educator and civil rights advocate.

POLITICS AND CIVIL RIGHTS

The Martin Luther King, Jr., Nonviolent Peace Prize is awarded to Bishop Desmond Tutu, an anti-apartheid leader in South Africa.

Martin Luther King, Jr.'s birthday, January 15, is officially celebrated as a federal holiday in the United States, the first such holiday to honor an African American.

Career diplomat Edward Perkins is named ambassador to the Republic of South Africa, the first black to serve in that capacity.

U.S. District Judge Leonard Sand orders Yonkers, New York, to build 1,000 housing units for families with low and moderate incomes in order to help correct over 40 years of intentional segregation in housing.

The NAACP moves its headquarters from New York to Baltimore. Two major reasons are high taxes and rent in New York, and Baltimore's majority black population.

Constance Baker Motley, who first gained prominence as an activist lawyer on behalf of civil rights during the 1960s, retires from her position as chief justice of the U.S. District Court for New York's Second District.

In the predominantly white Howard Beach section of New York, three black men looking for help in repairing their car are attacked by a gang of whites hurling racial epithets and wielding baseball bats. One of the black men, Michael Griffith, is hit and killed by a car while fleeing the gang. Three of the gang members are held without bail on second-degree murder charges.

BUSINESS AND EMPLOYMENT

The U.S. Supreme Court upholds affirmative action programs in hirings and promotions in a case involving a union of sheet metal workers in New York and New Jersey.

Lorimer Douglas, a leading banker and adviser to President Eisenhower and President Kennedy, dies February 8 in Atlanta.

RELIGION AND EDUCATION

According to the American Council on Higher Education, the number of black men enrolled in U.S. colleges and universities has steadily declined in the past decade, from 470,000 in 1976 to 436,000 in 1986. Meanwhile, the number of black women enrolled in U.S. colleges and universities has steadily increased, from 563,000 in 1976 to 645,000 in 1986.

At the Citadel military school in South Carolina, five white cadets

---

Contemporary Events, 1986 ■ The U.S. Air Force conducts a surprise attack on Tripoli, Libya, designed to destroy terrorist bases and undermine the confidence of Libyan leader Colonel Muammar al-Qaddafi. ■ New York celebrates the 100th anniversary of the Statue of Liberty.

James Baldwin

James Baldwin was one of America's great writers. His essay collections—**Notes of a Native Son** (1955), **Noboby Knows My Name** (1961), and **The Fire Next Time** (1963)—are classic works about the African-American experience. He also wrote highly acclaimed novels like **Go Tell It on the Mountain** (1953) and **Another Country** (1962) and a powerful drama, **Blues for Mister Charlie** (1964), based on the 1955 lynching of Emmett Till.

But when Baldwin's portrait appeared on the cover of **Time** magazine in 1963, the story was not under "Literature," but under "National Affairs," for having confronted Attorney General Robert Kennedy about civil rights. Baldwin was a vigorous spokesperson for African-American causes. He was also outspoken on homosexual rights. His novel **Giovanni's Room** (1956) dealt openly with his own homosexuality, and he continued to denounce prejudice against gays and lesbians. Baldwin felt compelled to make his home in France, where he could enjoy more freedom as a black gay man than he could in his native country. The French gave him their highest civilian award, naming him a commander in the Legion of Honor.

dressed in Ku Klux Klan garb harass a black cadet, Kevin Nesmith. Nesmith's subsequent resignation from the Citadel provokes censure of the school from prominent African-American leaders. A South Carolina state investigative committee attributes the incident to minimal black enrollment and recommends that black enrollment be increased from 6% to 10% in two years.

LITERATURE AND JOURNALISM

Actress and writer Ruby Dee publishes her collection of stories, poems, and essays, *My One Good Nerve: Rhythms, Rhymes, Reasons.*

Bill Cosby publishes his best-selling book *Fatherhood.*

France makes James Baldwin a commander in its Legion of Honor.

SCIENCE AND TECHNOLOGY

Ronald McNair, astronaut and physicist, is killed along with the other six crew members when the space shuttle *Challenger* explodes.

PERFORMING ARTS

Anthony Davis's opera *The Life and Times of Malcolm X*, based on the career of the Black Muslim and civil rights leader, is produced by the New York City Opera Company.

August Wilson's play *Fences*, with James Earl Jones, opens on Broadway. It will receive a Pulitzer Prize.

Debbie Allen stars in the musical *Sweet Charity* on Broadway.

Hollywood releases *'Round Midnight*, starring jazz musician Dexter Gordon, who earns an Oscar nomination for best supporting actor.

The film *Under the Cherry Moon*, starring rock composer and singer Prince, premieres.

The 1985 movie *The Color Purple* is nominated for 11 Oscars, including best picture, best actress (Whoopi Goldberg), and best supporting actress (both Margaret Avery and Oprah Winfrey). It does not win any awards.

Spike Lee's independently produced film *She's Gotta Have It* is a hit.

The Oprah Winfrey Show, based in Chicago, is syndicated on 128 TV stations across the United States. In addition, Oprah Winfrey, its star and producer, receives a "Woman of Achievement" award from the National Organization of Women and founds her own TV and movie production company, Harpo ("Oprah" spelled backwards).

Toni Morrison's play *Dreaming Emmet* is produced Off-Broadway.

Singers James Brown, Ray Charles, and Fats Domino are among the first group of inductees into the new Rock 'n' Roll Hall of Fame.

Singer Ray Charles receives the Kennedy Center Honors Award for Lifetime Achievement.

THE MILITARY

According to the Defense Department, over 400,000 African Americans serve in the U.S. Armed Forces.

SPORTS

Debi Thomas becomes the first African-American adult figure skating champion, winning both the U.S. and world championships.

Walter Payton, the all-time leading rusher in the National Football League, plays his last season as running back for the Chicago Bears.

POLITICS AND CIVIL RIGHTS

In Baltimore, attorney Kurt Schmoke is elected the first African-American mayor.

Marion S. Barry, Jr., is inaugurated for a record third term as mayor of Washington, D.C.

In Forsyth County, Georgia, 400 Ku Klux Klanspeople and other white supremacists throw rocks and bottles at 90 civil rights advocates conducting a peaceful "brotherhood walk" in honor of Martin Luther King, Jr. A week later, another "brotherhood walk" is staged along the same route by 20,000 people, who are protected by 3,000 police and National Guard officers.

In Tampa, a black man dies after police try to subdue him with a "choke hold." Two nights of rioting follow, ending when African-American leaders voluntarily patrol the streets to keep the peace.

In a TV interview, Supreme Court Justice Thurgood Marshall rates Ronald Reagan as the worst president in terms of his civil rights record. In a stinging public denouncement, Marshall states, "I don't care whether he's the president, the governor, the mayor, the sheriff, whoever calls the shots determines whether we have integration, segregation, or decency. . . . That starts exactly with the president."

In Wappingers Falls, New York, Tawana Brawley, a 16-year-old African American, reports she was abducted, sexually abused, and physi-

Contemporary Events, 1987 ■ The Reagan administration is plagued by the Iran-contra controversy over the alleged swap of arms for hostages in Iran. ■ President Reagan and Soviet Premier Mikhail Gorbachev sign a major arms-reduction treaty. ■ Evangelists Jim and Tammy Faye Baker are discredited.

cally tormented by a group of white men, possibly including police officers. To ensure that her case is not treated lightly due to racial bias, she is championed by high-profile black leaders, including Al Sharpton and Bill Cosby.

Shirley Chisholm, former congresswoman from New York, is the keynote speaker at the annual convention of the National Women's Political Caucus.

Civil rights leader Edgar Daniel "E.D." Nixon dies February 26 in Montgomery, Alabama.

Bayard Rustin, adviser to Martin Luther King, Jr., and executive director of the 1963 March on Washington, dies August 24 in New York.

Harold Washington, the first black mayor of Chicago, dies of a heart attack November 25, less than a year after being reelected.

Septima Clark, educator, civil rights activist, and recipient of a Living Legacy Award from President Carter, dies December 15 on St. John's Island, South Carolina.

BUSINESS AND EMPLOYMENT

Dick Gregory founds Correction Connection, Inc., a health and nutrition business to assist in weight loss and to market his "Bahamian Diet."

Publisher John H. Johnson is named "Businessman of the Decade" by *Black Enterprise* magazine.

LITERATURE AND JOURNALISM

A U.S. district court finds the *New York Daily News*, the nation's most widely circulated daily newspaper, guilty of retaliating against four African-American staff members—including an editor—because they complained of discriminatory treatment.

The National Association of Black Journalists reports that only 6.5% of American journalists belong to minority groups (a classification that also includes Latinos and Asians).

Toni Morrison's novel *Beloved* is published. It will win a Pulitzer Prize as well as nominations for the National Book Award and the National Book Critics Circle Award.

Rita Dove wins the Pulitzer Prize for her extended poem *Thomas and Beulah*.

Nikki Giovanni publishes her collection of poetry *Sacred Cows and Other Edibles*.

Toni Cade Bambara's novel *If Blessing Comes* is published.

Amiri Baraka publishes *The Music Makers: Reflections on Jazz and Blues.*

Terry McMillan publishes her novel *Mama.*

Henry Hampton produces the documentary *Eyes on the Prize,* about the civil rights struggle, which airs on PBS-TV.

Novelist John Oliver Killens dies October 27 in New York.

Novelist and essayist James Baldwin dies November 30 in St.-Paul-de-Vence, France.

SCIENCE AND TECHNOLOGY

Mae C. Jemison is the first African-American woman to become a U.S. astronaut.

The National Black Alcoholism Council, Inc., cites alcoholism as a serious threat to the welfare of black Americans. It refers to studies that show blacks are twice as likely to die from alcohol-induced cirrhosis than whites and that esophageal cancer, another potentially alcohol-related illness, is 10 times higher among blacks than whites.

Cancer researcher Jane Cooke Wright retires from her roles as professor of surgery and associate dean of New York Medical College.

PERFORMING ARTS

Alice Childress's play *Moms: A Praise Play for a Black Comedienne,* based on the life of Jackie "Moms" Mabley, is staged Off-Broadway.

On Broadway, Morgan Freeman stars as the chauffeur in the play *Driving Miss Daisy* and receives an Obie for his performance. In the same year he receives an Academy Award nomination as best supporting actor for his performance in the 1986 film *Street Smart.*

The action film *Lethal Weapon* is released, introducing the popular cop-buddy team of Danny Glover and Mel Gibson.

The movie *Cry Freedom* stars Denzel Washington as the murdered South African activist Steven Biko.

Rappers Salt-N-Pepa make their chart debut on March 21 with "My Mike Sounds Nice."

Soprano Barbara Hendricks makes her debut at the Metropolitan Opera House as "Sophie" in *Der Rosenkavalier.*

Michael Jackson releases his best-selling *Bad* album.

Aretha Franklin's double album of gospel music, *One Lord, One Faith, One Baptism,* is released.

Eddie Murphy Raw, a film of Murphy's comedy act, is a commercial success but earns criticism for its perceived slurs against women, gays, and Italians.

Mae C. Jemison

NASA's 1987 announcement that it had accepted Mae C. Jemison into the U.S. space program made her a national heroine and a role model for African-American women. Born October 17, 1956, in Decatur, Alabama, Jemison grew up in Chicago, graduated from Stanford University with a degree in chemical engineering, and went on to Cornell medical school. After spending two and a half years with the Peace Corps as a physician in West Africa and two years in a health maintenance organization in Los Angeles, she was chosen for NASA training from 2,000 applicants. She became the first African-American woman to penetrate outer space as a member of the 1992 **Endeavor** space shuttle crew.

25 Years After "I Have a Dream"

Across the country in August 1988, newspaper and TV commentators called attention to the 25th anniversary of Martin Luther King, Jr.'s "I Have a Dream" speech at the 1963 March on Washington rally. Most commentators acknowledged that African Americans had made significant political gains since 1963, recently illustrated by Jesse Jackson's campaign for the U.S. presidency. Nevertheless, these same commentators lamented that King's dream still seemed a dream rather than a reality. This quotation from an editorial in the **Salt Lake Tribune** on August 30, 1988, is representative:

"Dr. King wasn't talking about vote-getting or employment rewards, as crucial to the evaluation of a truly just and fair community as these manifestations are. He was, however, challenging this nation, people everywhere, to move permanently away from the poisonous distraction of racism so that more accurate, honest, and decent standards for evaluating human worth can reign."

VISUAL ARTS

The Studio Museum in Harlem launches a major touring show, "Harlem Renaissance: Art of Black America."

SPORTS

"Sugar" Ray Leonard wins the world's middleweight boxing championship by defeating "Marvelous" Marvin Hagler.

ADDITIONAL STATISTICS

According to the Center on Budget and Policy Priorities, a Washington research group, one in three African Americans is living below the poverty level. Among black children, 45.6% are living below the poverty level: the highest rate since the mid-1960s.

1988

POLITICS AND CIVIL RIGHTS

On January 18, a national holiday in honor of the birthday of Martin Luther King, Jr., thousands of demonstrators march through downtown Phoenix protesting Arizona's refusal to recognize the holiday. Other states that also refuse are Hawaii, Idaho, Montana, New Hampshire, South Dakota, and Wyoming. Celebrations occur in the other 43 states.

Jon Lester, a member of the white gang that caused the 1986 death of black youth Michael Griffith in the Howard Beach section of New York, is sentenced to prison for 10 to 30 years. Later, Jason Ladone, another member of the gang, receives a 5- to 15-year sentence.

The 20th anniversary of the 1968 Report of the President's Commission on Civil Disorders (the Kerner Commission report) is widely noted by urban experts and civil rights leaders. The report had predicted that the United States was moving toward two societies: one white and rich, the other black and poor. A follow-up report is published in March, claiming that the prediction has come true: "Segregation by race still sharply divides America . . . and the gap between [white] rich and [black] poor has widened."

President Ronald Reagan vetoes a civil rights bill designed to strengthen federal laws prohibiting discrimination. He claims that the bill allows for "unwarranted" government interference in the

---

Contemporary Events, 1988 ■ George Bush is elected U.S. president. ■ Over a million illegal aliens apply for amnesty under a new federal immigration policy. ■ Forest fires destroy huge sections of Yellowstone National Park.

activities of businesses and religious institutions. Later, Congress overrides the veto and the bill becomes law.

Jesse Jackson campaigns for the Democratic Party's nomination for president of the United States, winning over 6.6 million primary votes. At the Democratic National Convention, he delivers a stirring address, urging those who are suffering to "keep hope alive." He wins over 1,200 delgate votes, but loses the nomination to Michael Dukakis, governor of Massachusetts.

The NAACP denounces the states of Alabama and South Carolina for continuing to fly the Confederate flag, an emblem of the slave-holding states, over public buildings.

Over 55,000 blacks and whites march in Washington, D.C., to mark the 25th anniversary of Martin Luther King, Jr.'s 1963 March on Washington.

Jesse Jackson meets with Jewish leaders to try to allay growing tensions between African Americans and Jews in Chicago.

Bowing to pressure from civil rights groups, President Reagan signs into law a bill mandating stronger enforcement of previous federal "open housing" legislation.

A New York State grand jury concludes that Tawana Brawley, the black teenager who claimed to have been abducted and sexually abused by white men in Wappingers Falls, New York, made up her story, possibly to avoid being disciplined by her stepfather for staying away from home.

Clarence Pendleton, Jr., chairperson of the federal Civil Rights Commission, dies June 5 in San Diego.

M. Carl Holman, president of the National Urban Coalition, dies August 11 in Washington, D.C.

BUSINESS AND EMPLOYMENT

A U.S. Court of Appeals rules that an affirmative action plan aimed at increasing the number of black firefighters in the city is unconstitutional, a major blow against affirmative action programs.

Lee Roy Young becomes a Texas Ranger, the first African American in the police force's 165-year existence.

S. B. Fuller, founder of Fuller Products Company, dies October 26 in Blue Island, Illinois.

RELIGION AND EDUCATION

To protest alleged racial assaults, 200 African-American, Native American, and Latino students take over the New Africa House on the campus of the University of Massachusetts at Amherst. Six days later, the takeover ends when the administration agrees to expel any students who commit acts of racial violence and to promote a multi-cultural curriculum.

Boston University files suit against Coretta Scott King for the release of taped conversations and correspondence involving her husband, Martin Luther King, Jr. Boston University argues that the last will of Martin Luther King, Jr., an alumnus, left such materials to the university's collection of King-related documents. Earlier, Mrs. King had filed a suit against Boston University claiming that its collection of King-related documents belonged in the Martin Luther King, Jr., Center for Nonviolent Social Change in Atlanta.

Pope John Paul II names Eugene Marino archbishop of Atlanta, the first African American to become a Roman Catholic archbishop.

A landmark report entitled "One Third of a Nation," by the American Council on Education and the U.S. Education Commission, concludes that minority education must be improved or the nation will suffer. It states, "America is moving backward—not forward—in its efforts to achieve the full participation of minority citizens in the life and prosperity of the nation."

Historian William H. Harris is named president of Texas Southern University in Houston.

Entertainer Bill Cosby donates $20 million to Spelman College in Atlanta. It is the largest gift ever given to the college, and the largest donation to any college or university made by an African American.

The Project Excellence awards are established by newspaper columnist Carl T. Rowan to provide college scholarships to financially hindered youth in the Washington, D.C., metropolitan area.

LITERATURE AND JOURNALISM

Alice Walker's children's novel *To Hell with Dying* is published.

Julius Bernard Lester, writer, musician, and folklorist, publishes his autobiographical work *Lovesong: Becoming a Jew.*

Max Robinson, pioneering black television journalist and an anchor on ABC's *World News Tonight,* dies in December in Atlanta.

SCIENCE AND TECHNOLOGY

Bertram O. Fraser-Reid, a biochemist at Duke University, develops and patents a method for linking simple sugars together to form oligosaccharides, compounds that are vitally important in regulating various biological activities.

The National Center for Health Statistics reports that African-American men suffer much higher death rates from many major illnesses than white men: 68% higher for heart disease, 90% higher for strokes, 71% higher for cancer, 126% higher for liver-related ailments, and 86% higher for diabetes.

PERFORMING ARTS

Hollywood releases *Bird*, a film biography of jazz saxophonist Charlie "Bird" Parker, starring Forest Whitaker. At the Cannes Film Festival, Whitaker wins the best actor award for his performance.

August Wilson's play *Joe Turner's Come and Gone* opens on Broadway.

Michael Jackson goes on a highly successful international tour showcasing his most recent album, *Bad* (1987).

Eddie Murphy's movie *Coming to America* stars Murphy along with Arsenio Hall.

Spike Lee's film *School Daze* is released.

The rap group Public Enemy makes its chart debut February 6 with "Bring the Noise."

Rapper Ice-T makes his chart debut June 25 with the theme from the movie *Colors*.

VISUAL ARTS

The first annual National Black Arts Festival is held in Atlanta.

Hughie Lee-Smith has a major traveling show, beginning at the new Jersey State Museum in Trenton.

Artist Romare Bearden dies on March 12.

THE MILITARY

The U.S. Navy issues a report that cites "widespread but subtle bias against black and Hispanic sailors and other minorities in its ranks." A later report will indicate the navy has proportionately the fewest African Americans in the U.S. Armed Forces.

SPORTS

In Tokyo, Mike Tyson knocks out Tony Tubbs and retains his world heavyweight boxing championship.

Doug Williams, quarterback for the Washington Redskins, is named Most Valuable Player of the Super Bowl.

Debi Thomas wins the bronze medal in figure skating, becoming the first African American to win a medal in the Winter Olympics. At the Summer Olympics African-American gold medalists include Florence Griffith Joyner (100- and 200-meter dashes), Jackie Joyner-Kersee (long jump and heptathlon), Carl Lewis (100-meter dash and long jump), Steve Lewis (400-meter run), and Roger Kingdom (110-meter hurdles).

ADDITIONAL STATISTICS

According to the U.S. Census Bureau, almost 6 out of 10 African-American families with one or more children under the age of 18 are headed by a single parent (almost always the mother). The comparable single-parent rate among whites is 2 out of 10 families.

POLITICS AND CIVIL RIGHTS

Dexter Scott King, son of Martin Luther King, Jr., assumes the presidency of the Martin Luther King, Jr., Center for Nonviolent Social Change, after his mother, Coretta Scott King, retires from the position. He resigns several months later for undisclosed reasons.

While visiting the predominantly white Bensonhurst section of New York City to check out a car for sale, black youth Yusuf Hawkins is pursued and shot to death by a white gang. The highly publicized crime—and the arrests that follow—aggravate racial tensions throughout the city.

The Senate Judiciary Committee rejects President George Bush's nomination of African-American lawyer William C. Lucas to serve as the assistant attorney general for civil rights in the Justice Department. Lucas is faulted by some political liberals for lacking experience in civil rights litigation and opposing quotas.

U.S. Representative William Gray III is named House Majority Whip.

Ronald H. Brown is chosen chairperson of the Democratic National Committee February 10, making him the first African American to head a major U.S. political party.

L. Douglas Wilder is elected governor of Virginia, the state's first African-American governor.

David N. Dinkins is elected mayor of New York, the first African American to head the government of the nation's largest city.

The U.S. Senate impeaches U.S. District Court of Florida Judge Alcee Hastings on charges of conspiracy and perjury, the sixth such impeachment in U.S. history.

Contemporary Events, 1989 ■ Hurricane Hugo kills dozens of people across the Caribbean and southern Florida and causes billions of dollars in property damage. ■ The first woman cadet graduates from the U.S. Military Academy at West Point. ■ The **Exxon Valdez** oil spill damages Alaskan wildlife.

In Montgomery, Alabama, thousands attend a ceremony dedicating a monument to the martyrs of the Civil Rights Movement. The impressive monument by Maya Lin, designer of the Vietnam War Memorial in Washington, D.C., features 40 names of civil rights martyrs inscribed in a circular "table" of black granite. Over this table flows a thin sheet of water, symbolizing Martin Luther King, Jr.'s famous line, "We will not be satisfied until justice rolls down like water, and righteousness like a mighty stream."

U.S. Representative Mickey Leland, chairperson of the House Select Committee on World Hunger, is killed in a plane crash August 7 during a tour of Ethiopian refugee camps.

Louis Wade Sullivan, president of the Morehouse School of Medicine in Atlanta, becomes President Bush's secretary of health and human services.

Huey P. Newton, one of the founders of the Black Panthers Party in the 1960s, is shot to death August 22, for unknown reasons, in Oakland, California.

BUSINESS AND EMPLOYMENT

There are 37 black-owned banking institutions currently operating in the United States. The largest in terms of assets is IndeCorp Bank in Chicago.

The U.S. Supreme Court rules "unconstitutional" a Richmond, Virginia program requiring contractors for the city to give at least 30% of construction jobs to companies that are predominantly owned by minorities. The court calls the program "an unlawful form of reverse discrimination."

In a case involving firefighters in Birmingham, Alabama, the U.S. Supreme Court rules that workers who suffer as the result of court-sanctioned affirmative action programs may file lawsuits claiming discrimination.

Kenneth I. Chenault becomes president of the American Express Consumer Card and Financial Services Group, one of the highest corporate positions held by an African American.

RELIGION AND EDUCATION

Louis Farrakhan of the Nation of Islam makes his "Savior's Day Message" speech, in which he states African Americans are "being kept as nothing by the cruel hand of the government."

The Episcopal Church approves Barbara Harris, an African American, as its first female bishop. She is elected suffragan bishop and consecrated February 12 in the diocese of Massachusetts.

Joan Salmon Campbell of Philadelphia is elected moderator of the United Presbyterian Church in the USA, the first black woman to hold the position.

Student protestors staging a sit-in at Howard University in Washington, D.C., force Lee Atwater, the white chairperson of the Republican National Committee, to resign from the board of trustees. Among the protestors' charges against Atwater is that he had helped create a TV ad for George Bush's 1988 presidential campaign that catered to racism. The ad referred to the early release of Willie Horton, a convicted black rapist, by Bush's opponent, Governor Michael Dukakis of Massachusetts.

Atlanta University and Clark College merge to form Clark-Atlanta University. Thomas W. Cole is appointed president.

A *USA Today* report criticizes the Scholastic Aptitude Test, America's most commonly used college admissions test, for being biased against African Americans and other minorities by using language and situations that are more familiar to mainstream white culture than to other cultures.

Andrew F. Brimmer, former governor of the Federal Reserve Board, is named president of the Association for the Study of Afro-American Life and History.

LITERATURE AND JOURNALISM

Two new national magazines geared toward African-American readers make their premiere: *Sazz*, a women's fashion magazine, and *Emerge*, a news magazine.

Alice Walker publishes her novel *The Temple of My Familiar.*

Gloria Naylor's novel *Mama Day* wins the Lillian Smith Award, named for the white civil rights activist and author.

Ruby Dee's book of poetry *Two Ways to Count to Ten* is published.

Terry McMillan publishes her novel *Disappearing Acts.*

Clarence Page of the *Chicago Tribune* is the first African-American columnist to win the Pulitzer Prize for commentary.

John Steptoe, award-winning writer and illustrator of children's books, dies August 28 in New York.

SCIENCE AND TECHNOLOGY

Biochemist Bertram O. Fraser-Reid is honored with the title Senior Distinguished United States Scientist by the Alexander von Humboldt Foundation.

The federal government releases a report stating that the rate of

AIDS-virus infection among African Americans rose over 50% in the first part of the 1980s. Among black women, the rate rose 74%.

PERFORMING ARTS

At the Smithsonian Institution in Washington, D.C., the Rhythm and Blues Foundation bestows its first career achievement awards. Among those honored are Percy Sledge, Mary Wells, Charles Brown, and Ruth Brown, who all perform at the ceremony.

Spike Lee's film *Do the Right Thing* is both a critical and a commercial success.

Denzel Washington and Morgan Freeman star in the film *Glory*, about an African-American regiment during the Civil War. Washington will receive an Oscar as best supporting actor for his role.

The Arsenio Hall Show premieres on television.

Jessye Norman stars in the Metropolitan Opera Company's first one-person production, Schoenberg's *Erwartung*.

Janet Jackson releases her rock album *Rhythm Nation 1814*.

On September 9, the rappers 2 Live Crew make their chart debut.

Alvin Ailey, dancer, choreographer, and founder of the Alvin Ailey American Dance Theater, dies December 1 in New York City.

VISUAL ARTS

The exhibition "Black Art: Ancestral Legacy" opens at the Dallas Museum of Art.

Sculptor Martin Puryear represents the United States at the São Paulo Biennial in Brazil and wins first prize.

The Washington Project for the Arts in Washington, D.C., mounts the exhibit "The Blues Aesthetic: Black Culture and Modernism," featuring works by black artists that relate to blues music.

The Museum of Science and Industry in Chicago has a major group show, "Black Creativity 1989: Juried Art Exhibition of Black Artists."

Sculptor Richmond Barthé dies in Pasadena, California.

THE MILITARY

General Colin L. Powell of the U.S. Army is appointed chairperson of the U.S. Joint Chiefs of Staff, the nation's highest military post, the first African American to achieve this rank.

SPORTS

Bill White, former first baseman for the St. Louis Cardinals, the Philadelphia Phillies, and the New York and San Francisco Giants, is

Richmond Barthé

When Richmond Barthé, the African-American sculptor, died March 6, 1989, his obituary in the **Los Angeles Times** referred to him as "the man with the magic touch." His hands wrought powerful beauty in metal, clay, and wood, as his works in major American museums, such as the Metropolitan Museum of Art in New York, readily attest.

Barthé was born in Bay St. Louis, Mississippi, in 1901. Educated at the Art Institute of Chicago, he became one of the major figures in the Harlem Renaissance during the 1920s. Among his best-known works are **Singing Slave, Maurice Evans,** and **Henry O. Tanner.**

chosen as president of the National Baseball League. He is the first African American ever to hold the top executive position in a major U.S. professional sports league.

Mike Tyson knocks out Frank Bruno and, in a subsequent match, Carl Williams to retain his world heavyweight boxing championship.

Bertram Lee of Boston and Peter Bynoe of Chicago buy the Denver Nuggets of the National Basketball Association, thus becoming the first African Americans to own a professional sports team.

Art Shell, former lineman for the Oakland Raiders, is appointed head coach of the Los Angeles Raiders. He is the National Football League's first black head coach since 1925, when Fritz Pollard coached the Hammond (Indiana) Pros.

Businessman Comer Cottrell becomes co-owner of the Texas Rangers. He is the first African-American co-owner of a major league baseball team.

ADDITIONAL STATISTICS

According to the U.S. Census Bureau, New York State has the largest black population (2.7 million), but California (ranked second with 2.1 million blacks) has the fastest-growing black population. The bureau also states that four out of five African Americans live in metropolitan areas.

ADDITIONAL EVENTS

Debbye Turner of Missouri is crowned "Miss America," the third African American to hold the title.

POLITICS AND CIVIL RIGHTS

President George Bush vetoes the Civil Rights Bill of 1990, saying it would "introduce the destructive force of quotas" in the workplace. A Congressional attempt to override the veto narrowly fails to raise the necessary two-thirds majority. Civil rights leaders accuse Bush of trying to win favor with conservative whites.

Arthur A. Fletcher is appointed chairperson of the U.S. Commission on Civil Rights.

Contemporary Events, 1990 ■ President Bush commits over 500,000 American troops to Operation Desert Shield, to pressure Iraq to withdraw from Kuwait. ■ The U.S. treasury secretary reports that it could cost taxpayers $300 billion over 10 years to bail out insolvent savings and loan organizations.

The Supreme Court upholds an order by U.S. District Court Judge Leonard Sand requiring Yonkers, New York, to build 1,000 housing units for families with low and moderate incomes to help correct a 44-year history of segregated housing.

In New York, 19-year-old Joseph Fama of the Bensonhurst section of the city is convicted of being the trigger man in the death of Yusuf Hawkins, a black youth pursued and killed by a Bensonhurst gang. Fama is sentenced to over 32 years in prison. Another member of the white gang, Keith Mondello, is sentenced to 5 to 16 years in prison for inciting a riot and other charges.

Arizona votes against establishing a paid holiday for state workers in honor of Martin Luther King, Jr.'s birthday.

Marion S. Barry, Jr., mayor of Washington, D.C., is arrested for possession of cocaine in a sting operation at a city hotel. He pleads innocent but announces he will not run for a fourth term as mayor in the upcoming election.

Nelson Mandela, crusader against South Africa's policy of apartheid, visits the United States after serving 27 years in prison. He is given a tumultuous welcome in New York, where he speaks before the United Nations, and Washington, D.C., where he addresses a joint session of Congress.

Eight African Americans, including Abiyi Ford and Sheila Waker, participate with 130 other delegates from the Western Hemisphere, Africa, and Europe in the first international black "think tank," the Institute of Black Peoples, held in Ouagadougou, Burkina Faso.

Former Black Panther leader Bobby Rush becomes deputy chairperson of the Illinois Democratic Party.

Ralph Abernathy, minister, civil rights activist, and former SCLC president, dies April 17 in Atlanta.

BUSINESS AND EMPLOYMENT

Hilmon Sorey, Jr., of Chicago, becomes president of Hawthorn-Mellody, which is the largest minority-owned dairy operation in the United States.

In Harlem, the Freedom National Bank, with assests of over $120 million, is forced to cease business due to an alleged failure to meet federal regulation standards.

Black Expo, an annual networking and recruiting convention of black entrepeneurs, businesspeople, major corporations, and consumers from across the country, is held in Chicago.

Richard Parsons becomes chief executive officer of Dime Savings

"A Colorful Mosaic"

During the late 1980s and 1990, New York City suffered escalating racial tensions, most of which involved African Americans—by far the city's most populous minority. Blacks and Jews clashed in Williamsburg. Blacks and Italians fought in Bensonhurst. Blacks and Koreans boycotted each other in Harlem and Flatbush.

To try to resolve these enmities, Mayor David Dinkins held a historical Racial Unity Rally at the Cathedral of St. John the Divine on May 22, 1990. He referred to his 1989 campaign pledge to create "a colorful mosaic of race and religious faith" and said that the rally was designed to "create a wave of energy and unity so powerful that it could wash away the hate and hurt." While the rally did not put an end to race-related strife in the city, it did begin an ongoing dialogue among prominent spokespeople from the major minority groups.

Sammy Davis, Jr.

At the time of his death in 1990, Sammy Davis, Jr., was eulogized as the "world's greatest entertainer" during the last half of the 20th century. His career started in 1930, when he was five years old, singing and dancing in vaudeville and burlesque with his father and uncle. He went on to star in Broadway musicals—**Mr. Wonderful** (1956) and **Golden Boy** (1964)—and in many motion pictures, from **Porgy and Bess** (as "Sportin' Life," 1959) to **Tap** (1989). But he was most popular as a solo performer in nightclubs and concert halls, where he blazed a trail for black entertainers to follow.

Davis's personal life was often marked with suffering—racial discrimination, broken marriages, a near-fatal car accident that cost him an eye, professional betrayals, and a long, publicly waged bout with the throat cancer that ultimately killed him. Indeed, it was Davis's ability to rise above his difficulties that endeared him to all Americans. Among the honors bestowed upon him during his lifetime, the one he cherished most was the NAACP's Spingarn Medal for achievement in the entertainment industry and advancement of civil rights.

Bank, making him the first African American to head a major non-black U.S. savings association.

RELIGION AND EDUCATION

According to the Census Bureau, black Baptists constitute the fourth largest U.S. religious group, with 8.7 million members.

Walter H. Annenberg, a white businessman, pledges $50 million to the United Negro College Fund, the largest donation yet received by the fund.

George A. Stallings is consecrated by Old Catholics as bishop of the African American Catholic Church. Stallings, a Roman Catholic priest until 1989, broke away from the Roman Catholic Church, claiming that it did not adequately serve the needs of its African-American members.

Harold I. Bearden, former African Methodist Episcopal bishop in Cincinnati and civil rights leader, dies March 19 in Atlanta.

LITERATURE AND JOURNALISM

Charles R. Johnson wins the 1990 National Book Award for his novel *Middle Passage.*

Maya Angelou publishes her book of poems *I Shall Not Be Moved.*

Activist Angela Davis publishes *Women, Culture, and Politics.*

The Autobiography of Rosa Parks, who was hailed for launching the modern Civil Rights Movement by refusing to give up her bus seat to a white man in 1955, is published.

Shelby Steele publishes his critique *The Content of Our Character,* which wins the National Book Critics Circle Award.

PERFORMING ARTS

August Wilson's play *The Piano Lesson* opens on Broadway. It will win a Pulitzer Prize.

George C. Wolfe becomes the director of the New York Shakespeare Festival.

Michael Jackson releases his album anthology *Decade 1980–1990,* which is accompanied by a videotape.

Jazz singer Sarah Vaughan, often referred to as the "Divine One," dies April 4 in San Fernando Valley, California.

Entertainer Sammy Davis, Jr., dies May 16 in Beverly Hills.

Singer and actress Pearl Bailey dies August 17 in Philadelphia.

Jazz drummer and bandleader Art Blakey dies October 16 in New York.

VISUAL ARTS

In Atlanta, the New Visions gallery conducts a national Black Artists Invitational, entitled "Continuing Traditions . . . Contemporary African-American Crafts Artists."

Southeastern Center for Contemporary Arts in North Carolina mounts the show "Next Generation: Southern Black Aesthetic."

THE MILITARY

Marcelite J. Harris of Houston, becomes the first African-American woman to hold the rank of brigadier general in the U.S. Air Force.

SPORTS

In a major upset, James "Buster" Douglas knocks out Mike Tyson to win the world heavyweight boxing championship.

ADDITIONAL STATISTICS

According to the U.S. Census Bureau, there are 14.7 million black men and 16.8 million black women in the United States (total U.S. population is almost 249 million). Black women have consistently outnumbered black men since 1900, with the gap widening from 60,900 in 1900 to over 2 million in 1990.

The federal Center for Disease Control reports that the homicide rate among black males age 15 to 24 has risen 68% since 1984. Citing the rate as one in 1,000—nine times the rate for white males in the same age range. Robert G. Froehlke, author of the report, states, "In some areas of the country it is now more likely for a black male [in this age group] to die from homicide than it was for a U.S. soldier to be killed on a tour of duty during Vietnam."

ADDITIONAL EVENTS

Carole Gist of Detroit becomes the first African-American woman to win the "Miss USA" title.

POLITICS AND CIVIL RIGHTS

President George Bush signs the Civil Rights Act of 1991, a compromise between his administration and a more liberal Congress on the

---

Contemporary Events, 1991 ■ The U.S. economy enters a serious recession. National unemployment reaches 6.8%, and more banks fail than in any year since the Depression of the 1930s. ■ President Bush and Premier Gorbachev of the Soviet Union sign the historic Strategic Arms Reduction Treaty.

issue of enabling workers to sue in job-discrimination cases. Civil rights leaders attack the law as an assault on decades of civil rights progress.

Thurgood Marshall retires from the U.S. Supreme Court after serving as a justice for 24 years.

Clarence Thomas, a federal judge, becomes a U.S. Supreme Court Justice after the closest Senate confirmation vote in history. His appointment follows a nationally televised and highly acrimonious Senate Judiciary Committee investigation into charges that Thomas sexually harrassed Anita Hill, his legal assistant, 10 years previously.

Nelson Mandela, president of the African National Congress, makes his second visit to the United States to confer with President Bush and New York City Mayor David Dinkins about investment plans for a post-apartheid South Africa.

Rodney King is stopped by the police while driving his car in Los Angeles. An amateur videotaper records King being beaten by the police. Subsequent exposure of the videotape on nationwide television triggers a public outcry.

A huge turnout among African-American voters helps elect Edwin W. Edwards governor of Louisiana over former Ku Klux Klan leader David Duke.

Wellington Webb becomes the first black mayor of Denver.

Former Washington, D.C., mayor Marion S. Barry, Jr., is convicted on a misdemeanor charge of cocaine possession and sentenced to serve six months in jail.

BUSINESS AND EMPLOYMENT

A congressional poll finds that few African Americans benefit from affirmative action in federal government hiring. There are only two African Americans on President Bush's staff, and only 300 African Americans among the 8,200 congressional staffers.

Northwest Airlines creates a multi-million-dollar affirmative action program to settle job discrimination suits brought on behalf of thousands of its black employees, former employees, and job applicants.

President Bush awards the Medal of Freedom to Leon Sullivan of Phoenix, who spent his life developing job opportunities for blacks in the United States and Africa. Sullivan was the founder of Opportunities Industrialization Centers, which have provided job training for almost two million African-American men and women.

According to *Black Enterprise* magazine, the largest black-owned businesses fare better than the largest white-owned businesses.

Revenue for the top 100 African-American businesses jumps 10.4% from 1990 to $7.9 billion. Revenue for the top 100 white businesses increases only 1.8%.

RELIGION AND EDUCATION

Representative William Gray III (Democrat of Pennsylvania), the majority whip, resigns from Congress to become head of the United Negro College Fund.

Maryann B. Coffey, associate provost of Princeton University, becomes the first black person and first woman to chair the National Conference of Christians and Jews, a human relations organization.

James P. Lyke becomes archbishop of Atlanta, making him the highest-ranking African American in the Roman Catholic Church.

Nathan D. Baxter becomes dean of Washington [Episcopal] Cathedral in Washington, D.C.

According to the U.S. Bureau of the Census, 12% of African Americans 25 years of age and older have completed four years of college, compared to 22% of whites the same age.

The National Education Association reports a serious shortage of black teachers in public schools: only 8% of the total number, compared with 86.8% for white teachers.

LITERATURE AND JOURNALISM

In honor of Langston Hughes and the dedication of a theater in his name, his ashes are buried under Houston Conwill's sculpture in the floor of the Schomburg Center for Research in Black Culture in Harlem.

John Edgar Wideman's novel *Philadelphia Fire* wins the PEN/Faulkner Award for fiction.

Gordon Parks, photographer, film director, and writer, publishes *Gordon Parks, an Autobiography*.

Cable News Network (CNN) anchorman Bernard Shaw is named best newscaster of the year by the NAACP for his reporting skills during the Persian Gulf conflict.

Best-selling novelist Frank Yerby dies in Madrid.

SCIENCE AND TECHNOLOGY

The National Medal of Technology, the nation's highest award for technological achievement, is bestowed posthumously on Frederick M. Jones, who designed more than 60 devices to improve the preservation of food products.

Health and Human Services Secretary Louis Sullivan warns that in

1991: The Top 10 Black Businesses

1. TLC Beatrice International Holdings Inc. (New York): processing and distribution of food products; $1,542 million

2. Johnson Publishing Company (Chicago): publishing, broadcasting, cosmetics, hair care; $261.4 million

3. Philadelphia Coca-Cola Bottling Co., Inc. (Philadelphia): soft-drink bottling; $256 million

4. H. J. Russell & Co. (Atlanta): construction and development, food services; $143.6 million

5. Barden Communications, Inc. (Detroit): communications and real estate development; $91.2 million

6. Garden State Cable TV (New York): cable TV broadcasting; $88 million

7. Soft Sheen Products, Inc. (Chicago): hair-care products; $87.9 million

8. RMS Technologies (Marlton, New Jersey): computer and technical services; $79.9 million

9. Stop Shop And Save (Baltimore): supermarkets; $66 million

10. The Bing Group (Detroit): processing and metal-stamping: $64.9 million

two years, more than 125,000 African Americans (1 in 250) will have been diagnosed with the AIDS virus. He adds that blacks account for a disproportionate 28% of all AIDS-related cases in the United States, and that an estimated 40% of the black cases are the result of drug abuse.

PERFORMING ARTS

Whoopi Goldberg wins an Academy Award as best supporting actress for her role in *Ghost*.

At the TV industry's Emmy Awards ceremony, James Earl Jones is named best dramatic actor and Madge Sinclair best supporting dramatic actress for their work in *Gabriel's Fire*. Lynn Whitfield is named best actress in a miniseries for her role in *The Josephine Baker Story*.

The NAACP publishes a year-long study claiming that blacks are underrepresented in every aspect of the film and TV industry. It finds that "there is practically no representation in the top echelon of production."

Forbes magazine lists 9 blacks among the 40 richest people in the American entertainment business. They are (by rank): (1) Maurice Starr, producer and manager of New Kids on the Block: $115 million; (2) Bill Cosby: $113 million; (3) Oprah Winfrey: $80 million; (5) Michael Jackson: $60 million; (13) Janet Jackson: $43 million; (15) Eddie Murphy: $42 million; (19) M. C. Hammer: $33 million; (31) Prince: $25 million; and (35) Arsenio Hall: $23 million.

Spike Lee's film *Jungle Fever*, about an interracial love affair, is released.

John Singleton's film *Boyz N the Hood*, about gang violence in Los Angeles, is released. It will make Singleton the first African American to be nominated for an Academy Award for best director.

Singer Natalie Cole's album *Unforgettable with Love* becomes a bestseller. It features 22 songs made famous by her late father, Nat "King" Cole, one of which, "Unforgettable," is an electronically engineered duet between her and her father.

Miles Davis, jazz trumpeter, dies September 28 in Santa Monica, California.

Redd Foxx, comedian and TV star, dies October 11 of a heart attack on the set of his new TV series, *The Royal Family*, in Los Angeles.

Paul Russell, principal dancer with the Dance Theater of Harlem and San Francisco Ballet, dies February 15 in San Francisco.

VISUAL ARTS

Morgan State University in Baltimore names its art museum for retired art professor James E. Lewis. During his career, Lewis collected more than $11.5 million in African-American and African art, sculpted three major works, and directed an archeological dig in Nigeria.

Barbara Brandon becomes the first black female cartoonist nationally syndicated in the mainstream press. Her strip is called "Where I'm Coming From."

THE MILITARY

Among the 540,000 American troops who take part in Operation Desert Storm, the battle to liberate Kuwait from Iraq, 30% (or 162,000) are black. General Colin Powell emerges as a national hero for his leadership during the campaign and is awarded the NAACP's Spingarn Medal.

Corporal Freddie Stowers, killed in action during World War I, becomes the first black soldier in World War I to receive a Congressional Medal of Honor. The posthumous award is presented by President Bush to Stowers's two sisters.

A study conducted by *USA Today* finds that the U.S. military is one of the nation's most integrated institutions.

SPORTS

Baseball star Bobby Bonilla, a free agent, signs a five-year, $29 million contract with the New York Mets. This makes him the highest-paid sports figure in history until, later in the year, basketball star Patrick Ewing signs a six-year, $33 million contract with the New York Knicks.

Earvin "Magic" Johnson of the Los Angeles Lakers announces that he has tested positive for the AIDS virus and that he is retiring from the National Basketball Association. Later, he states that he will become a national spokesperson for AIDS awareness.

Muhammad Ali: His Life and Times, written by Thomas Haiser with the cooperation of the former heavyweight boxing champion, is published. In the book, Muhammad Ali admits that boxing was a major cause of his ongoing health problems.

Michael Jordan leads the Chicago Bulls to the NBA championship.

ADDITIONAL EVENTS

In a Gallup poll of the 10 most admired men in America, Earvin "Magic" Johnson is fifth, Nelson Mandela is ninth, and Jesse Jackson and Michael Jordan tie for tenth. Among the 10 most admired women, Oprah Winfrey ranks fifth.

The 1990 census is widely attacked for underreporting African Americans, especially in inner cities. The U.S. Census Bureau admits it may have missed up to 5.3 million blacks in its final count.

Comedian and TV talk-show host Arsenio Hall becomes a national ambassador for the DARE program (Drug Abuse Resistance and Education), which reaches about 20 million public school students.

Construction crews unearth a black colonial-era cemetery, known as the Negro Burial Ground, in downtown Manhattan.

Willie Duberry, the oldest living person ever recorded and certified, dies in Dorchester County, South Carolina at the age of 121 years.

POLITICS AND CIVIL RIGHTS

The U.S. Supreme Court sets limits on the 1965 Voting Rights Act by ruling that county commissions in two Alabama counties did not need federal approval to reorganize or diminish the authorities of individual commissioners.

From April 29 to May 1, rioting takes place in South Central Los Angeles following the acquittal of four white police officers on all but one charge relating to the videotaped beating of Rodney King. About 50 people, including 23 African Americans, are killed, and $2 billion in property is damaged, making it the deadliest and most costly race riot in U.S. history. Additional protests, ranging from minor riots to peaceful demonstrations, occur simultaneously in many other U.S. cities.

The U.S. Supreme Court strikes down a "hate crime" law in St. Paul, that bans cross burning and similar expressions of racial intolerance, claiming that the law infringes on a citizen's freedom of speech. The ruling casts doubt on numerous "hate crime" statutes across the United States.

As a result of November elections, the Congressional Black Caucus swells to a record 40 members. The total consists of 39 representatives (including newly elected Carrie Meek, the first African-American woman in Florida history to be sent to Congress) and newly elected Senator Carol Moseley Braun from Illinois, the first African-American woman to hold a U.S. Senate seat.

Contemporary Events, 1992 ■ Hurricane Andrew devastates Florida and Louisiana, killing 13 people, leaving 250,000 homeless, and causing $16.5 billion in insured damages. ■ Unemployment increases, reaching the highest level since 1984.

William "Bill" Clinton is elected president of the United States, thanks in part to heavy support from black voters disgruntled with George Bush and the Republican Party. Clinton appoints longtime civil rights leader Vernon Jordan to chair his transition team.

Willie W. Herenton is elected to be the first African-American mayor of Memphis, Tennessee.

Benjamin Hooks announces his retirement as executive director of the NAACP, a position he has held since 1977.

Willie L. Williams is sworn in as first African-American chief of police in Los Angeles.

The Birmingham Civil Rights Institute opens in Alabama, featuring exhibits that commemorate the struggle for civil rights.

BUSINESS AND EMPLOYMENT

According to the U.S. Census Bureau, blacks own a disproportionately low percentage of U.S. businesses—just 3%.

A presidential commission issues a two-year report calling for a major revamp of the $4 billion Federal Minority Business Plan. The report states that the plan crowds African Americans in unprofitable businesses while denying them sufficient capital to succeed.

Eric G. Johnson resigns as president and CEO of Johnson Products and buys Baldwin Ice Cream Company.

A nationwide survey of 7.8 million mortgages finds that over 33% of black applicants are rejected, compared with only 17% of whites with comparable income.

RELIGION AND EDUCATION

Frederick J. Streets becomes the first African American and the first Baptist to serve as chaplain at Yale University.

Spelman College in Atlanta receives a gift of $37 million from the DeWitt Wallace Fund established by the founder of Reader's Digest. It is the largest endowment ever bestowed on a historically black college or university.

The U.S. Department of Agriculture establishes a $2 million scholarship fund for students at 17 historically black land-grant colleges and universities.

African Americans earning their Ph.D's increase 13% since 1991, the first major jump since 1977. Altogether, 993 Ph.D's are awarded to blacks this year.

LITERATURE AND JOURNALISM

Pearl Stewart becomes editor of the *Oakland Tribune* in California,

The Birmingham Civil Rights Institute

Opened in 1992, the Birmingham Civil Rights Institute covers all aspects of the Civil Rights Movement of the 1960s. Among its most affecting exhibits are replicas of a "whites only" lunch counter, a segregated city bus, and a burnt-out "Freedom Riders" bus. The museum also displays television footage, photographs, newspaper clippings, and original documents relating to the struggle of black Americans for equality with white Americans under the law. It also has recordings of Martin Luther King, Jr., reading from his "Letter from Birmingham City Jail" and delivering his "I Have a Dream" speech.

1992 Statistics

Occupation (by percentage of black labor force; source: U.S. Bureau of the Census)

Professional/managerial:	17%
Technical/sales/	
administrative:	28%
Service occupations:	24%
Construction/repairs:	8%
Laborers/operators:	22%
Other:	1%

Family Income (source: U.S. Bureau of the Census)

Under $50,000:	84%
$50,000 to $74,999:	11%
$75,000 to $99,999:	3%
$100,000 and over:	2%

making her the first African-American woman to edit a major U.S. daily newspaper.

Cynthia Tucker is the first black woman appointed to edit the editorial page of a major U.S. daily, the *Atlanta Constitution*.

Terry McMillan publishes her best-selling novel *Waiting to Exhale*.

Alex Haley, author of *The Autobiography of Malcolm X* and *Roots*, dies February 10 in Seattle.

SCIENCE AND TECHNOLOGY

President Bush awards W. Lincoln Hawkins, researcher at Bell Telephone Systems, with the National Medal of Technology. Hawkins's work earned 18 U.S. and 129 foreign patents.

Mae C. Jemison, one of seven astronauts sent into earth orbit on the space shuttle *Endeavor*, becomes the first African-American woman in space.

The American Medical Association reports that only 3% of American doctors are black.

Edward S. Cooper of the Univeristy of Pennsylvania Medical School is the first black president of the American Heart Association.

A study by Paul H. Wise of the Harvard Medical School shows that black infants of college-educated parents are twice as likely to die as white infants of college-educated parents. Wise comments that "clearly a major portion of the problem is racism."

According to a survey published in *American Journal of Sociology*, blacks with lighter skins have demonstrably higher social status than their darker-skinned counterparts. Regardless of educational, occupational, or family background, lighter-skinned African Americans have 50% higher income.

PERFORMING ARTS

Gregory Hines wins a Tony Award for best actor in a musical for his starring role in the Broadway hit *Jelly's Last Jam*, based on the life of composer Jelly Roll Morton. Tonya Pinkins, also in *Jelly's Last Jam*, wins a Tony Award for best featured actress in a musical.

August Wilson's *Two Trains Running*, starring Roscoe Lee Browne and Laurence Fishburne, opens on Broadway. It wins the New York Drama Critics' Circle Award

Anna Deavere Smith's performance *Fires in the Mirror*, giving voice to different perspectives on the 1990 conflict between African Americans and Jews in the Crown Heights section of Brooklyn, opens Off-Broadway and is nominated for a Pulitzer Prize.

The two-part TV miniseries *The Jacksons: An American Dream* charts the rise of the 1960s group the Jackson Five and, subsequently, the independent singing careers of Michael, Janet, and LaToya Jackson.

Michael Jackson starts his "Dangerous" tour in Europe. It is widely heralded as the most spectacular tour of his career in terms of length, cost, projected attendance, stage effects, and choreography.

Hollywood releases Spike Lee's *Malcolm X*, starring Denzel Washington as the Black Muslim leader. Washington will win the Berlin International Film Festival's Silver Bear Award for this role.

Julie Dash's film *Daughters of the Dust*, featuring the heritage of the Sea Islanders in South Carolina, is released.

Morgan Freeman stars in the film *Unforgiven*.

Hollywood releases two movies starring Whoopi Goldberg: *Sarafina*, about schoolchildren challenging South Africa's policy of apartheid, and *Sister Act*. For the latter role, Goldberg will be named Female Star of the Year by the National Association of Theater Owners.

Whitney Houston stars in *The Bodyguard*, one of the top-grossing movies of 1992.

Jazz saxophonist Branford Marsalis becomes bandleader on NBC's *The Tonight Show*.

The final episode of the *Cosby* show is aired April 30, ending eight years of consistently top-10 programs. The broadcast attracts more viewers than have ever watched a farewell show on NBC-TV.

Jazz legend Lionel Hampton is saluted at the 15th annual Kennedy Center Honors.

Pioneer jazz drummer Ed Blackwell dies in Hartford, Connecticut.

R&B singer Mary Wells, famous for "My Guy," dies in Los Angeles.

Honi Coles, tap dancer in films and on Broadway, dies in New York.

Cleavon Little, Broadway actor, dies in California.

VISUAL ARTS

The Art Institute of Chicago, Studio Museum in Harlem, and other institutions hold a major retrospective of the work of Jacob Lawrence, widely described as the "greatest living black painter." The most prominent pieces are the closely related 32-panel *Frederick Douglass* series and 31-panel *Harriet Tubman* series.

The National Museum of Women in the Arts in Washington, D.C., exhibits the works of photographer Carrie Mae Weems.

The Whitney Museum of American Art mounts a posthumous retrospective of the work of painter Jean-Michel Basquiat.

Artist Camille Billops's *Finding Christa* wins the Grand Jury Prize for best documentary at the Sundance Film Festival.

The exhibit "Bridges and Boundaries: African Americans and American Jews" opens at the Jewish Museum in New York.

THE MILITARY

Doris Daniels becomes the first African-American woman to achieve the rank of lieutenant colonel in the U.S. Marines.

SPORTS

Deion Sanders rejoins the Atlanta Falcons after signing a $2 million one-year contract, making him the highest-paid defensive player in the history of the National Football League.

Cincinnati Reds owner Marge Schott is permanently suspended from baseball by the American League Executive Council for allegedly using racially disparaging terms in describing two former Reds players.

At the Olympic Games in Barcelona, Spain, the many African-American gold medalists include Michael Jordan and Earvin "Magic" Johnson of the basketball team (called the "Dream Team"), Gail Devers in the 100-meter dash, Jackie Joyner-Kersee in the heptathlon (her second consecutive gold in that event), Carl Lewis in the long jump (his third consecutive gold in that event), Gwen Torrence in the 200-meter dash, and Kevin Young in the 400-meter hurdles.

Tennis great Arthur Ashe reveals that he was diagnosed positive for the AIDS virus in 1988. He tells the press that he kept the diagnosis secret to preserve his privacy, but decided to speak out when he learned that several periodicals were about to break the news.

"Magic" Johnson, who retired after testing positive for the AIDS virus, announces his comeback with Los Angeles Lakers basketball team on September 29. Two months later, he withdraws from the team just before the season begins. He says that he wants to devote much more time to being a spokesperson for AIDS-related causes.

After several years of growing criticism regarding its failure to appoint a "fair" number of black coaches, the National Football League hires Stanford University coach Dennis Green to be the head coach of the Minnesota Vikings. Green joins the only other black head coach in the NFL, Art Shell of the Los Angeles Raiders.

World heavyweight champion Mike Tyson is sentenced to six years in prison for raping Desiree Washington while she was competing in the Miss Black America contest.

For the second year in a row, Michael Jordan helps the Chicago

Bulls win the National Basketball Association championship and is named NBA Most Valuable Player of both the year and the playoff.

ADDITIONAL STATISTICS

A survey conducted by Independent Sector, a nonprofit coalition of over 800 voluntary organizations, finds that blacks contribute more income to various causes than any other U.S. demographic group. The survey reveals that 64% of blacks contribute annually to voluntary organizations, and that the annual contribution per black household averages 2.7% of household income.

POLITICS AND CIVIL RIGHTS

The Clinton administration's five-day inaugural celebration in Washington, D.C., "An American Reunion," is attended by a record number of African Americans. Black entertainers present include Ray Charles, Luther Vandross, Aretha Franklin, Kathleen Battle, James Earl Jones, Sidney Poitier, Harry Belafonte, Oprah Winfrey, Whoopi Goldberg, Michael Jackson, Stevie Wonder, Wynton Marsalis, Chuck Berry, and Little Richard.

President Clinton appoints African Americans to several key cabinet positions: Hazel O'Leary as secretary of energy, Michael Espy as secretary of agriculture, Ronald Brown as secretary of commerce, Jesse Brown as secretary of veterans affairs, and Joycelyn Elders as surgeon-general.

For the first time since it was created as a national holiday in 1983, all 50 states observe Martin Luther King, Jr., Day on the third Monday in January.

John Jacob retires as president of the National Urban League.

David Dinkins, New York's first African-American mayor, loses his bid for reelection.

Jesse Jackson leads protests against the Clinton administration's Haiti policy.

Freeman Bosley, Jr., the grandson of slaves, is sworn in as St. Louis's first African-American mayor.

Benjamin Chavis, United Church of Christ minister and longtime

Michael Jordan

In 1992 Michael Jordan of the Chicago Bulls earned his sixth straight National Basketball League scoring title, prompting many experts to call him the most exciting person ever to play pro basketball. Earvin "Magic" Johnson, former Los Angeles Laker and, with Jordan, a member of the 1992 Olympics "Dream Team," summed it up at the time by saying, "Really, there's Michael and then there's everybody else." In 1993 Jordan surprised his fans by announcing his retirement from professional basketball.

Contemporary Events, 1993 ■ A 51-day seige of a religious group called the Branch Davidians in Waco, Texas, results in the deaths of over 75 people. ■ Devastating floodwaters in the Midwest cause widespread damage along a 500-mile stretch of the Mississippi River and its tributaries.

activist, becomes director of the NAACP, promising to shake up the organization and make it more relevant to black needs.

In August, citizens from around the nation converge in Washington, D.C., to commemorate the 30th anniversary of the historic March on Washington of August 28, 1963. The current march promotes the theme of "Jobs, Justice, and Peace." NAACP director Ben Chavis declares the march an expression of "faith in the future and our determination to translate that faith into fulfillment."

Attorney Alan Page, a former pro-football player in the National Football League's Hall of Fame, becomes the first African-American state supreme court justice in Minnesota.

Coleman Young, longtime mayor of Detroit, announces he will not seek reelection.

Jesse Jackson is awarded the Martin Luther King, Jr., Nonviolent Peace Prize, the highest award given by the Martin Luther King, Jr., Center for Nonviolent Social Change.

President Clinton's withdrawal of Lani Guinier to head the Justice Department's civil rights division (over her writings on racial quotas, minority voting, and legislative rights) evokes criticism from African-American political leaders and the heads of black organizations, who question the president's commitment to civil rights.

In response to a stand taken by Illinois Senator Carol Moseley Braun, the Senate votes 75 to 25 against allowing the United Daughters of the Confederacy to continue using the Confederate flag as part of their insignia, thus reversing a tradition of honoring the flag as "hallowed memorabilia." Moseley Braun argues that the Confederate flag "has no place in modern times . . . no place in this body . . . no place in society."

An FBI report indicates that 36% of bias crimes, the largest single group, are committed against African Americans.

African Americans gain control of the city council in Selma, Alabama, where on March 7, 1965, police responded to civil rights marchers with so much violence it influenced the passage of the Voting Rights Act of 1965. Blacks presently comprise 58% of the city population.

Evanston, Illinois, a suburb of Chicago, elects 74-year-old Lorraine H. Morton, a former city councilwoman and educator, as its first African-American mayor.

Thurgood Marshall dies January 24 at age 84 in the Betheseda Navy Medical Center after a distinguished 24-year career as NAACP attorney and the nation's first African-American Supreme Court justice.

James B. Parsons, the first African-American federal judge, appointed by President John F. Kennedy in 1961, dies at age 81 in Chicago.

BUSINESS AND EMPLOYMENT

Johnson Products, Inc., the Chicago hair-care company, is sold for $67 million to a white company.

Motown Records is sold to PolyGram for $301 million.

Entrepreneur and philanthropist Reginald F. Lewis, who orchestrated a leveraged buyout of the multinational food company Beatrice International in 1987 for $985 million, dies at age 50.

RELIGION AND EDUCATION

A Harvard study indicates that racial segregation is rising to levels not seen since 1968. The study shows that 66% of African-American students attend predominantly minority schools.

Spelman College in Atlanta, begun in 1881 as a school for former slave women, is ranked as the leading liberal arts college in the South. This is the first time a historically black institution of higher learning has placed first in a national survey of U.S. colleges.

Pope John Paul II apologizes for the Catholic Church's support of slavery.

Political science professor Condoleezza Rice is named provost of Stanford University, the first African-American chief academic and budget officer of that institution.

Surgeon-General Joycelyn Elders endorses sex education from kindergarten to grade 12 and the distribution of condoms in public schools to prevent the spread of sexually communicated diseases.

The House of Representatives authorizes the Smithsonian Institution to create a National African-American Museum to join the 15 other museums that comprise the Smithsonian.

The highest-ranking black Roman Catholic clergyman, Archbishop James Lyke, dies at age 53 in Atlanta, a diocese of 185,000 Catholics.

LITERATURE AND JOURNALISM

Maya Angelou reads her poem "On the Pulse of Morning" at the Clinton inauguration. She is the first poet to read since 1961, when Robert Frost participated in the Kennedy inauguration, and the first black poet to do so.

Toni Morrison becomes the first African American to win the Nobel Prize in literature. The Princeton University humanities professor is acclaimed by the Swedish Academy for creating prose "with the luster of poetry." Her works include *The Bluest Eye, Song of Solomon, Beloved,* and *Jazz.*

Basketball player "Magic" Johnson's autobiography, *My Life,* is published, reflecting on his childhood, athletic career, and fight against the AIDS virus.

Tennis star Arthur Ashe's memoirs, *Days of Grace,* written with Arnold Rampersad and completed a month before Ashe dies of AIDS, is published.

Rita Dove becomes the nation's poet laureate. She is the youngest at age 40 and the first African American to hold this office.

Historian John Hope Franklin receives a national humanities award from President Clinton.

Cornel West's study *Race Matters* becomes a best-seller. Director of Afro-American Studies at Princeton, West accepts a position in the Department of Afro-American Studies at Harvard.

Robert C. Maynard, former owner of the *Oakland Tribune,* dies in Oakland, California, at age 56.

Poet and feminist Audre Lorde dies November 17 in St. Croix.

SCIENCE AND TECHNOLOGY

David Satcher is appointed director of the Center for Disease Control and Prevention in Atlanta.

Barbara Ross-Lee becomes dean of Ohio University College of Osteopathic Medicine at Athens. She is the first African-American woman to head a U.S. medical school.

PERFORMING ARTS

Duke Ellington's opera *Queenie Pie* is performed at the Brooklyn Academy of Music to rave reviews by New York critics. Unfinished at the time of his death in 1974, the work contains 14 songs with music and lyrics by the master composer.

Rhythm and blues singer Ruth Brown is inducted into the Rock and Roll Hall of Fame on her 65th birthday. She popularized 1950s R&B tunes such as "Mama, He Treats Your Daughter Mean" and "Teardrops from My Eyes." Blues singer Etta James is also inducted into the Rock and Roll Hall of Fame. Among her most famous songs are "All I Could Do Was Cry" and "At Last."

The Horatio Alger Association of Distinguished Americans presents entertainer Oprah Winfrey with the Horatio Alger Award for those who overcome diversity to become leaders in their fields.

The People's Choice Awards honor Whoopi Goldberg as favorite comedy film actress and Whitney Houston as favorite female music performer.

Actor Sidney Poitier wins the National Black Theatre Festival's Living Legends Award.

President Clinton presents entertainer Cab Calloway, singer Ray Charles, and theatrical director Lloyd Richards with the National Medal of the Arts awards.

Angela Bassett and Laurence Fishburne star in the film *What's Love Got to Do with It,* about the life of Tina Turner.

Acclaimed opera singer Marian Anderson dies April 8 in Oregon.

Thomas Dorsey, the "Father of Gospel Music," dies at age 93 in Chicago. His first hit, in 1926, "If You See My Savior, Tell Him That You Saw Me," was translated into 50 languages. Other famous songs included "Peace in the Valley" and "Take My Hand, Precious Lord."

Jazz singer William Clarence "Billy" Eckstine dies at age 78.

Blues guitarist, composer, and performer James "Son" Thomas dies at age 66 in Greenville, Mississippi.

Jazz and avant-garde orchestra leader Sun Ra, formerly Herman "Sonny" Blount, dies at age 79 after a 60-year music career with over 200 albums and works in bop, gospel, blues, and electronic sounds.

Soul vocalist Marv Johnson dies at age 54. His 1959 hit, "Come to Me," was a precursor of the Motown sound.

Blues singer Albert Collins dies at age 61.

Jazz trumpeter John Birks "Dizzy" Gillespie dies in Englewood, New Jersey, at age 75.

Actress Claudia McNeil dies at age 77. She is remembered for her role as the matriarch in Lorraine Hansberry's *A Raisin in the Sun.*

Erskine Hawkins, a top jazz performers of the 1930s and 1940s and composer of "Tuxedo Junction," dies at age 79 in New Jersey.

VISUAL ARTS

Jacob Lawrence's *Migrants* series is shown in the Phillips Collection in Washington, D.C., for the first time in 20 years.

SPORTS

San Francisco Giants left-fielder Barry Bonds, a three-time All-Star player, becomes baseball's highest-paid player, with a $60 million dollar contract over six years.

Jim Law, a 76-year-old psychology professor at Johnson C. Smith University in Charlotte, North Carolina, sets a world record in the 400-meter and 200-meter runs, for the 65 to 69 age group.

Baseball slugger Reggie Jackson enters the Baseball Hall of Fame in Cooperstown, New York. His 563 career home runs place him sixth on the list of most home runs ever scored.

Chicago Bulls basketball great Michael Jordan retires at age 30, claiming "the thrill of the game is over." His nine-year career produced over $3 billion.

Heavyweight champion George Foreman retires after losing a match to Evander Holyfield.

Mannie Jackson, a former Harlem Globetrotter, becomes the first African American to own that famous basketball team.

Tennis star and human rights activist Arthur Ashe dies in New York. He was the first African-American male to win a Wimbledon title.

Don Barksdale, the first African-American National Basketball Association All-Star player, dies at age 69 in Oakland, California.

Boston Celtics star Reggie Lewis dies July 27 at age 27 in Waltham, Massachusetts.

Former Brooklyn Dodgers catcher Roy Campanella dies at age 71 in Woodland Hills, California.

THE MILITARY

General Colin Powell retires as chairman of the Joint Chiefs of Staff.

The last U.S. Buffalo soldier James Morgan dies at age 110 in Richmond, Virginia. A member of the army's black regiment during the Spanish-American War, Morgan also served in the West conducting wagon trains and fighting in the Indian wars.

ADDITIONAL EVENTS

In South Carolina, African-American volunteers plant sweetgrass in an acre plot on James Island to preserve the 300-year-old basket-weaving tradition that is threatened by shoreline development.

Eighteen-year-old Kimberly Aiken of Columbia, South Carolina, becomes the fifth African American (and the first from the South) to win the Miss America contest.

Heavyweight champion Joe Louis is the first boxer honored on a U.S. postage stamp. Other stamps honor rhythm and blues singer Clyde McPhatter, "Queen of the Blues" Dinah Washington, and soul singer Otis Redding.

Clara "Mother" Hale, founder of Hale House for HIV-infected babies in Harlem, dies December 18 in New York.

BIBLIOGRAPHY

American Heritage History of the 20s and 30s, The. New York: McGraw-Hill, 1970.

Aptheker, Herbert, ed. *A Documentary History of the Negro People in the United States,* vols. 1–4. New York: Citadel Press/Carol, 1990–92.

Asante, Molefi K., and Mark T. Mattson. *Historical and Cultural Atlas of African Americans.* New York: Macmillan, 1992.

Ashe, Arthur R., Jr. *A Hard Road to Glory: A History of the African-American Athlete,* vols. 1–3. New York: Warner, 1988.

Bailey, Thomas A. *A Diplomatic History of the American People.* New York: Meredith, 1964.

Barck, Oscar Theodore, Jr., and Hugh Talmage Lefler. *Colonial America.* New York: Macmillan, 1968.

Bearden, Romare, and Harry Henderson. *A History of African-American Artists.* New York: Pantheon, 1993.

Bennett, Lerone, Jr. *Before the Mayflower: A History of Black America,* 6th ed. New York: Penguin, 1988.

Bergman, Peter M. *The Chronological History of the Negro in America.* New York: Harper & Row, 1969.

Berlin, Ira, et al., eds. *Free at Last: A Documentary History of Slavery, Freedom, and the Civil War.* New York: New Press, 1992.

Billington, Ray Allen. *Westward Expansion.* New York: Macmillan, 1967.

Black Americans Information Directory. Detroit: Gale Research, 1992.

Black Art: Ancestral Legacy. Dallas/New York: Dallas Museum of Art/Abrams, 1989.

Bogle, Donald. *Toms, Coons, Mulattoes, Mammies, and Bucks: An Interpretive History of Blacks in American Films.* New York: Continuum, 1989.

Boorstin, Daniel J. *The Americans.* New York: Random House, 1973.

Bronson, Fred. *The Billboard Book of Number One Hits.* New York: Billboard, 1985.

Brown, H. Rapp. *Die Nigger Die!* New York: Dial Press, 1969.

Campbell, Edward D. C., Jr., with Kym S. Rice, eds. *Before Freedom Came: African-American Life in the Antebellum South.* Richmond/Charlottesville: Museum of the Confederacy/University Press of Virginia, 1991.

Driskell, David C. *Two Centuries of Black American Art.* New York: Random House, 1976.

Easton, Clement. *A History of the Old South.* New York: Macmillan, 1975.

Edelman, Marian Wright. *The Measure of Our Success.* New York: Harper Perennial, 1993.

Estell, Kenneth. *African America: Portrait of a People.* Detroit: Visible Ink Press, 1994.

Fax, Elton C. *Black Artists of the New Generation.* New York: Dodd, Mead, 1977.

Franklin, John Hope, and Alfred A. Moss, Jr. *From Slavery to Freedom,* 6th ed. New York: McGraw-Hill, 1988.

Garwood, Alfred N., ed. *Black America: A Statistical Source Book.* Boulder: Numbers & Concepts, 1990.

Grun, Bernard. *The Timetables of History.* New York: Simon & Schuster, 1979.

Hofstadter, Richard; William Miller; and Daniel Aaron. *The American Republic,* vols. 1–2. New York: Prentice-Hall, 1970.

Hopkins, Mary S. *Black American Poetry: A Selected Bibliography.* Plattsburgh, New York: Clinton-Essex-Franklin Library System, 1990.

Hornsby, Alton, Jr. *Milestones in 20th-Century African-American History.* Detroit: Visible Ink Press, 1993.

Huggins, Nathan Irvin. *Voices from the Harlem Renaissance.* New York: Oxford University Press, 1976.

Hughes, Langston; Milton Meltzer; and C. Eric Lincoln. *A Pictorial History of Blackamericans,* 5th rev. ed. New York: Crown, 1983.

Kranz, Rachel. *The Biographical Dictionary of Black Americans.* New York: Facts on File, 1992.

Lanker, Brian. *I Dream a World: Portraits of Black Women Who Changed America.* New York: Stewart, Tabori & Chang, 1989.

Lewis, David L. *When Harlem Was in Vogue.* New York: Knopf, 1981.

Logan, Rayford W., and Michael R. Winston. *Dictionary of American Negro Biography.* New York: Norton, 1982.

Magill, Frank N., ed. *Masterpieces of African-American Literature.* New York: HarperCollins, 1992.

Martin, Michael, and Leonard Gelber. *Dictionary of American History.* Totowa, New Jersey: Littlefield, Adams, 1966.

Matthews, Rupert. *Eyewitness to the 80s.* New York: Book People, 1990.

Meltzer, Milton, ed. *The Black Americans: A History in Their Own Words.* New York: Crowell, 1984.

Miller, John C. *This New Man, the American.* New York: McGraw-Hill, 1974.

Naltz, Bernard C. *Strength for the Fight: A History of Black Americans in the Military.* New York: Free Press, 1986.

Next Generation: Southern Black Aesthetic. Winston-Salem, North Carolina: Southeastern Center for Contemporary Art, 1990.

Phelps, Shirelle, ed. *Who's Who Among Black Americans,* 8th ed. Detroit: Gale Research, 1994.

Ploski, Harry A., and James Williams, eds. *The Negro Almanac,* 4th ed. New York: Wiley & Sons, 1983.

Reynolds, Barbara. *And Still We Rise: Interviews with 50 Black Role Models.* Washington, D.C.: Gannett, 1988.

Salzman, Jack, et al. *Bridges and Boundaries: African Americans and American Jews.* New York: Braziller/Jewish Museum, 1992.

Sloan, Irving J., ed. *The Blacks in America.* New York: Oceana, 1977.

Smith, Jessie Carney, ed. *Black Firsts.* Detroit: Visible Ink Press, 1994.

———. *Epic Lives: 100 Black Women Who Made a Difference.* Detroit: Visible Ink Press, 1993.

Smith, Valerie, ed. *African American Writers.* New York: Scribners, 1981.

Smythe, Mabel M., ed. *The Black American Reference Book.* New York: Prentice-Hall, 1976.

Southern, Eileen. *Biographical Dictionary of Afro-American and African Musicians.* Westport, Connecticut: Greenwood Press, 1982.

Story, Rosalyn M. *And So I Sing: African-American Divas of Opera and Concert.* New York: Warner, 1990.

Szwed, John F., ed. *Black America.* New York: Basic Books, 1970.

White, Timothy. *Rock Lives.* New York: Holt, 1990.

Williams, Juan. *Eyes on the Prize.* New York: Penguin, 1987.

Woods, Paula L., and Felix H. Liddell. *I, Too, Sing America.* New York: Workman, 1992.

Yount, Lisa. *Black Scientists.* New York: Facts on File, 1991.

INDEX

Kee, Solaria, 189
Kefauver, Estes, 227
Keith, George, 18
Kelley, William Melvin, 188, 242, 250, 255
Kelly, Leontine Turpeau Current, 158
Kelly, Patrick, 224
Kelly, Sharon Pratt Dixon, 203
Kennedy, Edward M., 301
Kennedy, Ethel, 258
Kennedy, John F., 227, 236, 241, 243, 244, 315, 343
Kennedy, Robert F., 236, 238, 252, 258, 316
Kerner Commission report, 257, 320
Kerouac, Jack, 229
Key, Francis Scott, 49
Khrushchev, Nikita, 241
Kilgore, Thomas, 262
Killens, John Oliver, 152, 224, 235, 245, 250, 256, 271, 319
Kincaid, Jamaica, 213
King, Billie Jean, 254
King, Coretta Scott, 169, 236, 258, 261, 264, 266, 283, 300, 322, 324
King, Dexter Scott, 324
King, Martin Luther, Jr., 167, 172, 225, 227, 229, 230, 231, 236, 239, 241, 244, 246, 248–9, 251, 253, 254, 257, 258, 279, 283, 291, 294, 296, 304, 318, 320, 321, 322, 324, 325, 337; birthday of, 264, 277, 306, 315, 320, 329, 341
King, Martin Luther, Sr., 286, 307, 310
King, Martin Luther, Sr., Mrs., 280
King, Riley B. B., 167, 278
King, Rodney, 332, 336
King, Woodie, Jr., 189, 274
King Philip's War, 16
King William's War, 17
Kingdom, Roger, 311, 324
Kinsey, Alfred, 211
Kirk, Andy, 129
Kirk, Roland, 186
Kitt, Eartha, 220, 233, 283, 293
Knight, Gladys, 204, 279
Knight and Bell, 77
Knights of Liberty, 71

Knoxville College, 103
Korean War, 215, 216, 218–9, 221
Kountz, Samuel L., 302
Ku Klux Klan, 90–1, 94, 95, 98–9, 100, 150, 158, 163, 164, 192, 248, 249, 294, 298, 306, 317, 332
Ku Mba Workshop, 285
Kwanza, 253

L

LaBelle, Patti, 204, 314
Lacoume, Emile "Stale Bread," 126
Ladone, Jason, 320
Lafayette, M., 32, 34
Lafayette Theater, 152, 184
Lamb, Pompey, 33
Lane, Isaac, 188
Lane, William Henry ("Juba"), 70
Lane College, 110, 188
Langston, John Mercer, 57, 80, 123
Lanker, Brian, 273
Lanusse, Armand, 70
Larsen, Nella, 119, 171, 172
Lathan, Stan, 311
Latimer, George, 68
Latimer, Lewis, 73, 109, 171
Lautier, L. R., 228
Lavalette, W. A., 106
Lavallade, Carmen de, 176, 226
Law, Jim, 345
Law, Oliver, 189
Lawless, Theodore, 224
Lawrence, Jacob, 154, 191, 193, 198, 228, 267, 271, 282, 308, 339, 345
Lawrence, Robert H., 256
League of Struggle for Negro Rights, 173
Leary, Lewis, 83
Ledbetter, Huddie "Leadbelly," 113
Lee, Bertram, 328
Lee, Canada, 140, 220
Lee, Don; *see* Madhubuti, Haki
Lee, George W., 181, 188
Lee, Harper, 235
Lee, Rebecca, 90
Lee, Robert E., 90
Lee, Spike, 230, 316, 323, 327, 334, 339
Lee-Smith, Hughie, 151, 323

Leftenant, Nancy, 212
Leidesdorff, William Alexander, 72
Leland, George, 291
Leland, Mickey, 325
LeMoyne-Owen College, 98
Lennon, John, 297
Leonard, "Sugar" Ray Charles, 229, 311, 320
Lester, John, 77
Lester, Jon, 320
Lester, Julius, 305, 322
Lewis, Arthur, 295
Lewis, Barrett, 108
Lewis, Carl, 311, 323, 340
Lewis, Edmonia, 70–1, 96, 104
Lewis, Henry, 260
Lewis, Isaac, 115
Lewis, James E., 335
Lewis, Jessie W., 278
Lewis, John, 159
Lewis, John Henry, 184
Lewis, Meade Lux, 190
Lewis, Norman, 143, 226, 245, 263
Lewis, Oliver, 103
Lewis, Reggie, 346
Lewis, Reginald F., 343
Lewis, Samella , 270
Lewis, Sinclair, 161, 173
Lewis, Steve, 324
Lewis, William Henry, 116, 121, 126
Liberty Party, 65, 69, 76, 80
Liberalist, 57
Liberator, 58–9
Lieber, Francis, 57
Liele, George, 30, 36
Lin, Maya, 325
Lincoln, Abraham, 61, 79, 83, 84, 85, 86, 88, 89, 90, 91, 178
Lincoln Brigade, 189
Lincoln Motion Picture Company, 157
Lincoln University, 79, 190
Lindbergh, Charles, 169, 177
Lindsay, Vachel, 155
Liston, Sonny, 243, 248
Little, Cleavon, 339
Little, Joan, 283
Little, Malcolm; *see* Malcolm X
Little Rock crisis, 230, 232, 234
Liuzzo, Viola Gregg, 248
Liverpool, Moses, 45
Llewellyn, J. Bruce, 313